"It's clear to me that pursuing action research is the best way to advance systems thinking and practice. This book is a significant step forward in that regard bringing together as it does systems theory, methodological practice and case studies".

Professor Mike C Jackson, *OBE, Emeritus Professor, University of Hull*

"Research with impact is challenging to do, this book shows a way to do this. It gives a detailed methodology and techniques, show how to abduct to theory and illustrates its narrative with beautiful diagrams from real cases".

Professor Janet Godsell, *Professor, Loughborough University*

"This book is highly recommended for its holistic and structured approach to understanding and improving organisational processes as dynamic, interrelated systems that drive sustainable performance. Although systems thinking underpins change it is difficult to practice; this book achieves this with gravitas".

Professor Umit Bititci, *Emeritus Professor, Herriot Watt University*

"Action research is about accessing meaning through rigorous attention to how issues are constructed, how actions are planned, implemented, and evaluated, and how learning captured informs practical and theoretical knowledge; it can benefit from the scholarly application of a well-defined methodology as presented in this book".

Professor Paul Coughlan, *Professor, Trinity College Dublin*

SYSTEMS THINKING AND ACTION RESEARCH FOR INNOVATION

Systems Thinking and Action Research for Innovation introduces the Process Oriented Holonic (PrOH) Modelling Methodology, a novel systems thinking methodology, combining academic rigour with practical guidance for conducting action research in organisations. It equips readers to conduct high-impact research and drive systemic transformation.

Readers will gain a comprehensive understanding of systems thinking and action research, with a focus on the innovative PrOH Modelling Methodology. This book provides detailed practical rules and guidelines, enabling readers to apply the PrOH Modelling Methodology effectively in action research projects. Engaging exercises and mini tests throughout the text help reinforce learning, while visually striking diagrams illustrate key concepts in an accessible manner. Real-world case studies from industries such as manufacturing, supply chain, legal and public services demonstrate the practical application of PrOH Models, offering insights into systemic success factors, process improvements and innovations. Reflections on theory link practice to foundational principles, ensuring readers develop theoretical, methodological and practical expertise. Additionally, the book explores advanced topics such as building holarchies, gamification and the future of holonic thinking, making it a definitive systems thinking and action research guide for academics and practitioners alike.

This book is intended for postgraduate students, doctoral researchers and management consultants specialising in organisational change, technical innovation and process improvement.

Additional resources are available from an author-maintained companion website dedicated to PrOH Modelling: https://prohmodel.org/

Ben Clegg is Professor of Operations Management and Systems Thinking and Founder of the PrOH Modelling Methodology. His research has received millions of pounds of funding from industry and government that has recently focused on the digitalisation of small-to-medium-sized organisations. He has previously worked with larger international companies and their supply chains to improve lean six sigma, concurrent engineering, enterprise management, service delivery and technical innovation. He specialises in MBA teaching and supervising researchers. He has 100+ publications including articles in top journals; he is the co-author of a leading textbook on Operations Management. He has been a Visiting Scholar at Stanford University and a European Operations Management Association (EurOMA) committee member. He is Advance-HE Fellow, Chartered Engineer and Fellow of the Institute of Engineering and Technology (IET). He has been Associate Dean for Business Engagement and Head of Department at Aston Business School. He is Editor-in-Chief of the *Systems* journal.

Krishna Chaitanya Balthu is Lecturer in Operations Management and Systems Thinking. His work focuses on applying systems thinking to design and implement change in organisations. He spent over a decade as a practitioner, leading process improvement and change initiatives across knowledge-intensive firms. Drawing on this industrial experience, Krishna has led industry-academia collaboration projects that bridge research and practice. He predominantly works on funded projects enabling organisations to adopt digital technologies, circular economy principles and systemic transformation using participatory approaches such as the PrOH Modelling Methodology. He has applied PrOH Modelling across diverse industrial contexts, enhancing and extending its application to deliver measurable impact. This body of work has featured in leading management journals and practitioner magazines. He is also actively involved in transnational education and capacity-building initiatives with India and Kenya, building collaborative learning and research partnerships. His teaching portfolio includes courses on Systems Thinking, Management Consultancy and Business Model Innovation.

SYSTEMS THINKING AND ACTION RESEARCH FOR INNOVATION

Theory and Practice of the Process Oriented Holonic (PrOH) Modelling Methodology

Ben Clegg and Krishna Chaitanya Balthu

Routledge
Taylor & Francis Group
LONDON AND NEW YORK

Designed cover image: Shutterstock

First edition published 2026
by Routledge
4 Park Square, Milton Park, Abingdon, Oxon, OX14 4RN

and by Routledge
605 Third Avenue, New York, NY 10158

Routledge is an imprint of the Taylor & Francis Group, an informa business

British Library Cataloguing-in-Publication Data
A catalogue record for this book is available from the British Library

ISBN: 9781032650418 (hbk)
ISBN: 9781032650449 (pbk)
ISBN: 9781032650425 (ebk)

DOI: 10.4324/ 9781032650425

Typeset in Times New Roman
by Deanta Global Publishing Services, Chennai, India

Ben thanks Anna, Harry and Ella and wider family and friends for their continual love and support.

Krishna thanks Tulya for her kindness and unwavering support throughout his scholastic journey, and Ben for his persistence and dedication in bringing this project to life.

The authors give special thanks to Richard Orme for his contributions to systems thinking and lean six sigma maturity models used with his permission throughout this book.

The authors also thank everyone we have ever worked with over recent decades in academia, industry and society who have influenced this book, who are too many to mention, but without whom we could not have written this book. You know who you are.

CONTENTS

PART II
The PrOH Modelling Methodology 57

FIGURES

TABLES

BOXES

Thinking Boxes

Action Boxes

ACKNOWLEDGEMENTS

The authors of this book would like to express their gratitude to the following colleagues and organisations, in no particular order, for their valuable contributions without which this book would probably not have been possible.

Glyn Morris, Ehsan Eslamian, John Edwards, Zulaiha Hamidu, Chris Owen, Ola Sanda, Balint Newton-Turcsanyi, Brian Ølgaard, Paul Hacker, Andrew Moss, Maya Vachkova, Innovate UK, The InterAct Project, Knowledge Transfer Partnerships, ESRC, EPSRC, Janet Godsell, Jill MacBryde, Iain Collis, Alison Boardman, Roya Gholami, Anuradha Kamble, Rob Brighouse, Amrik Sohal, George Feiger, Ian Briggs, Zoe Radnor, Chris Rees, Helen Higson, Mike Titchen, John Boardman, Stuart Wingrove, Julian Bulbeck, Higgs LLP, John Jostins, Aris Matopoulos, British Council, NIS, Duncan Shaw, Mario Binder, Nigel Driffield, Richard Orme, Marconi, Rolls-Royce Aerospace, BAE Systems, AMRC Sheffield, Pavel Albores, Sabah Al-Somali, Prasanta Dey, The IET, The Operations Research Society, European Operations Management Association, Production and Operations Management Society, Andy Neely, Mark Hart, Judy Scully, Ray Levitt, Tim Baines, Iain Reid, Chiltern Railways, MCT Aspire Engineering, Microcab, Louisa Huaccho-Huatuco, Alan Pilkington, Juliana Hsuan, Steve Paton, Metal Assemblies Ltd, James Mercy, Horizon Marketing, Newtown Packaging, Aurrigo PLC, Department for Business and Trade, Department for Work and Pensions, Simon Howells, Paul Taylor, David Bennett, Paul Hunt, University of Exeter, Birmingham Law School at University of Birmingham, De Montfort University, Stanford University and, of course, Aston University.

INTRODUCTION

This book is the definitive and most comprehensive text to date on the Process Oriented Holonic Modelling (PrOH) Methodology. 'PrOH' is pronounced as 'pro', in one syllable, with a silent 'h' to rhyme with 'show' as in 'show and tell'.

There are four parts to this book:

Part I gives an essential background to systems thinking in Chapter 1, particularly in respect to soft systems methodologies for organisational change and how they differ from other types of systems methodologies and techniques. Chapter 2 gives an essential background to action research. As each subject is extensive, chapters in Part I are not written to give comprehensive accounts but to give an essential context for the following parts of the book.

Part II discusses the PrOH Modelling Methodology and gives a full account of this unique soft systems methodology. Chapter 3 explains why the PrOH Modelling Methodology is needed, Chapter 4 explains how a single PrOH Model is constructed, and Chapter 5 describes how sets of PrOH Models are constructed and used to bring about organisational change.

Part III presents the PrOH Modelling Methodology case studies based on action research projects. Each case forms a separate chapter (Chapter 5–13). These cases have been carefully selected from a wider catalogue as collectively they show all aspects of the PrOH Modelling Methodology, give a variety of different case settings ranging from large to small organisations, service and manufacturing organisations and from the public and private sectors. These cases also address interesting topical issues.

Part IV reflects on PrOH Modelling Methodology for users and looks at the future for systems thinking and action research. Chapter 14 gives practical tips for users. Chapter 15 proposes how emerging frameworks and technologies may affect users of the PrOH Modelling Methodology in action research and suggests future topics suitable for PrOH Modelling Methodology research applications.

The tone of language throughout this book is aimed at the intellectually inquisitive systems thinker wanting to use systems thinking to change organisational systems by making them perform better; especially those having a process focus, and even more specifically, those that have a focus on creating value for customers and organisational stakeholders through innovative systemic thinking. The PrOH Modelling Methodology considers all organisational processes to be organisational systems composed broadly of social, human, technical and knowledge-based elements.

The authors hope that readers of this book will gain enough understanding of previous literature on systems thinking and action research to appreciate the unique benefits of using the PrOH Modelling Methodology as the authors believe that systems thinking and action research should constantly evolve, and this book is offered most humbly to the systems thinking and action research communities to hopefully make systems thinking and action research more robust and more adoptable. Thinking and Action Boxes are given (with answers at the end) to encourage independent thought. The authors of this book firmly believe that the World needs more systems thinking and more action research and hope that this book will contribute towards this aim.

PART I

A Short Guide to Systems Thinking and Action Research

Abstract

Chapter 1 of this book gives a review of systems thinking relevant to the Process Oriented Holonic (PrOH) Modelling Methodology, it is not intended to be a fully comprehensive account of all types of systems thinking. Instead, it focuses on types of systems thinking most closely associated with organisational change, particularly aspects linked to strategic, tactical, and operational structural, strategic, and cultural change in organizations. In other words, changes that might be considered as people-centred changes with objectives such as increasing efficiency and productivity, implementing productivity, increasing sustainable practices, digitalization, or lowering carbon footprints. This is because systems thinking is best used in organisations for challenging the status quo of current practice, attempting to see the bigger picture, encouraging consensus building, and catalysing change.

Chapter 2 covers action research as the predominant mode of research taken in this book where 'action' is management activity taken to give demonstrable changes in organizations, and 'research' is taken to be the delivery of generalizable findings for a wider audience to learn from, often through the developments of theory and or learning frameworks, based on practical experiences in organizations. Chapter 2 concludes with discussion on different types of logical reasoning in research to give broader context to how it is used in action research.

1

THE ESSENTIALS OF SYSTEMS THINKING

> Systems thinking is, "an approach aimed at understanding and intervening in complex systems by focusing on the relationships among a system's parts rather than treating components in isolation".
>
> *(Bertalanffy, 1968)*

This chapter will interest researchers who want to conduct action research using a systems approach to understand complex challenges in organisations, managers and management consultants planning change projects for impactful positive change in organisations, and, more generally, readers seeking a novel and creative way to get innovative things done.

Books on systems thinking tend to fall into three types:

(1) those that are comprehensive academic literature reviews of all systems thinkers – there are many of these already in existence which tend to be edited works from many different contributing authors (e.g. Ramage and Shipp, 2009; Jackson 2020);
(2) highly philosophical works on systems thinking portraying systems thinking as something spiritual, profound and revelatory which tend to offer few detailed rules and guidelines for practical use of systems thinking (e.g. Cabrera et al., 2024) – there are many of these already in existence;
(3) books whose purpose is to cover only one method in detail, set in a wider systems context, with instruction and cases. There are few good ones that do this well.

This book falls into the third type by giving the definitive and most comprehensive account of a unique type of systems thinking known as the Process Oriented Holonic (PrOH) Modelling Methodology. "PrOH" is pronounced as "PrO" with a silent "H" to rhyme with "show" as in "show and tell". This book covers work done over more than twenty years and sets the PrOH Modelling Methodology in a wider context of systems thinking and action research.

Consider for a moment the question in Thinking Box 1.

DOI: 10.4324/9781032650425-2

THINKING BOX 1: WHAT IS A "SYSTEM"?

Ackoff (1961, pp.26–42)	"any entity, conceptual or physical which consists of interdependent parts".
Von Bertalanffy (1968)	"a set of units with relationships among them".
Battista (1977)	"not a concrete thing but, rather, an abstract concept that refers to a particular relationship among things that can be actualised in a number of different ways".
Beckett (1971) is:	"a configuration of components interconnected for a purpose according to a plan. ... a continuous, boundary maintaining, variously related assembly of parts".

Think of organisational systems, both actual and conceptual, that you are familiar with and keep these in mind while reading this book.

Ludwig von Bertalanffy (1968), a pioneer of **General Systems Theory (GST)**, framed systems thinking as an approach for understanding and intervening in complex systems by focusing on the relationships among a system's parts rather than treating components in isolation (Bertalanffy, 1968), his emphasis on interconnectivity marked an early divergence from **reductionist** thought, positioning systems thinking as a holistic analytical framework. Richmond (1987) re-coined the term as "systems thinking" by describing it as "the art and science of making reliable inferences about behaviour by developing an increasingly deep understanding of underlying structure", his definition extends systems thinking into a methodological approach, emphasising the value of structural insight for explaining complex behaviour. Moreover, a very prominent definition emerged from Senge's contribution in The Fifth Discipline (Senge, 1990) and positioned systems thinking as "a framework for seeing interrelationships rather than things, for seeing patterns rather than static snapshots" (Senge, 1990). His interpretation gained considerable traction, as it articulates systems thinking as a means to transcend the constraints of rigidly defined fields, fostering insight through interdisciplinary thinking. Aronson's (1996) work on systems thinking defines and distinguishes it from reductionist thinking, and fundamentally diverges from traditional analytical methods; his view emphasises systems thinking as a radical departure from reductionism, favouring approaches that encompass *wholes* rather than *disaggregated parts*. Ramage and Shipp (2009) add further nuances to this discourse by portraying systems thinking as a means to understand complexity through a holistic orientation, positioning systems thinking as a worldview that favours integration over fragmentation.

Jackson's (2020) contemporary viewpoint defines systems thinking as "an approach to reasoning and treatment of real-world problems based on the fundamental notion of 'system'". Jackson's contribution underscores the role of systems thinking in practical problem-solving (Flood and Jackson,1991; Jackson, 2000) by bridging theoretical insights with real-world applications. His definition also emphasises the use of pragmatism as a foundational concept in addressing complex issues. Jackson (2024) proffers that systems thinking can offer a complementary approach to science where science struggles because of the complexity of the real world. This is especially the case in the human, social, political and environmental domains where science has and must continue to play a significant role in helping create a better world but struggles to provide comprehensive and absolute answers where systems thinking can contribute. So, without systems thinking, science is blind in some areas and, in the worst-case scenario, could potentially lead the human species towards destructive pathways. Therefore, science and actions in social, political, economic, legal and economic settings should be complemented with systems approaches to give more weight to interrelationships, organismic thinking, imagination, creation and flair to create equal societies and balance to our environments. The authors of this book believe wholeheartedly in these contemporary thoughts and focus the use of systems thinking on organisation-based challenges. As Churchman (1968) states:

> Systems are made up of sets of components that work together for the overall objective of the whole. The systems approach is simply a way of thinking about these total systems and their components.

General Systems Thinking

This chapter starts its account of modern systems thinking at the beginning of the 20th century with Western "traditional" systems thinking and majors on General Systems Thinking (GST) as its main foundation. GST was built on the ideas of Ludwig von Bertalanffy (Bertalanffy, 1969) and Kenneth Boulding (Boulding, 1956).

The traditional view of science for the first half of the 20th century was based on the **reductionist** viewpoint. In this context, the World could be understood by reducing it to fundamental terms; to simply illustrate, the field of biology could be understood through its decomposition to the field of chemistry, which could be understood through its decomposition to the field of physics, which represented a sort of absolute "truth". During the 20th century machines became increasingly complex, and initially, machines were simple enough to be within the competence of an engineer or group of engineers skilled in a particular field, such as automobile design. However, with increased complexities, such as with the development of the space programme, expertise from many fields was required, or as Bertalanffy termed it, an understanding of "heterogeneous technologies" was required. For instance, in the space programme, the integration of mathematical, mechanic, electronic and chemical engineering sciences, with the human skills of pilots, and, given the expense, the social, economic and ethical sciences of human beings became important. Thus, it became increasingly necessary to combine different sets of knowledge and expertise into a systems approach (or "expansionist viewpoint") to consider wider sets of knowledge in solving practical problems (Bertalanffy, 1969; Boulding, 1956; Ackoff, 1974). To complete these complex projects, involving great complexity, it became necessary to employ teams of systems specialists to produce optimal solutions based on many conflicting performance criteria. Systems specialists were needed to consider interactions between different possible solutions from each specialist field in addition to the performance of individual elements. For example, when considering social technical systems, specialists realised that it was unlikely that events could be explained by the actions of individuals alone, and thus, consequently, the tendency was to study increasingly larger sections of phenomena as systems rather than individual parts (Bertalanffy, 1969). In response GST was proposed as an attempt to provide theory where previously there was none and provide more generality than found in specific disciplines. In the words of Boulding (1956),

> General Systems Theory is a name which has come into use to describe a level of theoretical model-building which lies somewhere between the highly generalised constructions of pure mathematics and the specific theories of the specialized disciplines.

The goal of GST is to develop a body of systematic theoretical constructs which discuss the general relationships of the empirical world. However, GST is not concerned with creating a single self-contained general theory of practically everything, as a replacement for specific disciplinary theories, because "all we can say about practically everything is almost nothing" (Boulding, 1956). Rather GST attempts to develop an optimal degree of generality for each purpose and each level of abstraction that balances the general that has no content and the specific that has no wider meaning. In doing so, GST seeks to identify similarities between theoretical constructs and provide a language for communication between different disciplines, develop a "spectrum" of theories, "a system of systems", which may perform as a **Gestalt** entity in the construction of theory.

The development of a "system of systems" could point to gaps in theoretical models, potential methods of filling them and allow an interdisciplinary approach to problem solving rather than diversification into increasingly separate entities (Bertalanffy, 1969; Boulding, 1956; Checkland, 1999; Singhal and Singhal, 2012a, 2012b; Soltani et al., 2014). In applying GST, two possible approaches emerge. Firstly, the identification of phenomena that bridge several disciplines that may result in an overall theory, such as economic growth, interaction between "individuals" and their natural environment, population change (e.g. birth and death), communication and information control processes. Secondly, the development of a "system of systems" as a **hierarchy** (or **holarchy** – see Part II) of theoretical constructs based on the complexity of the systems they describe. However, due to the difficulty of observing systems as a whole, "systems" should probably only ever be **epistemological** devices used to facilitate understanding of the real world rather than its replication (Bertalanffy, 1969, pp.28–29), to this end Ackoff (1971) developed a classification of systems complexity to help think about systems complexity as summarised in Table 1.1, starting with the simplest level 1 and becoming increasingly complex towards level 9.

Most knowledge tends to reside in the first two levels of Table 1.1; however, knowledge at these levels is typically far from completely accurate. Fewer models exist at the intermediate third and fourth levels, and while considerable advances have been made since the work of Boulding and Bertalanffy, not least due to the now pervasive use of computers, there is still very limited knowledge. Above the fourth level, knowledge is even more limited because in these social-cultural system levels (e.g. level 8) there is very little uncontested work, particularly that which considers the topic of systems for organisational change as explored in Parts II and III of this book. Indeed, in the context of the organisational systems, one could argue that most uncontestable knowledge exists at levels 1 and 2 of Ackoff's classification (Table 1.1.) but should ideally be at higher levels 7 and 8, which itself remains a highly contestable point of discussion.

Ackoff's classification of systems complexity is complemented by Ackoff's (1971) "system of systems concepts" which seeks to define elements of systems, their relationships and maturity of purpose. In Ackoff's (1971) terms only systems that are consciously **goal-seeking**, as found in levels 6, 7 and 8 or higher, can exhibit learning behaviour. This is because:

TABLE 1.1 Classification of Systems Complexity Levels

Classification Level	*Description*
1. Frameworks of static structures	Outlines of the fixed or static structure of entities or systems that form the basis of further enquiry. In this situation no events (changes in system structure) occur during a relevant timeframe. For example, maps in geography, molecular structure in chemistry and the solar system.
2. Simple dynamic system	Systems that have predetermined and necessary motions where events occur during a relevant timeframe. For example, conventional physics and chemistry, simple machines, systems in equilibrium (at a very high level most social systems tend to equilibrium).
3. Control mechanism or cybernetic system	Differs from above in that it utilises the transmission and interpretation of information which on environmental changes will attempt to maintain equilibrium by making internal adjustments in addition to obeying equations. For example, homeostasis, chemical buffers and thermostats.
4. Open systems or self-maintaining systems	Open systems may exist for lower levels (e.g. flames) however with increasing complexity there is some element of throughput of material and energy as exhibited by "life" thereby being able to self-reproduce and self-maintain. For example, cells (through metabolism and DNA) and organisms in general.
5. Genetic-societal level or lower organisms	Could be considered as plants characterised by the division of labour between mutually dependent parts such as roots, leaves and stems, and the limited existence of sensory organs and therefore throughput of information.
6. Animal	Systems exhibit increased levels of mobility, **teleological** behaviour and self-awareness. Greater presence of information throughput and the development of an impression of the "world" as an image on which a response is made, interpretation of the information is necessarily different to the information itself. For example, learning and the beginnings of self-awareness.
7. Human	Humans considered as individual systems. Exhibits those characteristics of animals and that of self-consciousness. These are characterised by a **self-reflexive** ability, knowing that one knows, the ability to interpret symbols rather than signal, interpretation of existence in the context of abstract elements such as time, space and history.
8. Social organisations or social-cultural systems	Humans do not generally exist as individuals rather they tend to interact with other humans. This level is concerned with the social systems through which individual humans interact. These could be considered in terms of roles (although one must consider the human's effect on the role and the role's effect on the human) characterised by the content and meaning of symbols, culture, the nature of human society [This includes organisational systems].
9. Transcendental systems or symbolic systems	Questions that do not have answers, unknowable ultimates and absolutes. For example, language, logic, mathematics and arts.

Source: Adapted from Ackoff (1971). Increasing in complexity from simplest at the top to highly complex at the bottom.

- **goal-seeking systems** can respond differently to one or more different external or internal events in one or more of their different external or internal states; they can respond differently to particular events in an unchanging environment until they produce a particular state, their goal. A goal-seeking system has a choice of behaviour, which is responsive in character, and may be able to achieve its goal in different ways.
- **multi-goal-seeking systems** are goal-seeking in each of the two, or more, different initial external or internal states, and which seek different goals in at least two different states, the goal being determined by the initial state.
- **purposive systems** are multi-goal-seeking systems whose different goals exhibit a common property, the production of which is the system's purpose. Purposive systems can pursue different goals that are determined by the initiating event, rather than a choice by the system itself.
- **purposeful systems** can produce the same outcome in different ways in the same (internal and external) state and can produce different outcomes in the same and different states. Thus, a purposeful system is one that can change its goals under constant conditions; and therefore, display will (or **agency**) through the selection of both ends and means. A purposeful system can have goal(s), which can be achieved in a specific timeframe, and objectives, which may not be achieved in any specified period but over a longer timeframe.
- **ideal-seeking system** is a purposeful system which, on attainment of any of its goals or objectives, then seeks another goal and objective which more closely approximates its ideal. An ideal seeking system is thus one which has a concept of "perfection" or the "ultimately desirable" and pursues it systematically; that is, in interrelated steps. In this context, an ideal cannot be obtained within any particular time period but can be approached without limits.

This system of systems thinking is applicable to systems of organisation change and change management in general as organisational systems are usually purposeful systems that contain at least two purposeful elements which have a common purpose. To achieve this purpose there will be a functional division of labour as distinct subsets which can respond, through observation and communication, to one another's behaviour. And at least one subset of the system will have a system-control function. In this context, an organisation may be considered as a system of systems where several sub-systems function together to produce the organisation's purpose, that of the organisational sub-systems taken as a "whole".

In summary, GST aims to simultaneously provide a parsimonious and optimal degree of generality to facilitate theoretical construction. Organisational change systems (Part III cases) are interpreted in this research as **ideal-seeking systems** which contain **purposeful systems** and may contain purposive, **multi-goal-seeking** and/or **goal-seeking systems**. These multiple systems can be arranged into a "system of systems" to act as a **gestalt** entity to organise large sets of information from different sources to identify previously unobserved relationships or gaps in theory. However, due to the difficulty in observing these systems holistically, they are not objectively "real" rather human constructions that have been developed through historical and evolutionary adaptation to manage aspects of "reality"; thus, they result from the subjective perceptions and inferences of a systems thinker (Bertalanffy, 1969; Pidd, 1996; Pidd, 2004). In conclusion a "system of systems" is an entity which may contain subsystems, may be part of a larger system and can be defined by its constituents and contingency formed from its people, machines, critical success factors, inter-relationships, boundary, inputs, outputs, controls, name and environment (Clegg and Orme, 2012).

System thinking's breadth and diversity is a strength, but paradoxically it is also a weakness, as it can complicate one's attempts to define a unit of analysis whether tangible or conceptual. However, cultivating an intellectual curiosity based upon the tenets of systems thinking allows ongoing learning and insight. There are many derivatives of GST, two of which have influenced the development of the PrOH Modelling Methodology: Organisational Cybernetics and Critical Systems Thinking.

Organisational Cybernetics

The metaphor of organisational cybernetics is that organisations behave as organisms. It is the science of, "communication and control in the animal and the machine" (Weiner, 1948) or as an "effective organisation" (Beer, 1985). Organisational Cybernetics' primary concern, applied to management, is with the structure of organisations and the use of information and control systems. Systems structures are understood using the "black box" technique (input – self-contained process – output) to understand complexity, and self-regulation using negative feedback and **variety engineering** is used to address probabilism. The emphasis of organisational cybernetics literature is on the design of organisations to be self-regulating and self-organising. Ashby (1956) discusses what is meant by "variety" in this context; he established the "law of requisite variety" and introduced the use of causal-loop diagrams. Beer (1985) has been responsible for the development and application of management cybernetics, including a recursive view of systems using the **Viable Systems Model** (VSM). Users of VSM claim to be able to "diagnose" the operational effectiveness of any existing or proposed organisational design.

Organisational Cybernetics has found practical expression in **socio-technical systems** (STS) theory (or socio-technical design – STD). An account of STD is given by Rice (1963), who appreciates that "work organisations" have both social and technical aspects and must be optimised jointly to bring success. Rice advocates the creation of "autonomous work groups" to manage production processes and anticipated many organisational improvement initiatives to ensue from Organisational Cybernetic interventions. Kast (1979) draws on organic analogies to suggest that subsystems in organisations must be working well if they are to survive; it is then the job of management to co-ordinate these subsystems and fit an organisation to its environment. The common criticism aimed at **Organisational Cybernetics** is that it tends to embrace, rather too readily, the organic analogy.

Critical Systems Thinking

Critical Systems Thinking (CST) emerged in the 1980s. Ulrich (1983) is one of the authors who has made constructive endeavours in this area; he criticises "systems science" because in it the systems idea is only used in the context of "instrumental reason" to help us decide how to do things. Ulrich then sets out to develop the systems idea for use as part of "practical reason" to help us decide what we ought to do. Ulrich terms his approach as "critical" because it provides the means to reflect upon the propositions that enter any social systems design. Secondly, he sets out principles for a participative debate that must take place with all those affected by a design before that design can be regarded as validated and accepted for implementation. The metaphor that underpins critical systems thinking is that of the organisation as a **coercive system** (Jackson, 1991). The elaborate methodological arrangements recommended are to prevent the powerful in organisations using their influence for their own ends rather than in a process of whole systems improvement, although in response to Ulrich, Jackson states this needs further development (Jackson, 2003a).

Systems Thinking in Practice

When applying systems thinking it is necessary to define a "system" as "a cognitive construct for making sense of complexity and the organization of knowledge" (Barton and Haslett, 2007). This is true whether the system is viewed to be "real" or conceptual. From a more technical perspective, a system can be defined as a whole, which consists of a set of two or more inter-related elements, whether intangible or physical, which rather than being irreducible (in a reductionist sense) can be divided into parts. In this context the set of elements that form the whole, and any set of elements which form part of those elements, can be characterised by the following properties:

1. The properties and behaviour of each element, which constitute the set that makes up the whole, influence the properties or behaviours of the set taken as a whole.
2. The properties and behaviour of each element are affected by at least one other element of the set that constitutes the whole; therefore, no element has an independent effect on the whole.
3. Every possible subset of elements in the set that constitutes the whole has the first two properties; therefore, no subset has an independent effect on the whole. In this context, the set that constitutes the whole cannot be decomposed into independent subsets and remains a representative description of the whole, and a system cannot be subdivided into independent subsystems.

If these three properties hold true, then the set of elements that constitute the whole, taken as a whole, will always exhibit properties or behaviour that none of the elements or subsets can individually exhibit (Ackoff, 1974); and thus, these properties are referred to as "emergent properties". For instance, in a social system, such as an organisation implementing change, an individual will be constrained in actions they can take, due to organisational "rules". Conversely, they may be enabled to take actions they may otherwise be unable to do as an individual; for example, undergo expensive training. These are examples of "emergent properties" of systems.

The expansionist or holistic doctrine therefore considers elements or systems as parts of larger wholes and their roles within it, rather than wholes that should be decomposed to their parts. It also endorses the use of expansionism to develop synthetic thought (synthesis over decomposition) to explain properties and behaviour of individual and collective human systems, thoughts and *weltanschauung* (worldview) which cannot be obtained by objective analysis alone. Thus, when applied to systems problems, as a systems approach, problems are not solved by decomposition but by considering their parts in the larger whole. Such an approach is based on the observation that optimising the various elements and subsystems, based on their own criteria, rarely leads to the optimisation of the whole (Ackoff, 1974; Näslund, 2008).

The inclusion of the effect of the environment of a system leads to the inclusion of another form of cause and effect, additional to determinist cause and effect in a system, known as non-determinist cause and effect or "**producer-product**", in this context, the cause is necessary but not sufficient for the effect. For example, a supplier is necessary to provide input to produce a product; however, it is also necessary to have logistics to deliver it, which may require considerations of geography, traffic and resource availability and in general the environment of which it is part. These co-producers form the environment of an **open system** as opposed to the environment-free **closed system** of determinist cause and effect. Thus, **producer-product** is compatible with the idea of determinist cause and effect but provides a richer picture of it, including the consideration of **teleological** concepts such as **goal-seeking** and **purposeful** behaviour, thereby considering both what produced a property or behaviour and what it is meant to, or does, produce. **Teleologically** speaking, organisations and organisational change systems are therefore purposeful and contain purposeful systems of **producer-product** that can provide a richer understanding of the situation.

In summary, the expansionist viewpoint results from the realisation that it was necessary to consider wider aspects of reality as systems complexity increases. So, while "**machine age**" problems could be understood through the application of the reductionist doctrine and determinist cause and effect, as they are closed systems with passive parts which are fully observable, "systems age" problems are characterised by an expansionist viewpoint of open systems with purposeful parts which are only partially observable and teleologically explainable (Ackoff, 1974; Jackson and Keys, 1984).

Systems Thinking for Action Research

Systems thinking has emerged as a discipline to provide an antidote to the ills of conventional thinking, mainly to make sense of complex, messy systems that require interdisciplinary approaches to problem solving. For example, Senge (1990) defined systems thinking as a set of maxims that encourage "out-of-box" thinking and the use of a "holistic perspective" to complex problems and advocated that:

- Today's problems come from yesterday's solutions.
- Cause and effect are not closely related in time and space.
- Small changes can produce big results, but the best points of leverage can be the least obvious.
- The cure can be worse than the disease.
- The easy way out usually leads back in.
- Behaviour grows better before it grows worse.
- The harder you push, the harder the system pushes back.

Systems thinking has delivered positive results in organisations (Senge, 1990) when characterised by the following tenets:

- Representing both parts and wholes in a system through a holistic view.
- Highlighting interconnections between parts using feedback loops.
- Integrating people, processes and tools.

Senge's work became popular with practising managers as it was accessibly written even though it was criticised by academics for dumbing down systems science. Nevertheless, Senge's work often instilled enough confidence in its readers to "give system thinking a go" to create positive changes in their organisations.

Context of the Problem

The topic of how organisations implement change management programmes as a system-level intervention is inherently complex and requires the identification, selection and adoption of appropriate elements relating to specific organisational goals. To achieve this, the following types of questions must be considered:

- What assumptions exist from *a priori* literature on any given topic relevant to a system?
- Is the system being studied a complex purposeful system?
- Is there a definitive known model that could be adaptable to context (Albliwi et al., 2015)?
- Is the system process focused (Näslund, 2008)?
- How long will it take to implement improvement methodologies, and how can they evolve over time as the system under observation changes (Bessant, 2001)?
- Will model development be interpretive and subjective, or definitive and deductively testable?
- Is the opinion of decision makers on the "best" approach or "form" of any topic likely to be characterised by pluralistic viewpoints?

Two major features of these systems thinking challenges, according to Chapman (2004, p.14), are gaining a bigger picture, by going up a level of abstraction, and appreciating other people's perspectives. Therefore, designing and implementing any organisation change programme should be from both an interpretive and a non-determinist cause-and-effect viewpoint if a richer understanding of it is to be achieved.

Models of Systems

> All models are wrong, but some are useful.
>
> *(Attributed to A. Einstein, circa 1920)*

The context of the problem, how to design and implement an organisational change programme, is inherently complex and often difficult to observe as a "whole". Decisions in these types of complex situations are unlikely to be straightforward; therefore, they are unlikely to be made instantly, and it may not be clear what action should be taken, when it should be taken, and how long it will take. In these situations, there may be numerous possible courses of action; however, it is often impractical to implement or directly experiment on more than one of the possibilities. Hence, if there is a need to address some issue requiring some decision or control over the outcome, building models provides a practical option to allow "experimentation with reality" to examine the available options and choose the most appropriate course of action. This is particularly attractive if practical real-world experimentation is constrained by cost, time, ability to replicate under different conditions, high risks associated with inappropriate actions, and legality (Pidd, 2004). In the context of organisational change, real-world experimentation is highly likely to be extremely impractical due to these constraints, and, in the context of research, ethical issues will usually prohibit the "wrong" thing being done as an experiment in case irrecoverable harm occurs.

Models should act as simplifications of "reality" providing representation and approximation of the system of interest to facilitate interested parties' consideration and cognitive processing of a complex "reality". It is a model's simplification of complex "reality" that makes it *useful*. If a modelling process is to be successful, it must take a complex reality and express it more simply, and take the ill-defined subtle nature of reality and express it in well-defined concrete terms. Pidd (2004, p.12) states:

> a model is an external and explicit representation of part of reality as seen by the people who wish to use that model to understand, to change, to manage, and to control that part of reality.

Indeed, a systems model may not even be an explicit part of reality, as in PrOH Modelling, a model can represent a conceptual system – such as how to change "as-is" into "to-be" and so a PrOH Model represents a conceptual system rather than reality. This is discussed in depth in Parts II and III.

This poses the question: what level of detail and/or complexity should be contained in a model? Pidd (2004) suggests Occam's Razor (attributed to Occam, *circa* 1340) is a useful principle to decide what should or should not be included in a model. The principle states the formation of hypotheses, or hypothetical models, "do not use multiple entities unnecessarily" and "a plurality (of reasons) should not be posited without necessity". However, even though a systems model should be built parsimoniously and economically with the fewest number of assumptions possible, it is necessary to include **systemic success factors** of change known by its key stakeholders. From an ontological perspective, a systems model of "reality" (conceptual or tangibly real) constructed on this principle without stakeholder participation is useless. Thus, in terms of Occam's Razor, an organisational model of change should contain a sufficient level of complexity to allow a purposeful and critical appraisal of it in a holistic context and avoid easy incorrect explanations that may be instigated by reductionistic "**machine age**" approaches. Therefore, the construction of systems models to represent the complex reality of organisational change in simplified, explicit and concrete terms (using rules and guidelines) can facilitate the critical appraisal and implementation of complex organisational change programmes.

Systems thinking and systems model building for systems thinking is prolific in the field of Operations Research (OR), on applied and theoretical modelling, which originally developed when professional scientists joined groups responsible for the planning and execution of military operations during World War II. The military provided an assessment of the operational outlook and data to scientists, who would perform analysis using scientific methods to develop useful advice. Checkland (1999, pp.72–73) cites the Operations Research Society's (ORS") definition of OR as evidence of the transfer of this approach to management problems. Although the current remit of OR according to the ORS" website (theorsociety.com, 12 November 2024) has expanded this to be, "a community of problem-solvers", that includes problem structuring methods and "soft" OR. However, their focus remains on the application of simulation, probability, statistics and optimisation approaches characteristic of "hard" OR. A fundamental feature of this book is to constantly ask, "which methodological approach is best for modelling systems of organizational change: a hard methodological approach or a soft methodological approach, regarding their associated forms of modelling, and why?" These questions are explained below and revisited numerous times throughout this book.

Systems Methodologies

Historically OR has attempted to produce "scientific" models of extant real-world systems and, through the application of measurement criteria, has tried to test the effect of different decisions, strategies, or controls to scientifically determine policy and action (Checkland, 1999, pp.72–74; Ackoff, 1974). This is a "hard" OR approach which makes the implicit assumption that problem situations recur and that the form of the problem can be idealised and mathematically modelled to find *the* optimal "solution" (Checkland, 1971). This contrasts with the methodological view of "soft" OR (Checkland, 1999, pp.72–74) which argues that the "practice of management" of the problem should itself be considered as the "problem", due to its unique content and often unrepeatable actions, rather than the form the problem itself.

Hard Systems Methodologies

A "hard" systems approach is based on the view that there may be much to learn from natural systems and their behaviour, and the study of models of systems is used to help *solve problems in systems*, which may include those of human activity systems, rather than the *enquiry into the system*. For instance, the practice of systems engineering is primarily concerned with finding "solutions" to systems problems in systems judged on their practical assessment of how they operate and their fitness for purpose. For instance, the field of systems engineering has evolved into an effective means to design and implement physical and software information systems. In the belief that human beings are purposeful parts of such systems, from a "hard" systems (engineering) approach it makes sense to also try to engineer the human activity systems element, "fix" them and optimise them. Therefore, according to systems engineering it also follows that it may be possible that real world problems in predominantly **human activity systems** may be designed and implemented in the same way. In other words, human activity systems could be designed as one might design the physical assets of a chemical plant. This premise is, however, refuted by soft OR and soft modelling methodologies and the authors will seek to explain this refutation because *soft methodologies emphasise the process of enquiry into the system rather than analysis of the system itself.*

Systems Engineering and Systems Analysis

Systems engineering and traditional mathematical-based **systems analysis** both assume that problems can be formulated in the following manner: there is a current state and a desired state of a system, and the goal is to reduce the gap between them by moving the current state closer to the desired state, which can be addressed through problem solving (Checkland, 1975, 1978). Thus, in systems engineering, the gap defines the objective and systems analysis provides a systematic way of selecting the best alternative from the possible approaches to achieve the objective, as stated by (Checkland, 1999, p.138) "the belief that real-world problems can be formulated in this way is the distinguishing characteristic of all 'hard' systems thinking". The "hard" systems approach has been applied to "soft" problems; however, this has been criticised primarily because of the retention of focus on the system "objective" (Checkland, 1999, pp.140–146). This criticism centres on the assumption, in "hard" approaches, that there is a singular agreed-upon need or objective which can be met; thus, the question to be answered is "how" to achieve the objective rather than "what" the objective should be. While proponents acknowledge the need to ensure the "correct" choice of objective, it is assumed that a singular one exists. Further, it is assumed that issues of human behaviour can be explained systematically and predicted through theory. This may be appropriate for military systems (with their inherent high level of control) or those without a significant [controllable] element of human agency; however, it may be less appropriate for wider social systems [such as change systems] (Wilson, 2001, pp.19–22). Hence, the approach of systems engineering is to design a whole system and predict its emergent properties. In general terms, **systems engineering** attempts to achieve this through the following problem-solving sequence (Checkland, 1999, p.130):

- Problem definition, considered as the identification of the need.
- Choice of objectives, definition of the physical needs and set of values by which they are judged.
- Systems synthesis, the creation of possible alternative hypothetical systems.
- Systems analysis, analysis of the hypothetical systems against the objectives.
- Systems selection, selection of the "best" solution.
- System development, prototyping.
- Concurrent engineering, implementation of the solution and its assessment and/or modification.

Similarly, **systems analysis** is based on the approach of the RAND Corporation (RAND.org) from the 1940s and is detailed by Checkland (1999, p.130) in the following sequence:

- The selection of an objective or objectives we desire to accomplish.
- The selection of alternative techniques or instrumentalities (or "systems") by which the objective may be accomplished.
- The quantification of the cost or resources required by each system.
- The development of a mathematical model or models.
- The specification of a criterion, relating objectives and costs or resources for choosing the preferred or optimal alternative.

Information Systems Engineering (ISE)

As systems engineering and systems analysis, **information systems engineering (ISE)** applies a similar approach to the design of information systems. Three well-known methodologies for ISE are provided by Structured Systems Analysis and Design Methodology (SSADM) (CCTA, 1990), Information Engineering (Martin, 1986) and Multiview (Avison and Wood-Harper, 1990). As Checkland (1988a) states,

> when we examine the structure of thinking behind the ubiquitous accounts of the creation of computerised information systems via organised projects, the same ideas [as SE, OR, and SA] are revealed to be at work.

Soft Systems Methodologies

Systems thinking has been used as an intervention to deliver change, going back to some of the earliest writings produced at the beginning of the 20th century (Bogdanov, 1913–1917). With a long history of work in systems thinking geared to facilitating organisational change and wider social improvement (Midgley, 2003) especially in complex organisational settings. Complex systems are those with multiple causes and effects that are highly context-sensitive and do not respond to linear, prescriptive methods of intervention (Jackson, 2006). For instance, the delivery of legal services can be considered as a complex system because there are multiple stakeholders involved in the transaction and interactions between them, which can result in varied outcomes depending on contexts and decision-makers' opinions (Benedettini and Neely, 2012).

Soft systems thinking and its methodologies provide researchers with an interpretivist perspective of legal service as a complex system, and an approach to appreciate the interconnectedness of contextually dependent components (Clegg, 2007). The intuition provided by soft systems methodologies (SSMs) can enhance our worldview of legal service delivery by emphasising its systemic behaviour. More generally, SSM was developed to find a better way of dealing with situations that we continually face in our everyday lives, those which we feel "something needs to be done about this" – in other words, problematical organisational situations (Checkland and Poulter, 2006, p.3). Soft systems thinking and SSMs are especially useful for organisational change as, in contrast to hard systems thinking, they are purposed for sense-making, understanding and transformation of socio-technical, physical and cybernetic systems with an emphasis on human behaviour. In contrast, hard systems thinking and methodologies are purposed to recreate and optimise technical cybernetic systems with emphasis on mechanical devices.

The classical approach of systems engineering and systems analysis considers problems in terms of optimal outcomes based on stated goals. In this context, systems exist in the real world and can be modelled and engineered in a way that leads to a "correct" solution. Through his experience in organisations Checkland (1999) began to realise that "real-world" organisations exhibited different cultures, pluralistic viewpoints and histories which made it impractical to implement optimal solutions because stakeholders often held conflicting worldviews and aspirations. This led to the development of **Soft Systems Methodology** (SSM) and a philosophical basis for "soft" situations, such as understanding human activity systems, distinct from that of "hard" systems approaches (Checkland et al. 1990).

Checkland developed SSM through project work carried out in various organisations as part of research at Lancaster University (Checkland, 1999) in response to difficulties in defining organisational problems in the precise terms demanded by "hard" approaches. Applying "hard" approaches in these situations, without considering the possible range of different viewpoints, risked implementing solutions that were not appropriate for the "actual" problem experienced. Thus, SSM assumes that individuals or groups interpret their situations and characterise situations using an interpretive philosophical perspective, rather than hold true the detached objective view of *a priori* systems characteristics endorsed by "hard" approaches. Hence users of soft systems methodology must be conscious that organisational systems are not *ipso facto* and should generate systems models because of need and not necessarily because the systems they represent might already exist. This is a fundamental point that is an essential premise for PrOH Modelling – as the PrOH Modelling Methodology produces models of a conceptual change system.

In SSM the whole process is designed to facilitate learning about a problem situation (Checkland, 1999, pp.A7–A9). Those engaging in SSM are assumed to be in or observing a human activity system where they are attempting purposeful action that is meaningful to them.

This may include **goal-seeking behaviour**, when there is a well-defined objective, but is not restricted to it. Thus, the premise is to be,

> modelling purposeful 'human activity systems' as sets of linked activities which together exhibit the emergent property of purposefulness.

When trying to model purposeful activity as a means of exploring "real-world" action, it is probable there may be many interpretations of what the exact "purpose" is. Thus, it is necessary to consider what these definitions of purpose are, and which are relevant to the problem situation; thereby, an efficient number of the possible human activity system models can be built. Once completed, it is necessary, for each purposeful activity, to decide which worldview (i.e. *Weltanschauung*) will be applied when actioning from models. This is key because one must be clear on the assumptions that are applied when building the model for it to be constructively critiqued. It is important to declare the worldview which makes the model(s) relevant and determine the systems model's content; and given that there are many possible worldviews, more than one model may be in use rather than a single "correct" model. In this context, SSM should be considered as an enquiry or learning process into a system which is "soft" rather than "hard".

SSM *does not* therefore take the approach of systems engineering which assumes there is often an obvious problem which needs a solution; instead, it employs the idea that there is a situation that some stakeholders consider for various reasons to be problematical. Thus, SSM acts as a learning system by developing "human activity system" models based on different worldviews. Learning about the problematical situation is facilitated through the discussion and comparison of models. Lessons learned then lead to the development of new or refined models until the point is reached where participants can reach accommodations, a situation they can accept or live with, which allows for desirable, in terms of the analysis, and feasible, in terms of their history, culture and aspirations, leading to courses of action. The fundamental difference between a hard and soft approach is that hard systems approaches are optimising while SSM's emphasis is on learning and enquiry. SSM was primarily developed to help the design of information systems. PrOH Modelling has specifically been designed to learn about and instigate change in organisations.

Checkland (1999, pp.A50–A55) considers the philosophical position of SSM similar to work by Vickers as an epistemology "that can provide convincing accounts of the process by which human beings and human groups deliberate and act" (in Checkland, 1999, p.A53). Brocklesby (2007) complements Vickers' work by providing clarity on the cognitive aspects that constrain individual perceptions of reality. In this context, when applied to **human activity systems**, the goal-seeking paradigm by itself is considered inadequate because human activity is characterised by trying to maintain desirable relationships and avoid undesirable ones.

Hence, day-to-day human activity is characterised by **Lebenswelt**: "the interacting flux of events and ideas unfolding through time" (Checkland (1999, p.A50), this is considered to be an "appreciative system" where an observer-participant appreciates it by perceiving some aspect of reality and makes judgements about it, resulting in the contribution of ideas to **Lebenswelt**, leading to actions which result in events that are part of **Lebenswelt**. In summary, the key themes are:

- The use of reality judgements about what is the case and value judgements about what is humanly good or bad.
- The characterisation of human action as relationship-maintaining rather than goal-seeking.
- The concept of making judgements on action, based on judgements of reality and value. Checkland (1999, p.A52) expands this to include the modification of defined standards of reality and value.
- The notion that the cycle of judgements and actions based upon them is organised as a system.

Thus, appreciative systems may structurally remain the same, but their content and purpose may change continually through Lebenswelt, and because of component (sub-system) adaptation within the system, a concept known as **autopoiesis** is observable and therefore human activity systems are thought of as **autopoietic systems**. The main subject of enquiry in SSMs is the experiential world of human beings and all explanations, scientific or otherwise, which are observer-dependent, are not necessarily independently existing "real" phenomena, or are able to be objectively defined (Brocklesby, 2007). In conclusion "soft" systems approaches conceptualise and model reality or concepts through an interpretive ontology and are closely aligned to Vickers" epistemology of **Lebenswelt**.

Fitness for Purpose: Contrasting Hard Systems Methodologies to Soft Systems Methodologies

In summary, "hard" systems approaches assume that certain "types" of problems recur in different situations which can be idealised and optimised through the application of analysis (Checkland, 1978). All "hard" approaches assume that the goal or objective of a system can be explicitly and singularly defined as a gap between the desired and the actual situation. These "hard" systems assumptions and methodologies have been applied to numerous problems, including social systems, to engineer and analyse solutions; however, the application of "hard" systems assumptions to social systems has been challenged, most notably by Checkland as he realised that **human activity systems** were often multi-valued, characterised by a pluralist set of viewpoints and often contained many relevant and conflicting objectives and values. In these situations, proponents of "soft" systems approaches argue that "hard" approaches are inadequate as social situations often contain problem situations, rather than specific problems, which may be improved rather than optimised.

Wilson (2001, p.7) gives a direct, broad comparison of the systems engineering approaches and soft systems methodologies, which is summarised here to illustrate their differences. Wilson characterises **systems engineering** as being appropriate for the harder (well-defined) end of the problem spectrum and summarises **hard systems methodology** in the following sequence of stages:

1. Define the problem.
2. Assemble the appropriate techniques.
3. Use techniques to derive possible solutions.
4. Select the most cost-effective solution.
5. Implement the solution.

In the sequence, stages 2 and 3 may be iterative should the outcome of stage 3 be considered insufficient.

At the softer (ill-defined) end of the problem spectrum, it is often difficult to effectively conduct stage one of systems engineering above due to multiple interpretations of what the problem is, and so **soft systems methodologies** consist of the following sequence of stages:

1. Define the situation that is problematic.
2. Express the situation (using tools such as "rich picture").
3. Select concepts that may be relevant.
4. Assemble concepts into an intellectual structure.
5. Use this structure to explore the situation.
6. Define changes to the situation (i.e. problems to be tackled).
7. Implement change processes.

There may be situations where it is desirable to iterate between stages 3, 4 and 5.

SE, SA, hard OR and other hard systems methodologies (HSMs) were established before "soft" systems thinking had matured. ISE methodologies have been developed simultaneously with "soft" systems thinking, resulting in versions including some of the principles of "soft" systems methodologies (Patching, 1987; McLoughlin, 1986). Miles' (1985) methodology suggests two views of integrating "hard" and "soft" systems methodologies for ISE; he calls these "**grafting**" and "**embedding**". Grafting is where SSM happens before HSM, and embedding is where SSM acts as a meta-system analysis to more detailed specific HSMs. Authors of this book believe that these views have important implications for developing any process modelling technique attempting to incorporate elements of both "hard" and "soft" systems methodologies. The authors will expand upon these ideas later in Part II as this is relevant to developing PrOH Models.

Frameworks for the Selection of Systems Methodologies for Specific Purposes

Literature contains frameworks for choosing which systems approaches are appropriate for given situations. For the purposes of this book, two main approaches will be applied: Jackson and Keys (1984) *Towards a System of Systems Methodologies* along with Jackson's further work (Jackson, 1990) *Beyond a System of Systems Methodologies*, and Mingers' (2003) *A Classification of the Assumptions of Management Science Methods*. As neither approach is considered a definitive methodological framework beyond debate, each will be discussed in respect to SSMs and HSMs, and their relevance to the PrOH Modelling Methodology will be made explicit.

Jackson's System of Systems Framework

Jackson and Keys (1984) developed a system of systems methodologies as a classification of problem contexts in terms of the characteristics of the system within which the problem of concern is contained and the degree of agreement between decision makers, and later participants (Jackson, 1990). The system which contains the problem of concern is considered along a continuum from "simple" characteristic of Ackoff's (1974) **machine age** to "complex", characteristic of Ackoff's (1974) systems age. Simple systems contain a small number of elements with few or regular interactions which are fully observable, exhibiting well-defined laws of behaviour, in a relatively closed environment, passive subsystems and not influenced by behavioural issues. Complex systems contain many elements that are highly inter-related, only partly observable, exhibit probabilistic behaviour, are open to the environment, and exhibit behavioural characteristics. The objectives of decision makers may be unitary, where there is an agreed common set of goals on which decisions are based, or pluralist, where there is limited or no agreement on goals and decisions are made under differing objectives. In his development of his earlier work Jackson (1990) widens the scope of "decision makers" to participants including those who may be affected by the decision regardless of their effect on it.

Jackson and Keys (1984) adopt Ackoff's (1974) terminology by approximating "simple systems" to "mechanical" and "complex" to "systemic"; thus, four problem contexts were developed: mechanical-unitary, systemic-unitary, mechanical-pluralist and systemic-pluralist, which are discussed in more depth in Chapter 3. These evolved over time to become the more comprehensive System of Systems shown in Figure 1.1. *The PrOH Modelling Methodology sat in the original the Systemic-Pluralist category and now sits on the border of the later complex-pluralistic/complex-coercive zones of Jackson's Systems-of-Systems seen in* Figure 1.1.

Jackson (1990) emphasises that the application of "system of systems methodologies" should be a critical instrument which "must operate above the paradigms" and avoid being influenced by their theoretical assumptions. Problem contexts should be subordinated to critical thinking and provide guidance as, "'ideal type' classification of pure types of problem-context" making explicit the strengths and weaknesses of available techniques and the potential consequences of their use, which result from their assumptions. Thus, according to Jackson (1990) the "system of systems methodologies" (SOSM) (Figure 1.1) is applied as a part of critical thinking employed to select a methodology, rather than a prescription, that will serve the "knowledge" requirement.

At this point, it would seem appropriate to define *the problem* in more specific terms to facilitate an explanation of the reasoning behind methodological choices. Organisational systems, and systems for changing organisations, are characterised by elements and roles that are highly inter-related, where mathematical relationships are not clear (Shah and Ward, 2007; Alfieri et al., 2012), only partly observable at an organisational level, open to the environment and subject to the behavioural choices of the participants. The viewpoints of participants may be unitary in terms of the benefit of organisational change or improvement; however, in the absence of any definitive model, it is unlikely that there will be complete agreement on the structure and priorities of an organisational change programme (Albliwi et al., 2015). Furthermore, literature on

		Stakeholders		
		Unitary	**Pluralistic**	**Coercive**
Systems	**Complex**	Complex-unitary	Complex-pluralistic	Complex-coercive
	Complicated	Complicated-unitary	Complicated-pluralistic	Complicated-coercive
	Simple	Simple-unitary	Simple-pluralistic	Simple-coercive

FIGURE 1.1 Framework: Systems of System Methodologies/Problem Contexts.

Source: Adapted from Jackson (2019, p.164).

change management actively encourages innovations from employees, which requires them to challenge the *status quo*. This suggests that change is more effective in pluralist environments where employees can voice their opinions and are listened to (Eisenhardt, 2000; Morrison and Milliken, 2000). Therefore, the situation is likely, and possibly desirable, to be pluralist.

In conclusion, given the assumption that organisational systems (and organisational change systems) have a ("systemic-pluralist") "complex-pluralistic" context (Jackson and Keys, 1984), they are most approachable with Soft Systems Methodologies as the problem context is at the "soft" ill-defined end of the problem spectrum.

Minger's Classification of Management Science Methods

The work of Mingers (2003, p.562) classifies management science methods based on the **root definition** of a system, which he states as:

> A system to do the process specified by developing models of that assumed to exist, in the specified form of representation, based on necessary information, gained from particular sources, in order to assist users to achieve specified purposes.

Although authors have criticised Mingers" work (Gregory, 2003; Ormerod, 1992) for not classifying methods in terms of philosophical paradigms, Mingers (2005) clarifies this by stating "What I meant by this was that I was classifying the assumptions made by methods rather than the methods themselves". Nonetheless Gregory (2003) and Ormerod (1992) consider his approach as providing potentially useful descriptions and therefore Mingers" (2003) framework is a foundation for the purpose of the PrOH Modelling Methodology. Mingers' (2003) classification builds on the following underlying assumptions:

- **Ontology**, what the methodology assumes to exist (e.g. quantifiable "real" objects, causal relationships).
- **Epistemology**, the form of representation (e.g. diagrams).
- **Axiology**, necessary information (e.g. quantities, beliefs; sources of information used to build models, the appropriate users and the purpose of the methodology).

Mingers (2003) then continues to map each methodology onto a framework of problem context ("social", "personal" and "material") (Figure 1.2) against application criteria of what the methodology can do ("appreciation of", "analysis of", "assessment of" and "action to"). Thus, based on his framework, one can compare potential methodological approaches with the assumptions outlined about the problem and development of organisational systems. Mingers places SSM primarily in the central part of this grid: "Analysis of and Assessment of Personal contexts which have differing perceptions, personal rationality" with "alternative conceptualizations and constructions". But SSMs, such as the PrOH Modelling Methodology, also spill over into "Appreciation of social practices and power relationships" and "Action to select and implement best alternatives in a material context". All of which make SSM useful for organisational change. This is summarised by Figure 1.2.

SSM can be applied to all problem contexts; however, they are inefficient for all but "systemic-pluralist", analysis of and assessment of personal-social contexts. As this book

	Appreciation of	Analysis of	Assessment of	Action to
Social	Social practices, power relations	Distortions, conflicts, interests	Ways of altering existing structures	Generate empowerment and enlightenment
Personal	Individuals' beliefs, meanings, emotions	Differing perceptions, personal rationality	Alternative conceptualisations and constructions	Generate accommodations and consensus
Material	Physical circumstances	Underlying casual structure	Alternative physical and structural arrangements	Select and implements best alternatives

FIGURE 1.2 Framework: Classification of Management Science Methods.

is primarily concerned with these problem contexts, it will concentrate on SSM rather than HSMs from here onwards and only discuss HSMs in comparison.

Soft Systems Methodologies in More Depth

It is commonly accepted that three key authors in the development of "soft" systems methodologies are Churchman (1968), Ackoff (1971, 2010) and Checkland. Churchman's contribution is known as the "**Inquiring System**", Ackoff's is known as "**Interactive Planning**" and Checkland's is known as "**Soft Systems Methodology**" (SSM). The relationship between these is discussed fully by Jackson (1982, 1983). The authors of this book consider Checkland's SSM to have had more impact in the systems community than the others, especially in improving real-world problem situations. For this reason, the authors of this book concentrate on discussing Checkland's SSM, which has also had the most significance in the development of the PrOH Modelling Methodology.

Checkland's SSM

In general terms, Checkland's SSM is concerned with the improvement of problematical situations rather than the resolution of a given problem through a process of learning and reflective practice. These principles will be described in some detail as they also apply to Wilson's SSM and the PrOH Modelling Methodology. Checkland and Poulter (2006) state:

> SSM is an action-oriented process of inquiry into problematical situations in the everyday world; users learn their way from finding out about the situation to defining/taking action to improve it. The learning emerges via an organized process in which the real situation is explored, using intellectual devices – which serve to provide structure to discussion – to model purposeful activity built to encapsulate pure, stated worldviews.

Mingers (2003) summarises SSM as:

> a system to explore different worldviews relevant to a real-world situation and contrast them in a process of debate; Ontology: a real-world problem situation, conceptual human activity

systems (holons) and worldviews (W) are assumed to exist. Epistemology: system concepts, rich pictures, analyses 1, 2, 3, root definitions, conceptual models, and logical relations can be used to represent knowledge. Axiological: necessary information includes hard and soft information concerning structure, process, climate, and relevant worldviews; sources of information include concepts, language, logic, and participation by concerned actors; used by analysts, researchers, facilitators, and participants. Purpose: to learn about and improve a problematic situation by gaining agreement (accommodations) on feasible and desirable changes.

SSM utilises the "LUMAS" steps: "Learning **(L)** for a User by a Methodology-informed Approach to a Situation". In this context the "user **(U)** perceives a problem situation (S) and appreciating the methodology **(M)**, tailors the latter to the former to produce the specific approach **(A)** to be used in this situation **(S)**. This not only produces an improved situation but also yields learning (L)" (Checkland and Poulter, 2006, pp.19–20). The SSM learning cycle is summarised using seven principles which lead to five actions that can realise improvements in the problematical situation (Checkland and Poulter, 2006, pp.59–63).

Principle 1: the use of SSM to address a "real world problem" is incorporated in the concept of a "real world problematical situation" which represents a situation in the real world that someone whose worldview means they think needs improving.

Principle 2: individuals hold a particular worldview (weltanschauung) which characterises their assumptions and resulting interpretation of a "real world" situation. Thus, all critical appraisal and discussion of the "real world problematical situation" will be conditioned by the worldviews held by the participants.

Principle 3: it is assumed that every "real world problematical situation" will contain individuals who are trying to act purposefully; in other words, their activities are carried out to achieve some specific end. Thus "models of purposeful activity" must be created.

Principle 4: the models developed based on Principle 3 can be utilised as a source of questions to facilitate discussion and debate about the "real world problematical situation".

Principle 5: it is assumed that it is not possible to find optimised mathematical solutions that solve "real world problematical situations" rather it can only be improved by finding accommodations between different worldviews. Thus, through discussion and debate, embodied in Principle 4, an improved situation will entail an accommodation, a situation in which stakeholders can agree on collective action despite their differing worldviews and aspirations.

Principle 6: the process of inquiry embodied in Principles 1 to 5 is cyclical because the resulting accommodation entails a new (less) problematical situation with a new set of characteristics in which Principles 3 to 5 can be reapplied; representing a never-ending cycle of learning.

Principle 7: explicitly following the process of Principles 1 to 6 enables learning by facilitating conscious critical reflection about the situation and how one thinks about it. Thus, internalising SSM learning should lead to *reflective practice* where a practitioner reflects on the "real world *problematical situation*" prior to, during, and after interventions aimed at improving it.

These principles can be realised through the application of five actions in a cycle summarised in Figure 1.3 which makes an important distinction between the real world and systems

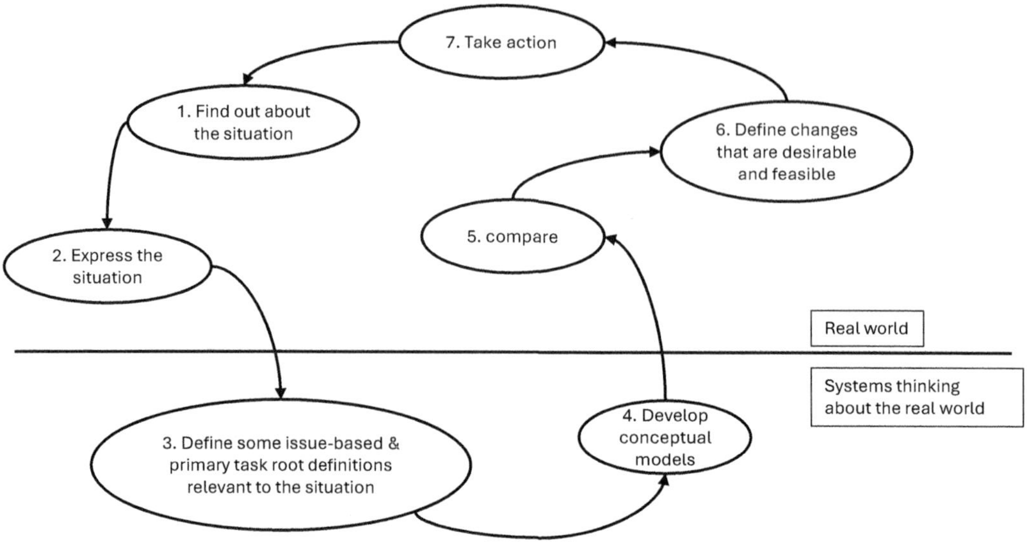

FIGURE 1.3 Checkland's SSM (2006).

thinking about the real world. This is because, from the philosophical perspective applied in SSM, systems of change do not objectively exist; rather, conceptual models or "human activity systems" are models "of a notional system containing the activities to undertake in order to pursue a particular purpose" such as change (Jackson, 2003, p.183). The five actions are:

- Finding out about the problem situation, utilising tools such as the **CATWOE (Customer, Agent, Transformation, Weltanschauung, Owner and Environment) Root Definition** of a system and E1, E2, E3 (1, 2 and 3 in Figure 1.3).
- Exploring the problematic situation through models of purposeful activity based on the different worldviews that are held by the participants and/or other relevant worldviews (Task 4 in Figure 1.3).
- Utilising the models to question the situation in a process of discussion and debate (Action 5 in Figure 1.3).
- Defining and taking action to improve the situation in a manner that can be accommodated by stakeholders to realise desirable and feasible changes (Tasks 6 and 7 in Figure 1.3).
- At a higher level, undergoing critical reflection on the whole process and learning about the situation and the SSM process as a whole.

The initial work to develop SSM was conducted by Checkland; however, other "versions" of SSM have been developed since then for specific situations, some of which are discussed below.

Salient Points to Note about Checkland's SSM

An Epistemological System

SSM is itself a system: an inquiring system for tackling ill-structured problems. This allows users to "learn" their way to improve a problematic situation. The enquiring system consists of two streams of analysis: the *logic-driven* strand and the *culture-driven* strand. The two streams interact, supporting and informing one another; these properties also make it suitable to be used for managing (Checkland, 1989).

The Concept of a Holon (née Human Activity System)

The term **Human Activity System** (HAS) was first coined by Blair and Whitson (1971) and has been popularised by Checkland. Checkland (1993) defines a system more specifically in terms of a HAS as:

> A model of a whole entity; when applied to human activity, the model is characterised fundamentally in terms of [~~hierarchical~~] structure, emergent properties, communication, and control. An observer may choose to relate this model to real-world activity. When applied to natural or man-made entities, the crucial characteristic is the emergent properties of the whole.

However, Checkland found two major problems with the term HAS that caused much confusion: firstly, trying to use everyday language (particularly the word "system") for serious professional discourse and, in doing so, trying to remember that conceptual models must not be treated as if they are part of reality. Systems scientists have striven to adopt a new term that removes these confusions. Gerard (1964) suggested the word "org", Jacob (1974) suggested "integron", and Koestler (1967) developed the concept of the "**holon**". It is the last word, "**holon**" that has come closest to catching on. Checkland adopted the term "**holon"** in his later work with Scholes (Checkland and Scholes, 1990a) to talk about the abstract notion of a whole instead of the term "system" when conceptualising and modelling HASs (Checkland, 1980b). Holon was coined to express the principle of layered structure, namely, an entity which is an autonomous whole at one level and is also a part of a higher-level whole. Allen and Starr (1982) give a definition of "**Holon**":

> The representation of an entity as a two-way window through which the environment influences the parts, through which the parts communicate as a unit to the rest of the universe. The have characteristic rates for their behaviour, and this places particular holons at certain levels in the [~~hierarchy~~] of holons. What a holon shall contain is determined by the observer.

Checkland and Allend and Starr's definitions are both interesting but are only partly agreed with by the authors of this book, because the *authors of this book do not agree that holons can be built as **hierarchies** but must be built as **holarchies***. Up until the development of the PrOH Modelling Methodology, this has not been **theorised**, developed as a methodology or clearly documented with examples, but this will be explained in more detail in Part II of this book. This book makes a novel contribution to "holon" construction and validation of their holarchical conceptualisation. Where the term "holon" is used by the authors to give a conceptual representation of a change system for a real-world "human activity system" within a holarchical set of models. The human activity can be real in the sense that it is a currently known and defined system; it can also be conceptual if it does not exist (e.g. a new process to be designed) or is so temporaneous that it is never defined or consciously recognised (e.g. a unique change process).

Checkland's SSM after Wilson

Wilson developed a different form of Checkland's SSM which adheres to the same philosophical perspective outlined above. Checkland (1999, p.257) considers Wilson's development as the application of SSM principles to the problem of making rational choices for organisation structure. In this context, the "relevant system" is a notional system (conceptual model) to carry out the organisation's primary task (or an aspect thereof). Once defined, the primary task leads to the development of **root definitions** which form the basis of conceptual models, which in turn form the rational basis of the organisational structure.

Wilson (2001) makes some refinements to the presentation of models including different arrow styles to represent information flows, more specific representation of monitoring and control activity, links between different subsystems and definitions of their boundaries (Wilson, 2001, pp.15–17), consideration of associated activities (Wilson, 2001, pp.63–65) and roles and responsibilities (Wilson, 2001, pp.91–140). The primary process is similar to Checkland's SSM; however, the difference is seen in the informational and structural aspects of the systems design as part of the "consensus primary task model" (CPTM).

Wilson's approach involves the use of an additional concept to Checkland's SSM known as the "Enterprise Model" embodied in the CPTM; this consists of

> a set of activities that represent its core process, i.e. its transformation process (T). There will be other activities (different in kind) which facilitate, or support, the process (S). Since the enterprise is bounded by some organization boundary, other activities must exist which Links its activities to its environment (L) and finally in a managed enterprise there will be activities to plan, monitor and control its destiny (P, M, C) (p.75). Each of the sets of activities T, S, L, and P, M, C is constructed in a similar fashion to Checkland SSM through a root definition, CATWOE analysis etc, the difference being .... There is not a neutral (non-contentious) model that forms a common set of activities in each system.
>
> *(Wilson, 2001, p.113)*

The process involves developing **root definitions** under each of the sets of activities T, S, L, and P, M, C, normally by constructing any one and adding each system to the model with appropriate connectivity, until the point is reached where a model of the organisational structure of the wider system and its information flows is created. The model or models can then be compared with the real-world situation to achieve an accommodation of views and consensus on action. Thus, in general terms, Wilson's SSM is similar to Checkland's approach, but it provides an additional methodological step to design organisational processes and assign responsibilities in more specific terms. Wilson's SSM is shown in Figure 1.4.

It is worth noting at this juncture that it seems to be an unwritten convention that soft systems methodologies use ovals and curved arrows, and hard methodologies use angular boxes and straight arrows with sharper corners to construct their diagrams. To the authors' knowledge, this has never been commented on until now, and we can offer no rational explanation for this other than maybe curves and circular icons subliminally give a softer, less engineered appearance to SSM models, which are supposed to present more philosophical and artistic interpretations.

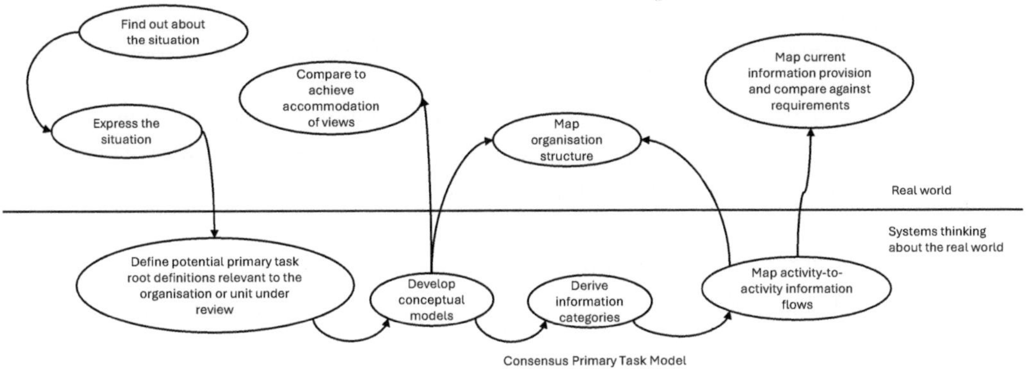

FIGURE 1.4 Checkland's SSM after Wilson (Wilson, 2001, p.8).

Critique of Checkland's SSM after Wilson by Authors

Despite its virtues, SSM is not without criticism. Checkland himself welcomes criticism to enrich and further establish soft systems thinking. Three of the main problems are highlighted below.

Regular Errors in Constructing Root Definitions and Conceptual Models

Checkland (1979) realises that the **root definitions** and conceptual models are problematic to construct and states that

- there is a tendency to formulate root definitions that contain several transformations and express several weltanschauungen;
- within **CATWOE** the most common mistake is to define a customer, the system's victims or beneficiaries, that is too far removed from the transformation;
- failures in logical dependency are common in constructing CMs;
- often the set of verb phrases (activities) used are outside the *minimal necessary set* (e.g. an operational level model should not contain the activity described by the verb phrase "generate profit" or "gain high reputation"); and
- the most common error is to slip into modelling part of the real world, rather than building a conceptual model of the system named in the root definition.

The Methodology Is Too General

Checkland has tried to construct a methodology for enquiring into any complex system. The authors of this book believe Checkland has fallen victim to and broken his own convictions because he emphasises the need for the right methodology for the right situation; this is the foundation of his criticism when "hard" methodologies are applied to complex and undefined problem situations. Checkland becomes guilty of doing just this even though it is at a lower level of application because, just as systems can be classified as "hard" or "soft", different types of "soft" systems can also be classified. Checkland alludes to these when he identifies conceptual models of "**holons** (or **human activity systems**) that are based on "primary root definitions" and those that are based on "issue-based root definitions". Furthermore, no honed techniques have been established in modelling from these different types of root definitions. Hence, the authors believe that Checkland's SSM is too general. Specialised techniques are needed to interpret the different nature of these root definitions. Also, new techniques are required to elucidate different properties exhibited by the processes in change management activities – these are discussed in depth in Part II.

Esoteric Theory Detached from Techniques

The authors believe that Checkland's soft systems methodology has much to offer but is not accessible to the uninitiated user as

1. the theoretical aspects are far too philosophical and esoteric to interest anyone who does not want to become a dedicated "systems thinker";
2. the conceptual models are the weakest part of the methodology as little practical guidance is offered by Checkland or his peers for how to build these. This causes people to choose more practical (usually "hard") methodologies in favour of Checkland's SSM; and
3. the theory and the practice do not relate well due to the incredible complexity of the foundations of his work and the shallowness of a finished conceptual model. This means that the good ideas contained in the philosophy are not apparent in the models produced by Checkland's SSM.

More work is required in the systems thinking field that offers a SSM that can be easily used by people who do not want to become full-time dedicated systems thinkers. This is a very serious problem which the authors believe stops SSMs becoming industrially recognised.

Other "Soft" Systems Approaches

The work of Ackoff (1981a, 1981b), Checkland and Churchman is taken to be representative of "soft" systems thinking. The emphasis in "soft" systems thinking is, "... on how to cope with ill-structured problems or 'messes' (Ackoff, 1981b). Rather than attempting to reduce the complexity of messes so that they can be modelled mathematically, "soft" systems thinkers seek to explore them by working with the different perceptions of them that exist in peoples' minds. Systems are seen as the mental constructs of observers rather than as entities with a real, objective existence in the world. Ackoff began as an OR researcher but despaired of the "predict and prepare" approach taken by OR. Instead, he established a social systems sciences' programme which was concerned with the development of **Interactive Planning**: a means of, "designing a desirable future and inventing ways of bringing it about".

The metaphor that most obviously underpins "soft" systems thinking is that of organisations as a "culture". Emphasis is placed upon the different values existing within the social system of concern. These should be surfaced, and their implications drawn out.

Interactive Planning

Mingers (2003) summarises Interactive Planning (IP) as:

a system to prepare a vision of how an organization should be and plan how to realise the design. **Ontology**: stakeholders with differing values that can be reconciled in designs for the future that are preferable for all are assumed to exist. **Epistemology**: constrained or unconstrained idealised designs that are technologically feasible operationally viable and improvable can be used to represent knowledge. **Axiology**: necessary information includes stakeholders' views about desirable designs for their own spheres of influence and their inter-relations; sources of information, involvement by all, the stakeholders in the design/planning process, used by analysts, facilitators, and stakeholders. Purpose: to plan and design futures that are desirable for different stakeholder groups and then jointly realise them.

On initial appraisal, IP would appear to be appropriate for use in organisations to develop an organisational change programme; however, there are several issues which would make it difficult or impractical to use in the context of research. Firstly, the development of an idealised design is context-specific and therefore is unlikely to be flexible enough to facilitate discussion in different contexts or stimulate discussion of alternative structures. Secondly, the IP methodology advocates the use of a particular organisational structure, the involvement of as many stakeholders as possible, the continuous review and development of plans and holistic management to integrate plans from different parts of the organisation (Ackoff, 1981a; Jackson and Keys, 1984; Sinn, 1998). Thus, the IP would be feasible for use in a single case study or intervention; however, it would require considerable resources to apply in several case studies to develop a more general model. Thus, from a practical perspective, SSM (Checkland or Wilson) and the PrOH Modelling Methodology (see Part II) have several advantages over IP (Sinn, 1998). SSM and PrOH do not require the consensus necessary for IP, have greater flexibility, can produce a greater diversity of models, do not require widespread participation of stakeholders and can articulate different worldviews for the change management. IP's main advantage over Checkland's SSM is its consideration of organisational structure (Sinn, 1998). While both Wilson's SSM and PrOH are specifically focused on organisational structure, in conclusion, IP is a valuable approach for the development of a change management programme; however, its need for a big resource commitment makes it impractical for many applications.

Viable Systems Model (VSM) Methodology

The Viable System Model (VSM) methodology is a conceptual framework developed by a British consultant, Stafford Beer, in the late 1960s and early 1970s. The model was first published in 1972 in Beer's book titled *Brain of the Firm (*Beer, 1972). He defined a viable system as a "system capable of independent existence". Beer's model focused on identifying patterns of communication in a network or teams, where he identified invariances which he posits can be applied universally regardless of size or nature. VSM has been applied in numerous firms ranging from SMEs to multinational corporations.

Beer (1984) suggests there are five essential subsystems interactively involved in any viable system of an organisation capable of maintaining its identity in any shared environment. In summary, these five subsystems are:

- **System 1 – The element that produces (operations).** This represents the team that produces the primary goods and services of an organisation and is responsible for carrying out the value-addition tasks of the goods and services produced in an organisation.
- **System 2 – The element that coordinates.** This ensures smooth communication and collaboration between the operational units in System 1. This element ensures flexibility and removes the traditional top-down control and directives.
- **System 3 – The element that controls.** This controls and monitors Systems 1 and 2 and adjusts as needed. By putting in place good reporting systems and an effective way of communication, the potential for supervisory requirements could be lessened.
- **System 4 – The element that gathers information/intelligence.** This is future-focused planning to ensure organisations adapt to rapidly changing environments by collecting and analysing data from both internal and external environments. It is a two-way link between the viable system and its external environment.
- **System 5 – The element that establishes objectives of the firm/policy.** This establishes policy and the overall direction of an organisation, serving as a guide to organisational processes. Its main goal is to provide clarity about the directions, objectives, values and goals of an organisation.

All five subsystems constitute the building blocks needed to construct a viable system.

While it is true that VSM questions the functions and structure of organisations, it is also a method that is complex and inaccessible to managers and requires dedication and extensive training to use effectively (Bititci, 2024, p.61; Burgess and Wake, 2013; Jackson, 2019, p.299). Also, it is a *huge irony*, that it uses *five* quite artificially separated conceptual systems to examine one actual real system. Authors of this book posit that this is surely the antithesis of holistic systems thinking, where effort is taken to keep parts of a (human activity) change system together as much as possible and look at its emergent (and hidden) behaviour. One might argue that the VSM method is more complicated than the actual real system under observation!?

Strategic Assumption and Surfacing Testing (SAST)

Strategic Assumption Surfacing and Testing (SAST) can be used to "Synthesise competing viewpoints about complex interactive messes". It attempts to identify and articulate contrasting competing views of groups and individuals regarding strategic options and reach a consensus through a process of debate (Mingers, 2003). From Mingers" (2003) perspective this would appear appropriate for problem solving; however, Jackson and Keys (1984) conclude that SAST focuses almost exclusively on addressing the pluralist aspects of problem contexts but does not provide a method for dealing with systemic aspects, assuming that once a consensus has been reached, the systemic aspects will be resolved.

Strategic Options Development Analysis (SODA)

Strategic Options Development Analysis (SODA) and cognitive mapping (Eden, 1995) can be used to "Surface and understand individual beliefs and generate consensus about possible strategic actions" (Mingers, 2003); however, a prerequisite for the use of the approach is that "The consultant will be more interested in designing and managing problem-solving workshops rather than in research and analysis of the problem characteristics" (Rosenhead and Mingers,

2001, p.22). Thus, SODA may be better suited to deciding what actions to take to change an organisational change programme rather than general research; additionally, the research is concerned with the extent of change programmes rather than individuals' perception of them (Rosenhead and Mingers, 2001, pp.21–60).

Strategic Choice Approach (SCA)

Strategic Choice Approach (SCA) (Rosenhead and Mingers, 2001, pp.115–150) can be used to "Structure decision choices under conditions of uncertainty and reach agreements and commitments for action" (Mingers, 2003). It considers decision problems based on three forms of uncertainty: uncertainty about *guiding values*, uncertainties about the *working environment* and uncertainties about choices on related agendas (Rosenhead and Mingers, 2001, pp.116–118). The approach employs four modes of thinking for decision makers; *shaping* the structure of the decision problems that are currently faced; *designing* the feasible courses of action based upon the current structure of the decision problems; *comparing* the implications of different courses of action; and *choosing* what actions should be taken currently and in the future (Rosenhead and Mingers, 2001, pp.118–150). SCA may be appropriate for the development of change management programmes; however, it is focused on a high level and is not designed to compare process redesign.

The above account of softer system thinking methodologies is given to appreciate some well-known methodologies. Other lesser-established areas of systems thinking include Visionary Systems Thinking (VST) (Filion, 1994) and Emancipatory Systems Thinking (EST) (Lane and Jackson, 1995).

Criticism of Soft Systems Methodologies in General

Criticism of "soft" methodologies often centres around Checkland's SSM due to its well-developed theoretical foundation and numerous published works. However, the common criticisms are listed below:

- SSM is unsuitable for the design of complex systems or if the situation is characterised by significant conflict and therefore accommodations cannot be reached (Jackson, 2003, pp.202–207).
- SSM has a limited ability to appreciate why problem situations occur, particularly if the design of complex systems requires practical expertise to derive rational solutions to problems.
- SSM adherence to an interpretive perspective, while theoretically sound, is criticised for discounting the possibility that "hard" approaches for managing complex adaptive systems can provide an objective approach to organisational design and management (Jackson, 2003, pp.202–207). However, although implementation is often considered soft, SSM does not preclude hard approaches; rather, once Stage 7 has been reached, hard approaches can then be applied (Wilson, 2001, p.8) by **grafting** (Miles, 1988).
- SSM focus on reaching accommodations tends to result in regulatory rather than radical change and assumes that social constraints, e.g. power relationships, do not affect the nature of those accommodations. It may not be realistic to ignore the role of existing structures

in creating worldviews which may not be possible to change without changing structure (Jackson, 2003; Rodríguez-Ulloa et al., 2011; Jackson and Keys, 1984).

- SSM does not provide guidelines on the construction of a "rich picture" of the real-world problem situation which may result in biased or incomplete representations (Rodríguez-Ulloa et al., 2011).
- Soft systems methodologies only produce "vague" solutions because actions are expressed verbally without a defined set of quantitative and qualitative measures to assess the effectiveness of agreed action in producing change and benefits in the real-world (Rodríguez-Ulloa et al., 2011).
- SSM offers little guidance on how proposed actions should be implemented in the real world and there is no clear consideration of practical aspects such as resource requirements, costs and responsibilities (Rodríguez-Ulloa et al., 2011). It should be noted that Wilson's (2001) SSM is better at addressing issues of responsibilities and SSM in general as it is not a fixed methodology.

There is no reason why the above criticisms could not be addressed through further developments, and despite the criticisms of SSM, it is considered to have several strong benefits:

- The SSM approach moves away from a goal-seeking approach to one utilising human activity system models to understand the important relationships between elements and reach accommodations on changes that are both desirable and feasible to stakeholders (Jackson, 2003, p.208).
- SSM does not require a clear set of goals before beginning problem-solving; rather, it mirrors normal managerial processes of development and consensus making.
- SSM offers a way of exploring possible solutions given different worldviews of participants.
- SSM provides a learning system by which to challenge existing perceptions and worldviews that can lead to novel solutions and new perspectives on problem situations.
- SSM is a way to understand the purpose of a system so that appropriate support systems and structures can be designed.

Several methods are available to support SSM approaches, and this book is mostly concerned with the developments that have been made in "soft" systems thinking, its associated methodologies and techniques for exploring undefined problem situations. However, to give these meaningful context, it is also necessary to discuss the methodologies and techniques associated with "hard" systems thinking and methodologies because the approaches are complementary and understanding one helps understanding the juxtaposition.

Hard Approaches

"Hard" systems thinkers view the real world as a system to optimise its performance in pursuit of some predetermined goal. Hard systems thinking embraces classical operational research (OR), systems analysis (SA), and systems engineering. As Checkland (1983) argues, these are all "based upon the assumption that the problem task they tackle is to select an efficient means of achieving a known and defined end". OR requires "formulation of the problem" (Churchman et al., 1957) based on the objectives to be achieved. SA requires "an objective or objectives which we desire to accomplish" (Hitch, 1985) and SE of, "a need to be met" (Hall, 1962). Once the problem of concern has been formulated, the system in which it is located is represented in a quantitative model, and experiments carried out which suggest an optimal solution that can then be implemented in the real world. The metaphor that underpins "hard" systems thinking is that of the organisation as a machine. It considers that an organisation can be designed in a similar fashion to a product. Managers are the rational decision makers in charge of ensuring the organisation structure is appropriately designed and controlled, in which measurable action can be taken. Social and behavioural issues do not normally strongly feature in hard methodology models.

Discrete Event Simulation

Mingers (2003) summarises (visual) Discrete Event Simulation (DES) as:

> A system to simulate the dynamic behaviour of physical and social flows and processes, and their causal relation. **Ontology**: entities and activities with stable patterns of statistical behaviour that form inter-linked processes. **Epistemology**: activity-cycle diagrams, entity life cycles, visual, interactive software. **Axiology** necessary information includes entities, their interactions, and the behavioural pattern; sources of information, observation and measurement of real-world entities and procedure, used by analysts. **Purpose**: to explore the operation of complex real-world interactions between discrete entities to aid understanding and control.

Literature contains many instances of the use of discrete event simulation, and simulation in general, to model organisations (Abdulmalek and Rajgopal, 2007; Detty and Yingling, 2000; Mandahawi et al., 2010; Robinson et al., 2012). However, much is concerned with the specifics of implementations, such as production or logistics, or as a method to facilitate discussion and understanding of organisational processes rather than the implementation of complex organisational change.

DES utilises activity-cycle diagrams to build simulations of entities of interest based on the interactions of entities and resources over time. Entities are the individual elements whose characteristics are being simulated and explicitly tracked (e.g. machines in a factory) and resources are individual countable elements that are treated as a group (e.g. the number of passengers waiting at a bus stop). Elements of the system are further sub-divided into classes, permanent elements that have identical or similar characteristics which may be modelled individually as sets, temporary groups of entities (e.g. members of a queue) and their attributes, with some discriminating or behavioural information that describes each entity. A simulation clock defines the time at which entities undergo operations which include events and the point in time when an entity changes state, such as activities moving from one state to another. Likewise, the chronological grouping of the sequence of events experienced by an entity or process (Pidd, 2004, pp.63–81). Thus, DES applies a bottom-up approach to constructing detailed models to *replicate* real-world (Schwaninger, 2006).

The application of DES may follow two possible approaches: event-based approaches considering the life cycle of each entity, which then decomposes into more performative parts defining all possible logical consequences of an event; or a process-based approach using a definition of the whole process of an entity and its constituent parts as the building block of a simulation (Pidd, 2004, pp.83–108). Hence, DES can provide understanding of underlying causal structures and examine alternative physical and structural arrangements. Despite the appropriateness of DES for detailed replications, it presents some practical challenges for change management. First, the bottom-up approach requires the definition of the characteristics of a high number of individual entities, which would require considerable resources and would be made difficult by the probable absence of data on which to base characteristics, causal inter-relationships and uncertainty of behaviours. Second, the application of DES to multiple case studies will greatly increase the number of entities and relationships that must be characterised, and the cross-case comparison will therefore become extremely complex should the characteristics change by context or maturity. Third, the probable lack of appropriate data necessary for a bottom-up approach will result in large numbers of assumptions, and therefore potential errors, which is undesirable (see Occam's Razor in Pidd, 2004) and could make essential validation infeasible. Thus, DES is not considered practical to facilitate the management of change to a conceptual system of systemic success factors, as it is too mechanistic and too reductionistic.

System Dynamics

System Dynamics is a relatively flexible modelling approach and can be combined with other methodologies (Schwaninger, 2006). According to Mingers (2003) System Dynamics is:

> A system to simulate the dynamic behaviour of physical and social flows and processes, and their causal relations. **Ontology**: material and immaterial stocks and flows, and their causal feedback relationships, information and decisions that link them. **Epistemology**: influence diagrams, systems dynamics diagrams, icon-based interactive software. **Axiology**: necessary information are structures of causal relations between flows, ideally with quantified data and mathematical relations; source of information observation and measurement of real world together with judgement and opinion user analyst. **Purpose**: to explore the operation of the complex real-world system to aid understanding and control.

As stated above, the main purpose of the application of a hard approach is to experiment with different options to identify the best structure to implement strategic actions (Snabe and Größler, 2006). System Dynamics attempts to identify key variables that affect a given outcome and define causal inter-relationships leading to observed or expected behaviours. These inter-relationships are articulated in a causal-loop diagram specifying interactions as positive and negative relationships, which can provide qualitative insights into a problem situation (Coyle, 2000). The causal-loop diagram can be further developed into a simulation model by defining the elements that accumulate and/or dissipate (stocks) and the physical or informational flows that lead to changes in the level of stocks (flows); this results in a stock and flow diagram. Mathematical relationships can then be derived to describe the expected behaviour as logical changes to causal assumptions play out in the model (Sterman, 2000).

Systems Dynamics is normally used in an exploratory manner to formulate strategies (Rodríguez-Ulloa et al., 2011) or to facilitate strategic implementation where general strategic decisions have already been made (Snabe and Größler, 2006). Hence *the scope of changes that can be made to the actual strategy is limited and the main purpose of systems dynamics modelling is understanding and refining a decision that has already been made.* In this context, strategy formulation and implementation are not separate but overlap; however, implementation modelling focuses on **intervention planning** including the definition of objectives, targets, roles, responsibilities and time and budget planning, stakeholder management including skills and "buy-in" and implementation planning including communication and roles.

The philosophical position of System Dynamics has not been resolved; or rather the theoretical assumptions of System Dynamics have been taken for granted and as such it may be applied under several philosophical positions (Lane, 2001, Part 1). It is often the case that System Dynamics is a "hard" methodology; however, this has been argued to stem from a poor understanding (Lane, 2000). Jackson (2003, pp.81–82) considers System Dynamics to have a functionalist perspective, focused on the objective understanding of the underlying structure of social systems while only giving limited attention to subjectivist viewpoints. However, system dynamics differs from other "hard" approaches by applying functionalism in terms of a structuralist epistemology; hence providing access to underlying causal structures that lead to systems behaviour rather than "surface details that, once logically examined, explain what is happening" (Jackson, 2003, p.82). Thus, System Dynamics "fits with Popper's view that the world is partly causal, partly probabilistic and partly open i.e. shapable by human will". (Lane, 2000, p.9).

Lane (2000) suggest it is superficial to consider System Dynamics as a "hard" purely functionalist and/or determinist approach; rather, it should be considered in terms of social theories that "seek to integrate the agency and structure views of social realms" (Lane, 2000, p.6) such as structuralism. In this and later work, Lane critiques the common criticisms and viewpoints on Systems Dynamics and clarifies the following philosophical position (Lane, 2000, 2001):

> System Dynamics helps people to think about the logical consequences of certain assumptions… but predictions are conditional on those assumptions. The point of an intervention is to aid in the creation of new assumptions, that is, guiding policies. (Lane, 1999, pp.7–9)

Human decision-making is conditioned on its environment while the environment is conditioned on human decisions. Therefore, System Dynamics is situated between determinism and human agency where "human decisions are only partly determined by system structure and that since the purpose of modelling is to make such influences explicit, the system may be recrafted advantageously" (Lane, 2000, p.10). Also, that System Dynamics is "concerned with aggregate social phenomena rather than individual meaningful action thus it puts forward a structural theory rather than a content theory and the level of aggregation, being above the individual, means it is reasonable to place less emphasis on human agency" (Lane, 2001, pp.11–15).

A System Dynamics model is concerned with framing a situation for a particular purpose, not because it is "correct" in a hard systems context. Thus, the judgements of a models" applicability are inherently subjective; therefore, it is entirely reasonable to construct several models based on different worldviews. Hence, users should avoid black-box models, aggregate models at a level away from individual decisions, and apply them as a system for learning (Lane, 2000 pp.15–17).

Criticisms levelled at System Dynamics are frequently based on the assumption that it follows a strict "hard" philosophy; however, the adoption of Lane's assumptions, outlined above, partly addresses some of these. Common criticisms are outlined below:

- The application of System Dynamics as an entirely "objective" methodology to describe a system and its inter-relationships denies human agency, assuming structure has complete control over human action; thus, individuals are considered unable to shape social systems, and the possibility of subjectivity and differing goals is neglected (Jackson, 2003; Lane, 2000).
- When adopting a realist philosophy, systems are assumed to exist in the real world and be governed by deterministic cause and effect, rather than being cognitive devices constructed by the modeller. Hence, systems can be objectively assessed and solved using "facts" (Rodríguez-Ulloa et al., 2011; Lane and Oliva, 1998; Lane, 2000). This approach assumes there is a singular problem; however, the problem is framed within the worldview of the modeller without that worldview being articulated and made explicit (Rodríguez-Ulloa et al., 2011).
- System Dynamics does not have a method for eliciting worldviews; thus, it is difficult to know on what basis to assess the model. Further, it is not possible to assess if an aggregate model or set of models has a coherent worldview(s) or if there are significant inconsistencies (Rodríguez-Ulloa et al., 2011; Lane, 2000, p.15).
- System Dynamics is too imprecise, which limits the "proper" representation of the initial state of the system and its usefulness in predicting behaviour (Jackson, 2003).
- System Dynamics has no specific method for the implementation of the policies chosen (Rodríguez-Ulloa et al., 2011). This criticism may be true of system dynamics models designed to describe behaviour; however, it is entirely possible to apply system dynamics as an implementation tool (Snabe and Größler, 2006).
- If there is no consideration of existing theory in the field of study, the resulting models can lack rigor. This is particularly the case if there is an over-reliance on system archetypes rather than an appropriate set of relationships when care has not been taken to collect all the necessary data for the model to be relevant (Sterman, 2000).

Despite the criticisms of system dynamics, it is considered to offer several benefits (Jackson, 2003):

- creates the ability to look beneath the surface for underlying structures responsible for behaviour;
- provides understanding of feedback and its relation to behaviour;
- avoids jumping to conclusions and considers what, potentially small, interventions can be made to make the greatest impact;
- avoids the blaming of individuals for problems that arise from a combination of events within the system;
- provides understanding of systemic relationships that can lead to double-loop learning;
- gives a top-down perspective of system dynamics (Schwaninger, 2006) making it easier to consider and select between a number of different structural arrangements or models than approaches such as DES, which require the definition of a much larger number of elements;
- gives a high-level perspective of systems dynamics, above the individual, enables the modelling of intangible elements (Warren, 2008, pp.575–626) based on "approximate" data rather than requiring the "exact" causal relationships necessary for other "hard" methodologies; and
- can be effectively combined with soft approaches, most notably with SSM (Rodríguez-Ulloa et al., 2011).

Overall System Dynamics can lead to models that can enable a non-superficial ability to understand the elements that make real change to the system (Jackson, 2003; Senge, 1990). Thus, organisational change agents can experiment with and learn about significant relationships, effects of assumptions, policies and delays that affect the implementation of possible actions to develop their programmes (Jackson, 2003; Senge, 1990; Mingers, 2003; Moorcroft, 2004).

Consider Action Box 1.

ACTION BOX 1: HARD OR SOFT METHODOLOGY?

Decide which of the following scenarios is best suited to hard systems methodologies and why:

1. Design of a new manufacturing system for sub-assembly for a radar system.
2. Designing a customer-facing service system for a rail operator.
3. Delivery of a high-volume low-variety legal system to provide legal services.
4. Redesign of an organisational system called "win new business".
5. Detail simulation of a conveyor belt system.
6. Designing a new engine sub-system.

Answers given at the back.

Summary

This chapter outlined systems approaches, each with their own methodologies and techniques. Soft systems approaches are most central to this book and have been juxtaposed to "hard" systems approaches. The authors of this book would like to make the following points in summary to contrast the positivist stance of "hard" systems methodologies with the interpretive phenomenological stance of "soft" systems methodologies, as the choice of methodology not only depends on the systems characteristics but also on the intentions of the systems analyst. In other words, *whether the systems analyst desires to optimise the chosen system or do they wish to understand and learn about the systems properties? And what happens if they desire to do both; which methodology should then be used?* These authors believe they have developed a hybrid "hard-soft" methodology in PrOH Modelling to suit the specific combinations of such scenarios by taking the following points into consideration. The main points are summarised below.

- The "Hard" and "Soft" Methodological Divide Is Too Great and Needs Bringing Together

Each systems thinking approach (methods or techniques) offers useful contributions in the endeavour to understand and improve organisational performance, but each taken separately harbours deficiencies. For example, SSMs do not offer enough guidance for building and achieving goals that are essential components for business strategic planning. HSMs, on the other hand, lack guidance to tackle organisational social and political issues. However, no organisation is directly applicable to either "hard" or "soft" systems theory, but this tends to be the way systems analysis is conducted due to the dichotomous nature of how systems methodologies are sometimes perceived. The authors of this book believe that the systems approach requires a pragmatic methodology that embraces elements of each approach for effective practical organisational process improvement.

- Development of "Soft" System Techniques Are Required

These authors have criticised Checkland's SSM for being too general and believe that this is caused by the application domain of SSM being too great. Every ill-structured problem will have many properties; Checkland mentions four (communication, emergent properties, hierarchy (incorrectly these authors argue) and control). It is improbable that these four properties could be the total and exhaustive correct set to be investigated in every circumstance. However, these authors believe that a more honed methodology can be developed if the systems analyst understands which properties he would like to investigate or optimise before a systems analysis begins. The primary concern of this book is precisely defined as the investigation and optimisation of organisational processes or procedures; these authors believe this set of properties should be reassessed considering this more precise application.

- Type of Observed System

Hard systems engineers tackle well-defined, **unitary problems** that reoccur in the real world. Soft systems methodologists address messy, pluralistic, ill-structured problem situations, which are often unique. For this reason, the approach used to analyse well-defined systems is often said to be "positivist" and for learning about ill-structured problem situations, it is said to be "phenomenological". A blend of both is needed.

- The Use of System Concepts

"Hard" systems thinking assumes the perceived world contains "holons"; "soft" systems thinking takes the stance that the methodology, the process of enquiry, can itself also be created as a "holon". Checkland's SSM is itself a "holonic" (previously called "systemic") process, which within its procedures happens to make use of models of "holons". The real distinction between hard and soft is the marked shift of assumed **systemicity**, from the real world into the process of enquiry into the world. The contrast between the two approaches is best summed up by Checkland and Scholes (1990) as:

> that which takes the world to be holonic ("hard systems thinking") and that which creates the process of enquiry as a holon. SSM is such a holon, a cyclic process of enquiry which happens also within its processes to makes use of holons. In everyday language we say that SSM is systemic [holonic] in two senses. It is a systemic process of enquiry, one which happens to make use of "systemic models". … those who write about "human activity systems" as if they exist in the real world, rather than being holons which can be compared with the world, are failing to grasp the essence of soft systems thinking.

"Hard" systems methodologies are *not* **teleological** as they do not ask what *purpose* is served by an object or system. "Soft" systems methodologies are teleological as they are learning systems about messy human situations (Khisty, 1993). Checkland (1983) states that, "*the weakness* *of OR, not less than that of SE and SA* ['hard' systems methodologies], *is that they are wedded to logic in situations in which logic is not necessarily paramount*".

- Holism Not Reductionism

HSMs are characterised by three principles: reductionism, repeatability and the refutation of (null) hypotheses expressed in the models. SSMs have the opposite approach by viewing problems *holistically*, dealing with unique situations and being exploratory. Therefore, SSMs do not seek to continuously divide and sub-divide the perceived real-world situations but try to preserve the holistic characteristics of the 'holon" to learn about its four major properties (holarchy (not hierarchy), communication, control and emergent properties) which are too nebulous to be usefully analysed through a HSM. Checkland (1980b) states that:

> The system movement, embodying holism rather than reductionism, offers the development of thinking in terms of whole entities which, exhibiting emergent properties cannot be reduced to their elements.

The problem of reductionism and fragmentation in analysis was one of the original impetuses to evolve SSM considering we are in the systems age.

- Validation

The distinction between "hard" and "soft" reflects the different nature of models in the two approaches. In a "hard" approach, models must be shown to adequately represent a part of the real world; in a "soft" approach, models have only to be verifiable, internally defensible, against a set of principles which define a particular kind of intellectual construct or a particular kind of epistemological device (Checkland, 1995). This gives SSMs better adaptability to represent political, social and cultural issues in their models.

- "Hard" System Methodologies Are a Subset of "Soft" Systems Methodologies

In one sense, it is wrong to even make a comparison between HSMs and SSMs because Checkland (1985) considers HSMs to be a subset, a special case, of SSMs when he states, "relations between hard and soft systems thinking are not like that between apples and pears; it is like that between apples and fruit". By this statement, Checkland means that an SSM could be used to analyse any problem situation that can be conceived as a system, whereas HSMs can only be used to analyse well-formulated systems that have clearly defined objectives. Therefore, following his logic, HSMs are a subset of SSMs. "Soft systems methodology can on occasion sharpen up into 'hard' methodology, which is a special case of it, but there can be no direct import of the 'hard' concepts into fuzzy ill-structured problems" (Checkland, 1993). However, if a problem is well formulated, it would probably be an overkill to apply an SSM, as a HSM would meet the desired need. Differences between HSMs and SSMs are discussed further by Khisty (1995) and Checkland (1993). It is summed up concisely by Woodburn (1988):

> Hard approach – the world is made up of systems, we can study it systematically. Soft approach – the world is problematic; we can study it systemically [holistically] (by thinking about it by means of a system of enquiry).

These concluding points are closely related and form part of the impetus for novel contributions made in the following parts of this book.

Further Reading

Bititci, U., and Spanellis, A. (2024), *Systems Thinking for Business and Management: Principles and Practice*. London: KoganPage.

Checkland, P., and Scholes, J. (1990), *Soft Systems Methodology in Action*. Chichester: Wiley.

Clegg, B.T. (1999), *A Systems Approach to Re-Engineering Business Processes Towards Concurrent Engineering Principles*. PhD Thesis. Chapter 2. De Montfort University and British Library.

Jackson, M.C. (2019), *Critical Systems Thinking and the Management of Complexity: Responsible Leadership for a Complex World*. Chichester: Wiley.

Orme. (2016), *A Systems Approach to Developing a Unified Methodology and Deployment Model to Help Maximize Impact of Lean Thinking and Six Sigma in Organizations*. PhD Thesis, Aston University.

Jackson, M.C. (2003), *Systems Thinking: Creative Holism for Managers*. Chichester: Wiley.

Ramage, M., and Shipp, K. (2020), *Systems Thinker's*. 2nd ed. Milton Keynes: Springer.

2

THE ACTION RESEARCH PARADIGM

A Research Paradigm

A **research paradigm** is a basic belief system that guides researchers in fundamental choices of ontology, epistemology and methodology (Guba and Lincoln, 1994). According to Guba (1990), paradigms can be characterised through three axioms:

- **ontology** which addresses the question of "What is the form and nature of reality and, therefore, what is there that can be known about it"?
- **epistemology** which addresses the question of "What is the nature of the relationship between the knower and what can be known"?
- **methodology** which addresses the question of "How can the knower go about finding out whatever he or she believes can be known"?

These axioms create a holistic view of how knowledge is viewed, how a researcher sees themselves in relation to this knowledge and the methodological means they use to discover it.

A research paradigm is best treated as the worldview (or weltanschauung) of a researcher. **Positivism** and **interpretivism** (sometimes known as **phenomenologicalism)** are two major prevalent worldviews. Table 2.1 contrasts positivist and interpretivist paradigms based on ontological, epistemological and methodological axioms.

In this book, the authors uphold the view that the reality of organisational change is subjective and context-sensitive, and the purpose of action research in organisational change is to explore, understand and explain the system. For instance, how a law firm operates within a wider legal system. Such an inquisition indicates that a researcher must have an **interpretive** perception worldview as dictated by the property of three axioms discussed in Table 2.1.

DOI: 10.4324/9781032650425-3

TABLE 2.1 Comparison between Positivist and Interpretivist Paradigms

	Definition	*Positivism*	*Interpretivism (Phenomenologicalism)*
Ontology	What is the form and nature of reality and, therefore, what is there that can be known about it?	Researcher and reality are separate	Researcher and the reality are inseparable
Epistemology	What is the nature of the relationship between the knower and what can be known?	Objective reality exists beyond the human mind – objectivist	Knowledge of the world is intentionally constituted through a person's lived experience – subjectivist
Methodology	How can the knower go about finding out whatever they believe can be known?	Experimental, verification of hypotheses, mainly quantitative methods – statistics, content analysis	Qualitative methods, use of Hermeneutics and Phenomenology

Source: Adapted from Guba and Lincoln (1994).

Interpretivism as a Dominant Paradigm for Action Research

Interpretivism is often the dominant paradigm used by researchers in organisational improvement and related theory development; and therefore, interpretivism and qualitative research are sometimes used interchangeably in a mixed method approach. For some, the former term is often taken to mean all those approaches in the human sciences that do not take a **hypothetico-deductive** approach to investigation, and qualitative research is itself characterised by an interpretive approach (Denzin and Lincoln, 1995, p.2). Either way, interpretivism can be understood as an umbrella term covering several traditions, in that the researchers have mostly followed **phenomenology** as a philosophy based on the premise that "one who is experiencing something can never stand apart from that experience" (Lee and Lings, 2008, p.59).

In this book, the authors have studied cases (Part III) acting in the role of an insider to understand the way operations management is practised (e.g. in the legal services or in a manufacturing plant) and have sought to generate new knowledge from these cases (Part III). Therefore, the authors of this book have been involved as participants in action research case studies where each case was selected for its potentially interesting socio-economic-technical management challenges. The qualifying factors for choosing each in-depth case study for action research were: (1) the possibility for rich data associated with an in-depth case study that could help probe the boundaries of organisational phenomena for wider learning opportunities; (2) time to allow these researchers to become familiar with the details of the profession, organisation and make a change and (3) the context specificity of the organisation and an authentic and willing desire to change the composition of operations (Lewis and Brown, 2012). Thus, this book presents phenomenologically based interventions that are derived from lived experiences in action research, where the researcher and reality are inseparable, using systems thinking methodology to make cultural and operational changes.

Action Research as a Process

Action research is a cyclical process where the researcher primarily selects a real-world situation, assigns respective roles to the people (participants) in that situation who begin to inquire about the situation to make improvements (Checkland, 1991). Simultaneously, both the researcher and participants start to make sense of the situation with the help of a declared framework and methodology. The procedure can be repeated as earlier stages can be reflected upon and new learning may be generated to further improve the situation. Ultimately, a researcher leaves the situation and reports the findings aiming to make new theorise-able findings from their observations and actions to add to the pool of prior knowledge about the topic being action-researched. A main feature of any action research methodology is that it comprises a series of successive research cycles, which when connected become a spiral (Saunders, 2003, p.95); as laid out by Coghlan and Brannick (2014). Figure 2.1 demonstrates the spiralling paradigmatic action research cycles (ARCs).

According to Carr and Kemmis (1986), action research can be classified into at least three different types, each type having different aims, roles and relationships between researcher and practitioner (Carr and Kemmis, 1986). Table 2.2 demonstrates these types. The focus of research in this book, using the PrOH Modelling Methodology, is on the *practical* type.

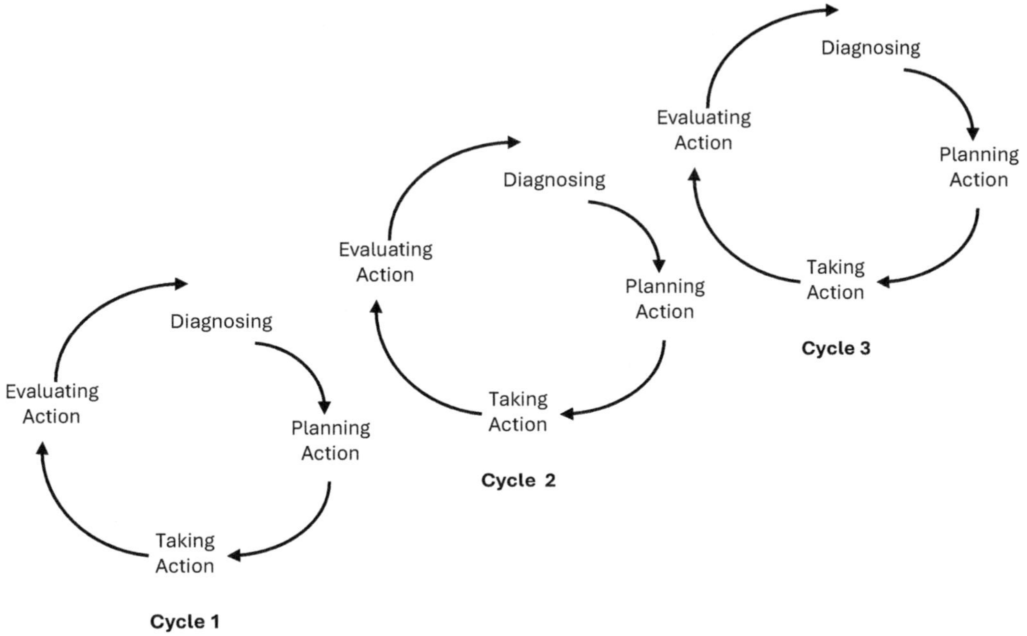

FIGURE 2.1 The Spiral of Action Research Cycles.

Source: Coghlan and Brannick (2014, p.110).

TABLE 2.2 Types of Action Research

Type of Research	*Aims*	*Facilitator Role*	*Researcher–Participant Relationship*
1. Technical	Informing	Expert	Participants dependent on researcher
2. Practical (interpretive)	Understanding	Participation	Process-oriented consultation
3. Emancipatory	Transformation	Moderator	Collaboration to expose injustices

Source: Adapted from Carr and Kemmis (1986).

These action research types are distinguished not by the methodologies they use but rather in the underlying assumptions and worldviews of their participants, which cause variations in methodological application (Grundy, 1988, p.363).

During action research cycles a researcher gets involved in action and performs the role of an insider influencing the collective action of the group; this is also known as **participatory research**. Action research of this nature has its philosophical roots in pragmatism (Greenwood and Levin, 1998). It mainly uses terms like "intervention" and "collaboration" or "interactivity" in defining the methods of doing things and how they relate to their field of study and activities as "applied research" (Eikeland, 2012, p.10).

Selener (1997) proposes that **participatory action research** has its theoretical roots in the liberationist writings of Karl Marx, which emphasises the importance of critical thinking to understand the ways in which they could develop their own organised action to address pertinent issues. Therefore, **action research** is understood to have two main objectives:

- produce knowledge and action directly useful to a group of people.
- empower people at a deeper level through the process of constructing and using their own knowledge (Reason, 2001).

According to Coghlan and Brannick (2014), **action research** is appropriate when a research question demands describing an unfolding series of actions over time in a given group, community or organisation; understanding as a member of the group how and why their action can change or improve the working of some aspects of a system; and understanding the process of change or improvement in order to learn from it.

Canonical Action Research

The **Canonical Action Research** (CAR) methodology, as proposed by Susman and Evered (1978) and adapted by others (e.g. Davison et al, 2004), is one of the foundational types of action research for the PrOH Modelling Methodology. There are five stages in the action research cycle (ARC), which are explained below and shown in Figure 2.2:

1. **Diagnosing/Initial Observation** – where a project aims to understand key areas with performance indicators to understand where improvement is needed within operational practices followed by the case study organisation. Data will be gathered using various

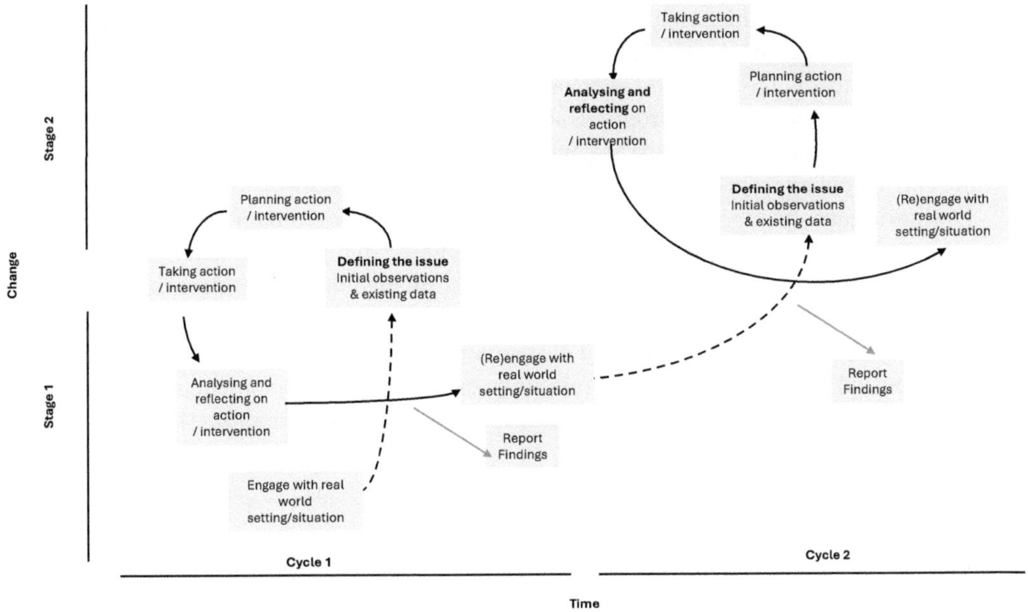

FIGURE 2.2 Canonical Action Research – A Foundation for the PrOH Modelling Methodology.

Source: Adapted from Susman and Evered (1978).

methods such as one-to-one interviews, focus groups and meetings with key stakeholders in respective areas.

2. **Action Planning** – where models, based on the initial diagnosis of human activity systems, will be built. Required actions to be taken for improving the problem situation will be identified during this stage. Models will be narrated and discussed with participants in a workshop where key stakeholders of that process are present. A model will be presented during which participants will discuss an alternative better approach and actively provide input that leads to the identification of factors and corresponding operational challenges in processes. Workshops will generate a list of key issues that need to be improved. These key issues will be categorised into different categories and tasks created against each that call for action. Models will be simultaneously validated during these sessions to see if they are defensible representations of the real world; they will also be verified to make sure that they are adhering to their own rules and guidelines. This process will ensure the "empirical evidence of [their] usability" (Fitzgerald, 1996, p.12). Once validated in this way, findings from models can be legitimately used, with permission of the case company, in dissemination to other wider audiences in later stages. Model iteration may be necessary to accommodate changes within the system, as in "**double loop learning**" (Argyris and Schon, 1978), or because of poor defensibility of the model. It should be rare that models will be completely indefensible, unless of course the model produced is so poor by not following a methodology or framework, as to not be useful. Should it not be useful, a more purposeful model should be constructed, and if necessary, more data collected until a saturated understanding of the system under observation has been achieved.

3. **Action Taking** – in this stage, action teams will be formed by drawing people from across different organisational parts, functions and departments. A researcher meets with separate action teams to agree on tasks and assigns them to leaders in the team. Each team would then go on to take appropriate action in fulfilling those tasks. An action researcher acts as a moderator in obtaining the output from each action team and ensures that actions are carried out appropriately as agreed.
4. **Evaluating/analysing/reflecting** – this stage occurs as a continuum during the process of action taking and afterwards. After the changes have been implemented by action teams, the outcome will be measured based on key performance indicators identified in Stage 1.
5. **Specifying learning/reporting findings** – where outcomes of actions and lessons generated in the process of observing and participating in the action research will be specified and reported. Any theoretical underpinnings that match the phenomenon observed in the process of action research will be discussed; this may be through **abductive thinking** and **abductive rationalisation**.

Case Studies in Action Research

Pure "case research" (Eisenhardt, 1989) consciously tries to separate the knower from what is to be known, and research is conducted from a distance. But action research differs from pure case study research as it is rooted in each participant's in-depth, critical and practical experience of the situation to be understood and acted in (Reason, 2001). According to Reason (2001), the most important characteristic of action research distinguishing it from other forms of enquiry is its *purpose*. The purpose of academic research is to contribute to a body of knowledge; however, it is argued that many academic theories are barely relevant and applicable to practitioners in the real world. Action research attempts to remedy this criticism by being driven by pragmatic challenges in **Mode 2 Research** (Coughlan and Coghlan, 2002; Maclean et al., 2002) because the primary purpose of action research is to develop learning that is directly applicable to the case being worked on and cognisable by others studying similar paradigms. Action researchers attempt to do this through their *communities of inquiry rooted in communities of practice* (Argyris and Schön, 1974; Senge, 1990).

According to Blichfeldt and Andersen (2006), both pure case study and action research case study are generic forms of research yet with significant diversity in theory and practice. While both are concerned with researchers' gaining in-depth understanding of specific phenomena (maybe through abduction) in real-world settings, action research offers a greater agency to the researcher in defining and changing issues to be addressed as "action research takes its cues, its questions, puzzles, and problems from the perceptions of practitioners within particular, local practice contexts". (Argyris and Schön, 1991, p.86) which concurs with **Mode 2** type research (Coghlan and Coughlan, 2002). In contrast purer action research (**Mode 1** type research) has more emphasis on observation with academic outputs than on intervention and action taking in practice.

Knowledge Creation through Action Research

Susman and Evered (1978, p.582) highlight a "crisis in the field of organizational science", as they state *research methods have become more sophisticated but simultaneously research became increasingly less useful for solving practical problems*. This is a view also endorsed by other authors who believe it is partly driven by the methodological pedantry of journal reviewers and editors who prioritise method over application, interest and relevance.

Susman and Evered (1978, p.582) also identify that management science has generated knowledge that has led to improvements in the efficacy of organisations, "but often at the expense of the quality of working life of their members"; this means if academic research is to have practicable "translation" of its results into management-language and practice it must also be grounded in reality. Authors of this book also believe that for research findings to be useful to both audiences, academic and practising-management, research methodologies must be rigorous enough for academics and relevant enough to deliver actions for practice, without being overly engineered in either regard.

Therefore, it is imperative for action research, although rooted in practice, to develop new knowledge and learning. Action research is specifically *concerned with three different areas of learning: practice, methodology and theory* and the combination and focus on all three is what distinguishes **action research** from a mere consultancy engagement, which is otherwise solely concerned with the change in the client's problem situation, without the need to generate and codify new knowledge and/or theory.

According to Checkland (1981), action research, which is an intervention into a problem situation, using a theoretical framework and a defined methodology, can contribute to each learning criterion; these principles are summarised well in Figure 2.3 where:

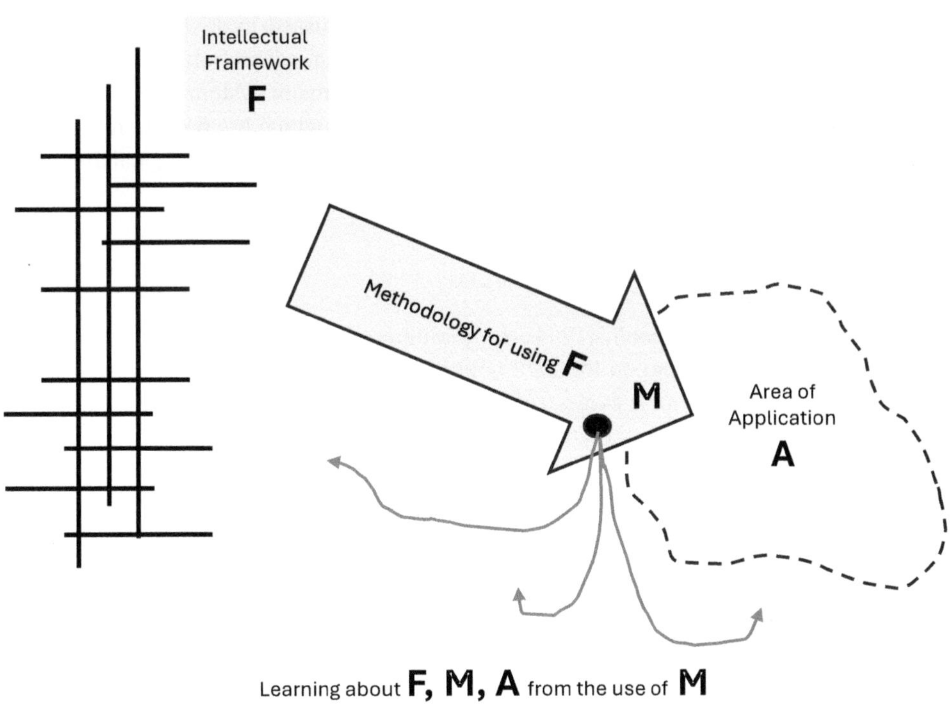

FIGURE 2.3 FMA Learning Outcomes from Action Research.

Source: Adapted from Checkland (1981).

1. the problem situation, area or system under observation of **Application** "A" is shown,
2. the ideas in the theoretical or intellectual **Framework** "F" used in action research [for possible abduction] are shown and
3. the specific approach or **Methodology** "M" used to improve the problem situation is shown.

Figure 2.3 illustrates these three learning objectives enabled through interventions with a case company and positions action research nicely somewhere between pure academic case research and pure consulting.

Therefore, when action research is viewed from FMA learning objectives (Checkland, 1981) in Figure 2.3, insights from action research can be categorised into three types:

a) **Lessons about the application** "A"/problem situation/system under observation: For instance, a "legal service operations improvement exercise", "a digitalisation transformation project" or a "lean six sigma change programme" (as discussed in Part III, Chapter 12).
b) **Lessons about the ideas in the theoretical or intellectual Framework** "F": For instance, use of Archetype Theory in professional service organisations (Pinnington and Morris' Professional-Partnership-Managed Professional Business (P2-MPB Framework), 2003) as discussed in the legal case in Part III (Chapter 11).
c) **Lessons about the methodology** "M": For instance, improving action research in general, or PrOH Modelling Methodology in particular, as discussed in depth in Part II. A good systems methodology should always be open to extension, adaptation to make it more purposeful. For example, links to other complementary forms of systems thinking and wider research techniques are often melded with one another, which are permissible if declared hand-in-hand with the theoretical findings and observations on the practical area.

Analysis and Validity in Action Research

Analysis

According to Denzin and Lincoln (1994), in qualitative research it is difficult to differentiate and draw a boundary between the data collection and analysis as action researchers will repeat stages of action research cycles repeatedly until sufficient action and/or findings are delivered. Myers (2009) suggests that a qualitative researcher ends up with huge amounts of data and it is not possible to include all data from a particular case when reporting findings of an action research project. Hence, data must be analysed to convey meaningful insights to facilitate understanding of the subject being researched rather than total data sets. Therefore, it is advisable to abridge and transform data to derive meaning and action from that meaning. Hence, PrOH Modelling Methodology is focused on understanding meaning and actions within a system, commensurate with the "hermeneutical" research tradition in natural science which focuses on understanding the world through meaning, interpretation and action. Lee and Lings (2008) describe hermeneutics as the process of understanding individual phenomena in respect to the larger whole from which they derive an understanding so that the whole is itself given meaning by its parts. Hermeneutics comprises various other axioms such as historicity, the hermeneutic circle, prejudice, autonomisation, appropriation and engagement.

Researchers who use a hermeneutical approach mostly depend on their intuition for analysing data with less need for employing text analysis software (such as NVivo). Yet, while dealing with large sets of data, suitable software can be used to interpret data, create memos, as well as mark, index and label data (Myers, 2009). For instance, the PrOH Modelling Methodology uses the PrOH Tool© (see prohmodel.org).

Validity

There is an emphasis on quality and relevance over traditional data validity when evaluating action research, as what is valid is what is perceived as correct by participants' viewpoints. There are various suggestions from authors about ensuring what quality validation is in action research. For example, there are four quality dimensions of organisation development through action research given by Coghlan and Shani (2014); five quality criteria proposed by Heikkinen et al. (2007); 15 characteristics of good action research given by Eden and Huxham (1996), and three criteria of rigour, reflection and relevance given by Pasmore et al. (2008). Bradbury-Huang (2010) advocates quality of data in action research as:

- proceeds from a praxis of participation (co-production);
- guided by practitioners' concerns for practicality (real-life problems);
- being inclusive of stakeholders' ways of knowing (joint-meaning construction); and
- propensity to build capacity for ongoing change efforts (workable solutions).

These action research quality principles, and especially those of Bradbury-Huang (2010) and Reason (2006), are adhered to in the PrOH Modelling Methodology and demonstrated in cases in Part II.

Success Criteria for Action Research

In action research, successful intervention and learning generated from it are interlinked with the management of any collaborative developments during a methodology deployment. According to Argyris et al. (1985), intervention is the action science analogue of experimentation in more positivistic experimental research. Thus, when clients involve themselves in change experiments, they engage in non-trivial learning, and they think and reflect seriously on what they are doing. Therefore, it is imperative to consider change in clients' situations when evaluating the success of action research interventions. Criteria for evaluating the success and quality of research are presented in Table 2.3 based on Checkland's (1981) 3E criteria (Efficacy, Efficiency and Effectiveness) for assessing the success of system interventions.

Ethical Considerations in Action Research

Basic ethical principles, in general, for action research are similar to other research methods. In brief, they are as follows:

- ensuring voluntary participation and obtaining informed consent from participants,
- anonymising and protecting confidentiality of the participants,
- storing data securely so that it does not fall into the wrong hands, and

TABLE 2.3 The 3E Criteria for Evaluating the Success of Action Research Intervention

3 E's	*Criteria: Examples*	*Performance Measures: Examples*	*Evidence: Example*
Efficacy	Does the research work? Does it meet the objectives set out initially? Is the transformation being done right?	The quality of the output as judged by the participants in terms of its usefulness to inform or change their practice.	Participant feedback, adoption of frameworks and tools developed.
Efficiency	Are minimum resources used in arriving at the results?	Additional expenditure on a project during the intervention phase. Time spent by people versus the value of the output they collectively generated.	List of tools developed in-house. Case study data highlighting participant time in each action research cycle.
Effectiveness	Does the output satisfy the expectations of the researcher and the case study organisation? Is the right thing being done?	Contribution made by the output to the wider organisation and the impact of it.	Change in perception of people towards change, improvement in the efficiency of operations, cost savings achieved.

Source: Adapted from Checkland (1981).

- non-disclosure agreements should be signed before commencing research and adhered to throughout the project and in any subsequent publications and public relations exercises.

Overall, keep the action research team working together closely, share data, and focus on purposeful goals while doing no maleficence to any project stakeholders.

Limitations of Action Research

There are inherent dilemmas for researchers doing action research. For example, having simultaneous and sometimes conflicting objectives of answering a research question as well as fulfilling a practical need (Rapoport, 1970). Also, the lack of ability to control processes and outcomes as well as their freedom to pick and choose problems (Baskerville and Lee, 1999). Furthermore, action researchers are widely critiqued for not declaring and discussing the intellectual framework of ideas they use in their projects (Checkland and Holwell, 1998) in advance. Checkland (1981, p.400) argues that "there must be an intellectual framework, declared in advance, in terms of which learning has been defined. Without such a framework, action research can quickly become indistinguishable from mere action". However, this statement is partially contended by the authors as a framework may also be declared *during* the action research process using **abductive reasoning** with prior published known frameworks for one-off cases, or by using **analogous reasoning** against other cases if enough cases are done during an action research project; or by using other very similar cases done by third parties. Therefore, the authors of this book agree that a framework for generating wider knowledge must be declared, but not necessarily before the project starts because quite often this is not possible as the problem and challenge in a case are often inexpressible at its onset.

Similar Approaches to Action Research

When discussing action research, one must also consider approaches such as Intervention Based Research (IBR) (Chandrasekaran et al., 2020) and Collaborative Management Research (CMR) (Pasmore et al., 2008, p.20) as these are names for similar ways to conduct research.

Intervention Based Research

The purpose of Intervention Based Research (IBR) is to "to publish high quality research articles that derive new theoretical and managerial insights by engaging with practice and solve complex field problems" (Van Aken et al., 2016, p.1). Some IBR authors have criticised some soft systems methods for being too theoretical as IBR is usually concerned with designing and implementing a solution whether this is a product, model, system or structure. IBR is designed to address organisational problems, intervene and then contribute. Notably, IBR researchers start by using **Design Science** (Baskerville et al., 2018) to develop intended contributions but also readily shift to **abducted reasoning** to find a workable solution, so that interventions may be put into motion when they do not go as planned. IBR is also characterised by cycles of interventions (Chandrasekaran et al., 2020), like action research, and builds on implementing pre-existing theory. In comparison to SSMs, the emphasis of IBR tends to be more on application and theorisation and less on methodology development.

Collaborative Management Research

Collaborative Management Research (CMR) is defined by Pasmore et al. (2008, p.20) as:

> an effort by two or more parties, at least one of whom is a member of an organization or system under study and at least one of whom is an external researcher, to work together in learning about how the behaviour of managers, management methods, or organizational arrangements affect outcomes in the system or systems under study, using methods that are scientifically based and intended to reduce the likelihood of drawing false conclusions from the data collected, with the intent of both improving performance of the system and adding to the broader body of knowledge in the field of management.

According to Coughlan et al. (2016), CMR is constructed from practitioner perceptions of key issues and themes.

Both IBR and CMR definitions closely resonate with how action research is conducted because the action researcher is often an outsider recruited to work for a specific time within the organisation supported by a third party, typically in a university–organisational or consultative–organisational partnership. Although distinctions exist at a detailed level, at a high level the spirit of action research, IBR and CMR approaches are similar.

Necessary Extensions to Action Research

Greater Impact Creation

Increasingly, action researchers are being asked to demonstrate the impact created through either demonstrable evidence, testimony, innovation or third-party endorsement. Some forms of action-taking are quicker and more direct than others in doing this. For instance, contrast:

- Survey deducing supply chain management practice where researchers collect and publish and hope for someone to use it and mention it – this is relatively slow and low.
- A set of case studies and/or interviews underpinned by a literature review inducing a new framework for supply chain practice might be used in the future and have some impact – this is relatively slow and low.
- An action research project using systems thinking to define and make simultaneous change using abduction will, by definition, create impact within the duration of a project – impact could be immediate and substantial.

This brings us on to a necessary and related field of thought: the use of logic in thinking in action research.

Novel Use of Logical Reasoning in Action Research

Too often, those who teach the use of logic in research polarise its application, simplify its use and typify it as either:

- **Inductive logic** – which is where research broadly starts off from a specific observation, which is then analysed for patterns resulting in propositions and theoretical generalisations. Data is usually empirical and **primary**.
- **Deductive logic** – which is where research typically starts off with a logical theory or hypothesis that is examined and tested with data to reach a specific conclusion. Data can be primary or **secondary**.

But arguably more relevant to quick high-impact research is that of the lesser-known **abductive logic** (sometimes also known as abductive rationalisation or abductive reasoning) where, for instance, in the context of organisational improvement, **abductive logic** requires a complex organisational system, sometimes described as a "wicked problem", to be investigated without necessarily having any *a priori* knowledge of the system or problem or a pre-selected theoretical framework; this provides the possibilities for quick and impactful research because action research does not need to start with a desk-based systematic literature review, which is much loved by classic academic researchers. Instead, using abductive logic the problem is primarily defined by the practical situation, the system under observation and then secondarily explained later through a postponed abductive rationalising thought process. Practical problems can therefore be investigated pragmatically and without prejudice, and reflection on theory for further insight and remedial action within the given situation can occur later for wider learning. This can give rise to quick and impactful action research once the situation under observation is **parsimoniously** and **holistically** understood. Consider Thinking Box 2.

THINKING BOX 2: ABDUCTIVE, DEDUCTIVE AND INDUCTIVE THINKING

If you have trouble differentiating *deduction*, *induction* and *abduction*, thinking about their roots might help. All three words are based on Latin *ducere*, meaning "to lead". The prefix de- means "from", and deduction derives *from* generally accepted statements or facts. The prefix in- means "to" or "toward", and induction leads you *to* a generalisation. The prefix ab- means "away", and you take *away* the best explanation in abduction. (Sætre and van de Ven, 2021a, 2021b).

In laypersons' terms, abductive thinking can be thought of like this: "if it looks like a duck, if it sounds like a duck and it smells like a duck, then it probably is a duck" (Anon, undatable). This means that if a theory fits and can be usefully used to explain a real-world scenario being researched, then use it. Through this process, developments can be made to the scenario and the theory. Also, perhaps the method used to acquire the data.

What type of thinking do you prefer and why?

Deductive research will start with an extensive desk-based literature review often steeped in academic jargon, theory and often outdated concepts, which are used to derive propositions and hypotheses to be tested using empirical data, attempting to prove hypotheses as true or false with as much certainty as possible, irrespective of whether the basis of the study was relevant to practice.

Inductive research will use a mix of literature, case studies and other various sources of empirical data to propose new ideas, such as frameworks, bodies of knowledge, models and/ or methods which then often need further validation and verification to make relevant and purposeful for practice.

Analogous logic (rationalising or reasoning), which is a lesser-known form of logic, relies on comparison with other similar cases. Analogous logic is where thinking relies upon an analogy. In action research this will be where different cases are compared with one another looking for similarities and differences. A pre-defined problem, framework or hypothesis is not required. This cross-case analysis can be done without necessarily declaring prior characteristics which can be evolved during the case study. This type of logic usually produces a general framework to support further learning. Further testing, validation and theorising is often required.

These logical approaches are summarised in the "**logic compass**" given in Figure 2.4.

Authors of this book summarise these four types of logical reasoning in what they refer to as the Logic Compass in Figure 2.4. Researchers should be clear about the type of logical reasoning they are using in their research. Action research will normally be placed somewhere in the abductive-analogous direction rather than the inductive-deductive direction, which is more suited to objective laboratory-style research where the researcher is separated from and does not attempt to influence the data they are observing.

In an organisational change context, action research is used within case comparisons of organisational data looking for an explanation, which may be followed up with or complemented by theory induction, extension or modification or testing of formulated hypotheses.

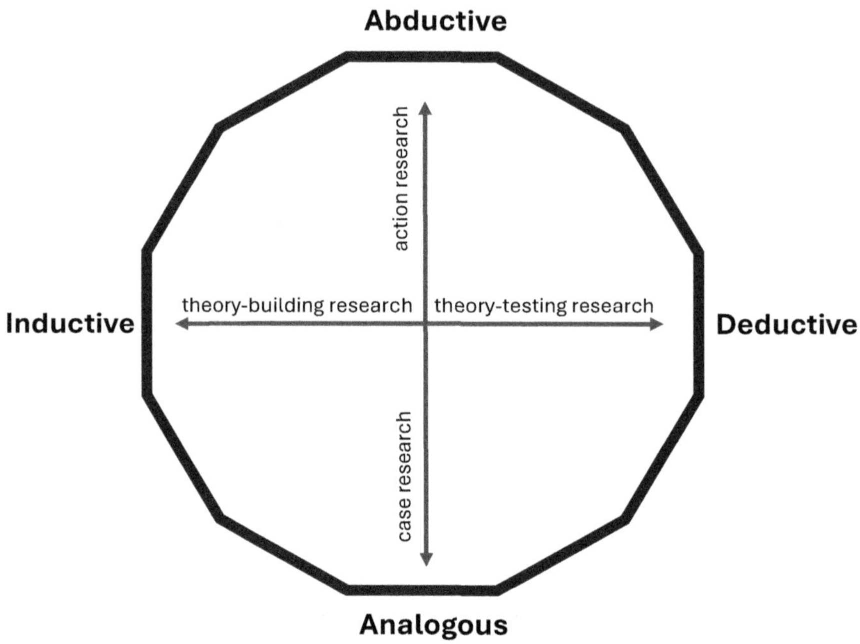

FIGURE 2.4 The Logic Compass: Relationship between Different Types of Logical Reasoning.

ACTION BOX 2: SCENARIO BASED LOGIC

If you were about to start on some research, try deciding which of the following scenarios is best suited to each type of logic:

1. An action research case study with an unclear purpose.
2. A lab-based experiment to optimise the output of a robot making sweets.
3. A desk-based literature review on topics relating to an emerging area of research.
4. A group of different teams of researchers investigating the same topic, using the same methodology, across several different organisations.
5. Writing a story based on no evidence.

Answers at the back of the book.

Different stages in a research project may use different types of logic. Labels on the direction finders in Figure 2.4 show the prevailing type of research associated with each type of logic.

Summary

The main point is that to define a real-world system requires interviewing agents, collecting data on the system, extracting logic of workflow systems – physical, cybernetic and human – and making sense of these. Action research and systems thinking can be used to define complex problems in real-world organisational systems, after which practical action can be taken by agents in the real world to remedy problems and/or improve systems improvements, thus creating positive impacts. This will normally be through either abductive rationalisation, if a single case is used, or through a combination of abduction with analogous rationalisation if more cases, or sub-cases within a case, become involved in sense-making.

Further Reading

Balthu, K. (2021), *Applying Systems Thinking to Improve Professional Service Operations.* Ph.D Thesis, Aston University.
Coughlan, D. (2019), *Doing Research in Your Own Organization*, 5th ed. London: Sage.
Karlsson, C. (2016), *Research Methods for Operations Management*, 2nd ed. London: Routledge.
Sekaran, U., and Bougie, R. (2010), *Research Methods for Business*, 5th ed. London: Wiley.

PART II

The PrOH Modelling Methodology

Abstract

Part II of this book builds on the general background to systems thinking and action research given in Part I and describes why the PrOH Modelling Methodology was developed and its unique properties making it purposeful for organisational change and its ability to create high impact.

Chapter 3 focuses on the development rationale for the unique PrOH Modelling Methodology.

Chapter 4 describes how to create, storyboard and gamify individual PrOH models.

Chapter 5 details the principles and techniques for advanced PrOH Modelling for situations where more than one model is required by building a set of PrOH Models known as a *holarchy*. Steps for creating more than one model at the same level are given – for both *serial models* and for *parallel models* and for *holarchic abstraction* and *enrichment* to build sets of organisational models pitched at different organisational levels. Examples are used to illustrate how abstraction and enrichment is done for both *serial models* and for *parallel models*.

Part II also shows how *emergent* and *hidden properties* of systems are revealed by modelling in *holarchies*. The advantages of the PrOH Modelling Methodology are discussed in comparison to other comparable approaches.

3

RATIONALE FOR WHY THE PROH MODELLING METHODOLOGY IS NEEDED

Introducing the PrOH Modelling Methodology as a Derivation from Checkland's SSM

The Process Oriented Holonic (PrOH) Modelling Methodology is a relatively new type of soft systems methodology specifically designed to catalyse organisational change (Clegg, 2006, 2007; Clegg and Shaw, 2008). While PrOH is derived from Checkland's SSM, PrOH Modelling is more focused on organisational processes than Checkland's SSM and PrOH Models are more focused on process change than Wilson's SSM by combining "aspects of softer and harder approaches to aid modellers in designing business processes" (Clegg and Shaw, 2008, p.447). Theoretically, PrOH Modelling attempts to "overcome the narrowness of many existing approaches and their rigidity in use" (Clegg and Shaw, 2008, p.448) and practically aims to "satisfy the need of managers in organizations to better understand their organization's processes" (Clegg and Shaw, 2008, p.448).

The PrOH Modelling Methodology uniquely employs the concept of "pitch", "width" and "length" to define the granularity of a PrOH Model and help clarify the worldview employed during model construction. Systemic Success Factors (SSFs) of organisational process change are defined in terms of their purpose, roles, artefacts and inter-relationships using jargon-free natural language which can be formalised in a SIPOC (Supplier-Input-Process-Output-Customer) table before drawing a PrOH Model.

Structured data from a SIPOC (Brown, 2019) type analysis in a table can be used to construct colourful PrOH Models which can be "storyboarded" to visualise SSFs of organisational change. PrOH Models are simplified parsimonious representations of the process of change and their associated systemic success factors (SSFs), and *do not* attempt to recreate or reproduce organisational processes *per se* in their present current state or in their future intended state. Therefore, PrOH Models are models of a conceptual system of change and are not models of "as-is" or "to-be" processes; this is one of the PrOH Modelling Methodologies' unique features.

The PrOH Modelling Methodology is strong in situations where processes are difficult to define, such as those with low volume and/or high variety, which are characterised by change

DOI: 10.4324/9781032650425-5

through extended time periods and/or offer limited opportunities for learning. Thus, while incorporating aspects of "hard" systems approaches, PrOH Modelling possesses "softer" aspects which more closely resemble a problem structuring method that is better for accommodating different stakeholder viewpoints on a change situation than purely "hard" systems analysis methods, such as systems engineering, which are more focused on optimisations of closed, well-defined and well-known systems. Clegg and Shaw (2008, p.457) summarise,

> The foundations of PrOH help to decide the right granularity for the models (according to pitch, length and width), build models with explicit objectives and which reflect the situation accurately while maximizing the use of normal language to encourage stakeholder engagement. As [sets of] models are built, details are added to enrich them and enhance their usability for analysing the process. The models aim to be a device through which stakeholders can come to learn more about the processes and so collectively agree their (re)design.

As a development of SSM the PrOH Modelling Methodology (Clegg and Shaw, 2008, p.470)

- has the same philosophical approach to modelling as SSM;
- uses models to build a defensible representation of a situation and not necessarily attempt to recreate it faithfully and exhaustively;
- uses models to stimulate debate and select "feasible and desirable" changes; and
- realises that the performance of a complex human activity system (e.g. a production process or a service delivery system) is not able to be optimised in the same way as a physical system but is only capable of becoming better through improved understanding of it.

Each PrOH Model is built around a core process for change, based on Juran's process chain (Juran, 1988) which describes the Supplier-Input-Process-Output-Customer (SIPOC) dependencies. In addition to this, PrOH Models also define the "objective" of the change process. Additional information on relevant supporting processes is then added to the core (SIPOC) process to describe the system in terms of its defined pitch: strategic, tactical or operational. This approach offers a significant advantage over traditional process mapping and/or flowcharting because it provides a coherent methodology for simplifying organisational systems, based on stated worldviews, avoiding excessive detail and increasing a modellers' understanding for change.

The structuring of PrOH Models in terms of worldviews at several pitches leads to another unique aspect of the PrOH Modelling Methodology, which are its rules for abstracting and enriching to produce a set of models known as a "**holarchy**" (Clegg, 2007). Individual PrOH Models at a given "pitch" can be linked together through their input and output relationships to form a set of interlinked PrOH Models representing processes at a given level. A PrOH Model at a given "pitch" can be **enriched** by focusing on artefacts and roles from that "pitch" and constructing a new PrOH Model at a lower "pitch" containing a new core process, with artefacts and roles relevant to that level or worldview, for example by moving from a strategic to a tactical worldview. **Abstraction** is achieved by reversing this process, where artefacts and roles from the core process of the lower level are extracted and form part of the higher-level PrOH Model, which has a different core process and worldview, for example by moving from a tactical to a strategic worldview.

The advantage of a **holarchy** over a hierarchical set of models is the maintenance or re-expression of a relationship, through common artefacts or actors, across differently pitched PrOH Models constructed under different worldviews. Therefore, recontextualisation of relationships can occur in PrOH Modelling, meaning that the PrOH Modelling is unconstrained by child-parent inheritance of properties, which is a problematic and restrictive feature of harder systems methodologies.

Thus, the PrOH Modelling Methodology is a problem structuring systems methodology that combines the most suitable aspects of "soft" and "hard" approaches to guide users in the development of representative models of change by learning about organisational systems of change behaviours. While the PrOH Modelling Methodology employs the same philosophical approach to modelling as Checkland and Wilson (1980) the PrOH Modelling Methodology provides more specific rules on the construction of its models and how they interrelate, more characteristic of harder systems methodologies.

Consider Thinking Box 3.

THINKING BOX 3: WHAT IS HOLONIC THINKING?

Think about modelling organisation processes. Most modellers try to model "as-is" and "to-be" processes in an organisation which is a relatively hard systems approach to organisational process improvement. Soft systems methodologies such as PrOH Modelling focus on the conceptual system of change that transforms "as-is" into "to-be".

1. Name some typical organisation processes.
2. Try to name typical organisation processes systems of change.

At first this may seem a subtle and inconsequential difference, but as one becomes a more experienced modeller of change systems, it becomes fundamental to a modeller's view of change.

While the first question is easy to do because these are identifiable as "real" processes in the "real world" the second question is relatively difficult as these are conceptual systems, and creating models of conceptual systems is an intuitive thing to do.

Holonic thinking is a useful way of thinking about building models of conceptual systems.

See back of book for answers.

Systems Thinking: Holism or Reductionism?

When a person or group of people select an organisational problem to be resolved or process to be improved and subsequently develop or select an approach to facilitate its resolution or improvement, they are most likely to do so based on their philosophical viewpoint or *Weltanschauung* (worldview). Thus,

> A person's ability to manage his or her society's affairs depend more on his understanding of, and attitudes toward, the World that contains him than on his problem-solving methods.

> Put another way, his success depends more on his view of the World and the philosophy he lives by than it does on his science and technology.
>
> *(Ackoff, 1974, p.7)*

In this context, successful problem-solving involves not only the resolution of the "real-world problem situation" but also the selection of the correct problem to resolve; more simply, finding the right solution to the right problem. Further, effective problem resolution requires both the application of the "correct" tools and the appropriate philosophical approach to apply them (Ackoff, 1974; Ackoff, 2006; Checkland and Poulter, 2006). Ackoff (1974a) divides philosophical approaches into "**machine age**" and "**systems age**".

"**Machine age**" thinking applies an analytical approach and takes a viewpoint where the relationships that govern "reality" follow the doctrine of mechanism, which can be understood through the application of reductionism. The reductionist doctrine maintains that all things can be divided into smaller and smaller elements until one arrives at an indivisible part or parts. To illustrate, in chemistry, molecules are made from atoms which are made from protons, neutrons and electrons which are in turn made of particles such as "quarks", "bosons" and "leptons" which are now considered to be "elementary" or "fundamental" particles; formerly, this was the atom. This might be considered in the light of the development of "science". Consequently, following this line of thought, it is entirely reasonable to apply a reductionist approach to all aspects of enquiry, where nature is consistent with the **hierarchical** and causal view of "science". To use a chemistry analogy again, fundamental particles cause the properties of atoms of which they are part, and atoms cause the properties of the molecules of which they are part. Thus, analytical thinking, based on a reductionist worldview, can be applied to explain and understand any problem by breaking it down into its constituent parts. By aggregating this understanding of the constituent parts, one can predict and explain the behaviour of any whole of which they comprise.

Thus, the "**machine age**" perspective when confronted with any problem breaks the "whole" problem into smaller independent "sub-problems" that can be individually resolved and summed together to provide the solution to the "whole" problem. One can disassemble a problem into independent "sub-problems" that can be understood through the inter-relationships of its component parts, where one part causes the behaviour of another as a *cause-and-effect* relationship. Determinist cause and effect states that the cause is necessary and sufficient to produce the effect; if the cause occurs the effect will be observed, and the cause is the only thing required to explain the effect. In this context, causes are environment-free and are consistent with the idea of a "closed-system", which is applied or at least approximated in laboratory environments to eliminate any alternative causes and thereby determine a singular cause and effect. Thus, effects are entirely determined by causes and behaviours of anything can be explained in a deterministic manner. Every effect is the result of the cause that preceded it, and as such, the universe is considered to behave as a mechanism where teleological concepts such as function, goals, purposes, choice, and free will are unnecessary to explain natural phenomena (Ackoff, 1974). It should be noted that the reductionist approach has provided much scientific insight and may possibly, if "complete" provide an explanation of everything; however, this may well be impossible and is certainly currently infeasible in the context of social systems.

Bennis and O'Toole (2005, p.98) question the appropriateness of a reductionist approach to the study of businesses and management as they argue that it is a "faulty assumption that business is an academic discipline like chemistry or geology"; rather it is a profession that calls on many disciplines, and as such, may be "ill-equipped to wrangle with complex, unquantifiable issues – in other words, the stuff of management" (Bennis and O'Toole, 2005, p.96). "When applied to business – essentially a human activity in which judgements are made with messy, incomplete data" (Bennis and O'Toole, 2005, p.99) questions of interest are not easily the subject of scientific experiment or validation. Further, the more complex the problem is, for example, strategic decision making, the more difficult it is to "get right" based on purely quantitative factors; consequently, the need to consider qualitative factors becomes important; however, such factors are inherently difficult to measure. In conclusion, a reductionist approach cannot provide a solution for managerial problems as it is removed from the realities of organisations which cannot be appropriately considered as environment-free closed systems.

In contrast, Ackoff's (1974) "**systems age**" is built based on expansionism, teleology and "systems thinking" which he considers a modification of, but compatible with, the reductionist, mechanistic viewpoint and analytical thought. Expansionism acknowledges that "wholes" consist of parts; however, rather than focusing on their decomposition to identify ultimate elements, it focuses on wholes consisting of inter-related parts. Thus, expansionism "maintains that all objects, events, and experiences of them are parts of larger wholes" which will from now on be referred to as *systems*. The work of Boulding (1956) states that the key aim of General Systems Thinking (GST) was to develop a parsimonious or optimal level of *generality*, which could fill the gap between the highly generalised relationships of mathematics and the specific theories of specialised disciplines that may enable better understanding of biological, behavioural and social phenomena where the level of scientific knowledge was, and still is, somewhat limited (Boulding, 1956; Bertalanffy, 1969). This consideration of systems has become increasingly important in organising social and scientific worldviews (Ackoff, 1974).

Hard Systems Methodologies versus Soft Systems Methodologies

Authors of this book believe that systems thinking should be the philosophical foundations for most contemporary ideas about how to manage the process of organisational change. In the 20th-century systems thinking has contributed greatly to many management initiatives. However, this is rarely acknowledged or even realised by many management theorists. Some early protagonists who made the connection included Beer (1959) and Bertalanffy (1969); and more recently, Weinburg (1975) and Senge (1990) have contributed. Jackson's (1995) inaugural paper contrasts the,

> well researched work in systems thinking with the somewhat cavalier approach adopted by the people who propagate management fads (guru theory, TQM, BPR and the learning organisation).

ACTION BOX 3: THE CONCEPT OF PARSIMONY AND EFFICIENCY IN BUILDING CONCEPTUAL MODELS

The parsimony principle is a foundation to all science and tells us to use the simplest scientific evidence that fits the evidence. This principle can also be applied to methodologies.

"Parsimony is an important principle of the scientific method for two reasons. First and most fundamentally, parsimony is important because the entire scientific enterprise has never produced, and never will produce, a single conclusion without invoking parsimony. Parsimony is absolutely essential and pervasive" Gauch (2015, pp.269–326).

Try defining a conceptual system of change as simply as possible, using a practical but systems-based methodology, while retaining all essential properties of a system.

Answer: see back of book.

Jackson makes three main points which distinguish "systems thinking" from "management fads"

- to do serious research, it is necessary to set-up strong hypotheses, which you seek to refute over an extended period of time. Those who propagate the fads often appear to know the answers before they actually do the research. We need to carry out more serious research and not jump to conclusions, as it seems that advocates of the various fads do;
- the solution offered by the fads often seems extremely partial … propagators of new fads are continually finding new pieces of the jigsaw but are failing to fit them in properly; and
- fad writers do not, for the most part, explore the theories underlying their recommendations; they do not ask what they are taking for granted about organisations in intervening in them in particular ways.

The authors of this book believe that the failure to reflect on the theory on which process improvement recommendations are based means that advocates of these fads cannot relate their experiences back to theory to learn why some interventions succeed while others fail. Theory has much to contribute when trying to elucidate issues concerning **hierarchy** and/or **holarchy**, **"holons"** (conceptual parts and wholes), life-cycle milestones, supply-chains and control and communication within organisational processes. Hence, the authors of this book adopt the axiom that any well-founded management theory should endorse the fundamentals of systems thinking. From all the greatly diverse literature on systems thinking, the work of Peter Checkland on soft systems methodology (SSM) has been most significant in influencing the development of the PrOH Modelling Methodology. Checkland's SSM is systematic in its method of enquiry and systemic (**holonic**) in its representation of **human activity systems (HASs)** as **holons** which are perceived systems that give insight into the real world. Checkland's SSM is typically used for exploring ill-defined problems in HASs (Clegg and Boardman, 1998a).

However, to meet a slightly different and narrower purpose, the authors of this book have focused on new technique developments specifically to investigate, represent and instigate business, operational strategy and organisational change, which have concentrated on producing what Checkland calls "**primary task based**" models, making the PrOH Modelling Methodology and its techniques migrate away from the "softer" end of Checkland's modelling spectrum. **Primary task** is a term initially used by Rice (1958) and later adopted by Checkland and the Tavistock Institute to describe the task which an organisation is "created to perform" or "the task which … an enterprise must perform if it is to survive". On the other hand, "**Issue based**" models are more likely to represent the "softer" "or latent issues that relate to functions which may or may not be recognised by the people in the system under observation. In developing the PrOH Modelling methodology, its authors have tried to produce a usable set of techniques that emphasise the **primary task**" in the core process statement (as in Checkland's root definition) of a PrOH Model but can still depict the "softer issues" in its **Systemic Success Factors** and supporting process statements. The reason for this emphasis is influenced by Checkland (1980) as he states that,

> In choosing the type of relevant system, the selection of a primary system will be most appropriate (a) if the problem is perceived to be one of organisational design or information system provision, (b) if the task itself is not controversial. In such cases a primary task root definition is probably the best way of initiating the debate about change.

"Hard" process modelling techniques include IDEF (and GRAI), data flow diagrams (DFDs), critical path analysis (CPA) and business process petri-nets (BP nets) (Clegg, 1999). Research conducted by the authors of this book into business strategies and processes has led to their firm conviction that the "harder" the technique, the more its representation of the real world tends to neglect the principles of systems thinking, which is ironic because the intention is often the exact opposite. This means that the representation is less able to represent the "softness" of the systems perceived to exist in the real world; and, if the "soft" issues of a business strategy or process cannot be elucidated through a modelling exercise, then there is little point in conducting it. "Hard" methodologies for process modelling are often applied too functionally and too mechanistically; this discourages holistic thinking and often fails to deliver a systemic (holonic) perspective of either a strategy or a process, or its system of change. Change methodologies need to represent both "hard" and "soft" aspects of any process change in an integrated fashion; this is also recognised by Woodcock (1996) when he states that,

> The easiest processes to identify are those that relate to the supply chain with one or both ends outside the company. These are often referred to as "hard processes". Processes for developing new products and services require a structure and activities that create the best conditions for combining design and operational skills. The "soft" support processes, usually related to people, planning, communication and culture, were more difficult to define but are critical to longer-term success. In fact, the "soft" processes appear to represent the most important components for fundamental change in the new business environment.

It is interesting to note that Checkland believes that "**primary task**" based models give the most potential to encourage process improvement, and Woodcock believes that the "soft" issues give the greatest potential. The authors of this book believe there is a need to develop a hybrid "hard-soft" systems-based modelling methodology for process change. The methodology for enquiry and the real-world representation of Checkland's SSM have both been specifically adapted to suit business process change rather than general problem definition within HAS's. This potential has been seen, although not fully developed by others, such as Vidgen et al. (1994) when he sates,

> SSM models are models of purposeful human activity ideally suited to BPR [business process reengineering] process modelling, since they cope with basic processes as well as abstract and intangible processes … The modelling of "relevant systems" and the clear status of SSM models as "holons" (logically consistent potentially operable systems,

not representations of the real world) offer a rigorous way of structuring thinking about re-conceptualisation.

However, Vidgen provides no evidence of either methodology or techniques being adapted for this specific application. For such reasons, the academic and business worlds are a long way apart on using systems thinking, the former concentrating their efforts on developing and testing theory, which, in many cases, is not penetrating the more pragmatic world of business; and the latter reverting to HSMs. The unique PrOH Modelling Methodology discussed explicitly at length in this book retains the fundamental principles of systems thinking, but they are now more pragmatic as they move away from pure SSM and adopt the most appropriate aspects of HSMs as the primary task of systems of change is focused on.

Modelling Organisational Processes

The employment of graphical modelling has long been endorsed by practices such as systems thinking, business process re-engineering, concurrent engineering (Clegg, 1996a, Gatenby et al, 1994) and other change methods for operations, service and digitalisation improvement. This is true for HSMs and SSMs as graphical modelling (e.g. a picture) can help to

- give objectivity to a process;
- develop consensus on a process;
- discuss pitfalls of a process and possible improvements;
- provide a presentation and/or learning medium; and
- develop system requirements.

Different techniques vary in their ability to meet the above points as it is imperative that a modeller chooses the correct techniques for

- the type of real-world system as they differ greatly (i.e. human activity system or a mechanical-oriented system) and
- the desired purpose of the model (i.e. strategic process envisioning or software requirements capture).

This chapter follows the taxonomy of systems methodologies given previously in Chapter 1 and adds detail to "hard" and "soft" *methodologies* by briefly describing different forms of graphical modelling used via typical applications, strengths and weaknesses.

"Hard" Modelling for "Hard" Systems

Hard modelling methods and techniques are oriented on detailed objectives of processes; they feature heavily on identifying inputs, outputs, transformations and resources. However, they lack richness to explicitly convey complexity or ambiguity in entity relationships and transformations and therefore also lack the ability to convey the **"holonic"** properties of concepts and strategies. This makes them limited to applications such as

TABLE 3.1 Types and Applications of "Hard" Modelling Methods and Techniques

Name	*Key Authors*	*Application Domain*
SADT™	Marca (1987)	Requirements definition (software development)
IDEF0	U.S. Airforce (1981)	Functional representations of processes (static)
IDEF1x	U.S. Airforce (1982)	Relationship representations between entities (dynamic)
GRAI	Doumeingts (1984)	Manufacturing systems
Petri Nets	Dicesare (1993)	Mathematical analysis of systems logic
Network Analysis/Critical Path Analysis (CPA)/PERT Charts	Barnetson (1978)	Project planning – resource allocation
Gantt Charts	Gantt	Project planning (critical path)
"Simple" Flow Charts	Various	General process representation
IFLO	Prasad and Strand (1993)	General process representation
Quality Process Language (QPL)	Born (1994)	Quality accreditation
Data Flow Diagrams (DFD)/ Structured Systems Analysis	Gane and Sarson (1979)	Software requirement definition
Systems Dynamics	Sterman (2000)	Casual quantitative dynamics of systems
Yourdon	Yourdon and Constantine (1978), De Marco (1978)	Software requirement definition

- product data modelling;
- establishing software requirements when it is explicitly not a requirement to show ambiguity in transformations of information or entity relationships; and
- project management where the models are only required to represent task dependency in a project, calculate lead time, resources and critical paths. They have limited application to represent a process of a project and have a minimal ability to place the project in the context of the wider system of which the project is part.

Table 3.1 names some significant modelling techniques breakthroughs considered to be "hard"; some of these are briefly discussed, and a summary of their "strengths, weaknesses, opportunities and threats" (SWOT) is given later. See Table 3.2.

Structured Analysis and Design Technique (SADT™)

SADT™ (a trademark of Softech Inc., Massachusetts) is the foundation of all IDEF derived methods. It was introduced in the 1980s; since then, it has been used on a wide variety of problems: telephonic software, long-range and strategic planning, computer-aided manufacture, computer system configuration and inventory control. The Integrated Computer Aided Manufacturing (ICAM) programme of the US Department of Defence recognised the utility of SADT™ by standardising and making public a subset of it called IDEF0. IDEF0 is most used for functional representations of activities during process modelling. IDEF1x is a derivation of IDEF0 and is best suited for representing information flows. IDEF2 is a derivation used for sharing the dynamic flows in a system. However, Buchel (1984) "it does not provide … any

TABLE 3.2 SWOT Analysis of "Hard" Graphical Process Modelling

Strengths	Weaknesses
• Highly structured and coded to reduce ambiguity for software requirements and provide software designers and customers with a highly defined "top-down" structure for programming. • Widely adopted by industry (military driven in the case of SADT techniques). • Activities on the critical path of a project can be shown by CPA and Network Analysis. • Suited for discrete event simulation of real-world processes.	• Flow charting techniques are undisciplined and have limited adoption of "systems thinking". • Poor for continuous event simulation. • Human activity system (holons) descriptions are compromised due to high codifiability of software modelling techniques. • IDEF0 encounters difficulty since it does not allow any flexibility (Weltanschauung) between the different modelling levels. • IDEF0 has no method for distinguishing between different types of communication or entity. • Petri Nets require an extensive set of logical dependencies to be able to represent the simplest of "soft" issues. • Gantt charts cannot express inter-relationships between activities. • Poor qualities for knowledge presentation and dissemination. • Cannot cope with the stochastic nature of human activity systems as holons.
Opportunities	Threats
• Most "hard" techniques can be verified against a specification document (e.g. Yourdon) or mathematically (e.g. Petri Nets).	• Rich description of relationships between entities is lost in codification. • Often infer artificial accuracy. • Critical path analysis, network analysis and Gantt charts are often wrongly used as a process representation. • "Simple" flow charts are often developed to context specific notation. • Do not have to be oriented around the purpose (objectives and sub-objectives) of the process being modelled.

problem-solving model … it relies on the resourcefulness of the designer to do such things properly" and Coulson-Thomas (1994) advises that, "Although this technique is widely used by consultants (because of the rigorous approach) we believe that this approach should not be used in the early stages of a BPR initiative".

Another adaptation of IDEF0 is that by Ang and Gay (1993) who has tried to apply it to project risk assessment; however, the authors of this book believe they introduced even more notation and complexity into it. Ang and Gay (1993) criticise the IDEF notation as they say that "because the three IDEF methodologies are independent, the complete IDEF modelling process can be very time consuming and involve a tremendous amount of wasteful effort in repeated capturing of the same data". The generic faults of IDEF0 notation are highlighted by Zaff (1991); when he states that

- "decision making criteria are only apparent at the lowest level of the diagrams ... neither the cognitive processes nor the perceptual-action-environment interactions are apparent. The diagram provides a functional knowledge representation that is oriented towards resources and results but fails to show (i) the underlying decision rules, criteria, or alternatives; and (ii) the perceptual discriminations necessary for situated actions".
- "it is structured with precisely defined boundaries. This weakness becomes a major problem for the modelling of extremely complex and dynamic environments where boundaries are fluid, and the task priorities, conditions, and interrelationships are continuously changing".
- "the simplicity offered by pictorial representation is easily overwhelmed by the use of annotation and symbology. As a consequence, it becomes difficult to independently validate, with a cross-check by domain experts, the information that is represented. For this reason, the diagrams remain representative of the analyst's perspective of the user requirements rather than depicting the user's perspective of their own requirements for the task".

Despite all the known problems with IDEF0 in a survey by Small et al. (1998) 38% (3rd highest) of the surveyed companies had had experience of using them for process modelling; however, since then, use has declined and the method has become less prominent.

Petri Nets

Petri Nets are a mathematical representation of the logic within a process; analysis of Petri Net models shows both the structure and dynamic behaviour of the modelled process (by constructing reachability trees); they capture the controls associated with the process but little about "soft issues". Thus, mathematically, Petri Nets are even more rigorous than IDEF0 but are not useful for process change analysis from a product design and realisation viewpoint (Peterson, 1981), or for business process reengineering, although attempts have been made to do this by Aalst and Hee (1994). Cecil et al. (1992) points out that

- they also suffer from a lack of a general methodology for construction in a system analysis and
- the diagrams can become cluttered when attempting to model complicated systems.

In the survey conducted by Small et al. (1998) only 9% of the surveyed companies had had experiences of using these for process modelling, and since then, use has further declined.

Project-Based Modelling Techniques

If correctly applied, Gantt, CPA and Network Analysis techniques can be used to support project management. However, the authors of this book have seen these misapplied in industry as process modelling techniques, and we suspect this is because they are simple to use; however, the ability to represent the wider system is negligible, and the threshold for even basic process representation is soon reached. (Note: these were quite rightly not included in Small's (1998) survey). The use of these is very popular in business planning and wrongly applied to modelling systems of change.

Flow Chart Modelling Techniques

Simple flow charting is used widely and is commonly adapted by individual users who develop their own hybrid to suit their purpose; for instance, Prasad and Strand (1993) developed ILFO. If not adapted, they are often poorly disciplined and lack richness of description. Flow chart modelling techniques are used in quality accreditation (e.g. Born, 1994) where written prose is now considered too verbose by many, and diagrams are favoured. This is true for the ISO 9001, the Malcolm Baldrige Quality Award (used in the United States), and the European Quality Award.

The most common form of flow chart is the Data Flow Diagram (DFD), which is less rigorous than others such as IDEF0 and has no explicit rules for governing either the number of process boxes at a particular level or cross-checking of data and/or object flows. Martin (1988) suggests that

> DFDs are deceptively simple, and that their use can produce models that look right, but which on further and more critical examination are likely to be full of inconsistencies … DFDs should only be used to give an overview of the document and or material flows within a system.

Authors of this book, along with Coulson-Thomas (1994) and Wastell (1994), believe DFDs to be very limited in their ability to model systems of change.

In the survey conducted by Small (1998) a massive 64% of the surveyed companies had had experiences of using these for process modelling, despite being considered the worst technique by experienced modellers. This suggests that knowledge, training and therefore confidence about systems thinking is not being transferred from academia to industry.

Yourdon

Yourdon and SSADM type modelling techniques are designed to facilitate software design: they try to help by allowing

- an analyst to learn about the organisation to see the system requirements through users" eyes;
- people in the user community to know what is feasible and what isn't;
- an analyst to manage the business criteria and the technical details of the new system; and
- creation of documents setting out the details of a new system (i.e. system specification) to form a contract between the user department and the systems development group.

SWOT of HSMs

HSMs are a medium that users in a designing community can adopt as a common language as these must conclude in an unambiguous model that can be converted into computer code or a product specification. However, often the codification of data becomes very cryptic and hence the usefulness of HSM models is reduced as they do not have the expressive abilities to adequately represent "softer" organisational issues.

In the survey conducted by Small (1998) 49% (2nd highest) of the surveyed companies had experiences of using HSMs for process modelling. This is a worrying statistic as it suggests that industry does business process modelling as a step to designing new software, rather than for purposes of organisational process improvement associated with the non-IT and non-product aspects of the business.

"Soft" Process Modelling for Human Activity Systems (Holons)

Although this group is far smaller in number than the "hard" modelling techniques, they are more central to the key theme of this book. They are used widely in academia and have highly expressive abilities to describe entities and activities relationships. SSMs were introduced in Part II, and some of their techniques are summarised in Table 3.3.

Concept Mapping

Concept mapping is a technique that results in the externalisation of an individual's knowledge in a format that is believed to be consistent with the individual's cognitive structure through the construction of a concept map; this is designed to allow a way of escaping the restrictiveness of the linear thought process reflected in both written and spoken language (Lambiotte et al., 1989). In pedagogical settings, Novak and Gowin (1984) states that conceptual mapping has proven to be a useful technique for

- transferring information from one individual to another;
- for identifying key ideas within a given subject;
- for improving a formalism that is closely analogous to the mental organisation of the individual being mapped; and
- summarising a given cognitive domain.

Concept mapping is also uniquely regarded as a flexible non-obtrusive knowledge acquisition technique, and it bears close resemblance to Checkland's "rich pictures". A SWOT analysis of these techniques is given in Table 3.4. Authors of this book believe that at present the main problems with these techniques are that they are too general and that specific techniques for narrower applications should be developed. This is reinforced by Ormerod (1992) when he stated that:

> I do see a lot of opportunity to explore more fully the use of SSM as the first stage in systems identification and would encourage researchers to concentrate on the potential role of SSM in specific defined contexts. SSM could provide the tool to investigate the context, the systems development process, and the people engaged in it.

TABLE 3.3 Types and Applications of "Soft" Modelling Techniques

Name	*Key Authors*	*Application Domain*
SSM: rich pictures, root definitions and conceptual models	Checkland (1981)	Problem analysis in Human Activity Systems/Holons
Conceptual Mapping	Eden et al. (1983)	Paradigm analysis

TABLE 3.4 SWOT Analysis of "Soft" Graphical Process Modelling

Strengths	Weaknesses
• Very high expressive ability essential for business process redesign exercises, promoting team working and learning. • Visually appealing. • People oriented. • Process envisioning capabilities.	• Notional & conceptual. • Lack of formal approach and formal validation and verification techniques. • Lack efficiency.
Opportunities	**Threats**
• Great potential for improving techniques for drawing, validation & verification (subject of this book). • "May" have the benefit of "top-down", bottom-up" and "middle-out" views to process modelling.	• Industry suspicion of academic approaches (systems thinking ideas about "soft" issues in human activity systems and "hard" systems).

In general, concept mapping is often perceived to be too conceptual by industrialists and therefore it lacks their confidence to be practically used and hence gain their buy-in.

These sentiments are reinforced by Small et al.s' (1998) survey because only 8% of the surveyed companies had any experience of using SSM, and one should note that Concept Mapping was not even included. It therefore should come as no surprise to learn that industry does not use these "softer" graphical representations, and the authors of this book suspect it is because of the reasons stated above. Small et al. (1998) states that industry demands "simple methods requiring short development times, at a minimal cost to the company and which can produce simplistic easily amended models". This description does not seem to be regarded by industry as applicable to "soft" methodologies and techniques. The authors of this book have built upon these identified strengths and opportunities and claim to have reduced most of the threats and weaknesses as *the founding purpose of the PrOH Modelling Methodology was to appropriately draw on both hard and soft techniques that can be practically used to recommend strategic and operational improvements whilst embodying hard-soft systems thinking principles emphasising the softer aspects.*

Integrating "Hard" and "Soft": A Better Graphical Methodology

What becomes apparent from the above is that to achieve strategic change in either service or design and manufacturing organisations, it is pointless to look at isolated activities (i.e. raising a purchase order) or even two activities (i.e. vetting an order and shop floor loading). Ideally, to maximise the potential of any change management philosophy, it is appropriate to examine an appropriate selection of tasks and/or processes in a "**primary**" and/or "**supporting**" role. This examination must be conducted in a systemic (holonic) fashion, looking at the *processes* of change and not limiting thinking to *function, structural or* organisational *control* reconfiguration. Specifically, the authors of this book believe there is a clear need to address the *human issues* in strategic and operational process change (Clegg et al., 1996b). Managers of process change (i.e. agents of change) must be given the opportunity to learn to work as a team to develop shared ownership of their processes and use it to achieve common goals with greater efficiency. If a team of people do not understand the common goals they are trying to achieve or the process they are supposed to use to achieve this, there can be little hope of ever improving the process or efficaciously achieving its goals.

Authors of this book believe that a new methodology and techniques are required to group together and portray key information and impressions about complex process change in a structured and evocative manner that gives stakeholders great agency for change because once change agents understand the context of the processes that they are involved in, they become a greater asset to their organisation. However, achieving this is a non-trivial exercise, and a systems approach to capture and promulgate the message would help. The authors of this book believe that applying a "soft" systems approach in an integrated hybrid hard-soft technique within a methodology is the best way to do this as also suggested by Mingers (2000) and Mingers and Brocklesby (1997). There are two perspectives that will achieve this integration, "**grafting**" and "**embedding**" which are discussed below.

Grafting versus Embedding Perspectives to Integration

The "soft" systems approach addresses problem situations in which the designation of goals is itself problematical, such as those endemic in human affairs and human activity systems. Unlike the "hard" systems tradition, the "soft" systems approach enables progress to be made without the prerequisite of defining the problem in terms of a means-end schema. To combine both "hard" and "soft" approaches into some kind of "hard-soft" methodological framework of practical and consistent usage is not straightforward. However, these authors believed that doing this would give rise to some interesting systemic insights. Two perspectives considered suitable to achieve this were "grafting" or "embedding".

The "grafting" perspective's distinguishing characteristic is that the "soft" systems stage is grafted onto the front end of the conventional "hard" systems methodology. This is shown in Figure 3.1.

The "embedding" perspective can be described in terms of two interrelated levels of methodological deployment where "hard" methodologies are used at a subordinate level to the "soft" methodology. The "soft" methodology operates at a meta-level of iterations or **action research cycles** within which the "hard" systems methodology is used.

It is at the meta-level that systemically desirable and culturally feasible changes to the real-world situation are identified and agreed upon. Once the context of a problem situation is defined

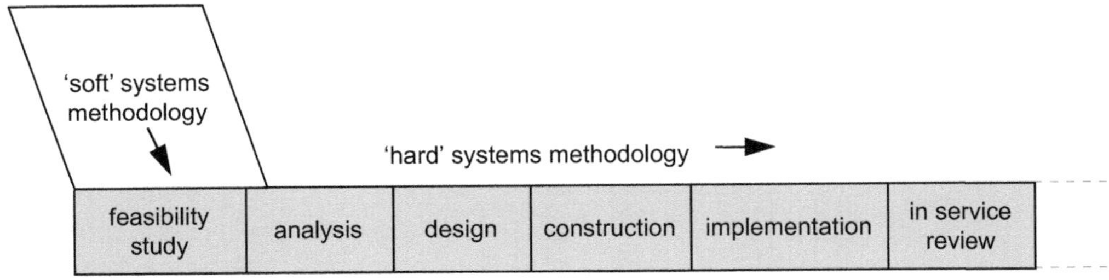

FIGURE 3.1 The Grafting Perspective for Graphical Modelling Techniques.

Source: Adapted from Miles (1988).

using the "soft" methodology, then a specific solution can be objectified and realised by deploying a suitable "hard" methodology. The "embedding" perspective is shown in Figure 3.2.

The main contrast between the perspectives is that "embedding" uses "soft" methodologies as a potentially on-going iteration of **action research cycles** within which to deploy "hard" methodologies and, "grafting" uses "soft" systems ideas in an *initial* analytical thrust to clarify objectives at the fuzzy front end of a project where there are many unknown unknowns.

These perspectives are discussed further by Miles (1988), and Savage and Mingers (1996), where most of the discussion revolves around methodological integration. Authors of this book believe the "embedded" perspective is more suitable to use in the context of PrOH Modelling" application because

- Checkland considers "hard" methodologies to be a subset of "soft" methodologies and therefore the author believes their associated techniques will follow the same relationship;
- techniques operate within a methodological framework and so by "grafting" one technique onto another you are effectively merging methodologies; and
- it retains a multiplicity of perspectives at a meta-level throughout by making the "hard" methodologies subordinate.

Grounded research for this book has created new "hard-soft" process modelling techniques with an "embedded" perspective to allow

- a better integration of "hard" and "soft" systems thinking and
- a useable medium has been reached between the need for pragmatic application of "harder" methodologies and the "softer" ontological correctness of representations of perceived human activity systems.

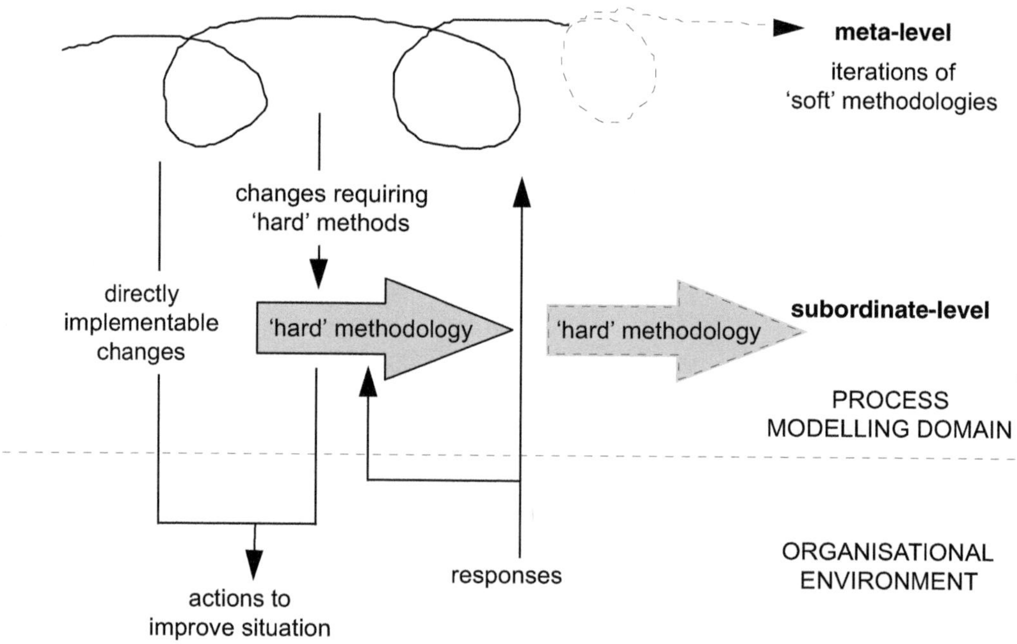

FIGURE 3.2 The Embedding Perspective for Graphical Modelling Techniques.

Type of Application Scenario

When a new set of techniques or a methodology is defined, it is necessary to be aware of developmental perspectives, as in Design Science (Johannesson and Perjons, 2021) to be aware of the context in which the new techniques are intended to be deployed because this greatly affects the form of the methodology, and in this book, the modelling representation and execution of the methodology. Checkland (1972) suggests that,

> problem situations facing organisations can be thought of as falling in a spectrum from "soft" to "hard". "Soft" problems are those with a predominance of human content and relatively little technology i.e. the problem is about the interrelationships between purposeful systems.

Based on this definition, the novel PrOH Modelling Methodology and its new techniques are intended to have a slight bias towards the "softer" end of the "hard-soft" spectrum but not to be as "soft" as classical Checkland SSM.

The authors of this book locate the application of the PrOH Modelling Methodology and its new techniques by referring once again to Jackson's (1984) work on "problem contexts" (see Figure 1.1, Chapter 1). Jackson's simplest categorisation identifies four contexts, which are: **mechanical-unitary**, **systemic-unitary**, **mechanical-pluralist** and **systemic-pluralist**. Readers should be familiar with the specific meanings of "mechanical" (**machine age**) and "systemic" (**system age**) in the context of systems thinking from Ackoff's work discussed earlier. In addition, readers need to be aware of "**unitary**" and "**pluralistic**" terms that have specific meanings: where a problem context is "**unitary**" if the set of decision makers all agree on a common set of goals for the whole system and make their decisions in accordance with these goals; and, in contrast, "**pluralist**" if the set of decision makers cannot agree on a common set of goals and make decisions which are in accordance with differing objectives. In more detail:

- **Mechanical-unitary** contexts can be dealt with adequately by classical OR, SA or SE techniques.
- **Systemic-unitary** contexts are complex, probabilistic systems. They have many elements in close inter-relationship and exhibit behaviour that is difficult to predict. Furthermore, these systems are open to their environments and include purposeful parts; for instance, Socio-technical-systems theory (Trist et al., 1963) is regarded as being well suited to exploring this context.
- **Mechanical-pluralist** contexts concern the interaction of mechanical parts that are passive and not purposeful. Therefore, the pluralism concerns differences among decision makers outside the system about the goals served by that system. If disagreement among the decision makers can be resolved, then the problems remaining can be solved using the "hard" systems methodologies previously examined. Perhaps one of the most sophisticated attempts to develop a methodology to bring about a synthesis among decision makers, so that action can be taken, is that of Churchman's (1968) GST. Mason and Mitroff (1981) then developed Churchman's ideas further into "Strategic Assumption Surfacing and Testing" (SAST).
- **Systemic-pluralist** contexts are those most relevant to the PrOH Modelling Methodology, as it is here that the "soft" systems approach of Checkland also seems most appropriate. This context is characterised by organisations that are purposeful systems which contain

purposeful parts, and which are themselves parts of larger purposeful systems. Hence, "organisations have responsibilities to their own purposes, to the purposes of their parts and to the purposes of the larger systems of which they are parts" (Ackoff, 1974). These purposes are often considered to conflict and thought of as "pluralistic". The conflict at different levels of systems (conceived as "**holons**" in "**holarchies**") is a major consideration in the development of the PrOH Modelling Methodology.

Authors of this book constrained the developments of the PrOH Modelling Methodology to "**systemic-pluralist**" contexts (Jackson, 2019; Figure 1.1; Chapter 1) so they essentially become adaptations of "soft" systems thinking, with elements of "hard" techniques "embedded" and believe that to approach its development from the opposite way around would be meaningless because

- it would not be considered methodologically feasible to "embed" "soft" techniques into a "hard" methodology and
- if any result was achieved, it would not be suited to achieving the improvement of human issues towards the best practice of change because it would require a pre-defined end objective, which is a fundamental of all "hard" methodologies, to be stated, which is not always culturally feasible or desirable when improving business strategy, operations and processes.

However, authors of this book disagree with Jackson on these last two points about the development of new methodologies and techniques because Jackson believes that it would be possible to take either path by taking the above as the authors have done; or, to "soften-up" a "mechanical-unitary" problem.

Soft Systems Models: Validation and Verification

Under Checkland's soft philosophical worldview where there will be several viewpoints on what the "problem situation" is, which can be improved by reaching accommodations on action rather than the development of a "correct solution to *the* problem" as in systems engineering. Hence "soft" models are not measured by their representativeness of the real world rather as "in Soft Systems Methodology models are not part of the real world; they are only relevant to debate about the real world and are used in a cyclical learning process" (Checkland, 1995). Given that soft models do not either claim to be "would-be" descriptions of extant systems in the real world they cannot be tested as representations of it. Instead, they are "epistemological devices" that must be assessed as good or bad devices; in other words, are they *valid*. The **validation** question then becomes whether the model is relevant to the problem situation or conceptual system. Thus, softer models can become more relevant through iterative cycles of learning and model reviews, and modification of a model of a concept, subsequently to new empirical evidence and insight.

Verification is the question of whether a model is competently constructed according to its own rules and guidelines; in the context of the PrOH Modelling Methodology this is done using a holonic temple to define its core process (equivalent to the **root definition** in Checkland's SSM) and supporting issues of a worldview (strategic, tactical or operational) which must be demonstrable and defendable in respect to the template which embodies essential **systemicity**. Thus,

> in a "soft" approach models have only to be internally valid [i.e. verified], that is to say internally defensible against a set of principles which define a particular kind of intellectual construct, or a particular kind of epistemological device.
>
> *(Checkland and Holwell, 1998)*

An additional criterion for validity advocated by Checkland and Holwell (1998) involves the concept of "recoverability". In experimental research, repeatability is an important validation check; however, such an approach is not possible in "soft" approaches; nonetheless, one should aim for more than mere plausibility of the research "story". To achieve this, a researcher should use a declared-in-advance methodology and describe the epistemological basis of the methodology so that interested parties can understand how the ideas and assumptions that were applied in the research and how researchers arrived at their conclusions. By doing this, it is possible for interested parties to critically assess the research because the methodology is "recoverable".

> The aim was [is] to make clear to interested observers the thought processes and models which enabled the team (researcher) to make their interpretations and draw their conclusions. Those observers may not accept the team's (researcher's) interpretations; then a debate about the work can take place which is sufficiently well structured as to be coherent
>
> *(Checkland and Holwell, 1998)*

Hard Systems Models: Validation and Verification

The process of model validation in hard systems methodologies (e.g. System Dynamics, SD) involves some level of validation at every stage through judgments of fitness for purpose; however, assessments of the validity of the usefulness of the purpose itself are essentially a qualitative process (Barlas, 1996; Checkland, 1999, 2006). Thus, questions of model validity are similar to those addressed by Checkland, above. Therefore, Systems Dynamics as applied under the "soft" end of the spectrum does not represent an objective truth and therefore from a critical perspective model validation is impossible (Sterman, 2000, pp.846–850). Consequently, Sterman (2000, p.890) states:

> The word validation should be struck from the vocabulary of modelers. All models are wrong, so no models are valid or verifiable in the sense of establishing their truth. The question facing clients and modelers is never whether a model is true but whether it is useful. The choice is never whether to use a model. The only choice is which model to use. Selecting the most appropriate model is always a value judgement to be made by reference to the purpose. Without a clear understanding of the purpose for which the model is to be used, it is impossible to determine whether you should use it as a basis for action.

Similarly, despite the impossibility of validating a model Pidd (2004, p.293) states that validation should be: "regarded as an ideal toward which we must strive if we are to be at all faithful to the idea that Management Science aims to support action in the real world". Thus, Sterman (2000, p.850) suggests that,

Instead of presenting evidence that the model is valid, good modellers focus the client on the limitations of the model so it can be improved, and so clients will not misuse it

To achieve this, it is necessary to be clear on the purpose of a model. The purpose of a model for change is to attempt to provide a basis, predicated on organisational process structure and a maturity model, for testing different assumptions about the outcomes of proposed actions to increase the maturity of an organisation's improvement programme (Snabe and Größler, 2006) in whatever criteria are deemed desirable. Thus, the use of harder systems methodologies (e.g. systems dynamics) provides a framework for the measurement of the performance of the organisational improvement programme and the experimentation with different proposed actions and worldviews.

Verification for HSMs is done by checking against their rules and guidelines; in the case of HSMs these are likely to be more perfunctory and easier to do than with SSMs.

Validation: How Valid Is Validation?

The mode (e.g. Modes 1, 2 and 3 as discussed in Chapter 2) of application of the model relates directly to the process by which it should be validated. Barlas (1996) considers two types of model

- "correlational" for purely data-driven "black-box" models associated with harder techniques and
- "causal descriptive" for theory-like "white box" models associated with softer techniques.

"Black box" models represent the aggregate output behaviour of the model; validity can be "easily" assessed as whether the output of the model matches that observed in the real-world (Barlas, 1996), or more precisely that the predictions of the model and those observed in the real world are close enough to demonstrate adequate validity (Pidd, 2004, pp.289–299). Given these assumptions and the nature of organisational improvement implementations, it would be infeasible to produce "black box" models of change. The stated purpose of a harder systems methodology model, such as an SD model, is to experiment with different proposed courses of action, which will inherently involve a change to the modelled system and being context specific cannot reliably import data from another *similar* system. Therefore, one might argue that it is illogical to validate against historical or imported data which will inevitably represent a different context; meanwhile, post-hoc assessment of the model's predictions, based solely on "black box" output, is insufficient without some confirmation that a model's structure, and therefore the actions taken, in some way caused the observed post-hoc behaviour. Further post-hoc examination may be useful for the assessment of "black box" model assumptions regarding expected behaviour but will still represent historical data from a different past lost context; thus, a hard systems methodology model must be sufficient to experiment with different proposed actions and at least represent the expected behaviour of those actions to aid implementation (Snabe and Größler, 2006) in similar but not the same context; which to do so, must function more as a "white-box" model context.

"White box" models are essentially statements about the operation of real systems; in this case output behaviour is insufficient to validate the model; additionally, the internal structure must also be validated. The internal structure is hence considered valid through the validated case study data collated in the form of the SIPOC table in PrOH Modelling. Thus, a model must produce the right behaviour for the right reasons and therefore explain the behaviour (Barlas, 1996; Pidd, 2004, pp.299–300). Validation of model structure is not a simple thing to do for two main reasons: the first is philosophical, in which a positivist standpoint would hold that a model is correct or incorrect, while a more interpretive approach would argue that a model is one of many possible models. Under the philosophical standpoints applied in this book, the latter, interpretive, context is appropriate; thus, validation cannot be entirely objective; rather, it is a process of building confidence in the model as being adequate for purpose. Thus, using models in a "reflective" mode (Sterman, 2000, p.858) "in which testing is designed to uncover flaws and hidden assumptions, challenge preconceptions, and expose assumptions for critique and improvement" becomes more appropriate as models become softer in their purpose.

Derived Requirements for the PrOH Modelling Methodology and Its Techniques

New process modelling methodology and its techniques were deemed necessary by this book's authors to capture "hard-soft" process change issues and disseminate these in a manner that was uncodified to retain the richness of the original semantics in which the data were collected. Philosophically speaking, "soft" system methodologies are most relevant to this type of application, but often they sadly lack adequate diagrammatic techniques. These techniques need to be able to depict "hard-soft" issues discussed in this and previous chapters.

The authors of this book make no differentiation between different change management "fads" (such as total quality management (TQM) or business process reengineering (BPR)), because fundamentally they are all considered to be founded on the principles of systems thinking, although this is rarely acknowledged or even understood. Consequently, epistemologically it follows that any method of enquiry should also be founded on the same systems thinking principles. The PrOH Modelling Methodology and its new techniques evolved with these facts in mind, so it did not fall into the trap of being too mechanistic ("hard") with its inquiry and representation. However, these authors have tried to remove some of the esoteric properties that are common criticisms of Checkland's SSM, which make it unsuitable for organisational strategic or process change modelling.

The PrOH Modelling Methodology is an attempt to make soft systems methodologies usable by others apart from guru-consultants or specialised academics; *the authors of this book have attempted to narrow the cognitive dissonance between the purposefulness of perceived "soft" systems and the objectives and goals of primary "hard" systems.* A possible way of achieving this is to reduce a perceived "soft" system's purpose to a series of phases (with constituent serial sub-phases) which are conceived as ***"quasi-hard" systems*** with goals and objectives.

This book's authors believe a "quasi-hard" system is what a few authors might have referred to before as a "hard-soft" system. Very little work has been done on this system's ontology and therefore there has been no methodology or technique development. These authors believe they can begin to explain this system's ontology (Clegg, 1997). When a modeller undertakes a "soft" systems analysis, they analyse the purpose of a "holon". When modellers analyse "hard" systems, they analyse the objective of a "system". To analyse a "quasi-hard" system a modeller should analyse the purpose of each "holon's" objectives, which we believe facilitates the provenance of the whole system and its **emergent** and **hidden properties**.

The stance taken by a "soft" systems modeller is said to be phenomenological because they will give precedence to the mental perceptions solicited from the real-world process agents (Checkland terms this as "Weltanshauung"). A "hard" systems modeller will take a positivist stance as they will give precedence to historical or scientific experimental evidence.

To model a "quasi-hard" system a modeller must use a phenomenological stance to define the "dimensions" of each of the "holons", because these are part of the perceived conceptual "soft" system. As Gregory (1993) states, "there is no single 'holon' that is correct in regard to any given situation". However, once the "dimensions" of each "holon" have been defined a "hard-soft" modeller must use a positivist stance to attribute a goal, objective and/or milestone to each. This is possible because process milestones can be documented with actual evidence from the "real-world".

Figure 3.3 depicts the ontological space between perceived "soft" systems (full of human activity) and actual "hard" systems in which "quasi-hard" systems exist; it also shows where the new concept of the "**process oriented holon**" sits between purely "soft" and purely "hard" modelling representations. This central ground was the "yet to be explored" gap that drove the development of the Process Oriented Holonic Modelling Methodology. *Thus, this is how Process Oriented Holonic Modelling derives its methodological name.*

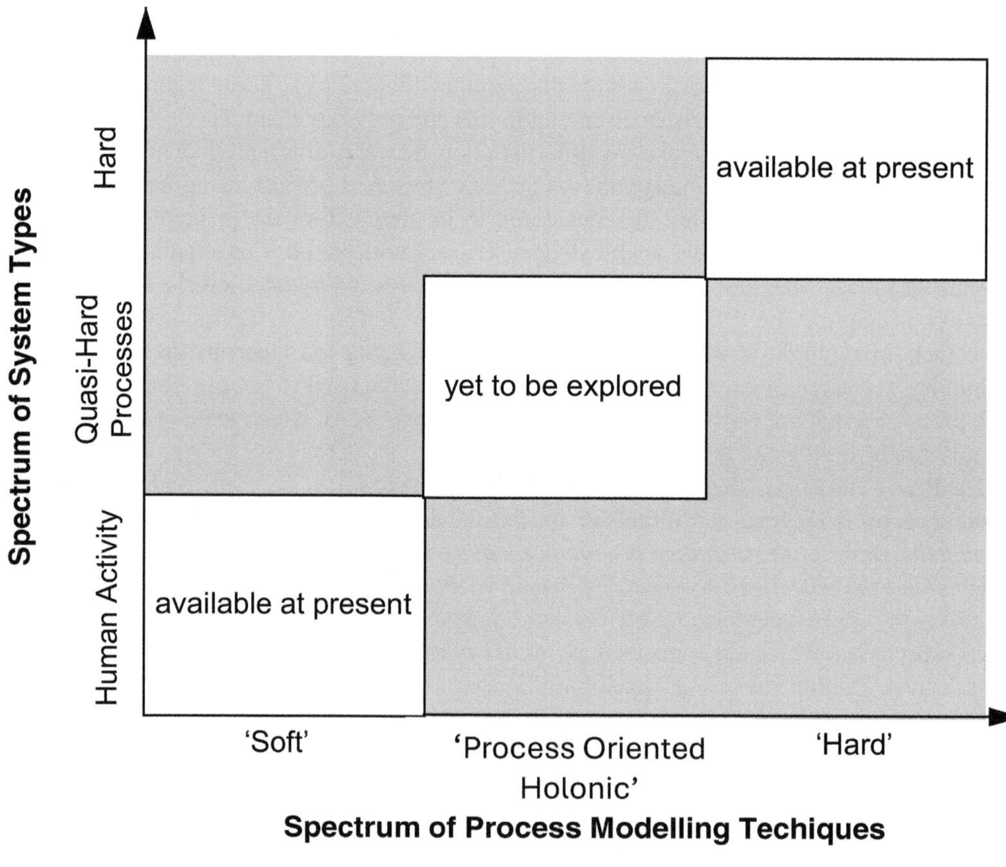

FIGURE 3.3 New Process Modelling Requirements for a New Systems Ontology.

Source: Clegg, 1999, p.102.

A Holonic Ontology for Operations and Strategy

Documented application of "holonic" thinking began in the 1990s when the PrOH Modelling Methodology was being developed, and it is still very limited. It was mostly limited to manufacturing domains Dong (1995) who investigated the underlying principles of "holonic" manufacturing. They see "holonic" manufacturing as a means to emphasise the human-technical interface and increase agility in manufacturing:

> Holonic manufacturing systems are composed of "holons". Each "holon" is a system building block which is both autonomous and co-operative. A manufacturing "holon" may transform, transport, store and/or validate information and physical objects. The "holon" consists of an information processing part and often a physical processing part and can be part of another "holon".

Dong (1995) introduces new terms for describing such "holonic" thinking; the most poignant is "**holarchy**" which defines basic rules for co-operation between the "**holons**" and therefore limits their autonomy. Unfortunately, no methodology or "**holarchy**" rule base is offered for their "**holonic**" ontology; instead, they have developed an object-oriented window-based activity information model. On a larger scale, "holonic" thinking was applied to manufacturing enterprises by McHugh et al. (1997) as they define a "holonic network" as a

> set of companies that acts integratedley and organically; it is constantly reconfigured to manage each business opportunity a customer presents. Each company in the network provides a different process capability and is called a "holon". Each configuration of process capabilities is called a virtual company.

The primary author of this book believes that "holonic thinking" was at the time of developing PrOH Modelling becoming in danger of being dismissed as the next "management fad". However, he believes that careful application of academic research from recent years could save it from an undeserved debunking. In fact, at the time of writing, holistic thinking has not yet become popular mainstream theory and has perhaps been waiting for advances in technology (i.e. artificial intelligence and large language models) to catch up with the theory and make it a reality. Some work in this area continues, but there is currently still little consensus (Kruger, 2018; McFarlane, 2000).

Summary

The main point is that the process of implementing change towards any ideal purpose within an organisation is always difficult, and the degree of difficulty varies exponentially with the increasing size of the organisation, the length of time the change process takes, and its perceived complexity. With this in mind, Checkland's methodology has been adapted to meet a specific need, as others have done so before (Watson and Smith, 1988; Wilson, 1984). SSM was initially developed to provide an insight into the real world for defining problem areas with quite unlimited application. This book's authors have developed a derivation of SSM to meet the specific set of requirements outlined by the rationale of systems thinking and action research set out in Chapters 1 and 2.

In following Chapters 4 and 5, the principles of a system remain the same, but a narrower application domain means that a more prescriptive set of techniques can be used by a modeller. This is a deliberate attempt to make SSM more user-friendly to potential industrial users. As Checkland (1979) states,

> the diagrams of such [human activity] systems are so bad that some progress towards better diagrams is urgently needed.

This has been achieved by migrating towards the "harder" end of the spectrum of process modelling techniques and having a smaller application domain. The position of the new type of system ontology and the requirement for the new process modelling methodology and techniques relative to the existing ones is depicted in Figure 3.3. A fundamental construct on which the PrOH Modelling methodology is built is the **process oriented holon**.

The authors are conscious that process modellers will tend to "always seeing the world in terms of their favourite problem-solving technique" (Jackson, 1984) and so this book's authors might be guilty of being overenthusiastic about the PrOH Modelling Methodology. However, we would like to share it with the world; methodology, techniques and all, and we do this in Chapters 4 and 5 with illustrative cases in Part III. Further details of the PrOH Modelling Methodology's origins and derivation can be read in Clegg (1999).

Further Reading

Clegg, B.T. (1999), *A Systems Approach to Re-Engineering Business Processes Towards Concurrent Engineering Principles*. PhD Thesis. Chapter 5. De Montfort University and British Library.

4

THE PROH MODELLING METHODOLOGY

How to Construct a Single PrOH Model

The PrOH Modelling Methodology

This section gives an overview of the Process Oriented Holonic (PrOH) Modelling Methodology which is depicted in Figure 4.1. At a methodological level, the PrOH Modelling Methodology is founded on the principles of systems thinking as given in Chapters 1 and action research set out in Chapter 2, which have been adapted in response to new development requirements as proposed in Chapter 3.

The PrOH Modelling Methodology is made accessible and useable for those unfamiliar with the scholarly works given in previous chapters by following a popularist change methodology depiction, as used by Edward Deming in his **Plan-Do-Study-Act (PDSA)** cycle (Deming, 1986, 1993; Moen and Norman, 2010). Earlier similar versions of The PrOH Modelling Methodology diagram seen in Figure 4.1 have been published (Clegg, 2006, 2020; Clegg and Shaw, 2008) but are now superseded by this latest version given in Figure 4.1.

The PrOH Modelling Methodology in Figure 4.1 has systems thinking and action research **embedded** within an adapted **Plan-Do-Check-Study-Act (PDSA)** cycle (Deming, 1986).

Demings' PDSA cycle emphasises practical impact making. In contrast, action research and systems thinking approaches have more emphasis on academic theorising to promote research and pedagogical deliverables. Together, all three combine into the PrOH Modelling Methodology to give a pragmatic methodology capable of delivering practical impactful change in organisations with associated academic outputs.

Uniquely PrOH Modelling combines the worlds of academia and practice in a **Planning + Researching**, **Doing + Systems Thinking**, **Studying + Actioning**, **Acting + Impacting** methodology as follows:

1. **Planning**: Scope granularity of real-world human activity system to change in an organisation (e.g. process) and define its minimum viable elements as a system with reason(s) for its change.

DOI: 10.4324/9781032650425-6

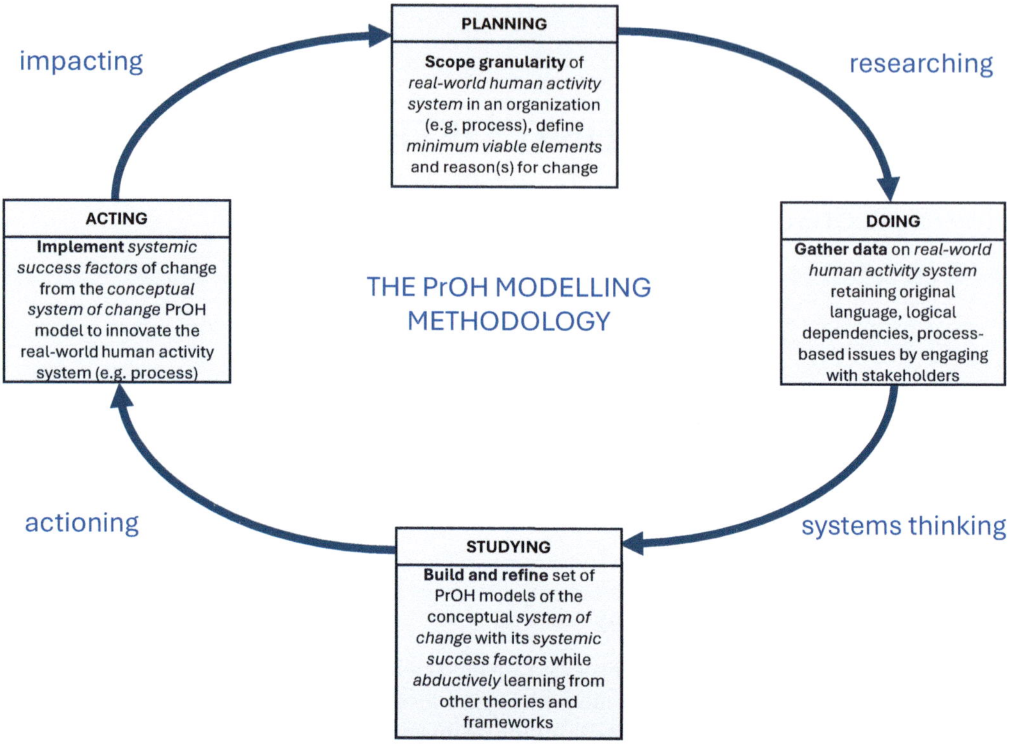

FIGURE 4.1 The PrOH Modelling Methodology.

Researching – secondary planning to contextualise practical study in a wider field-of-use using secondary research.

2. **Doing**: Gather data on real-world human activity system retaining original language, logical dependencies and process-based issues by engaging with stakeholders.

   Systems Thinking – conceptualising a system of change from the real-world system under observation (e.g. a process) rather than "as-is" and "to-be" thinking.

3. **Studying**: Build and refine a (set of) PrOH Models of the conceptual system of change with its systemic success factors while abductively learning from other theories and frameworks.

   Actioning – drawing on best practice research and practice from other sources.

4. **Acting**: Implement *systemic success factors* of change from the PrOH Model of the *conceptual system of change* to innovate the real-world human activity system (e.g. process).

   Impacting – practical knowledge transfer and imbibement of actions into practice and collect evidence of impact.

Chapter 4 is structured using this PrOH Modelling Methodology above and seen in Figure 4.1.

Planning and Researching

Organisational elements shown in PrOH Models may include the following: people, machines, knowledge, IT systems, products and services; further examples of systems elements are given in Table 4.1.

When using the PrOH Modelling Methodology, a process to be observed becomes the subject of a system of change, which can most simply be thought of as the construct shown in Figure 4.2, depicting the **minimum viable elements** of a system. This could be applied to the system under observation (e.g. a real-world process) or to a system for change (e.g. a conceptual model using the PrOH Methodology).

Scoping an Organisational System under Observation

The first step to composing a PrOH Model of a change system is to scope the dimensions of its system under observation (e.g. the "real-world" process), which if done correctly, should define the:

- **Pitch** – is the level of managerial thinking reflected in a PrOH Model. Typically, it will be any one or combination of three levels either strategic, tactical or operational. For example, a strategic model of a furniture manufacturing factory will have the core of the model pitched on a high-level concept of a product's look and feel, range of products, company growth, turnover, etcetera and is likely to have a clear focus on gross revenue and net profit margins. In contrast, tactical models of the same factory would focus on three sequential models of "pre-manufacture", "manufacture" and "post-manufacture". Operational models in the same factory would focus on sub-systems of change for each tactical model. For instance, for the manufacturing tactical model, the operational models of change are likely to be something such as "machine set-up", "machine monitoring and operation" and "product checking and quality approval".
- **Length** – is where a PrOH Model starts and finishes understanding. There will be a "**pick-up point**" where the model of an organisational system starts and a "**drop-off point**" where the model of an organisational system stops. For example, for a factory making furniture the "**pick-up point**" of the strategic model might be "client enquiry" and the "**drop-off point** be 'installed furniture at clients' premises". For lower pitched models at tactical levels these points will be re-pitched; accordingly, for example, the "manufacturing" tactical model "**pick-up point** would become 'set up of manufacturing requirements planning (MRP) system'" and the "**drop-off point**" would be "completed furniture". Operational models at a lower pitch would be even more detailed, starting with lower-level pitched "pick-up points" such as "machine loading" of a product and "drop-off" with something such as "change over" to another product.
- **Width** – is how far a model digresses from the core (**primary-task**) process description in a PrOH Model Template. A PrOH Model may not digress too much from the core process statement and therefore have a narrow **width**; or might be quite expansive and divergent and more remote in what it includes in respect to the core process description and will therefore have a much broader **width**. For example, a PrOH Model describing a furniture

TABLE 4.1 Examples of Elements of an Organisational System from Manufacturing and Service

	Organisation	
	High Street Bank	*Washing Machine Manufacturer*
System	Customer relationship management (CRM) system	Production System
System Inputs	New customer with no profile	Sheet Metal
Feedback Loops (keep the system in control)	Data-mining techniques to check the effectiveness of marketing promotions	ISO 9001 quality procedures, ISO14001 environmental regulations, total productivity maintenance, shareholder meetings, health and safety regulations
Elements **Transforming Resources** – those that do not become part of the final product or service but are used to make and deliver these **Transformed Resources** – those that are being processed and may end up as part of the final product and service	People – marketing department Financial – employee incentives Tangible – computer hardware Intangible – intellectual property CRM softwarePersonalised and updated customer profiles to facilitate a more personalised service	Human – machine operators Financial – working capital Tangible – machines Intangibles – operating procedures Parts, materials and sub-assemblies to make finished products for the consumer
Relationships between Elements (make these activities occur)	Customers (system inputs) are transformed by employees (who are a transforming resource) e.g. customer profiles are updated by the CRM software every time a transaction is made	Tangible materials (system inputs) are transformed by humans and machines (transforming resources) e.g. people use machines and materials to make other machines
System Boundary(establishes authority and influence)	Limit of channel interfaces with customers and bank that can produce valuable communication	The interface with suppliers at one end customers at the other end
Environment(to link a system with the rest of the world – which is itself made up of other systems)	Competition and regulation of the high street banking sector	Competition and regulation (e.g. health and safety, export laws)
System Outputs (the creations of the systems – which are hopefully value adding)	Transformed resources – e.g. loyal customers with a fully customised profile	Transformed resources – e.g. parts and materials become washing machines

Source: Adapted from Paton et al., 2021, p.142.

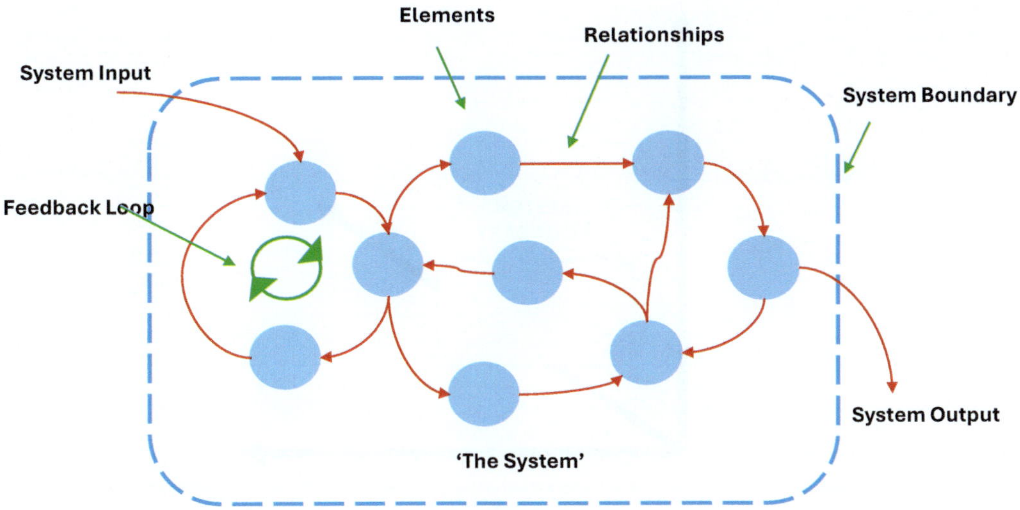

FIGURE 4.2 A System.
Source: Adapted from Paton et al., 2021, p.141.

making factory would have a narrow width if it only focused on the physical production of the furniture, but it would have a much broader **width** if the model included financing of the furniture manufacturing company, human resourcing planning and discussed its relationships with its partners and contract manufacturers. If PrOH Models need to be very broad it may be appropriate to think about using **parallel** rather than **serial** rules of PrOH Modelling as discussed in more detail in Chapter 5.

The **pitch**, **length** and **width** dimensions for scoping a systems model are shown in Figure 4.2 and can be applied to define the system boundaries for individual models or to a set of models and in doing so will clarify the purpose of the PrOH Modelling exercise, encourage parsimony and clarity among modellers, contributors and audiences of the models. The blue lozenge in the centre of Figure 4.3 (Clegg, 2007) represents the minimum viable elements of a system as shown in Figure 4.2.

In this Chapter 4 we will only consider building a single PrOH Model. PrOH Modelling considers a single PrOH Model to be a **holon** that represents a system of change containing **Systemic Success Factors** for change. A **Process Matrix** may be used to define a set of PrOH Models in the same way, as discussed in Chapter 4.

Researching – Other Related Areas

While defining the system under observation (SuO), a PrOH Modeller will start to get a feel for its **primary task** and **issue-based SSFs**; although at this early stage, these may not be fully understood. Therefore, a PrOH Modeller must begin to read materials on related subject areas such as digitalisation, circular economy, efficiency, productivity, carbon reduction, leanness or agility in a scholarly way; this brings a broader context to the PrOH Methodology and distinguishes it from mere action-taking or consulting, as rigorous objective topical knowledge will

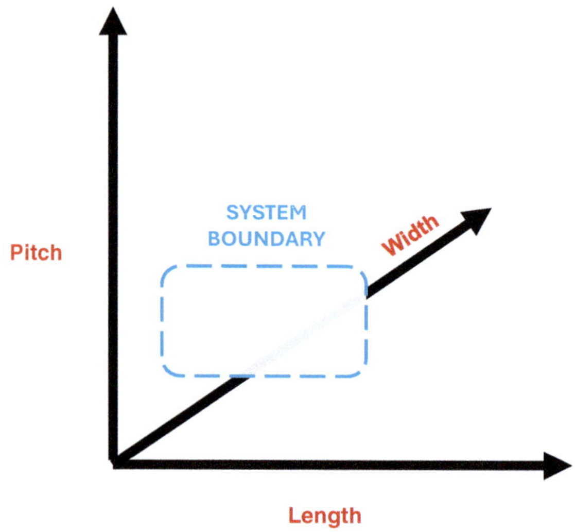

FIGURE 4.3 Scoping Dimensions for a Model of Systemic Change.

Source: Adapted from Clegg, 2007.

be transferred into the theme of the system under observation. Researching will also help give context to findings from the case, which can then be more purposefully and impactfully disseminated to third parties for practice or for theorising. As the PrOH Modelling Methodology primarily uses **abductive reasoning**, it is not necessary to declare at the earliest stage which frameworks and methods will be used, as these can be decided on and evolved later during "Doing and Systems Thinking" and "Studying and Actioning" when the SuO is better understood.

Doing and Systems Thinking

Engaging with Stakeholders of the Primary Task

This section describes how primary data is collected for an action research case and structured prior to drawing a PrOH Model. It is important to go through all these steps prior to drawing PrOH Models although as a modeller becomes more proficient in using PrOH Modelling, they may be able to do some of these data structuring steps in their head rather than explicitly writing these down.

Once the organisational system has been scoped, and a feel for its size has been grasped, a PrOH Modeller must think whether they are going to perform PrOH Modelling as a "top-down" macro exercise starting with the strategic level, or perform it as a "bottom-up" micro exercise starting with operational activities, or indeed as a "middle-out" exercise by starting with the meso "tactical" level. All three of these approaches are designed for and allowed in the PrOH Modelling Methodology making PrOH Modelling unique in comparison to other methodologies. What determines this is whatever the stakeholders of the system for change are interested in and the confidence of the modeller. However, it is often easier to start with a "top-down" modelling approach to get a rough feel for how many models need to be done, and whether these will be at a strategic, tactical or operational level.

There will always be only one strategic level model in a set of models. Three to five tactical models can normally be produced from one strategic model, and three to five operational models may be produced from each tactical model in operationally pitched models. Creating between three to five models from a higher-level model is a favourable "**span-of-enrichment**".

Using a Process Matrix to Scope Phases of a Process

Defining a span-of-enrichment means that the number of phases at each process pitch must be decided using a **Process Matrix**. For instance, a manufacturing process modelled at the tactical level may be divided into four process phases called, "pre-contract award", "set-up and planning", "manufacturing" and "post manufacturing shipping and delivery". At this stage, only inputs and outputs of each phase will be required; the details of what happens within each phase will be ascertained when constructing a PrOH Model for each phase; more detail on the structure of a **Process Matrix** is given in Chapter 5.

During any **span-of-enrichment** it is not necessary to create an equal number of models at a lower level for each higher-level model. In fact, as long as two or more lower-level models are created via **enrichment** then any number of lower-level models may be created for any number of higher-level PrOH Models. Creation of PrOH Models should be driven by stakeholders" interests. Sub-phases are again defined using a **Process Matrix**.

At the onset of PrOH Modelling, it is unnecessary to have a whole **holarchy** defined in **Process Matrices**, as a PrOH Modeller may choose to start with a "middle-out" meso exercise consisting of three tactical models followed by an **abstraction** to deliver a single top-level strategic model or enrich any one tactical model into five operational models. All these sequences, and many others, are possible.

Steps for **enrichment** and **abstraction** to form a **holarchy** are explained in Chapter 5; for now, in this Chapter 4, we will focus on the **refinement** of a single PrOH Model.

Data Collection

It is crucial to consult with all key stakeholders in a **system under observation** so a holistic understanding can be constructed. Usually, each stakeholder will have a slightly different understanding (Weltanschauung) of the System under Observation (SuO) in which they operate due to what they do on a day-to-day basis, how they do it, their role, their responsibilities and their previous experiences and personal biases (whether conscious or subconscious); and therefore, **multiple tenable viewpoints** are permissible and must be included in a PrOH Model. Sometimes some stakeholders may even try to obscure the truth, as they often have incentives or biases to make the system of change work to their advantage; and so, therefore, by triangulation of different views of the system, a moderated systemic view can be produced and presented in the PrOH Model system of change.

PrOH Modelling should strive to use as much **primary data** (e.g. interviews and focus groups) as possible as this makes the PrOH Model more relevant and keeps stakeholders engaged in the change management process. Secondary data (e.g. documents produced for other purposes) can be used in support, such as organisational procedures, documentation, quality metrics, reports, along with items such as product or service brochures.

The most efficient method of data extraction for PrOH Modelling has been to interview stakeholders separately. This is best done in a quiet room sitting at a table sketching on a large (flipchart sized) piece of paper using a soft pencil and an eraser. Alternatively, this can be done online using conferencing systems (e.g. Microsoft Teams) to conduct the interview, record and transcribe the interview (e.g. using artificial intelligence software) where drawing tools (e.g. MS Visio) can draw flowcharts of the system under observation on the fly while interviewing.

Once settled and free from distractions, an interviewer should set the interviewee at ease and ask them to tell a chronological process story of typical events in the **system under observation** as they see it, which should be a process that they work in daily. Interviewees should be encouraged not to worry too much about the official rules and regulations of the organisation, as this is not intended to be an official process audit, but to focus on what actually happens. It should be made clear to interviewees that their data is confidential, that they are not being tested, and that their data will become anonymised within a consolidated PrOH Model.

Very few, if any, interviewees will truly be able to think in a systemic way about any real-world process, let alone about a conceptual system for change, so it is best to ask interviewees to think of events in a linear serial chronology for a real-world system (e.g. an organisational-based process). For instance, if a modeller is interviewing someone about an "order winning" process, then a linear serial chronological process with tasks such as "find new business", "quote business", "negotiate business" etcetera should unfold, which should be achievable for most interviewees. A standard flow chart (using software such as MS Visio) can be sketched to represent an individual's account of a process as long as a few simple rules are followed:

- the process must have a start and finish point;
- use as few symbols as possible;
  - lozenges for start of finish points,
  - rectangles for activity boxes,
  - parallelograms for inputs and outputs, and
  - diamonds for decision points.
- rectangles with double lines at their sides for destinations of outputs and sources of inputs, or for aspects of the process outside of the system under observation (e.g. subcontracted activities, parts of a bidding process where a customer is evaluating a proposal, or where a supplier is responding to a request for a quotation);
- each activity rectangle must include an agent (the person(s)) responsible for doing it (e.g. "purchasing manager issues request for "quote"), an input (e.g. technical specification) and an output (request for quote); and
- the process must have decision points with three possible outcomes: feedforward loops, feedback loops and stops so a process can be terminated.

Flow charts form the raw **primary task** data source about the system under observation (e.g. operational process) in the real world, from which to later construct the conceptual holonic-based PrOH Models of the system for change. See Figure 4.4 for a simple example of what an interviewee's process flow chart may look like.

Once a flowchart has been sketched, the interviewer can then reflect on it by asking the interviewee to describe what parts of the process cause problems and why. Noting these on the flowchart paper as the respondent is speaking helps to initiate **critical systems thinking** (Jackson, 2019, 2024) by the interviewee on **issue-based** tasks to better understand the **systemic success factors** for change in the system for change. Once the **primary task** process and the **issues-based** tasks have been noted, the flowchart should be signed and dated by the

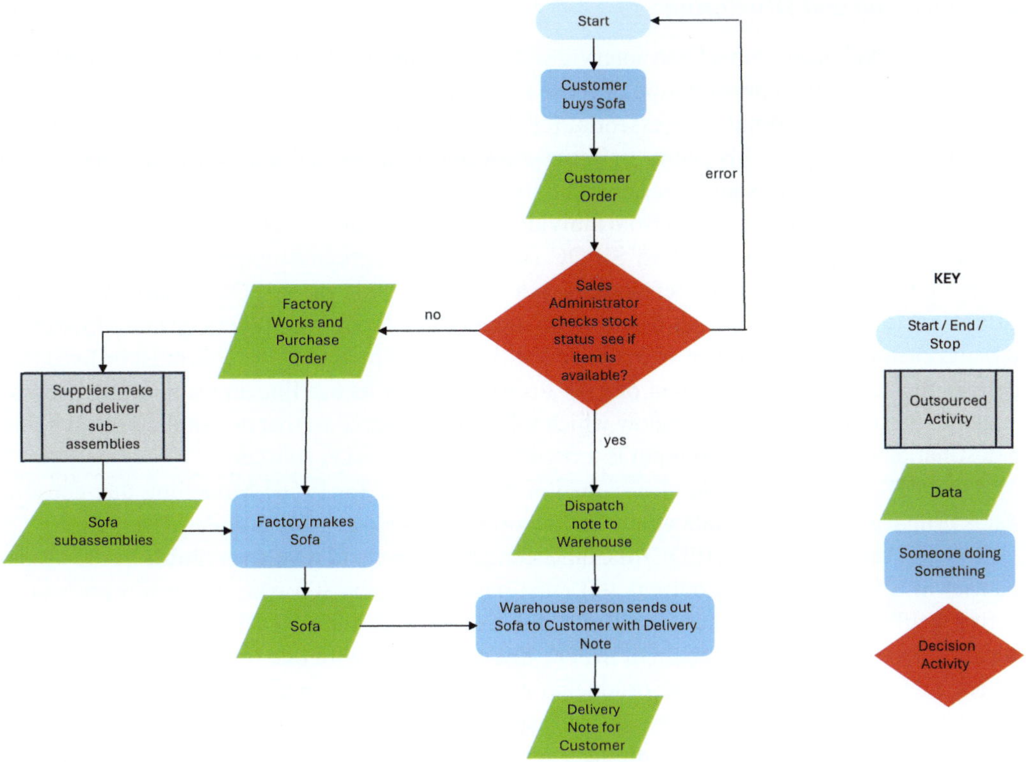

FIGURE 4.4 Flowchart (Possibly with Annotated Issues) of the Real-World Process.

Source: Adapted from Paton et al. 2021, p.153.

interviewee; this becomes raw data for an action researcher. During the interview, the interviewer-cum-modeller must take care not to offer any interpretation or additional input to data and must remain impartial and unbiased. At this point, if needs be, data can be anonymised to form a dataset for use by third parties for other purposes and stored securely for later analysis.

A researcher may well ask: *why do interviews separately*? Well, the answer to this is that all stakeholders must have their say and not, at this stage, be influenced by other stakeholders, as some stakeholders will be more vocal, powerful and knowledgeable than others. The interviewer must take care to consider all stakeholder perspectives and preserve their sense of primary **agency** in the process. Even if some stakeholders may be less knowledgeable, newer to the organisation, confused by certain aspects or misled, all viewpoints are valid in the sense that if these facts are what people genuinely believe happens, then it is self-fulfilling that these are likely to occur to some greater or lesser extent and become manifest in the overall behaviour of the system under observation; consequently, all perspectives need to be considered when creating the system for change in a PrOH Model.

Data Cleaning and Structuring

Once key stakeholders have been interviewed and produced, their flowcharts annotated with critical reflection, the consolidation of these multiple tenable viewpoints can be melded into a PrOH Model. At this point, it is essential for the systems thinking lens of a PrOH Modeller's mind to kick in. Up to this point, **primary-task** and **issue-based** data will often have been partial, fragmented and sometimes contradictory.

To integrate and structure data from individual interviews, the PrOH Modelling Methodology uses a table rather like a standard SIPOC (supplier-input-process-output-customer) table as given in Table 4.2 sometimes referred to as a "SIPOC" table or "SIPOC" chart. A standard SIPOC table has a line for each task for the supplier (S), input (I), process or task (P), output (O) and customer (C); however, in PrOH Modelling, an adapted SIPOC table must be used that defines the core process statement of each PrOH Model in its top line and supporting process statements constructed in lines below which follow in sequence so that no output is left without a destination (i.e. sink) and no input is left without an origin (i.e. source).

Table 4.2 gives an example of a sequential SIPOC table for PrOH Modelling that consolidates primary interviewee data about a real-world process (e.g. system under observation).

To make this sequential SIPOC-like table comprehensive and give a **verifiable** PrOH Model dataset in SIPOC terms, its outputs (O) must have customers (C) who perform a process or activity (P) that gives another output (O) that becomes an input (I) for the next process or activity, and so on. Hence, a chain of SIPOC links is formed with one link per line on the table where each line defines an agent producing an output that then becomes an input to another line in the SIPOC table. Links between lines are formed by notes in the extreme right-hand side and left-hand side columns. Accordingly, each activity (an agent doing something) will appear three times in three separate lines; firstly, as a customer (sink) of an output from a previous activity in the far-right hand column, secondly, as an **active agent** in the central column of the table, and thirdly, as a supplier (source) of an input to another **active agent** in the far-left hand column. Hence, no output is left without a destination, and no input will appear without a source. However, it is possible that inputs can have more than one source (see Table 4.2), and outputs can have more than one destination (or "sink"), as shown by greyed-out lines in a PrOH SIPOC Table (see case studies in Part III).

Decision points are shown as a person (or agent) doing something in the middle two columns of the table with more than one outcome. Decisions in a sequential SIPOC table outcomes are usually mutually exclusive. For instance, if there are three possible outcomes to a decision such as "approve bid", the outcomes might be to "stop" bid if no more work should happen, "approve" bid if it is ready to be issued to the customer, or "rework" bid if more work is needed before it is ready; no more than one option is possible in each line. Each outcome will be a separate line in the SIPOC table with greyed-out line(s) under the inputs, agent and activity. The greying out represents a repeat of the text in the line above. Each outcome of the decision will begin with "OR:" (e.g. "OR: stop", "OR: approve", "OR: rework"). In the PrOH Model, each outcome is represented as a sub-bubble in a **complex bubble** with a dotted outline that signifies that the bubble is a **decision bubble**, and the sub-bubbles are possibly mutually exclusive outcomes of that decision. In a PrOH Model, each outcome would start a new sentence describing the behaviour of the System for Change in a PrOH Model. **Complex** bubbles used to show decisions in this way are called **decision bubbles**.

TABLE 4.2 PrOH Sequential SIPOC Table (Core Process Statement at Top under Column Headings)

Previous key human resource	*Input*	*Key human resource*	*Performs an activity*	*Outputs*	*Next key human resource and activity*
Input from previous process phase: key human resource of previous phase produced core inputs	**Core inputs to be transformed**	**Key human resource of current process phase**	**Produces core transformed output**	**Core transformed output**	Output to next process phase: key human resource of next phase manages next phase
		Key human resource of current process phase oversees resources	Oversees processing of resources for micro-operations	Resources for micro-operations	**Output to next process phase**: key human resources of next process phase manage next process phase
		Supporting human resources	Uses resources essential for producing transformed output	Resources for micro-operations	**Output to next process phase**: key human resource of next phase manages next phase

Another type of **complex bubble** is a **containment bubble**, which is a bubble with other bubbles inside and has a solid outer line that indicates that all the sub-bubbles contained within it are part of the larger containment bubble; rather like an "AND" in logic or in a Venn diagram. In a **PrOH SIPOC** Table, sub-bubble items are shown after the label of a **containment bubble**, and each sub-bubble label is given in a separate bracket. If necessary, **sub-sub-bubbles** can be used and shown in a SIPOC table as brackets within brackets after the label of the **complex bubble**. See Figure 4.5 to see representations of **complex bubbles**.

Constructing this sequential SIPOC table is comprehensive and exhaustive and ensures that all entities (people, physical artefacts, intangible artefacts) and key decisions are defined, and all relationships (active and passive) expressed using bubbles, bubbles within bubbles with different outlines and directional links that may use different colours or patterns to ease reading of the PrOH Model.

The purpose of constructing this sequential SIPOC-like table is to consolidate, clean and structure data; to make sure terms are used consistently, that **systemicity** is not compromised, that data is left without dead ends, deadlocks or live locks. *But most importantly to amalgamate different **process flowcharts** of the real-world system into one coherent table of data that can be used to produce a PrOH Model of the SSFs of change for a system under observation (e.g. an operational process).* Building a sequential SIPOC table from such data for a PrOH Model is best done using a spreadsheet application (e.g. MS Excel) as detailed SIPOC tables may have dozens of lines which makes spreadsheets currently the best-known non-proprietary way to manage it. A PrOH Modeller can use PrOH Tool© on prohmodel.org which uses a special

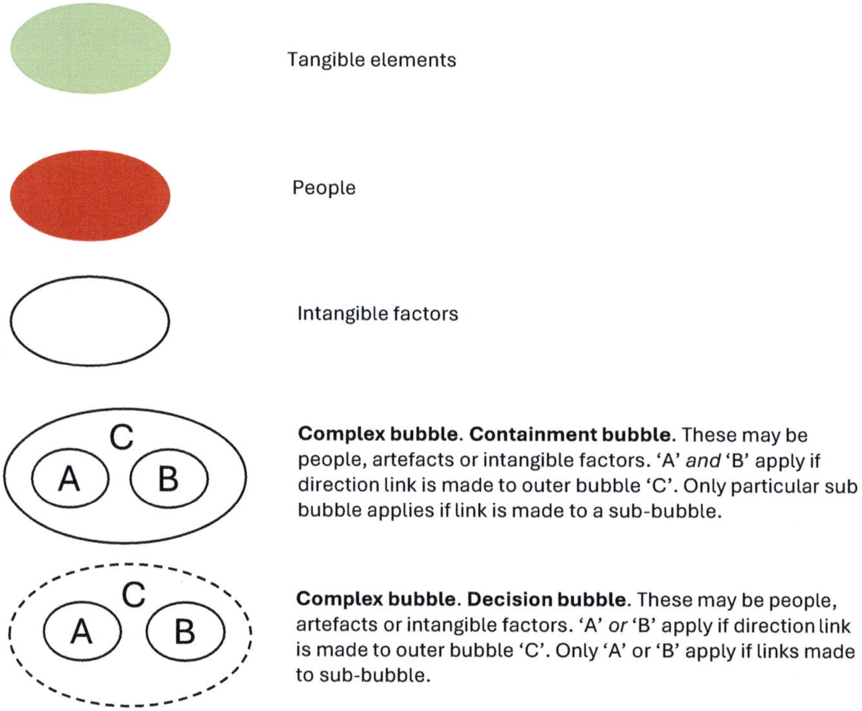

FIGURE 4.5 Bubble Types in a PrOH Model Representing Elements in a System of Change.

downloadable MS Excel spreadsheet that can be reuploaded to give the beginnings of a PrOH Model drawing.

A Drawing Palette for PrOH Models

Creating PrOH Models of organisational change systems requires only a limited palette of images and simple notations. Other modelling methodologies often have too many symbols that are too complex to use and obfuscate rather than elucidate a change system and its SSFs. For this reason, the PrOH Modelling uniquely minimises codification, maximises the use of (English) natural language and places more emphasis on rules and guidelines that encourage holonic thinking rather than emphasising use of a huge lexicon of symbology.

In PrOH Modelling elements are represented as labelled bubbles with phrases containing noun-based phrases and relationships between elements expressed on directional links (i.e. like arrows) labelled with verb-based phrases. Bubbles with noun phrases can represent

- people or groups of people (e.g. managers, customers, suppliers, regulators) and are coloured in red;
- tangible (physical) elements (e.g. machines, documents, products, materials) and are coloured in green; and
- intangible entities (e.g. knowledge, data, metrics and key performance indicators) and are coloured in white; see Figure 4.5.

Verb phrases are placed on directional links to show how to read a PrOH Model, see Figure 4.6. The more active the verb phrase is (being action focused or dynamic) the more potential the directional link, and hence the PrOH Model, will be able to elucidate SSFs and inspire changes. Common active verb phrases used in PrOH Modelling are: "designed by", "reviewed by", "analysed by", "must be planned for", "will be defined by", "need to be examined by", "delegated to", etc. All these being types of activities are used to describe connection between

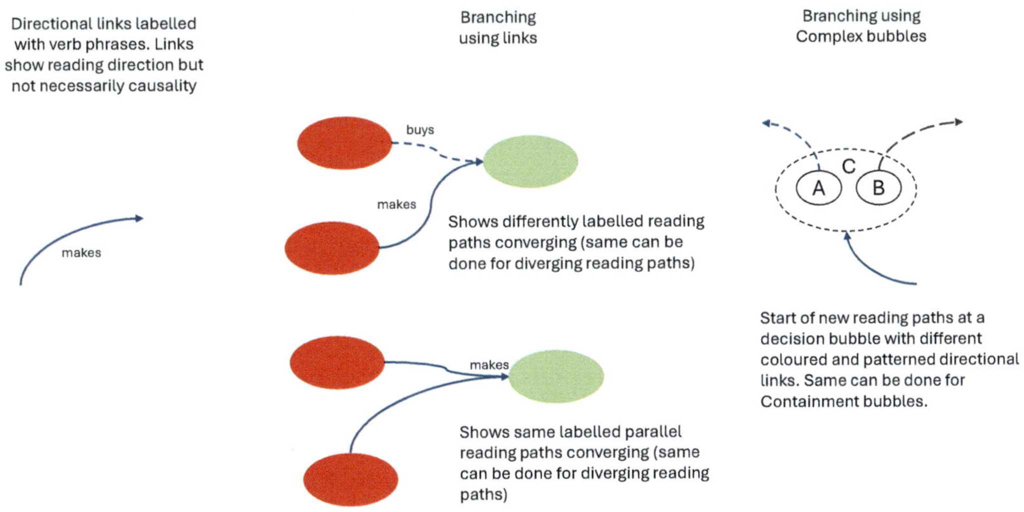

FIGURE 4.6 PrOH Model Relationship Activities Described Using Verb Phrases on Directional Links.

elements within a system. However, it is not possible to always use active verbs in which case less active or more passive verb phrases will suffice, such as: "was given to", "sent to", and "were received by". These are typically used in PrOH Models to fill in between stronger less passive verb phrases to make a PrOH Model readable and formulated into interesting, interconnected sentences. Tenses of verbs may be past, future, present or imperfect depending on what the PrOH Modeller wants to say. These passive phrases tend to be used to connect different lines on the SIPOC and contrast with more active verb phrases that will represent the central columns on a SIPOC where an agent is actively doing something.

Modellers are encouraged to use a broad vocabulary to bring PrOH Models to life. The use of **natural language** in hard systems modelling methodologies is negligible; however, it is actively encouraged in soft systems modelling but often poorly deployed. Uniquely, in contrast, PrOH Modelling strongly encourages the use of rich **natural language** instead of large lexicons of symbology.

Put together the noun phrases in bubbles and the verb phrases on the directional links to form readable sentences that describe the **system of change** through a systemic lens. Sentences interlink with one another to form an integrated description. One of the most important rules for PrOH Modelling is that an element (e.g. bubble) can *never* be repeated in the same model. This seems a simple rule, and one might ask, *so what, why*? But in application, this rule encourages the modeller to think holonically, which increases the **systemicity** of the model.

It is good practice to have readable sentences either starting and finishing at the core process statement or at **complex bubbles**. Further rules and guidelines are described later.

Modelling a Holon Using a PrOH Model Template

Holonic thinking can be applied and defined using the PrOH Modelling Template given in Figure 4.7 on which all PrOH Models are based. Bubbles will change in size, shape and labels, as will the shape of and labels on any directional links.

The PrOH Model Template in Figure 4.7 describes:

- **The boundary of the system under observation**: This is depicted by the large blue dotted lozenge shape in which all, but the previous phase boundary and following phase boundary sit. The PrOH Model may be a phase of a system if a model is part of a larger set of PrOH Models.
- **The objective of the system under observation**: which can be quoted as a short natural language sentence read from the core process statement in the PrOH Template as a red person bubble (noun phrase) – link (active verb phrase) – green or white bubble (noun phrase); in the PrOH Template the default sentence starts as, "the person in charge of this present phase produces output to present phase/input to next phase".
- **The preceding phase that came before this phase**: as the holonic template allows the model to be connected to the preceding phase of the larger system.
- **The following phase that comes after this phase**: as the holonic template allows the model to be connected to a following phase of the larger system.
- **Input or inputs**: to this phase that are the same as outputs from the previous phase.
- **Output or outputs**: from this phase which are the same as inputs into the following phase.
- **Agent (e.g. person(s) or artificial intelligence agent) in charge of the previous phase**: who will have the greatest agency, responsibility or accountability for the previous phase.

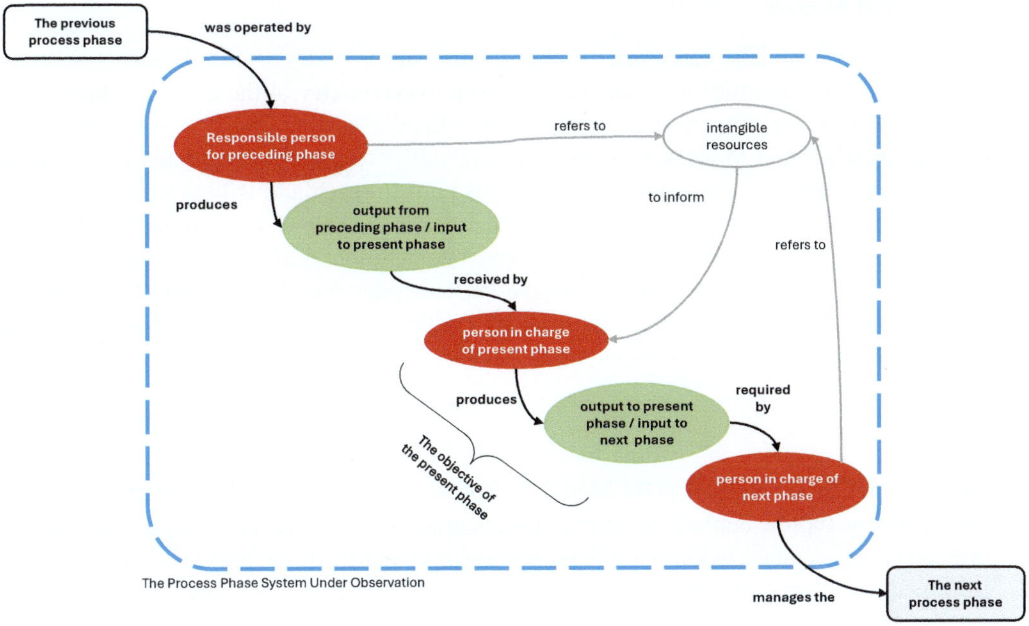

FIGURE 4.7 PrOH Model Template for a Single PrOH Model.

- **Agent (e.g. person, people or artificial intelligence agent) in charge of this phase**: who will have the greatest agency, responsibility or accountability for this phase.
- **Agent (e.g. person(s) or artificial intelligence agent) in charge of the next phase**: who will have the greatest agency, responsibility or accountability for the following phase.

To date, the PrOH Model Template has been able to fit any purposive organisational system of process change across all known cases. As a minimum, a PrOH Model must contain all elements of the PrOH Model Template, which are regarded as the **Minimum Viable Elements** of a PrOH Model. The PrOH Template is focused on a core process (**primary task**) description that creates output from an input and forms the backbone or mainstay of the rest of the holonic model similarly to Checkland's SSM Root Definition. Each agent (person or artificial agent) identified in the core process statement must be unique and distinctly different from others, appearing only once in the model as must any inputs and outputs. If a PrOH Modeller is struggling to do this, it probably means that the holon is poorly conceived and is likely to have low **systemicity**. Consequently, more system thinking is needed, guided by the rules and guidelines of PrOH Modelling.

As further description of a system is achieved by adding more elements and directional links to the core process through what is referred to as the **refinement** of the PrOH Model; by doing this, a PrOH Model becomes a better semblance of the system for change. **Refinement** changes a coarse PrOH Model into something more detailed. The opposite of refinement is **de-refinement**, when details of a PrOH Model are stripped out of a PrOH Model to make it **coarser**; this might be done to simplify a PrOH Model prior to gamifying it.

Drawing PrOH Models

As with all drawn models, some artistry lies in drawing a PrOH Model. Drawing a PrOH Model provides an opportunity to enhance the visual **systemicity** of the model, although the chronological sequence of events has already been defined in a SIPOC table. A PrOH Modeller should construct a PrOH Model so relationships in the SIPOC tables are depicted in a visually appealing way. Like all artistic endeavours, this is hard to teach and is best learned through practice by applying the chronological structure defined in the SIPOC table to the PrOH Model Template (Figure 4.7). Start with the core process statement found in the topline of the SIPOC table to form the core process statement in the PrOH Model Template running from top-left to bottom-right. Rules and guidelines for drawing the PrOH Model are given below. The rules must always be followed.

Drawing Rules:

- **Always start by using the PrOH Model Template** – and formulate the core process statement from the topline defined in the PrOH sequential SIPOC table. This will ensure that the previous process phase is known, the person/agent in charge of the previous process phase is known, the output of the previous phase/input into this phase is known, the significant person(s)/agent in charge of this phase is known, the main core process activity (verbs) is known, the outputs of this phase/input into the next process phase are known, and the next process phase is known. All of these are essential to define before any other part of a PrOH Model can be drawn.
- **Never repeat a bubble** (an entity) – this ensures more explicit **systemicity** in a PrOH Model. It is okay to repeat verb phrases on directional links.
- **Use complex bubbles** – complex bubbles are bubbles that contain other bubbles to show grouping of alike people, artefacts or intangible elements. Complex bubbles can be inclusive (rather like an "and" in Boolean logic (Martin and Metcalf, 2011) or in a Venn diagram) and will have a solid outer line, or mutually exclusive (rather like an "or" in logic or in a Venn diagram (Habib, 2015) and will have a dotted outer line.
- **Never have directional links crossing one another** – If necessary, directional links can pass through **complex bubbles** between the sub-bubbles.
- **Always have alternating people and non-people bubbles** – which preserves logic from PrOH SIPOC Tables and increases **systemicity** of the model.
- **Be sure to include at least one decision bubble in each model** – A PrOH Model without at least one decision bubble is likely to be ill-conceived and have a low level of **systemicity**. Decision bubbles have a dotted outer line.
- **Make sure a PrOH Model fits into one readable view** – this normally means one sheet of paper or one computer screen when viewed at an A4 size.
- **Keep to standard colour codes** – red for people/agents, green for physical items, white for intangible items. Sub bubbles in complex nodes will all be white but will still be the same class of entity as the outer bubble (e.g. a white sub-bubble in a complex red bubble will still be a person/agents).
- **Use verb phrases on directional links** – Do not put nouns on the directional links.

In addition to the above rules, PrOH Modellers should try to follow guidelines whenever possible as they portray good practice; these are given below.

Guidelines:

- **Put feedback loops in the top right-hand corner of a PrOH Model** above the core process statement when **refining** a model by adding additional supporting statements.
- **Put feedforward loops in the bottom left-hand corner below the core process statement** when **refining** a model by adding supporting statements.
- **Use complex bubbles as the core process bubbles where possible** because the core process statement bubbles are the focus of the PrOH Model and so often require more in-depth detail. The use of complex bubbles will also enable directional links to cross the core process statement by passing through the complex bubble if required.
- **Use the richness of natural (English) language** to express relationships between entities on verb phrases on directional links.

In a PrOH Model SIPOC table, **chronological thinking (chrono-logicalism)** prevails where all relationships are expressed chronologically. Relationships are also expressed with **direct causality**. For instance, a person/agent does something and produces an output which is an input for another person/agent to do something. This represents the logic in the real-world process.

The act of consolidating the logic of individual flowcharts into a sequential SIPOC table emphasises the logical chronology of a real-world process. Producing a holonic-based PrOH Model of its system of change requires a change in the epistemological mind-set of the modeller from the chronological flow of real-world process data into a **holonical** epistemological mind-set for data visualisation using **holonical-logicalism** with **indirect causality** for describing behaviours commensurate with high degrees of **systemicity**. For instance, all relationships and entity descriptions found in PrOH Model sentences are assumed to affect one another either directly or indirectly as described by the natural language used. This change in episteme is required because holistic thinking in PrOH Model holons represents systemic success factors (SSFs) of change in a conceptual system of change, rather than the chronological thinking found in the sequential SIPOC-like tables based on raw data flowcharts of process logic from real-world process systems (e.g. an organisational process).

A PrOH Modeller's epistemological mind-shift is supported by the PrOH Modelling Template as it is constructed in such a way as to embody PrOH Modelling rules and guidelines as rules for formulating core process statements that err towards explicit causality and **chrono-logicalism** formulated in the topline of the sequential SIPOC table and further supporting statements encouraging a **refined** PrOH Model erring towards **indirect causality** of **holonical-logicalism** commensurate with higher degrees of **systemicity**. Together all statements readable from the core process statement and in refined supporting statements should give a hybrid **chrono-holonical-logicalism** account of the system of change. Within this, the chronological components in the core process statement talk more of the direct logic found in real-world organisational processes and the **refining** supporting sentence statements talk more of the indirect **holonical-logicalism** of systemic success factors for change. Collectively giving purpose to entities and activities, groupings of entities, behaviours, decisions, feedback and feedforward activities.

It is important to remember that PrOH Models are not designed to show the logic or chronology of a real-world process *per se* but to show people-of-agency how to instigate the SSFs of change, as **issues-based** factors, in the conceptual system for change. As a result, it becomes more important to express **systemicity** in a PrOH Model rather than chronology or explicit logic, as would be found in a flowchart representing the chronological flow of tasks in an unchanging real-world process. It is, however, important to retain some semblance of logicalism at the core of the PrOH Model, namely, the process chronology of the primary task in the core process statement.

ACTION BOX 4: REAL PROCESS SYSTEMS AND CONCEPTUAL SYSTEMS OF CHANGE

The system represented by a PrOH Model *does not* actually exist in the real world as a physical system because it is a model of a conceptual system for change showing the systemic success factors for transitions in a real-world process from one state to another and thus only exists as a temporary and transitionary concept.

The PrOH Modelling Methodology consolidates multiple individual chronological flow models to form an amalgamated sequential chronological SIPOC table which is then transformed into **chrono-holonical-logicalism** in a Process-Oriented Holonic Model (PrOH Model) for catalysing changes to the chronological process into which it gives insights. This is done via its **primary task** defined in the core process statement and **refined** by other supporting **issue-based tasks** or **SSF** statements.

Have you ever previously considered the difference between modelling real-world systems and conceptual systems? Are you clear on the difference? Try to explain this to yourself.

Becoming a Soft Systems Thinker

During in-depth data collection, data structuring, drawing and redrawing of a PrOH Model, a PrOH Modeller will begin to own, live and breathe the data and start to think about the nature and composition of the real world and its related system of change with its associated SSFs. This will give a PrOH Modeller credibility as an expert, authenticate data and have hands-on experiences of the real-world system under observation.

Systems thinking is initially likely to begin with chronological thinking about the real-world process system from interviews performed and further practical systems experiences by being involved with mechanical, data processing, authorisation, health and safety, technical and legal tasks. Later a PrOH Modeller's thoughts should gravitate towards more holistic thinking of SSFs within the system of change and in this way, thoughts should slowly become more profound, purposive and have greater value for its stakeholders in change. To increase the chances of this happening practical research should follow from some initial academic scholarly research followed by some further practical benchmarking of the case from relevant industries and bodies of commerce.

Studying and Actioning

Focus on Dynamic Systemic Success Factors (SSFs) of Change in a "Could 'n' Should" Model rather Than on Static Logic in "As-Is" or "To-Be" Models

When thinking in systems, it is important to try and include as many elements and relationships of a **system under observation (SuO)** as possible. However, if one tries to do this, one will soon find that this is very difficult, if not impossible, and should probably not be attempted as it is likely to end in failure and disappointment. Instead, one should focus on the dynamic **Systemic Success Factors (SSFs)** of change in its conceptual system of change, which are properties that can influence change to the process system under observation in its wider context while enabling the model of change to be relatively parsimonious.

Therefore, it is not essential or even desirable to try to faithfully recreate all elements of change for a system under observation but to choose and focus on relationships between parts of the system that can be remedied in systemic challenges and improve the behavioural characteristics of the system. This requires PrOH Modellers to think about the change system rather than modelling the real-world process system-under-observation itself, which is an unusual way of thinking in systems.

Most traditional modellers will advocate modelling what the world is today as people see it in an "**as-is**" model and tell stories about that. The traditional modeller will then often advocate creating another "**to-be**" model of what the world should be once intervention has occurred. However, the "**as-is**" model can never be entirely created as it is often partly undefinable, too complex, too stochastic and too large. Likewise, models that claim to be of a future "**to-be**" state of a system are likely to be fanciful, fictional and unauthentic because even if changes were made, partially or wholly, to achieve the desired future state this could often not be proven beyond reasonable doubt within an observable timeframe. Thus, changes are unlikely to be approved, unimplemented, never officially endorsed and unadopted as futuristic constructs and ironically, may remain so in perpetuity. Given these assumptions **agents** in a **system under observation**, when interviewed, will effectively be stating *what "should be"* or *what "could be"* in a system. A PrOH Modeller is therefore creating a model of what "*could* 'n' *should*" be in a model, without realising it, but is still likely to claim that it is an "**as-is**" model or a "**to-be**" model. So, if a model and modeller are inclined to include what "could 'n' should" be then the model should call it a "**could 'n' should**" model and make therefore make a more authentic claim of what the model actually is. This difference is fundamental and is a unique feature of PrOH Modelling where "**as-is**" and "**to-be**" models *are not* created, instead a "'**could 'n' should**" model is deliberately created featuring the dynamic **Systemic Success Factors** of change in the system of change. Improvements and iterations of the "**could 'n' should**" model will be variants of the same "**could 'n' should**" model which are likely to be made during **validations** and/or **verifications** of a PrOH Model. PrOH Modelling is one of a few **soft systems methodologies** that explicitly acknowledges it is better to model the *system of change* for a system rather than modelling the real-world system under observation itself.

Modelling the "**could 'n' should**" of a system is likely to produce a model that is more authentic, if less conventional. "**Could 'n' should**" models need to depict the current concerns of people, be timely, topical, pertinent and personal, expressing issues that need to be addressed by people identified within the PrOH Model. Modelling the "**could 'n' should**" rather than "**as-is**" and "**to-be**" also makes the change process more efficient (one of Checkland's "E's")

(Checkland, 1981) quicker to accomplish and more value adding. To stress this issue further, readers of this book should ask themselves:

- *Where is the value in creating a model of "**as-is**" if this is to be immediately changed for something else?*
- *Where is the value in creating something that is perpetually futuristic and fanciful, which is unlikely to become adopted, is also probably a waste of time?*

This is not to say that further versions of a "**could 'n' should**" model of the same system will not be created, as they are very likely to be, but these later "**could 'n' should**" models will show other or different **systemic success factors** of future systems for change as the SuO's conditions, issues and environment change. It is prudent at later time periods for modellers to update the scope of the model to keep the model timely, topical, pertinent and personal. These will be different versions of the *same* "**could 'n' should**" PrOH Model.

Holon and Holarchy

The word "system" is often an imprecise and ambiguous term which is unhelpful when a more thorough analysis of systems is required. Hence, the PrOH Modelling Methodology uses the term "**holon**" and "**holarchy**" which have more precise definitions.

Each PrOH Model can be thought of as a **holon** where this is used in an organisational context to describe the behaviour of a system of change within a set of PrOH Models of conceptual systems (sometimes known as a **system-within-systems** or a **system-of-systems** construct).

The PrOH Modelling Methodology refers to a set of PrOH Models as a **holarchy** and there are (currently) two ways to compose a **holarchy** in PrOH Modelling: in **series** or in **parallel**; these are explained in more detail in Chapter 5.

Relationships between elements in a holon describe the systemic behaviours of a holon with a holistic lens where each element affects the other elements. To define purposive organisational holons is not easy as these are borne from the mind's eye of a PrOH Modeller verified through a holonic lens (e.g. the **PrOH Model Template**) and validated with those in the organisation being modelled. **Holons** should be valid for the agents (people) in the real-world model and purposeful for the **sponsor** (and/or **champion**) of any change activity while being true to the wider properties of **human activity systems** (discussed in Part I). Thus, for PrOH Modelling, holonic lenses are best focused on changing processes that are supplier-customer facing, such as the design and delivery of a strategy, service or product, where each **holon** contains elements from different IT systems, functional departments and prominent organisational themes within a supplier-customer facing process that aims to create value for its stakeholders and needs performance improvement.

In contrast, functional models that depict organisational departmental activities make for a poor holonic lens because these holons typically have no process focus. Similarly, purely ad-hoc **issue-based** models also make a poor holonic lens because these are often isolated events without **purposive** process context.

THINKING BOX 4: WHAT IS A "HOLON"?

A holon is an entity that is simultaneously a whole system, part of a larger system, and contains other systems; and as such, the holon is a construct that can address the dichotomy between parts and wholes. The term "holon" as a concept is largely attributed to Arthur Koestler in his book, *The Ghost in the Machine* (Chapter III, 1967) when he refers to holons as "Janus faced entities" due to their many contradictory properties. Koestler stated that,

> "There is no satisfactory word in our vocabulary to refer to these Janus-faced entities: to talk of sub-wholes (or sub-assemblies, sub-structures, sub-systems) is awkward and tedious. It seems preferable to coin a new term to designate these nodes on the hierarchic tree which behave partly as wholes or wholly as parts, according to the way you look at them. The term I would propose is 'holon', from the Greek holos = whole, with the suffix '-on' which, as in prot<u>on</u> or neutr<u>on</u>, suggests a particle or part" (p.48).

The term was first applied to natural organisms but can be applied to socio, behavioural and organisational contexts. Koestler states that,

> "It [the Holon] also symbolises the missing link – or rather series of links – between the atomistic approach of the Behavourist and the holistic approach of the Gestalt psychologist". and that "The Gestalt school has considerably enriched our knowledge of visual perception and succeeded in softening up the rigid attitude of its opponents to some extent. But in spite of its lasting merits, 'holism' as a general attitude to psychology turned out to be as one-sided as atomism was [from the Behaviourists], because both treated 'whole' and 'part' as absolutes ... we can say that the Behaviourist never gets higher up than the bottom layer of stones, and the holist never gets down from the apex. In fact, the concept of the 'whole' proved just as elusive as that of the elementary part, and when he discusses language, the Gestaltist finds himself in the same quandary as the Behaviourist" (p.49).

Holons are entities that are quasi-independent and can take actions with effects without having to check or interact with higher systems as they are somewhat autonomous but are concomitantly subject to control by these higher systems. Thus,

> "The rules of conduct of a social holon [as found in organisations] are not reducible to the rules of conduct of its members" (p.58)

However confusingly, it is not until later in his book, in Chapter VII, that Koestler introduces the other concept of *holism*, that of the *holarchy* in which sets of *holons* are placed, that things become clearer. *This adds to the confusion that holons are built into holarchies and not into hierarchies, whose difference is uniquely defined, conceptually, methodologically and technically in PrOH Modelling.* This has been a blocking factor in the development of holons and holonic thinking until the development of the PrOH Modelling Methodology.

Excerpts from *The Ghost in the Machine* (Arthur Koestler, 1967).

Verification of PrOH Models

Once a PrOH Model has been drawn, it can then be **verified**. This is the act of making sure that a PrOH Model has been drawn correctly, where all rules have been followed and all guidelines have been adhered to as closely as possible. This ensures a PrOH Model has good *verity*.

Verification should be done by an independent competent PrOH Modeller. The verifier should reflect on rules and guidelines and ensure the model is **purposive**, interesting and generally makes good sense. The overall **systemicity** of the model should also be reviewed; in other words, does it describe a system of change well enough to be useful for its audience and/or stakeholders?

During **verification**, it is also a good time to question whether the PrOH Modelling Methodology could be adapted or extended, especially if the PrOH Modelling Methodology has been applied to a new scenario that has not been modelled before and may possibly raise the need for new techniques.

Also, more broadly than just PrOH Modelling, it is also good to see if the PrOH Modeller has had any thoughts on action research and systems thinking, as users of these encourage their evolution based on practical experiences and epistemic cogitations.

Abductive Thinking

At this point, wider scholarly research done in "Planning and Researching" should be married up with practical research done in practical benchmarked activities in "Systems Thinking and Studying" to encourage breakthrough eureka moments where, through **abductive thinking**, the practices and themes of the real-world process under observation and wider context from academic research come together as the researcher-cum-modeller-cum-actioner is able to put their finger on theories or frameworks they can apply, adapt or extend to give value-added perceptions into their action research project.

This is always an anxious part of the project for all involved as it can be make-or-break whether a set of incremental or radical changes are actioned. This is where innovation is most likely to occur in the project brought about by a deep understanding of the SuO, discontinuous thinking from its stakeholders within a wider context and benchmarking against other industry solutions and wider academic reading. One hopes at this juncture mutual knowledge exchange occurs between all parties involved in the project and some truly radical non-linear systems innovations will occur. This is hopefully where the 'magic" of innovation can happen.

Actioning – Another Round of Abductive Thinking

By taking action at this point, the PrOH Modeller-cum-consultant is aiming to impart as much knowledge from themselves and collegiate researchers to those in the process system under observation. This is done by building rapport, having empathy and being disciplined and productive. At the same time, educating the practice stakeholders about new insights from wider academic research and industry-based benchmarking. The whole team, through engagement with the PrOH Modelling Methodology, should be starting to think together, and the two worlds of academia and practice should become conjoined and work harmoniously together, which is the focus of the remaining parts of the PrOH Modelling Methodology.

Acting and Impacting

Storyboarding

If done thoroughly, a PrOH Model can contain so much tacit and explicit knowledge about a system for change and its SSF issues that it is often too much to digest in one view, and so PrOH Models are best served up to an audience in manageable storyboarded scenes. As the name "storyboarding" suggests, storyboarding is a way of presenting a lot of detailed information to an audience piece by piece. This is like a moviemaker making a series of hand-drawn sketches (or cartoons) to explain a concept for how to shoot a movie sequence to a production crew, *taking it from a script to a recorded film*. In a similar way, a PrOH Modeller of change systems should present parts of the system for change scene by scene, with its SSFs, to explain how an organisational system can transform from "as-is" practice towards "to-be" practice. So just as a complex concept for a movie shoot is explained to the production crew, the complex SSFs of a change system can be explained to its stakeholders.

Each scene should have a digestible amount of process knowledge from the PrOH Model, and each scene will be annotated with systemic success factors, noted as issue-based bullet points, contributed by its stakeholders during their interviews and annotated on their raw data flowcharts. These SSFs have been derived during the translation of the data from **chrono-logicalism** (in sequential SIPOC tables) to **holonical-logicalism** (in a Process Oriented Holonic Model) and are the equivalence of thematic codes in approaches such as Template Analysis (King, 2004) or Grounded Theory (Glaser and Strauss, 1967; Strauss and Corbin, 1998).

The skill of a storyboarder is to get an appropriate number of scenes, about four to six, appended with interesting and reflexive systemic success factors (SSFs) which may catalyse change, as perceived by its stakeholders. Put another way, storyboard scenes should tell an interesting story about how to change the process under observation that will engage its audience.

The presentation of a PrOH Model storyboard to the audience from which the raw data came is also a type of validation, and if correctly done, should be more than just a validation exercise, as it should produce actions to be agreed upon and taken by its stakeholders to make changes to the real-world process.

How to Make a Storyboard from a PrOH Model

Storyboarding is performed by:

1. Taking a fully completed storyboard (produced in a package such as MS PowerPoint or PrOH Tool© on promodel.org) and making multiple copies of it (i.e. one MS PowerPoint slide becomes six identical PowerPoint slides in the same file).
2. Once saved, the first slide should have all but the core process statement deleted so that the core process for change can be explained in the first slide, so that the primary task of change becomes the focus. This creates Scene 1 of the storyboard.
3. Using animation and bullet points, add SSFs for change into the scene, added together or one by one, as relevant. Each SSF should be useful enough to discuss for a good time with the audience. This creates Scene 1 of the storyboard with its SSFs.

4. Go to the next slide that has your whole model in and remove fewer parts of the model this time, and by doing so again retain the core process statement (Scene 1) and start to add back in to the PrOH Model supporting process descriptions. This creates Scene 2 of the storyboard.
5. Add the SSFs to Scene 2, again using an animation or bullet point functionality of the software you are using, as in Step 3.
6. Repeat the above steps until all supporting sentences in the model are shown along with their SSFs.

The last scene of the PrOH Model should show the complete model with SSFs that relate to the last scene of the storyboard. A simple model should be presentable in 3–4 scenes while a more complicated model may take 5–6 scenes. For each scene, there is no set amount of SSFs that should be bullet-pointed, but seven, plus or minus two, is a good guide. Fewer SSFs are also acceptable, although more is inadvisable, and the storyboarder should create more storyboard scenes.

By starting with the whole PrOH Model and cutting down the model, a better presentation is given, as by doing this all slides will be identical and redrawing work is minimised. Any changes made to any scenes must be replicated on all other scenes. Therefore, it is best to make sure the model is verified before storyboarding and validation commences. An example of a storyboard using six scenes, as thumbnail sketches, is given in Figure 4.8 to give a notion about storyboarding. The full-sized storyboard can be seen in Part II, Chapter 7, Case 2.

Validation of PrOH Models

Once a PrOH Model has been drawn and verified, storyboarding validation can commence. Validation is arguably one of the most important parts of PrOH Modelling as, with any form of soft systems modelling, validation is the act of critiquing proposed process changes to the real world through the SSFs of the PrOH Model conceptual system of change – giving useful insight into the real world. The success of this can be attributed to the **systemicity** of the model, the efficacy of the storyboarded scenes, and the engaging nature of the modeller-cum-storyteller.

Validation of a PrOH Model storyboard in a stakeholder workshop can serve several purposes: (1) **authentication validation** – given to those who contributed the original data – to ensure the relevance of the model; (2) **dissemination validation** – given to those not contributing to the original data but who operate in the system under observation – to actively involve more people in the system of change; (3) **promulgation validation** – given to those who neither contributed the raw data nor operate in the system under observation but have a related interest, such as those who may work in different phases of the process, earlier or later, to create wider cultural buy-in to change activities. Or, indeed, to those who work in higher or lower-level pitches of the process. For instance, in the case of a tactical model, these would be stakeholders in higher-level pitches, senior managers and those in lower-level pitches, being operatives. These validation types are best used in the given order to snowball buy-in and deepen and broaden change activities.

As organisational change is often about gathering information, making holistic sense of systemic success factors for change in a process and validating these in different ways, the importance of validation is paramount. Arguably, this is where most value is created as people debate the issue presented within a given system model boundary. From such debates,

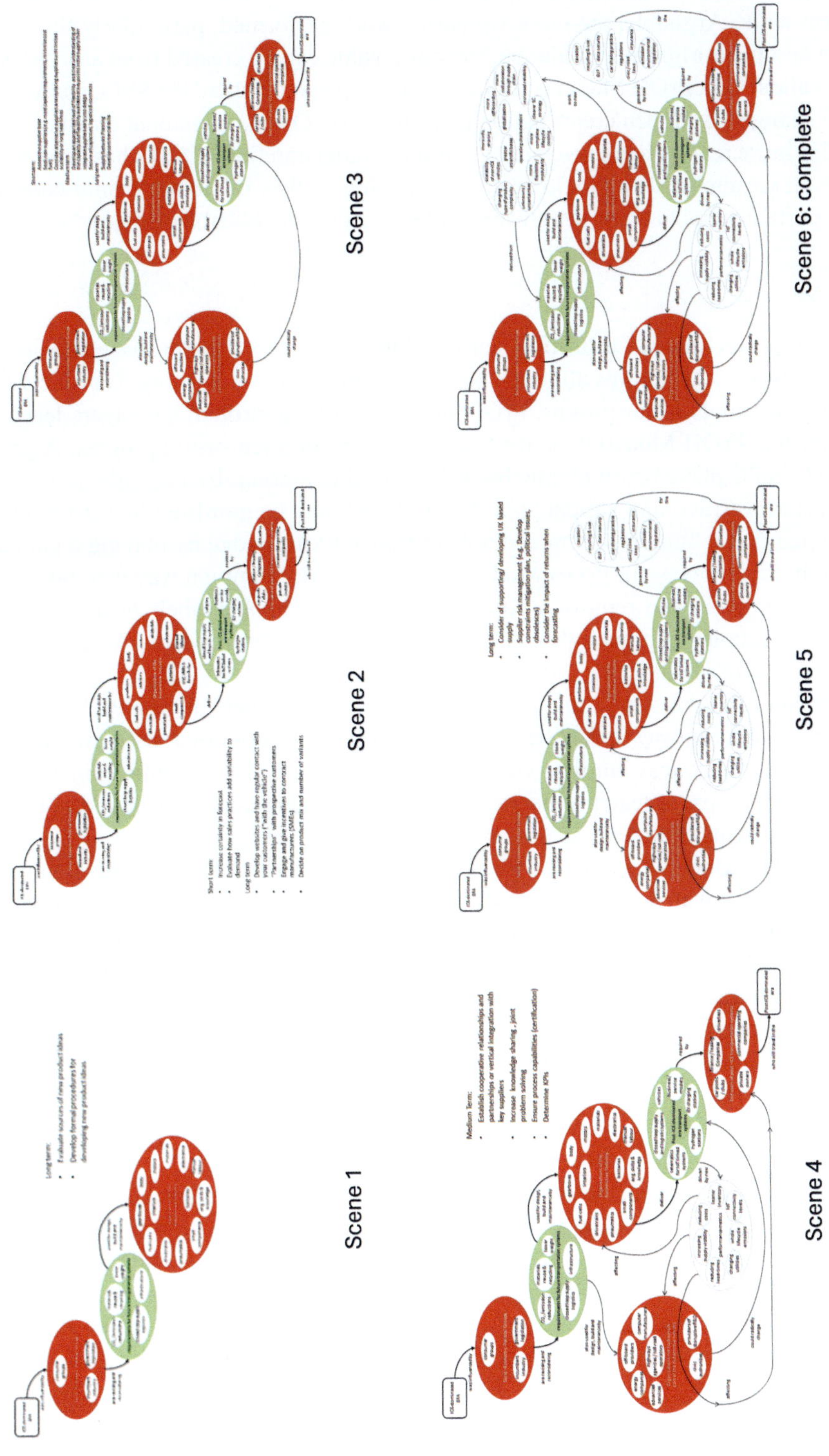

FIGURE 4.8 A PrOH Model Storyboard.

SSFs should end with actions being agreed, with timescales, by those responsible for doing the improvement work. Arguably, the more validation work performed, particularly through **dissemination** and **promulgation** validation, the more value can be created from a PrOH Model. The aim in validating a PrOH Model is to check that people understand the SSFs, agree on what needs to be changed, and then create action plans to do so. Often, agreement on what needs to be changed is more readily achieved once a common understanding of **SSFs** has been reached. This is why all the above steps should be done; even though they might seem time-consuming, they are important steps in a journey towards affecting positive holistic change.

Gamification

Gamification is a technique for turning learning into fun, with a competitive element, so that people (e.g. players) learn things almost without realising they are learning. Gamification can be done for individuals or for groups. PrOH models can be **gamified**, so players learn about systems thinking, PrOH Modelling and a change system for a real-world process. A gamified PrOH Model can be played individually but is best used in a group-based workshop.

Once created, verified and validated, a PrOH Model may be **gamified** by turning it into a learning device that is fun, engaging and able to transfer knowledge by playing a game. This can be done in several ways in PrOH Modelling, but the most common way is to take a whole un-storyboarded model and remove a combination of some bubble labels or directional link labels from it while leaving enough natural language on the PrOH Model for the players to recognise the system of change.

As validation can take some time to do properly, a gamified version of a PrOH Model can often be a quick and fun way to further share knowledge in group-based dissemination activities. Perhaps with those less familiar with the system, as part of an organisational induction programme; or perhaps, to teach someone to think using holonic-logicalism and to become a more effective systems changer.

Gamified PrOH Models can be used for students as well as part of short professional education courses for those who do not necessarily want to learn how to produce a PrOH Model from scratch or act on changing a process but want a quick introduction to systems thinking and action research using PrOH Modelling. A PrOH Model game can be printed on large sheets of paper (ideally A3 sized), printed out and then used in group exercises in training sessions on PrOH Modelling or to come up with further SSFs. Alternatively, this can be done online using the PrOH Model Game©, see prohmodel.org.

A gamified PrOH Model might look something like Figure 4.9; where those new to systems thinking and PrOH Modelling can "have a go" and "fill in the blanks" without too much prior knowledge.

The aim of a PrOH Game© is to fill in the blank spaces with defensible and useful text. If the players should get the same as the original full PrOH Model, then all well and good. However, this is not necessarily the main purpose of the game, as players might come up with other viable solutions, insights and suggestions, which may be even better than those in the original model. The point of this exercise is to get players to think about elements and relationships in a system of change, its SSFs, then discuss, debate and decide how most effectively the

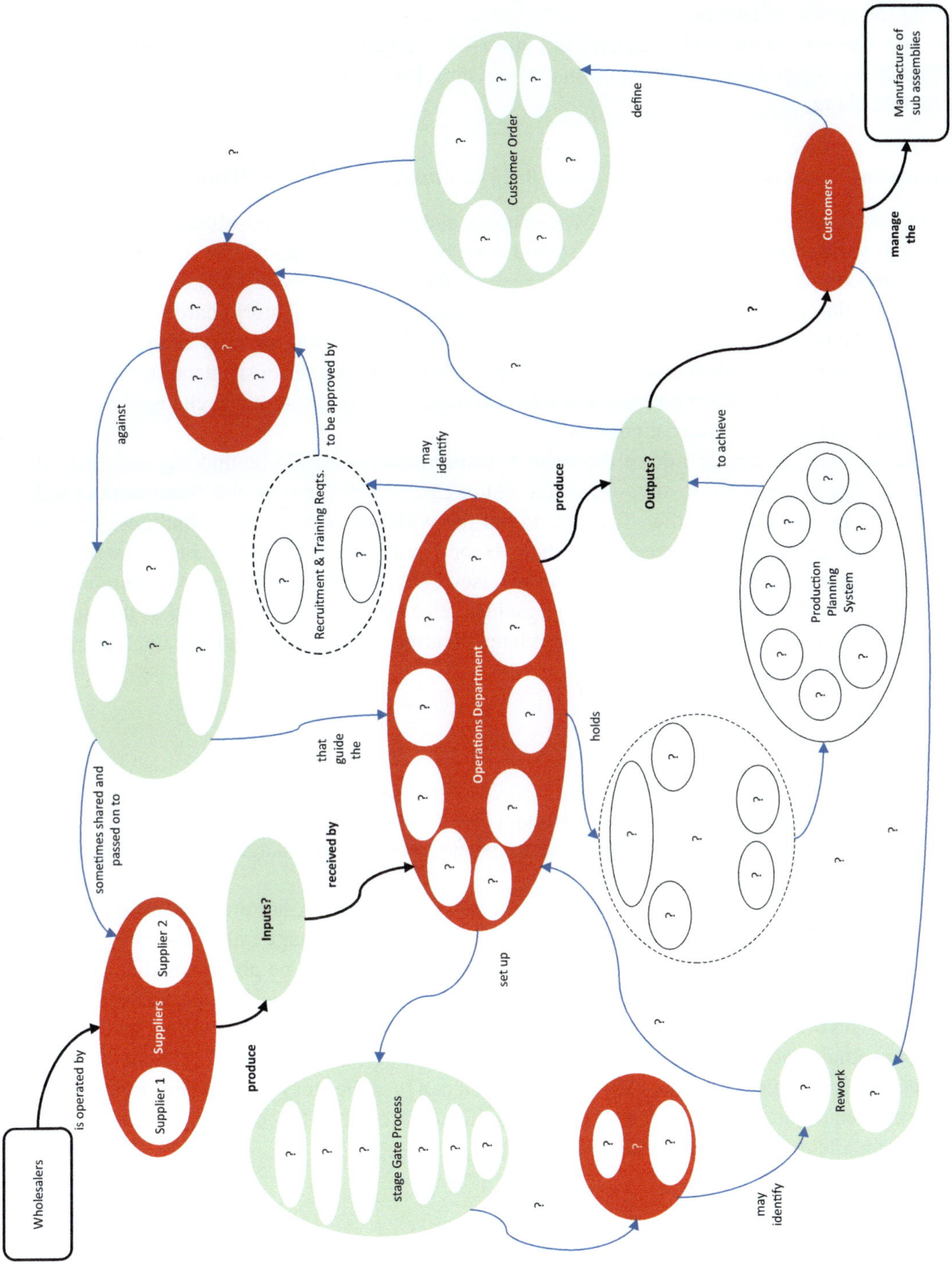

FIGURE 4.9 A Gamified PrOH Model.

system-under-observation can be improved. Like the PrOH Model on which it is based, the point of the PrOH Game© is to socialise (Nonaka et al., 2000) and exchange ideas, in this case about the system of change.

The 'answer" to the PrOH Game© in Figure 4.9 is given in the Metal Assemblies Case 5, Chapter 10, Figure 10.6 in Part III of this book. Other PrOH Game© examples can be seen on prohmodel.org.

Impacting – from the System of Change Back to Impacting the Real-World

Activities from the PrOH Modelling Methodology and associated socialisation of its outcomes through **validation** and **gamification** should have brought about innovative ideas for change that can be implemented by practising managers in the real-world process system under observation. Action points placed in PrOH Modelling workshops, using storyboarding or gamifications, should involve aspects of new technology implementation, process change, cultural changes, training and education. All these, if they are to be taken seriously, need funding, project managing and allocating to accountable individuals to make actionable changes. Nothing practical should be left unaccounted for.

On the more academic side of the project, team members should be making sure that all possible data is collected to support, adapt and/or extend any theories and frameworks used in knowledge transfer in either direction to aid the wider dissemination of findings. At this stage, these pedagogical devices (e.g. theories or frameworks "F") must be declared and robustly applied so that they could be repeated elsewhere with similar outcomes. Testimonials, anonymised data, videos, blogs, trade magazines, etcetera should be produced at this stage, leading to more robust referred publications later, creating wider impact with greater longevity.

Summary

The main points are given below.

- PrOH Modelling does not attempt to model "**as-is**" or "**to-be**" version of a process system under observation but models the systemic success factors of change within a "**could 'n' should**" model.
- PrOH Models are a model of the system of change and its SSFs, not the real-world process system. As such, a PrOH Model is a picture of the **system of change** rather than the **process system under observation**. The storyboarding session should be about whether process changes are valid to make or not and not whether the PrOH Model is a perfectly faithful representation of the process – because it is not intended to be and cannot be, as it is the conceptual model of change. This difference should be made clear by the modeler-cum-presenter, and if not clearly positioned as such, it can turn the storyboarding exercise into an event debunking the PrOH Model rather than focusing on the SSFs of change in the change system affecting the real-world process.

- **Holons *are not* part of a hierarchy but *are* part of a holarchy.** *Holons should not be considered as parts of a **hierarchy*** but must be considered in a ***holarchy*** as the nature of holons does not follow the rules of a hierarchy but, contrastingly, follow the rules of a **holarchy**. *The terms hierarchy and holarchy should not be used interchangeably* as they do not mean the same thing and are strongly contrasting. Much confusion occurs in literature where this has occurred. Even Koestler himself has occasionally done this. In this book, hierarchy and holarchy will remain distinctly different. This is a deliberate demarcation that will hopefully help to popularise and clarify **holonic** and **holarchic** constructs made during the development of the PrOH Modelling Methodology. Misunderstandings may, in part, be due to misleading historical visualisation of **holons** and **holarchies** and compositional rules and guidelines at a methodological and technique level. This book, through rules and guidelines for developing PrOH Models and new graphics of sets of PrOH Models and its associated methodology, seeks to right these visual and compositional misunderstandings.

Further Reading

Clegg, B.T. (1999), *A Systems Approach to Re-Engineering Business Processes Towards Concurrent Engineering Principles*. PhD Thesis. Chapter 6. De Montfort University and British Library.

Paton, S., Clegg, B., Pilkington, A., and Hsuan, J. (2021), *Operations Management*, 2nd ed. London: McGraw-Hill. Higher Education. Chapter 5.

5

THE PROH MODELLING METHODOLOGY

Building Sets of PrOH Models as Holarchies

Chapter 5 follows on from how to build a single PrOH Model in Chapter 4 and it is necessary to have read and understood Chapter 4 before reading Chapter 5, because Chapter 5 gives instruction to PrOH Modellers on how to build a set of PrOH Models using holarchical rules and guidelines.

Sets of Models

It is often possible to represent a relatively small system of change in a single PrOH Model. However, to represent a system of change for a larger organisation or one of greater complexity, it is more likely that more than one PrOH Model will be needed. The most conventional way of doing this is to start with a single strategic top-level PrOH Model and use this to gauge the level of complexity and number of PrOH Modelling phases required in lower-level tactical PrOH Modelling. A top-level strategic model will be a single PrOH Model representing the highest currently known level of strategic thinking.

A single model is usually able to be **enriched** by creating between two and five lower-pitched models. Likewise, each of those lower-level models may, in turn, be able to be **enriched** into lower-pitched models at an operational level, and so on. Three levels of PrOH Modelling should, however, be enough to cover any system of change if thoughtfully composed.

Sometimes a PrOH Model will be produced by a PrOH Modeller who thought, at the time, it was to be the highest-level model, but full deployment of the PrOH Methodology may reveal issues pertaining to an even higher-level system of change, such as a supply chain level system of change. If so, the initial model can become part of a higher-level model, for instance, a company within a supply chain. Accurately pitching levels of systems thinking can be something of a chicken-and-egg situation, which is fine if a modelling methodology can deal with it. PrOH Modelling can, because it allows for any PrOH Model to become part of a higher-level set of models through **abstraction**, or to be explained in a more detailed set of models through **enrichment**.

DOI: 10.4324/9781032650425-7

Conversely, if a PrOH Modeller wants to start a PrOH Modelling exercise by modelling a system of change for an operational process which will have more than one phase of modelling, the PrOH Modeller should define how many phases there are and what each of these are called, even if only one model is initially produced; a PrOH **Process Matrix** is used for this. Clarity on the number of phases and meaningful names, with the main inputs and outputs for each of these phases, will enable easier construction of other phase models and/or **abstraction** and **enrichment** of model or models at a different pitch later in the exercise as may be required.

PrOH Models can be connected at the same pitch of PrOH Modelling by splitting the system of change into PrOH Modelling **phases**, and a **Process Matrix** is used to do this.

Process Matrix to Define Phases and Sub-Phase of a System of Change

A **Process Matrix** is a table, normally built in a spreadsheet, that defines phases of the system of change, which may be connected serially or in parallel. A **Process Matrix** will define the name of each phase or sub-phase, its external inputs, its external outputs and who does what. At this point further details about the sequence of activities are not required. A **Process Matrix** is a first pass at understanding parts of the bigger picture which follows on to more detailed SIPOC tables for each of the phases or sub-phases, see Figure 5.1 for the generic structure of a Process Matrix table. A detailed populated example can be seen later in Chapter 9, Case 4 (GMRDASL Part 2, Figure 9.2).

PrOH Model Icon

An icon is used to represent a single PrOH Model in a set of models as shown in Figure 5.2 which is used as a "thumbnail" representation of the **PrOH Model Template** given in Figure 4.8; this is known as a **PrOH Model Icon**. The PrOH Model Icon looks like the PrOH Model Template and represents the same elements: the system boundary, the core process statement, elements in the core process and elements in supporting process descriptions (e.g. red people bubbles, green tangible bubbles and white intangible bubbles) and previous and next phases of the system under observation are identifiable. The PrOH Model Icon is used when discussing the composition of a set of PrOH Models, rather than the internal elements of a single PrOH Model, when it is more important to focus on relationships between different PrOH Models in different phases of a system of change.

	Name pf Phase				
	Phase 1	**Phase 2**	**Phase 3**	**Phase 4**	**Phase n ...**
Inputs					
Agent	*activities descriptions*				
Agent	*activities descriptions*				
Outputs					

FIGURE 5.1 Process Matrix Structure.

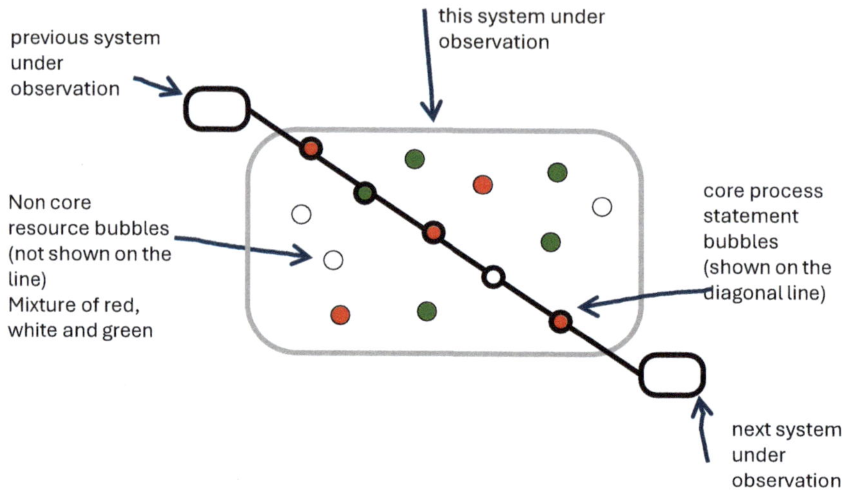

FIGURE 5.2 A PrOH Model Icon Used to Represent a Single PrOH Model.

THINKING BOX 5: WHY DO MODELLING USING A HOLARCHY RATHER THAN A HIERARCHY?

The suffix "archy" means a rule or governance. Let's think what this means in the context of organisational change and modelling systems of change.

HIERARCHY

Let's start with the more commonly understood term "**hierarchy**" which is rather like a taxonomy of parts of an organisation that has a top, a middle, and a bottom. In an organisational taxonomy, the top parts will be large units (e.g. a holding company), middle level units may be sub-divisions (e.g. an autonomous company in a holding company), and the bottom level may be sub-sub-divisions (e.g. departments within an organisation). Leaders of larger and/or higher-level parts of an organisation typically have more authority, more power and therefore more agency.

In a hierarchy, sub-parts are formed by breaking up the larger parts through a **hierarchical ontology** that uses **reductionism** and **aggregationism**. Reductionism assumes that all sub-parts of a higher-level unit inherit properties from its higher level and are subject to its rules and laws, and where no **hidden properties** are found to exist. Inversely, in a hierarchy, larger parts can be formed in an opposite action to **reductionism** through what is known as **aggregationism**, which involves joining together smaller parts to form larger parts where the smaller and larger parts have the same properties. Hierarchies are normally drawn as a pyramid with the pointy "strategic apex" at the top. Hierarchies are good to use for unambiguous sets of entities that are easily classifiable and hence divisible and re-joinable.

HOLARCHY

A **holarchy** is a set of parts called **holons** that make up a whole where sub-parts are autonomous. Holarchies are **gestalt** entities and so are collectively more than the sum of their parts. Holarchies are *not* composed or structured in the same way as hierarchies as they are formed through a **holistic ontology** that uses **abstraction** and **enrichment** *where the purposes, relationships and systemic success factors between organisational holons and their elements are its focus rather than its entities per se.* When building a holarchy from a set of models, some **emergent properties** and **hidden properties** are expected.

"This can be demonstrated in the holarchic relationship where each holon is a 'level' of organization ... and, like a fractal, the patterns evident at one level can be similar to those at another". Spangler, D. In PrOH Modelling this fractal pattern is the **PrOH Model Template** found to repeat at all levels and can be connected to other models at either the same or different levels.

Holarchies are best drawn as sets within sets – rather like a **Venn diagram**. Holarchies are best used for **soft systems modelling methodologies** that model conceptual systems.

CONTRAST BETWEEN HOLARCHY AND HIERARCHY

Spangler, D., *In a hierarchy, participants can be compared and evaluated by position, rank, relative power, seniority and the like. But in a holarchy each person's value comes from his or her individuality and uniqueness and the capacity to engage and interact with others to make the fruits of that uniqueness available.* Thus, the **holistic** principles of holarchies and holarchical thinking are useful and suitable for making models of conceptual systems of change for organisations as they resemble the characteristics of a **holarchy** more closely than they do a **hierarchy**.

Sets of PrOH Models – Serial PrOH Modelling

Serial PrOH Modelling is appropriate when PrOH Models represent phases in a system of change that follow one another in a chronological sequence. In a manufacturing process, these phases may be called "design", "set-up and planning", "production" and "post-production delivery". In a professional service organisation, such as an architects' partnership, these phases might be called "client on-boarding", "designing", "planning approval", "project management of construction", "completion" and "certification".

Sets of PrOH Models – Parallel PrOH Modelling

Parallel PrOH Modelling is appropriate when models of organisational change run side by side, in other words, change models of processes that run almost independently from one another and are not serially connected. A good example of this would be when different legal services in a law firm run independently of one another and only become connected in higher-level systems of change concerning senior partners of a law firm strategising at a top level. One might also argue that parallel models should also be connected at a lower tactical level as they will often share the same office facilities, support staff and perhaps the same core company IT systems and policies. As such, at a middle operational level, even though the different service lines may not be in the same system of change, they may be part of the same wider system of change at strategic and/or operational levels.

ACTION BOX 5: SERIAL OR PARALLEL?

Think of an organisation you have worked with. Using a simple **Process Matrix**, try to sketch at an operational level (1) a serial process that can be modelled in four phases of change and (2) an organisation with four parallel phases of change.

Question: For each ask yourself, are you clear on this difference? If not, then keep practising.

Similarly, in a manufacturing organisation, parallel systems of change might be where different production lines have very different products being made on them, and where products at no point change from one production line to another. Therefore, there is no direct connection between changes on production lines at an operational level. There will, however, be a connection at a higher strategic level, most likely by using shared capital resources and contributions to the financial bottom line. There may also be connections at a lower tactical level, similarly to a service company, where operations perhaps share the same company IT, HR systems, suppliers and procurement policies.

Enrichment and Abstraction of Serial Models

When creating models of organisational systems of change at different pitches, one must clearly define what each level contains. To do this consistently, one should stick closely to the level defined in the **core process statement**, which is sometimes referred to as the **granularity of a process**. Each level will have its own **granularity,** and these granular descriptions should not be muddled. Muddling differently pitched levels of thinking in a single level is likely to cause confusion to an audience unless this mix is vital to show poignant SSFs. If so, the best way to achieve this is by including more detail within sub-bubbles of **complex bubbles**.

A major challenge for any systems thinker and systems modeller is to maintain consistent granularity of process description within a particular pitch, to differentiate between different pitches, and simultaneously flit between differently pitched levels as required. Concomitantly, a meaningful connection from one level to another needs to be made.

At this juncture, it is important for a systems thinker to be reminded about the differences between "**hard systems methodologies**" and "**soft systems methodologies**" (Chapters 1 and 3), and as PrOH Modelling is a **soft systems methodology**, it is not necessary to show comprehensive **inheritance of properties** from one level to another, but only **provenance of origin** instead. This is because a PrOH Model is a conceptual system of change and not an organisational process *per se*. Inheritance of properties between differently pitched levels of modelling is only necessary when using **hard systems methodologies** in a parent-child relationship for modelling real-world systems such as products, physical systems, or mechanical organisational processes, but is not necessary for conceptual systems for entities such as organisational systems of change; this is because **soft systems methodologies** allow reinterpretation and re-contextualisation of descriptions of their elements in respect to different pitches of modelling.

Serial Abstraction of PrOH Models

Serial abstraction is when a set of serial PrOH Models of the same pitch are summarised at a higher-level pitch into a single PrOH Model. Steps to achieve serial **abstraction** are as follows:

1. Select all the bubbles from all the **core process statements** of a set of models at the same **pitch** and use all of these in the higher pitched PrOH Model remembering to remove any bubbles repeated across separate PrOH Models.
2. Use the **PrOH SIPOC Table** to abstract one new core process statement from either (1) the lower-level series of models' **core process statement** bubbles or (2) from newly introduced bubbles. Ensure the "**pick-up**" and "**drop off**" points for the lower-level series of PrOH Models are the same as the newly constructed higher-level PrOH Model. For that reason, the initial input and final output of the lower series of models will be the same as the initial input and final output of the higher-level model but the previous process phase and following process phase names will differ because of the difference in modelling pitch. The higher pitched PrOH Model connects to higher pitched PrOH Models preceding and following the current system phases, and the lower pitched phases connecting with lower pitched preceding and following system phases.
3. Using a **PrOH SIPOC Table** define supporting process statements while ensuring that all bubbles from lower-level core process statements are used if they have not already been used in new higher-level **core process statement**. Some new process descriptions can be introduced to **refine** the newly created model which are pertinent to the higher pitched level of modelling. Some detailed process descriptions from a series of lower-level models will be omitted, as the redefinition and re-contextualisation modelling means they are unlikely to remain pertinent, as is the nature of **abstraction**.
4. Draw the higher-level PrOH Model. See rules and guidelines to do this in Chapter 4.

From these four steps one can see how fundamental the construction of a **core process statement** is to a **holarchy**, and how it creates provenance between the originating and generated levels without needing absolute and explicit properties of inheritance, which are not required when performing abstractions in conceptual models using a soft systems thinking, which is a unique characteristic of the PrOH Modelling Methodology.

Using the **PrOH Model icon** for a single PrOH Model, as seen in Figure 5.2 these steps are depicted in Figure 5.3.

The purpose of abstraction is to put the detail of lower-level PrOH Models into a higher context and reveal "**emergent properties**" of a higher-level system.

Serial Enrichment of PrOH Models

Serial enrichment is when a single higher-level model is expressed in enhanced detail as a series of lower-level models and is the reverse of **serial abstraction**. **Serial enrichment** is achieved by:

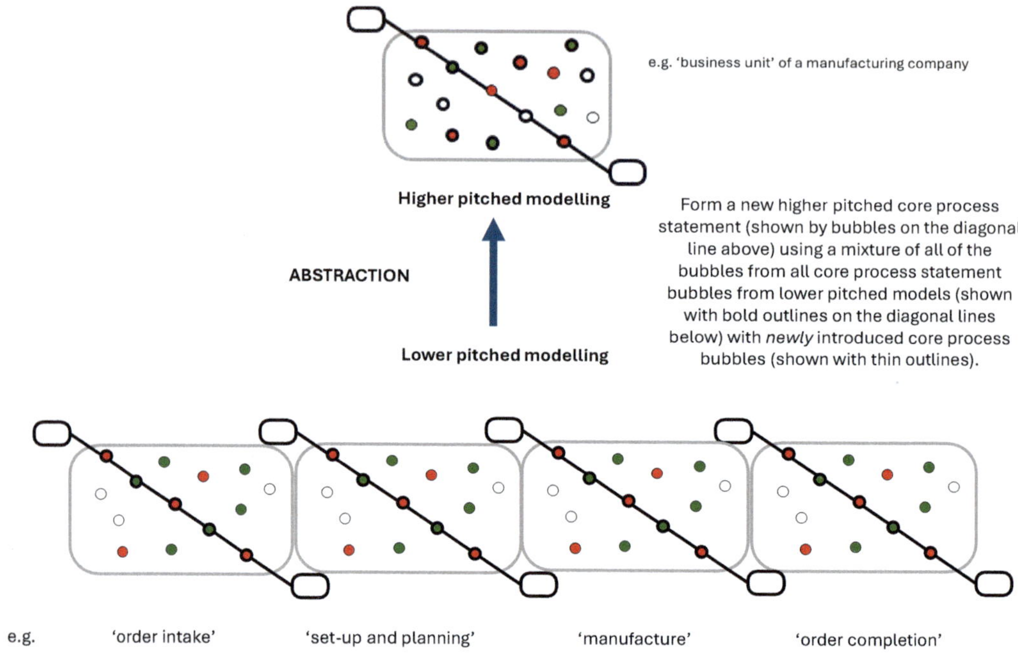

FIGURE 5.3 Holarchical Composition: Serial Abstraction of PrOH Models Using the PrOH Model Icon.

1. Defining a series of **core process descriptions** made from bubbles and activity links to describe the system in more detail at a lower-level pitch of modelling. If more than one serial model is to be produced, then these new core process statements must be linked by inputs, outputs and supplying and receiving agents (e.g. human resources).
2. For each new serial model to be enriched at a lower-level pitch, define a new **core process statement** made entirely from bubbles contained in the higher pitched level. Use a separate **PrOH SIPOC Table** to define each of these new core process statements. Do not introduce new bubbles into these new **core process descriptions**.
3. Add in new supporting resources (new bubbles) and their relationships using directional link descriptions to create new supporting descriptions for all new lower-level PrOH Models; this is known as **refining** PrOH Models by adding in more detail into a single PrOH Model. A **PrOH SIPOC Table** should be used to do this.
4. Draw the new lower-level models – see Chapter 4 for rules and guidelines.

Using a **PrOH Model Icon** of a single PrOH Model as given in Figure 5.1 a depiction of serial enrichment in a holarchy can be seen in Figure 5.4.

The purpose of serial enrichment is to show more detail at a lower level of PrOH Modelling and reveal "**hidden properties**" of a change system.

Enrichment and Abstraction of Parallel Models

Parallel models can be **abstracted** and **enriched** into a set of holarchical models using the same principles as serial abstraction and enrichment; details are given below.

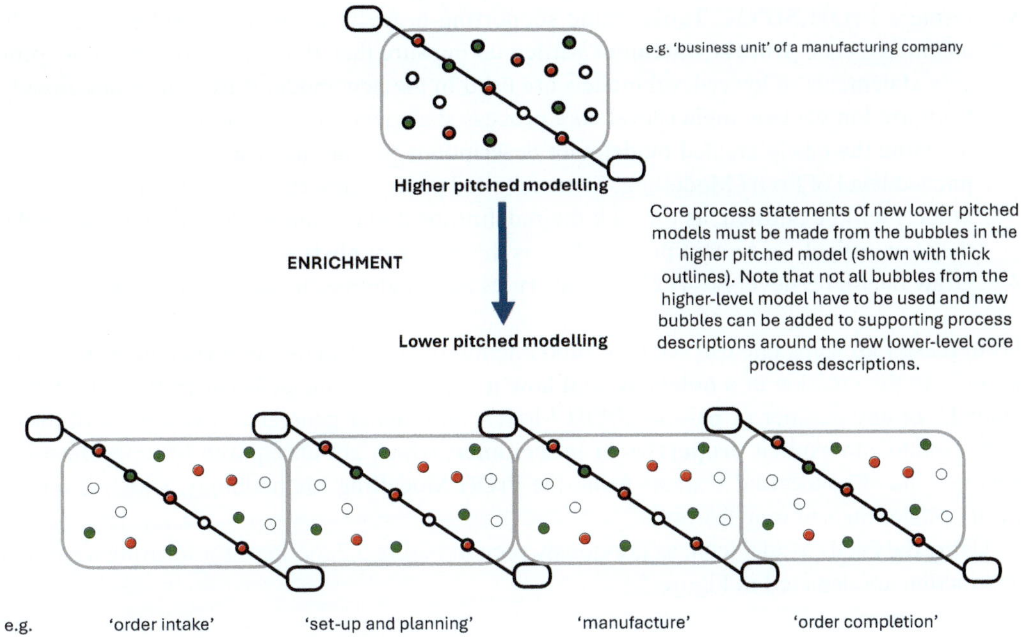

FIGURE 5.4 Holarchical Composition: Serial Enrichment using the PrOH Model Icon.

Parallel Abstraction of PrOH Models

Parallel abstraction is when any number of parallel PrOH Models at the same pitch are summarised at a higher-level modelling pitch in a single PrOH Model. Steps to achieve parallel abstraction are as follows:

1. Select all bubbles from all the **core process statements** of a "bunch" of any number of parallel models at the same pitch and use these bubbles in the higher pitched PrOH Model remembering to remove any bubbles repeated across separate models.
2. Use the **PrOH SIPOC Table** to define a new core process statement from either (1) the lower-level set of model core process statement bubbles *and* (2) from newly introduced bubbles. New bubbles *must* be introduced into the new core process statement that were not previously in the lower-level core process statements to reflect the new higher-level pitch of the model. Ensure that the "**pick-up**" and "**drop off**" points for the lower-level set of models are the same as the newly constructed higher-level model; this should be easy to do because all the lower-level models run in parallel and, by definition, will have the same "**pick-up**" and "**drop-off**" points. For that reason, the initial input and final output of the lower set of models will be the same as the input and output of the higher-level model but the previous process phase and following process phase names will differ because of the difference in modelling pitch. The higher pitched model connects with higher pitched preceding and following phases and the lower pitched phases connecting with lower pitched preceding and following phases. Effectual practice to achieve parallel abstraction is to use **complex containment bubbles** in the newly abstracted core process statement and include relevant bubbles from the lower-level core process statements within these as sub-bubbles.

3. Using a **PrOH SIPOC Table** define supporting process statements to **refine** the newly abstracted **core process statement** while making sure that all bubbles from the core process statements of lower-level models are used in the new model if they have not already been used in the new higher-level core process statement. New process descriptions need to **refine** the newly created model with descriptions that are more pertinent to the higher pitched level of PrOH Modelling. Some detailed process descriptions from the lower-level models will be omitted, as through the redefinition and re-contextualisation of the model they are unlikely to remain pertinent, as is the nature of **abstraction**.
4. Draw the higher-level PrOH Model; see rules and guidelines to do this in Chapter 4.

From these four steps one can see how fundamental the construction of a **core process statement** is to the creation of a **holarchy**, and how it creates provenance between the originating "bunch" of any number of parallel PrOH Models and higher generated levels without needing absolute and explicit **properties of inheritance**, which are unrequired when performing abstractions of conceptual systems using the PrOH Modelling Methodology, which is one of PrOH Modelling's unique features.

Using the PrOH Model Icon, as previously seen in Figure 5.2 the steps for forming a parallel abstraction are depicted in Figure 5.5.

Parallel Enrichment of PrOH Models

Parallel enrichment is when a single higher-level model is expressed in enhanced detail in a "bunch" of lower-level models. It is the reverse of **parallel abstraction** for parallel PrOH Models. **Parallel enrichment** is achieved by:

1. Defining a **core process description** made up of bubbles and directional activity links that need to be described in more detail at a lower pitched level. If more than one model needs to be produced in parallel then the new core process statements should be derived from bubbles found in the higher-level model, or from potential sub-bubbles pertaining to **complex bubbles** in the original higher-level model.
2. For each new model enriched at a lower pitched level define a **new core process statement** made entirely from bubbles contained in the higher pitched level. Use a separate **PrOH SIPOC Table** to define each of these new core process statements. Introduce new bubbles into the core process descriptions – even though these may be containment bubbles containing bubbles from the lower-level models as sub-bubbles. For parallel models produced by enrichment the "**pick-up**" and "**drop-off**" points for all models should be the same as one another and the same as the higher-level model.
3. Add in new supporting resources (new bubbles) and their relationships in directional link descriptions to create new supporting descriptions for all new lower-level models; this is known as **refining** PrOH Models with more detailed descriptions of entities, and their relationships not found in the higher-level model. A **PrOH SIPOC Table** should be used to define these.
4. Draw the new lower-level models – see Chapter 4 for rules and guidelines.

Using a PrOH Model Icon as given in Figure 5.2 is used to depict parallel enrichment as shown in Figure 5.6.

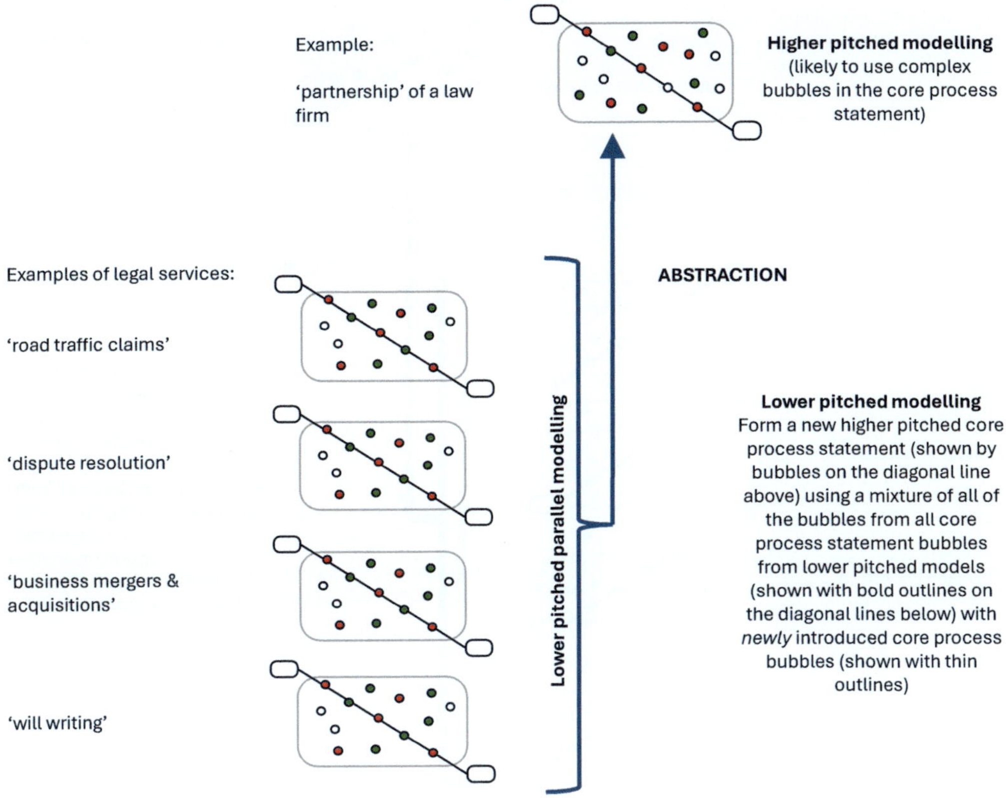

FIGURE 5.5 Parallel Abstraction of a Bunch of Parallel PrOH Models Using the PrOH Model Icon.

One can be seen how fundamental the thoughtful and purposeful definition of a **core process statement** is to the formation of a **holarchy**, either through **abstraction** or through **enrichment**.

Hidden and Emergent Properties Shown by Holarchies Produced from PrOH Models

Systemic properties that appear through **enrichment** are known as **hidden properties**. Systemic properties that appear through **abstraction** are known as **emergent properties**. This is true whether a set of models is composed as models in **series** or in **parallel**.

Through **abstraction** new properties can be added to the model that are only apparent and pertinent to the higher level. For example, going upward from a tactical level to a strategic level in a service company could mean that more external forces, such as those exerted by customer, suppliers and regulators come into effect. In contrast, through **enrichment** in a manufacturing company, **enrichment** may mean that new hidden properties may become apparent that were not relevant or impactful at a higher level. For instance, tactical modelling in manufacturing may be more about production planning, while at the operational level, it may be more about machine monitoring and set-up procedures. Further examples are given in Table 5.1.

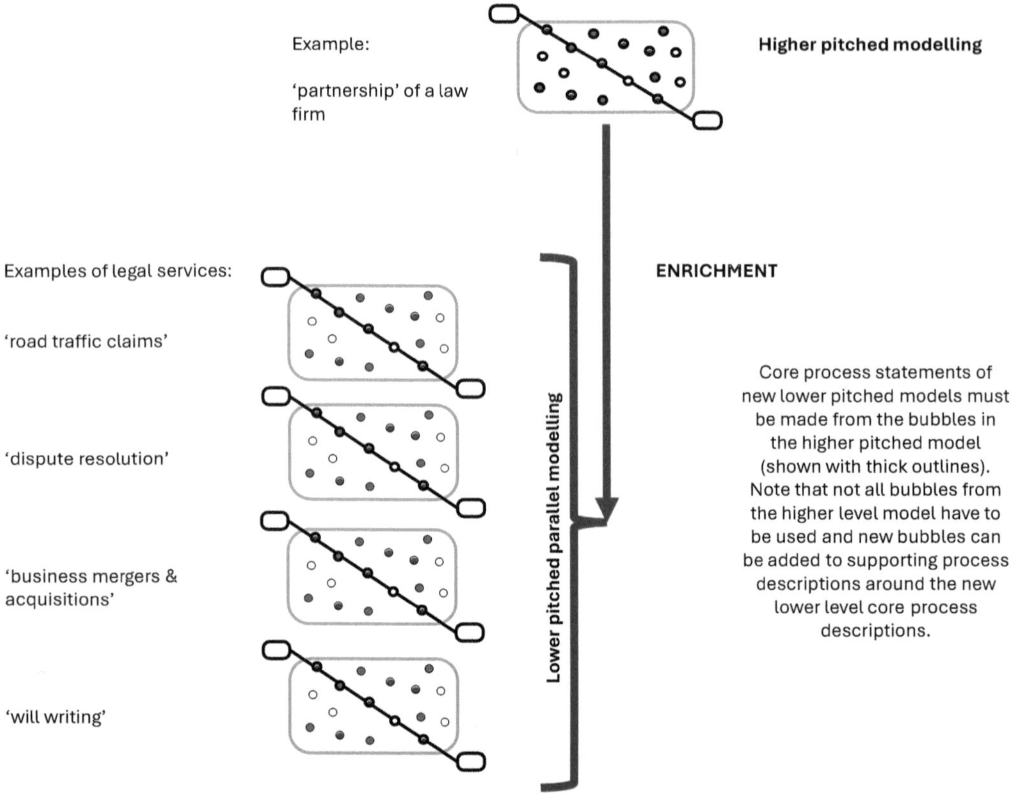

FIGURE 5.6 Parallel Enrichment of a PrOH Model into a Bunch of PrOH Models Using the PrOH Model Icon.

Although each example in Table 5.1, for service and manufacturing, is connected and interdependent with those at different levels, the different **pitch** of modelling requires names of artefacts and people (agents) and their relationships to be refreshed and re-expressed for a different **pitch** to tell more poignant stories on **systemic success factors** for change.

A visualisation of sets of PrOH Models in a serially composed **holarchy** is given in Figures 5.7 and a parallel composed holarchy is Figure 5.8. These are drawn in this way to suggest models within models to represent systems-within-systems or systems-of-systems in holistic thinking. These contrast with graphical compositions of hierarchical sets of models normally represented in pyramidal construction, emphasising dominance and agency strength at its pointed apex. In contrast Figures 5.7 and 5.8 are more like **Venn** diagrams than traditional pyramidal organigrams of hierarchy, power and control.

This alternative "system-of-systems" view of organisational structure is another defining difference between **holarchical** and **hierarchical** thinking.

Maturity Level Modelling Using PrOH Models

Maturity Levels are commonly used to discuss levels of achievement in properties such as functionality, discipline, practice or bodies of knowledge, and the concept of maturity is often

TABLE 5.1 Examples of SSFs That Might Be Apparent at One Level and not at Another

Level of Systemic Success Factor (SSF)	*Manufacturing (e.g. making metal panels)*	*Service (e.g. legal services)*
Strategic	• Price of raw materials and energy • Access to casual labour markets • Possible changing of company ownership	• Partner and ownership politics • Changing regulatory environment • Moving or developing new offices
Tactical	• Production planning and control • Maintenance scheduling for machinery • Developing new manufacturing capacity	• Managing each specialised legal service • Interacting with third parties (e.g. insurance companies) • Providing audit and compliance materials
Operational	• Machine setting and calibration • Set-up and machine monitoring • Error detection and quality sampling in products	• Case file management – use of digital systems • Booking hours to clients bills and issuing bills • Client relationship building activities

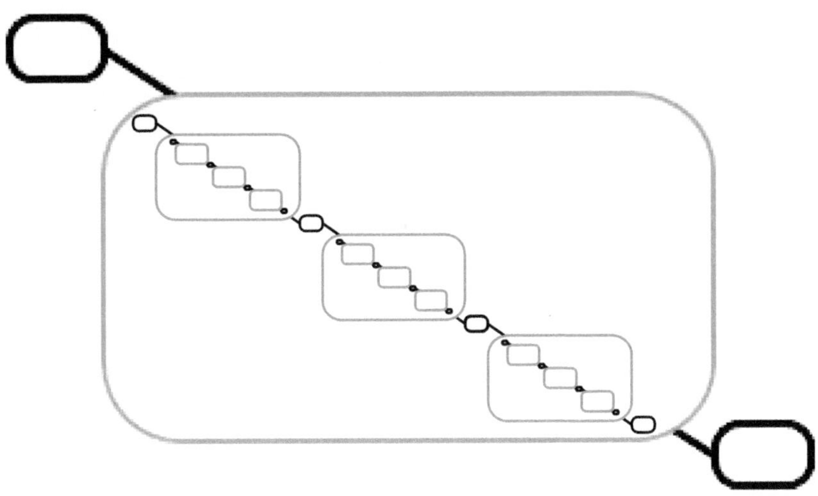

FIGURE 5.7 A Holarchy of PrOH Models Composed in Series – Using the PrOH Model Icon.

used in research studies to develop generic reference frameworks for benchmarking one example against another in **analogous rationalisation** and **logic**. For instance, a maturity level can be constructed for supply chain readiness, digital maturity, corporate social responsibility (CSR) or Equality, Diversity and Inclusion (EDI) or indeed many other management topics.

For example, PrOH Modelling has been used to show the maturity of lean six sigma practice. Lean six sigma (LSS) is a team-focused managerial approach that seeks to improve

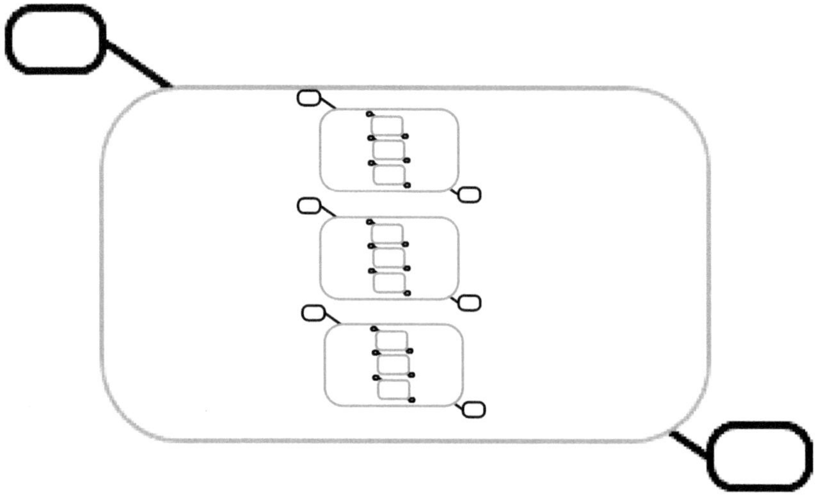

FIGURE 5.8 A Holarchy of PrOH Models Composed in Parallel – Using the PrOH Model Icon.

performance by eliminating waste and errors. Lean thinking focuses on reducing resource waste, thus becoming leaner, while the six sigma concerns the removal of errors, thus making a process more productive. Increasing leanness and reducing errors will result in higher levels of Lean Six Sigma maturity. An example is given in Part III, Chapter 12, Case 7. The maturity level of the LSS system for change denotes, among other things, how comprehensive, sophisticated and technically competent an LSS implementation is. The PrOH Model was constructed following the same rules and guidelines as any other PrOH Model. **Storyboarding** told the story of change from moving from a low level of maturity towards a higher level of LSS maturity.

Similarly, PrOH Models have been used to show supply chain readiness levels in a maturity model for upscaling electric vehicle supply chains. Supply chain maturity models help organisations to gauge the efficiency and effectiveness of their company to integrate with other companies to create value and growth in respect of the delivery of a product or service, in this case an electric powered vehicle. An example is given in Part III, Chapter 7, Case 2.

A maturity level variant of PrOH Modelling is important to mention in this section of this book because it is another significant way to show that a PrOH Model has been used in a new way to its original application.

A maturity level PrOH Model is constructed in the following way. Firstly, by constructing the full PrOH Model showing the system in a complete and comprehensive state; then secondly, by removing parts of it to show how a less sophisticated, less capable, less technical and less effectual system would operate. Thirdly, by then presenting this in reverse order to an audience in a **storyboard** to explain how an organisation would progress and develop these different elements to develop increasing levels of LSS or electric vehicle supply chain maturity.

Maturity level models are currently the least well-applied type of PrOH Modelling and cases are currently limited to LSS (Part III, Chapter 12, Case 7) and supply chain readiness (SCR) (Part III, Chapter 7, Case 2). Further work is needed in this area and would be a fertile area of research that could reveal another way of building a holarchy.

Summary

The main points are summarised below.

- It may be possible that there are other ways to conceive and construct a **holarchy** using PrOH Modelling that could be found by applying it to other diverse cases, and so this is a fertile area for further methodological and philosophical research. Indeed, the authors of this book would encourage readers and researchers of this work to try to do this through **abductive logic** and experiment with concepts in systems thinking.
- One experiment that comes to mind is to see how a set of models in a hybrid parallel–serial composition would work, and scenarios where and why this might be useful. Or whether this level of complexity would ever be required. Also, it would be interesting to see how PrOH Modelling could be combined with other, more quantitative systems analysis methods. New applications, technical developments and suggested further work are picked up in Part IV of this book.

Further Reading

Balthu, K.C. (2021). *Applying Systems Thinking to Improve Professional Service Operations*. PhD Thesis, Aston University.

Clegg, B.T. (1999) *A Systems Approach to Re-Engineering Business Processes Towards Concurrent Engineering Principles*. PhD Thesis. Chapter 6. De Montfort University and British Library.

Orme, R.A. (2016), '*A Systems Approach to Developing a Unified Methodology and Deployment Model to Help Maximize Impact of Lean Thinking and Six Sigma in Organizations*. PhD Thesis, Aston University.

PART III
Cases

Abstract

Part three gives detailed case studies that have used the PrOH Modelling Methodology to develop understanding about changing complex organisational system and their systemic success factors to improve operations, processes, technology, strategy, and methods of working and training.

Cases have primarily been selected to show the practical application of the PrOH Modelling in action research projects; collectively the cases show all aspects of the PrOH Modelling Methodology rules and guidelines.

Cases are based on real projects performed with manufacturing and service organizations including large multinational companies and small-to-medium sized enterprises to show insights into different organisations challenges and topics. Most of these projects were done under a formal contract between a university, a case company with third-party research funder.

These diverse cases are presented in a similar structure. Firstly, the context and purpose for doing each case is introduced. Secondly, the PrOH Models, their SSFs, impacts and innovations for the case company are given. Thirdly, reflections on abducted theories are given. Fourthly, reflections on PrOH Modelling Methodology rules, guidelines and nuances are given. A summary concludes each case.

Each case varied in duration and the extent to which the PrOH Modelling Methodology was deployed. In some cases, a single PrOH Model was produced and in other cases, two or three different pitches of PrOH Modelling were produced using several PrOH Models at multiple holarchical levels.

6

CASE 1: GMRDSL'S SRL FACTORY – A STRATEGIC MODEL

Part 1

This case shows how data from interviews is structured to create a SIPOC Table and a PrOH Model. It is based on a large international manufacturing company's factory making radar systems for commercial and military use. This is a two-part case study; the first part presents a single top-level strategic PrOH Model, and the second part builds it into a holarchical set of PrOH Models.

Context

The case company is referred to as GMRDSL, who designed and manufactured radar systems which are installed across the World for military and civil aviation purposes, many seen at regular commercial airports. At the time of writing, its main factory, called the "SRL Factory", was based in the Midlands in the UK, with headquarters in London and numerous other smaller factories across the UK and Europe. They originally invented the radar and many of their products have been in service for more than 50 years across the world. At the time of conducting this case study, there were major cuts in UK defence budgets and hence radical downsizing and efficiency drives were necessary in GMRDSL. The chosen way to achieve this was to try to implement the principles of **concurrent engineering** (Boardman and Clegg, 2001; Koufteros et al., 2001) to make the design and manufacture of new radar systems and the redesign and servicing of after-sales services more efficient. This was largely done through abductive thinking.

PrOH Modelling Using a SIPOC Table

This action research case study lasted for 12 months and consisted of one systems-level strategic PrOH Model, four phase operational level PrOH Models and eleven sub-phase tactical level PrOH Models. In this chapter, to keep things simple, we only consider the formation of the strategic PrOH Model. Data interviews and collection, data structuring into a SIPOC table and drawing of the PrOH Model followed rules and guidelines given in Chapter 4:

- Interviews were conducted with shopfloor factory workers and managers involved in core factory processes from order intake, manufacturing set-up and planning, manufacturing

DOI: 10.4324/9781032650425-9

and dispatch. Each interview was recorded as an individual flow chart depicting interviewees' perceived sequence of actions that occurred in the process and their related challenges. Individuals who interfaced with the factory from headquarters, suppliers, subcontractors and other business units (BU) who managed the commercial aspects of factory work orders were also interviewed. These raw data source materials are not shown here, as they were extensive and, in themselves, are not novel aspects of PrOH Modelling, even though they are a vital first step to gaining a deeper understanding of the system under observation (SuO), which in this case is the design, manufacture and servicing of a radar systems.
- Individual interviews, recorded as flow charts, were then consolidated into the SIPOC Table shown in Table 6.1. To simplify reading this SIPOC Table, colour coding has been used to trace activities. The same colour is used to show a person (or agent) doing something in the centre two columns of the SIPOC Table, indicating which person's activity feeds it as its originator and which activity follows. Colour coding becomes more important when SIPOC Tables get larger. Grey shading in a SIPOC Table, as defined in Chapter 4, shows where there is more than one input or output from a central activity. Where grey shading is given, the reader should use the text immediately above; this practice reduces data duplication and makes the SIPOC Table easier and quicker to read.
- The SIPOC Table in Figure 6.1 was used to draw the PrOH Model in Figure 6.1 following the PrOH Modelling Methodological steps in Chapter 4.

The PrOH Model in Figure 6.1 follows rules and guidelines in Chapter 4. Some features of Figure 6.1 to note as specific interpretations of *guidelines* are:

- Branching and joining of directional links. This is to reduce the number of directional links on the PrOH Model, so it is clearer to read.
- It has two instances of green bubbles following one another. This is occasionally permissible but unadvisable as each occurrence reduces **systemicity**.
- It has no decision bubble – this is inadvisable as a system should ideally always have at least one decision bubble as each occurrence will increase **systemicity**.

Logic in SIPOC Table in Table 6.1 can be seen in descriptions in the PrOH Model in Figure 6.1 although of course artistic interpretation is allowed to give readable sentences and an impactful visual representation that can be **storyboarded**.

The storyboard for this PrOH Model is not shown for this case as the purpose of this case is to show (1) how to get from a single SIPOC Table to a single PrOH Model, (2) to show PrOH Modelling application to a manufacturing factory and (3) how guidelines can be cautiously interpreted. However, a storyboard would contain the points given in the "lessons learned" section about **concurrent engineering** below as bulleted points on each storyboard scene.

Abducted Thinking: Lessons Learned about Concurrent Engineering for GMRDSL's SRL Factory

- Manufacturing was done on many sites and was commercially uncoordinated for the customer.
- Multiple interfacing with different manufacturing business units (BUs) throughout the project resulted in process delays.
- Commercial relationships between other BUs need to improve, removing the need for internal part-to-part company contracts.

TABLE 6.1 GMRDSL SRL Factory – Strategic Level SIPOC Table

SYSTEM INPUT: customer (Chelmsford BU), (other BU, external customer) defines manufacturing requirement	**potential orders (works requisitions, RFQ and data pack)**	**SRL management team (materials, accounts, quality, operations, programmes, personnel, purchasing)**	**must manage delivery of assembled units**	**assembled units**	**SYSTEM OUTPUT: customer gains utility from assembled and shippable units**
SYSTEM INPUT: customer (Other BU, External customer) defines manufacturing requirement	potential orders (RFQ and data pack)	project manager (programmes/bid dept)	aims to bid successfully to solicit a prime purchase order and data pack	contractual documents (new PO/ SOW/ITP), (PO/ SOW Amendment)	project manager (programmes/ bid dept) can manage set-up of manufacturing control documents (MRP ECO), (MMR)
project manager (programmes/bid dept) aims to bid successfully to solicit a prime purchase order and data pack	contractual documents (new PO/ SOW/ITP), (PO/SOW Amendment)	project manager (programmes/bid dept)	can manage set-up of manufacturing control documents (MRP ECO), (MMR)	manufacturing control documents (MRP ECO), (MMR)	operations department ensure the first MRP run
SYSTEM INPUT: customer (Chelmsford, BU) defines manufacturing requirement	potential orders (works requisitions)	project manager (spares cell), (repairs cell)	can directly manage set-up of manufacturing control documents (MRP ECO, MMR)	manufacturing control documents (MRP ECO, MMR)	operations department ensure the first MRP run
project manager (programmes/bid dept) can manage set-up of manufacturing control documents (MRP ECO), (MMR)	manufacturing control documents (MRP ECO)	operations department	ensure the first MRP run	first MRP run	operations department must complete manufacturing with assembled units

(Continued)

TABLE 6.1 (Continued)

project manager (spares cell), (repairs cell) can directly manage set-up of manufacturing control documents (MRP ECO, MMR)					
operations department ensure the first MRP run	first MRP run	operations department	must complete manufacturing with assembled units	assembled units	**SYSTEM OUTPUT: customer gains utility from assembled and shippable items**
					project manager (programmes/bid dept), (spares cell), (repairs cell) takes action in order to close the order
operations department must complete manufacturing with assembled units	assembled units	project manager (programmes/bid dept), (spares cell), (repairs cell) takes action in order to close the order	project manager (programmes/bid dept) takes action in order to close the order	closed orders	SRL management team (materials, accounts, quality, operations, programmes, personnel, purchasing) are directed by GMRDS policy

(Continued)

TABLE 6.1 (Continued)

SYSTEM INPUT: GMRDS senior management define GMRDS policy (profit targets, strategic goals and working practices, turnover targets, constant change for improvement, order intake targets)	GMRDS policy (profit targets, strategic goals and working practices, turnover targets, constant change for improvement, order intake targets)	SRL management team (materials, accounts, quality, operations, programmes, personnel, purchasing)	are directed by GMRDS policy	periodical status reports (UBR pack)	**SYSTEM OUTPUT: GMRDS senior management are kept informed of SRL progress**
SYSTEM INPUT: customer (Other BU), (External customer), (Chelmsford BU) defines manufacturing requirement	potential orders (RFQ and data pack), (works requisitions)				
project manager (programmes/bid dept), (spares cell), (repairs cell) takes action in order to close the order	closed orders				

Abbreviations: BU = Business Unit, UBR = Unit Business Review, RFQ = Request for Quote, MRP = Materials Requirement Planning, ECO = Engineering Change Order. PO = Purchase Order, SOW = Statement of Work, ITP = Instruction to Proceed. MMR = Master Manufacturing Document. GMRDSL = company name. SRL = Factory name.

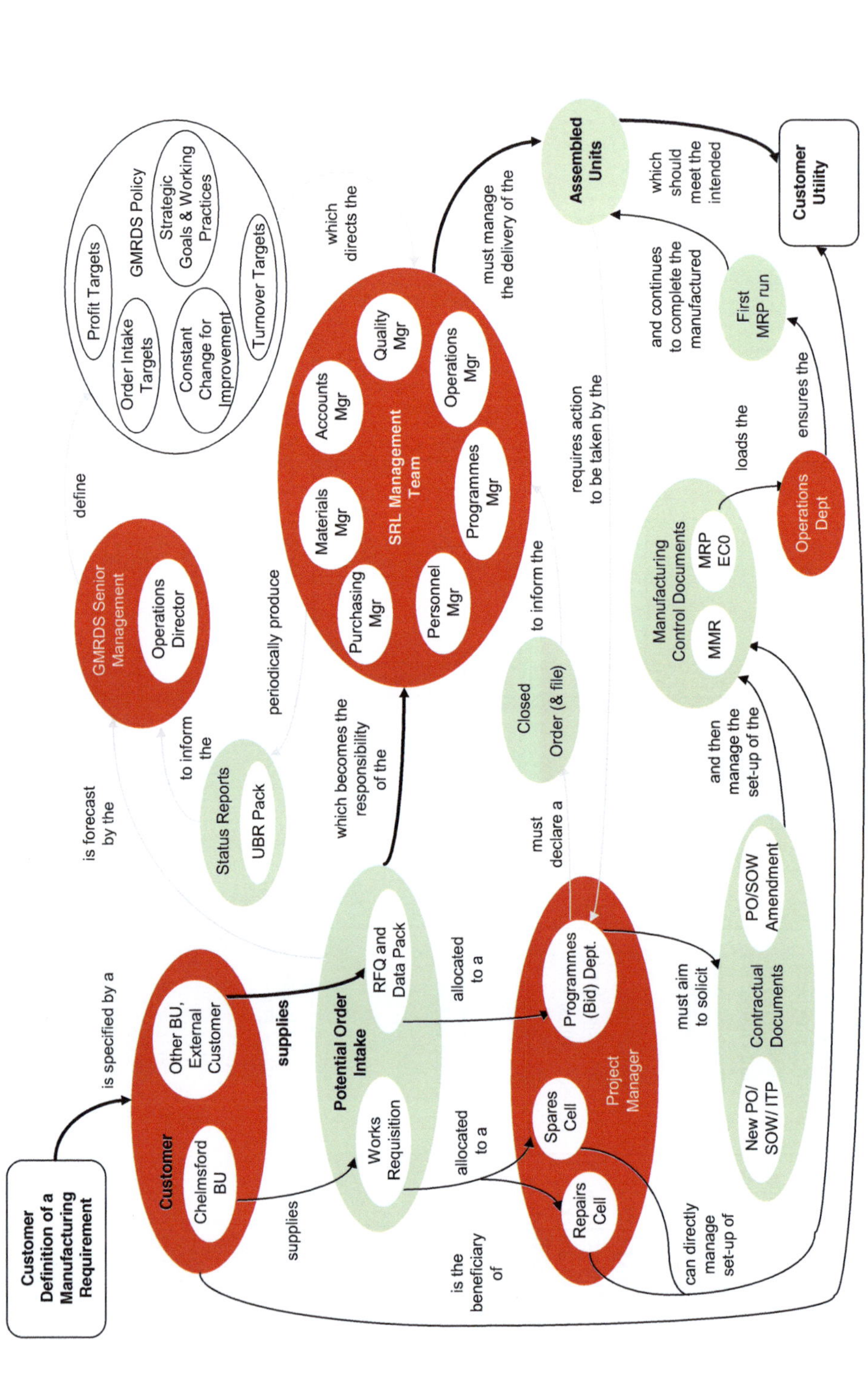

FIGURE 6.1 MRDSL Strategic Level – Factory PrOH Model.

Abbreviations: BU = Business Unit, UBR = Unit Business Review, RFQ = Request for Quote, MRP = Materials Requirement Planning, ECO = Engineering Change Order. PO = Purchase Order, SOW = Statement of Work, ITP = Instruction to Proceed. MMR = Master Manufacturing Document. GMRDSL = company name. SRL = Factory name.

- The spares and repairs cells were recently introduced to achieve high volume, lower-value and fast throughput processes (25% lead-time reduction) which could possibly be a pilot rolled out across the whole factory.
- Different sites are the same company, and not customer and supplier, although often treated as such and made to compete for profit.
- There is debate about which site takes the profit and who takes the losses.
- Long paper chains of documents with much bureaucracy resulting in higher operational costs needed to be automated and digitalised.
- Lack of customer focus is giving customer dissatisfaction.
- Enquiry, order processing, project management, engineering and accounts IT systems were all independent, and more integration was needed.

The combination of these negative effects made it difficult to implement concurrent engineering principles, which require joined-up thinking between product design authorities, designers and builders of integrated product service systems. Further reading on concurrent engineering principles in this case can be found in Clegg (1999), Clegg and Boardman (1996) and Clegg et al. (1996a, 1996b).

Methodological Reflections

The single PrOH Model in Figure 6.1 is part of a larger action research case that gave recommendations for improvement to how GMRDSL's SRL factory operated and interfaced with other parts of the company and external organisations.

A **Process Matrix** (Clegg, 1999, Appendix 8) was used to define phases within the system of change, or, in systems-thinking terms **holons** within **holons**. This **Process Matrix** is given in Part 2 of this case (Chapter 9, Table 9.2) where each column lists, without logical dependencies, the activities most likely to go into each phase.

Similarly, a **Process Matrix** can be used to identify **Sub-Phases** from **Phases**. A **Process Matrix** is a useful exercise to do before embarking on in-depth interviews and should be used to scope a set of PrOH Models. Scoping can initially be done from secondary documented data and later revised as needed when primary data has been collected.

Summary

This case provides an introduction to a typical context and use for the PrOH Modelling Methodology which, at its onset, had a general objective to improve efficiency and productivity in one of their factories. However, after some initial systemic-based investigations and further research and engagement with the client, it became apparent that, through **abductive thinking**, **concurrent engineering** was a useful body of theoretical knowledge to use to further explore and critique GMRDSL's practices to this end.

Thus, in a simple way this case shows what data was used in a PrOH Model and what a strategic PrOH Model looks like and its SSFs that can be included in a storyboarded version of a PrOH Model. Further pointers to theoretical expositions via **concurrent engineering** and action research-based interventions to effect practical changes followed. Further enrichments of this case's features can be read about in Part 2 in Chapter 9.

Further Reading

Clegg, B. (1999), *A Systems Approach to Reengineering Business Processes Towards Concurrent Engineering Principles*. PhD Thesis. De Montfort University.

7

CASE 2: MICROCAB

Upscaling Supply Chains for the Manufacture of Electric Vehicles

The Organisational Challenge

This case set out to investigate how to upscale the supply chain of a small hydrogen fuel-celled electric vehicle, known as a Hybrid Electric Vehicle (HEV). Figure 7.1 shows Microcab's two-seater electric car. Microcab is a research and design focused company. This case focuses on resource dependencies between suppliers of different drivetrain parts in the hydrogen fuel-cell drive train. This challenge is interesting as there is currently huge potential for the widespread use of hydrogen-powered vehicles as hydrogen is a plentiful, clean and potentially cost-effective fuel which is a potentially viable replacement for internal combustion engine (ICE) drivetrains.

However, there are challenges to building hydrogen fuel-cell vehicles in large volumes as the UK supply chain, customer base and operating environment are not yet fully developed. At the time of writing, Microcab was a small-to-medium sized enterprise (SME) based in the UK Midlands, producing small volumes of vehicles in a job-shop set-up. They aspire to produce larger output volumes to supply bigger clients such as metropolitan car-share schemes across Europe and in the Far East. The massive increase in volume demanded by such customers involves upscaling production from five vehicles to 30,000 vehicles per year in five years' time. The challenge of this case was to see how prepared and how enthusiastic Microcab's suppliers were for such massive change.

Action Research and Systems Thinking Approach

An inter-organisation case study method was used in this action research. Data was collected via interviews from Microcab, two of its tier-one suppliers and five of its tier-two suppliers involved in the design, build and servicing of the hydrogen fuel cell drive train.

By using the PrOH Modelling Methodology, as described in Chapters 4 and 5, a strategic-level overview was created to visualise the systemic success factors of a dynamically changing automotive industry in a predominantly, but rapidly disappearing, internal combustion engine

DOI: 10.4324/9781032650425-10

FIGURE 7.1 Microcab's Two-Seater Hydrogen Fuel-Cell Car.

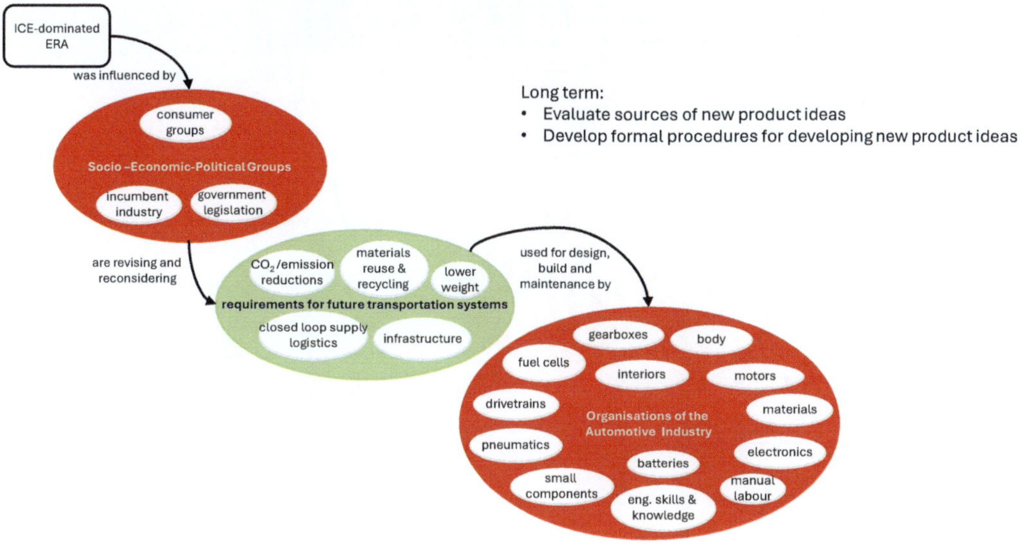

FIGURE 7.2 Scene 1 – A Roadmap: Organisations of the Automotive Industry Deliver Post-ICE-Dominated Era Transport Systems – with SSFs.

dominated era. The PrOH Modelling Methodology gave insight into better understanding of how to change systemic success factors, whether these be social, economic, political or technological and their impacts on other systemic success factors across the business and their supply chain. The PrOH Model based on this data with its systemic success factors is given in a six-scene storyboard shown in Figures 7.2–7.7. This case is given to demonstrate how a storyboard is developed.

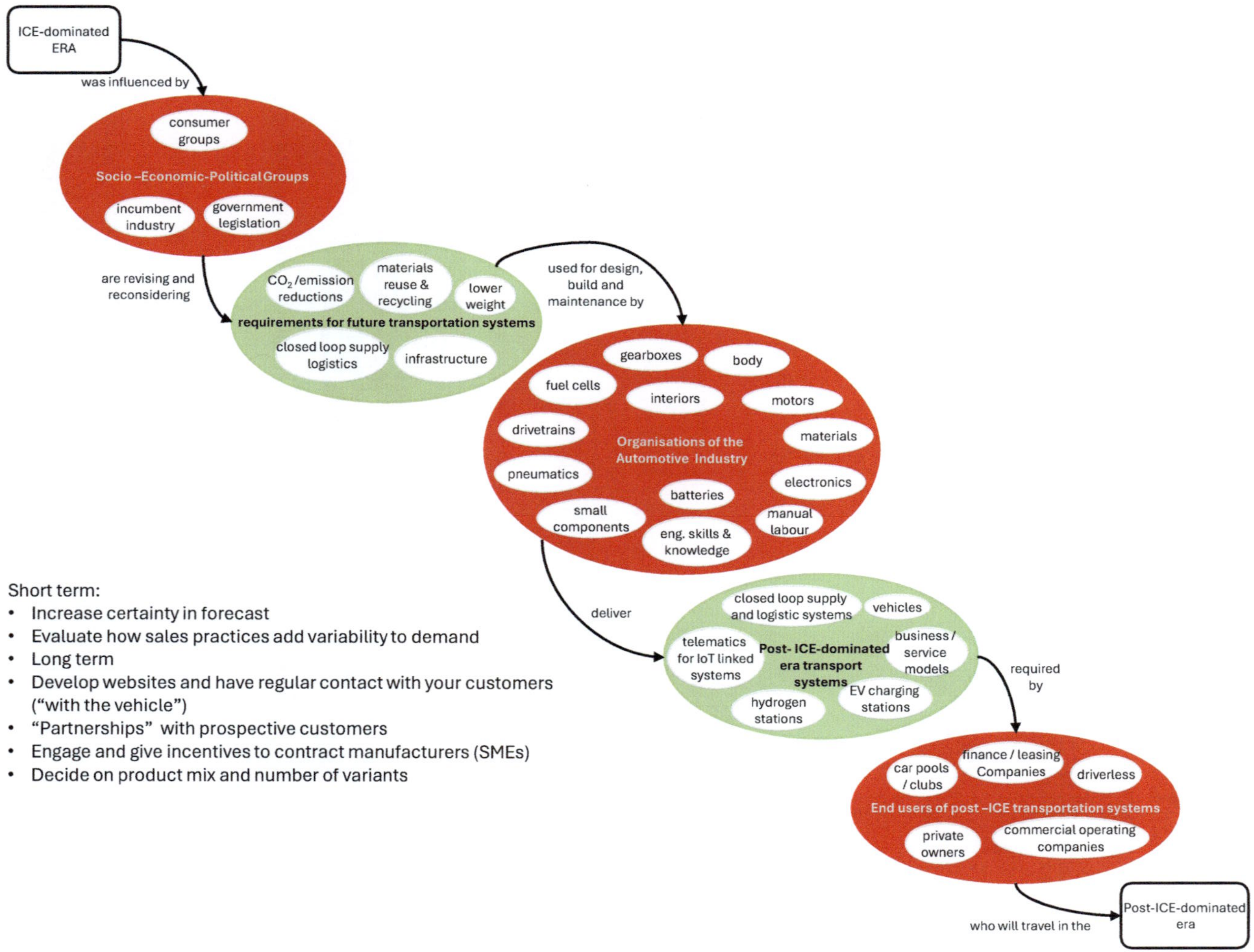

FIGURE 7.3 Scene 2 – A Roadmap: Organisations of the Automotive Industry Deliver Post-ICE-Dominated Era Transport Systems – with SSFs.

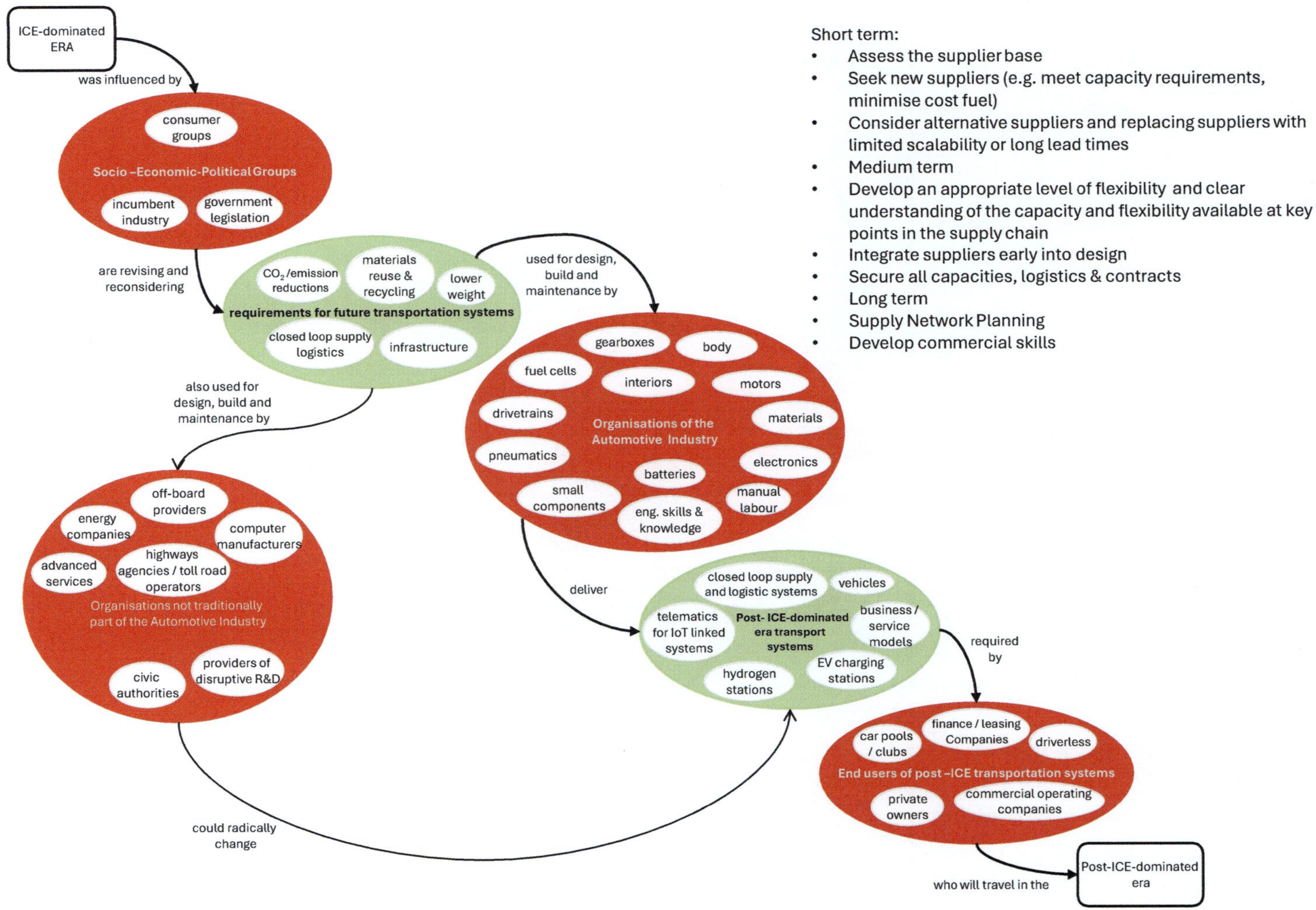

FIGURE 7.4 Scene 3 – A Roadmap: Organisations of the Automotive Industry Deliver Post-ICE-Dominated Era Transport Systems – with SSFs.

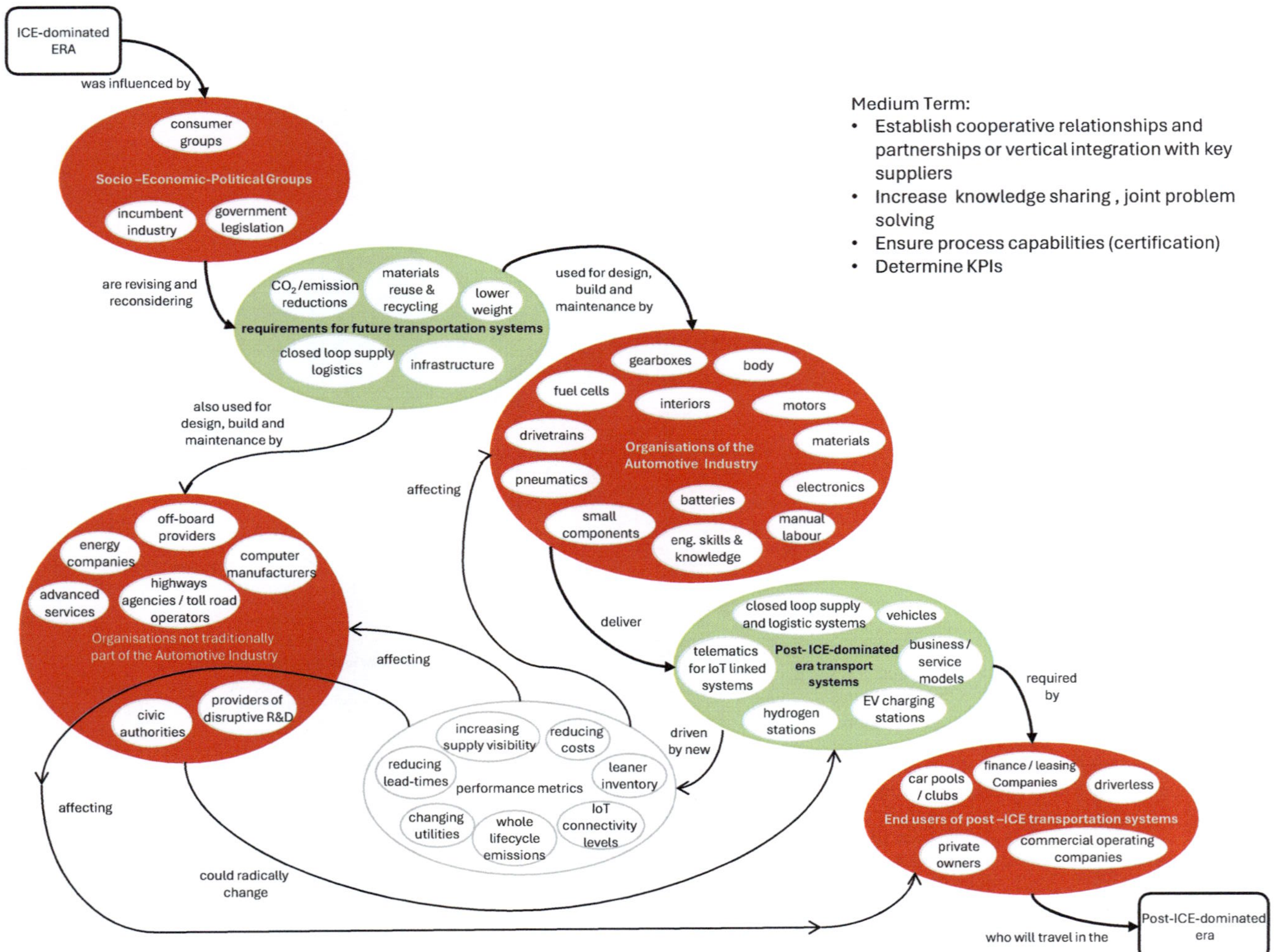

FIGURE 7.5 Scene 4 – A Roadmap: Organisations of the Automotive Industry Deliver Post-ICE-Dominated Era Transport Systems – with SSFs.

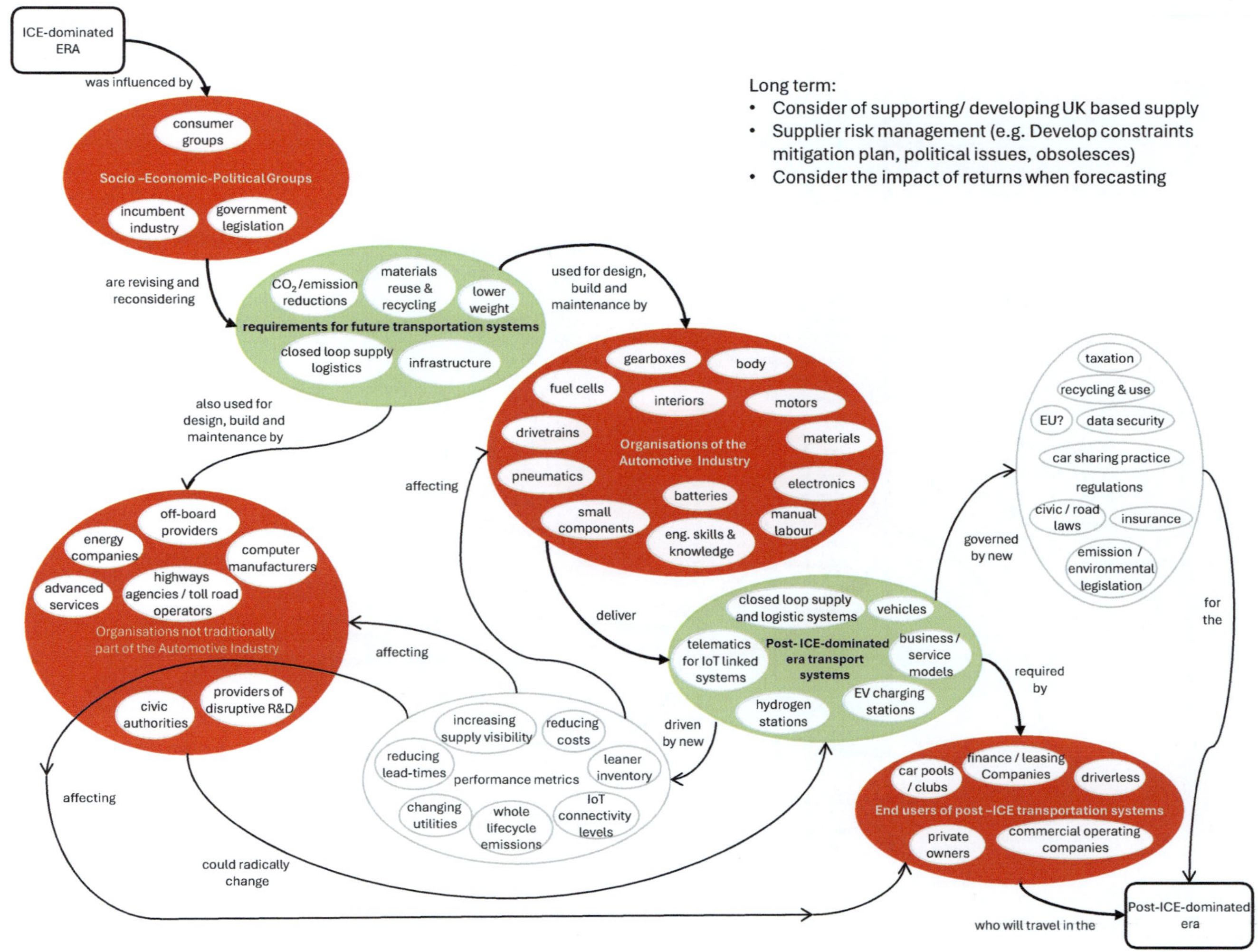

FIGURE 7.6 Scene 5 – A Roadmap: Organisations of the Automotive Industry Deliver Post-ICE-Dominated Era Transport Systems – with SSFs.

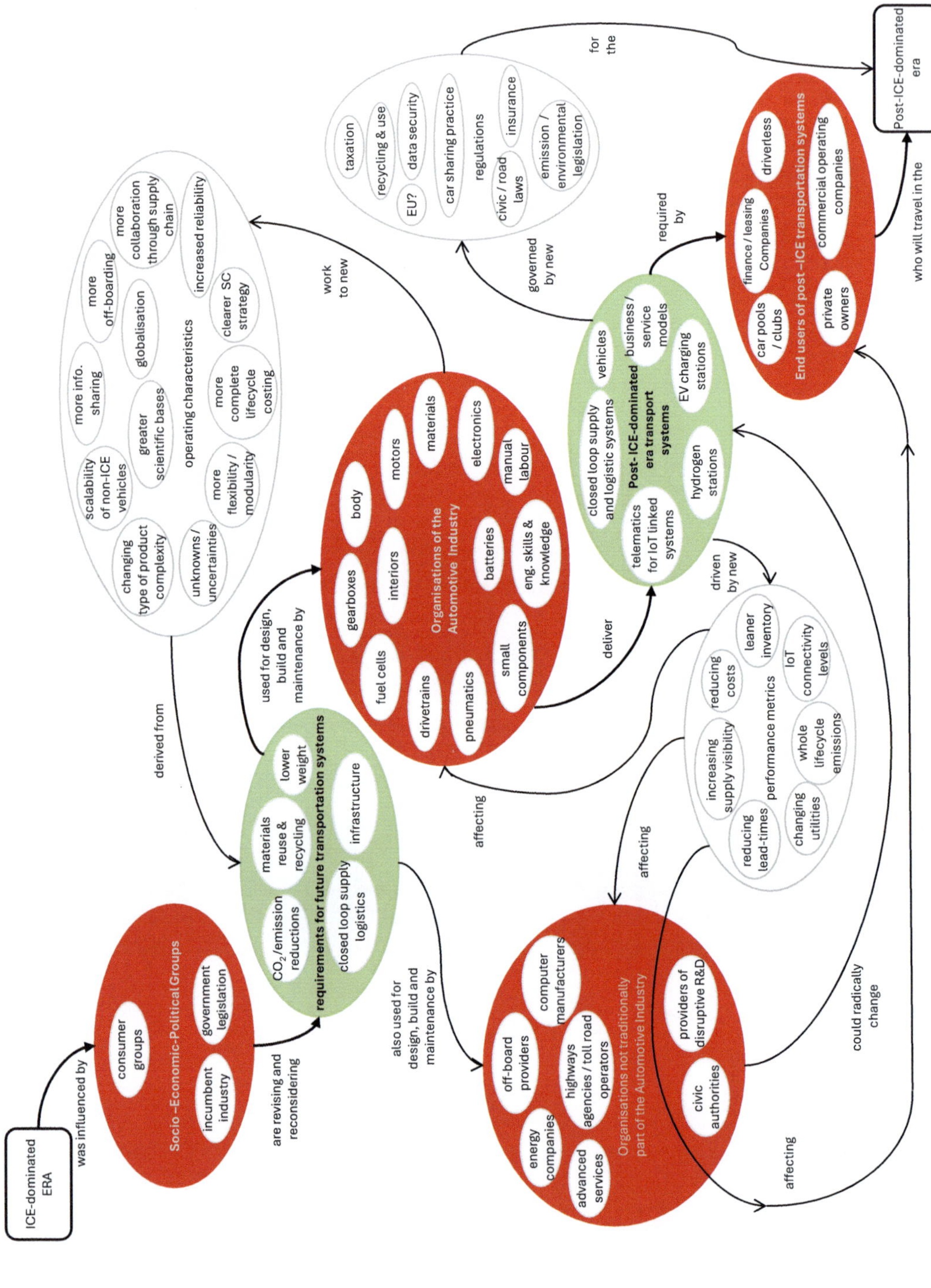

FIGURE 7.7 Scene 6 – A Roadmap: Organisations of the Automotive Industry Deliver Post-ICE-Dominated Era Transport Systems.

Practical Systemic Success Factors of Change as a PrOH Model Storyboard

A variety of strategic success factors (SSFs) of change were observed and acted upon to help Microcab managers avoid and/or reduce critical inter-firm resource dependencies during production upscaling.

For instance, as planned production volumes increase, it was anticipated that developmental relationships were needed in inter-company relationships across their supply chain, rather than short-term transactional relationships. Also, another interesting finding was how certain pivotal key suppliers, far larger than Microcab, were orchestrating and managing the entire supply chain and could either hinder or help niche electric vehicle manufacturers, such as Microcab, to design and operationalise their core processes towards higher volume output. These systemic success factors are shown scene by scene.

The first scene in Figure 7.2 shows the first half of the PrOH Model core process statement, and the second scene given in Figure 7.3 shows the other half of the core process statement. The core PrOH Model statement focuses on how the "Organizations of the Automotive Industry" must consider "requirements for future transportation" systems from "Socio-Economic-Political Groups" and "deliver post-ICE dominated era transportation systems" for "End users of post-ICE transportation systems". Each scene includes its SSFs; for instance, in scene one these are "evaluate sources of new product ideas" and "develop formal procedures for developing new product ideas" and should be read accordingly. Subsequent PrOH Model scenes in Figures 7.3–7.7 are presented similarly, and the model and their SSFs should be similarly read to understand this system of change. It is convention that when PrOH Model scenes are presented, the PrOH Model scene is initially read verbatim so the action researcher can focus the minds of stakeholders in the audience to ensure a common understanding of the system of change is achieved. Once this has been accomplished, the SSFs are then presented and discussed as much as possible. Each PrOH Model scene is placed on a separate slide (using MS PowerPoint where SSFs appear using the "animation" function). In this case, due to the complexity of the PrOH Model in Scene 6 (Figure 7.7), the SSFs are presented beneath the PrOH Model rather than on it; however, in the actual PrOH Modelling storyboarding event, these were shown as an animation to appear over the PrOH Model.

For Scene 6 in Figure 7.7 the SSFs were:

Short term:

- Design bill of materials (BOM) to be accurate and financially precise with documents, (e.g. CAD files, supplier appraisals).

Medium term:

- Identify product rollout issues and constraints.
- Finalising and validating product designs.
- Develop needed skills and hire people with the correct skills.

Long Term:

- Explore technologies that would aid with the synchronisation process across supply chain partners.
- Get rid of assemblies, parts and techniques that prohibit reuse and remanufacture of end products.

Theoretical Considerations

Resource Dependence Theory (RDT) was used in abductive rationalisation to analyse and explain the changing inter-organisational interdependencies throughout the planning and execution of up-scaling. RDT revealed how Microcab was better able to manage its suppliers and their resource interdependencies. This abductive rationalisation is explained in more detail in Kalaitzi et al. (2019) in respect to different resources, supplier substitutability, discretion over who has control over which resources to develop *bridging* and *buffering* strategies that can be deployed by members of a supply chain to mitigate supply risk as advocated by RDT.

Methodological Considerations

In respect to PrOH Modelling:

- This model was pitched at the supply chain organisational level rather than an individual company level and therefore shows the changing roles of different players in future supply chains. Only one PrOH Model was necessary to run a series of effective workshops on the system of change.
- This project was delivered as part of a relatively short piece of intervention-based action research run over six months.
- This project produced a positive strategic impact for Microcab, and findings were published in a leading academic journal (Kalaitzi et al., 2019).

Summary

This case focuses on resource dependencies in the production of hydrogen electric vehicles, which differ from conventional vehicles, as the key players have changed and performance metrics differ. Whereas innovation in the conventional automotive industry tends to be driven by a few large organisations, mainly OEMs and large tier-one suppliers, innovation in the EV industry can come from both large and small companies. Specifically, SMEs are playing a more crucial role, as either suppliers and/or vehicle manufacturers. Moreover, the power is shifting in the supply chain away from conventional vehicle manufacturers and generic automotive companies, towards specialist newcomer suppliers (Bierau et al., 2015) who deliver electrical and electronic components focused on a battery and/or fuel-cell drive trains. It is expected that around eight million electric vehicles will be on UK roads by 2040, and a long-term transformation of the automotive industry will be needed (Fojcik, 2013).

Further Reading

Kalaitzi, D., Matopoulos, A., and Clegg, B. (2019), 'Managing Resource Dependencies in Electric Vehicle Supply Chains: A Multi-Tier Case Study', *Supply Chain Management: An International Journal*, Vol. 24, Iss. 2, pp. 256–270.

8

CASE 3: CHILTERN RAILWAYS

Improving Passenger Information during Disruptions for a Train Operating Company

The Organisational Challenge

However well-planned passenger rail services are performed, they will always be subject to disruptions for many reasons – some due to the train operating companies (TOCs) themselves (e.g. not having enough staff, poorly maintained assets or a mismatch of schedules to passenger demand) and some which are totally outside a TOC's control (e.g. due to the rail network operator's negligence, poor weather conditions, accidents or strikes). As such, it is a constant challenge for TOCs to try to prevent disruptions but also to plan for recovery after disruptions to service have occurred, and a key aspect of this is their ability for *managing passenger information during disruptions*. In 2014, the Passenger Focus report revealed that three of the top twelve rail passengers' improvement priorities directly related to information use during disruptions, such as: "train companies [need to] keep passengers informed about delays" (5th), "accurate and timelier information [must be] available at stations" (8th) and "accurate and timelier information [must be] provided on trains" (12th) (Passenger Focus, 2014). Disruptions require the replanning of services and may last from hours to days (Pender et al., 2012).

Managing passenger information during disruption, or "PIDD" as it is commonly known, is a significant factor in running effective and quick-to-recover rail operations. Disruptions are unpredictable, and their timely resolution is ultimately dependent on the expert knowledge of experienced frontline staff. The development of frontline staff by their employers usually takes the form of reviews of practice and "on-the-job learning". Occasionally, frontline staff also participate in more academic education that tends to major on theoretical approaches and classroom-based teaching; however, this is typically less common due to the time and cost commitment involved. This case study is based on an industry-based action research project that developed a serious game (the "Rail Disruption Game") combining theory and practice to train frontline staff to make them better equipped to deal with disruptions more quickly and more effectively. This case study provides insight into how to design, make and deploy a serious learning game as part of a gamified management process (Clegg et al.,2018) based on

DOI: 10.4324/9781032650425-11

a systems thinking action research project using the PrOH Modelling Methodology to understand the challenges and develop an innovative solution to address some known issues.

The Practical Systemic Success Factors of Change in a PrOH Model Storyboard

Systems thinking was used to investigate the complex system that delivers rail services and resolve service disruption. The focus of this case was not on disruption prevention, which is another topic, but on effective disruption resolution focusing on which frontline staff behaviours are most effective and how actions can most speedily resolve the disruption and resume service to normality for passengers.

Numerous interviews were conducted with frontline staff in accordance with the PrOH Modelling Methodology as defined in Chapters 4 and 5. Frontline staff were interviewed who work on station platforms and on trains, as well as those in signalling, media and ticketing, as well as staff from other key stakeholders such as Network Rail, the Office for Road and Rail (ORR), British Transport Police (BTP), etcetera. A strategic level PrOH Model was created from this data and socialised around different parts of the company. The storyboard for this PrOH Model is given in Figures 8.1–8.5; it was presented to the senior management board of this TOC, who discussed it at great length and set in motion a series of intervention-based actions relating to its systemic success factors for change. The most innovative of which was to commission the design, construction and use of a serious learning game to gamify learning within the PIDD process for frontline staff. Furthermore, to show passengers benefited from this, as demonstrated in passenger feedback surveys.

Innovations

Interventions based on action research in this case took many forms but perhaps the most innovative was the conceptualisation, construction, implementation and use of a training board game that embedded the systemic knowledge gained from the PrOH Modelling in a board game with an interactive video which was designed for use by the TOC's training department in regular staff training events. Since adoption, the Rail Disruption Game has been used with hundreds of frontline staff over many years.

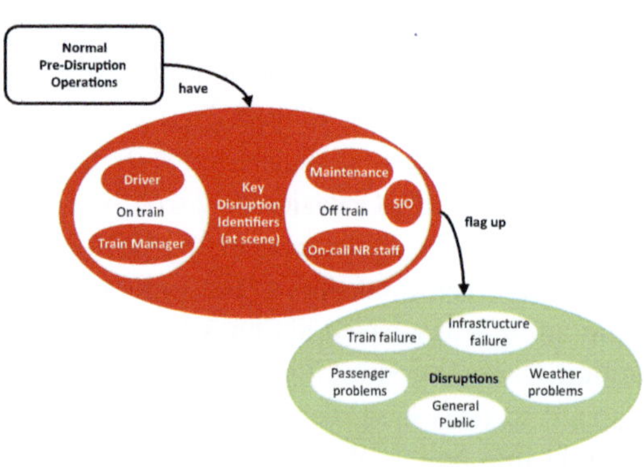

- Seems to be no formal decision-making forum for bringing together 'at scene identifiers' with 'disruption solvers'. Perhaps need to make duty control managers more informed using a many-to-many open communication channel.
- A better ability to send, track and record messages between 'identifiers' and 'resolvers'. A GSM-R phone would be useful (particularly hands free similar to airline pilots).
- Remote logging on to engines by drivers (e.g. as used by other TOCs) would facilitate knowing which trains drivers were on, and which cabs they are in.

FIGURE 8.1 Scene 1 – Disruption Solvers (Duty Control Managers) Make Recovery Plans – with SSFs.

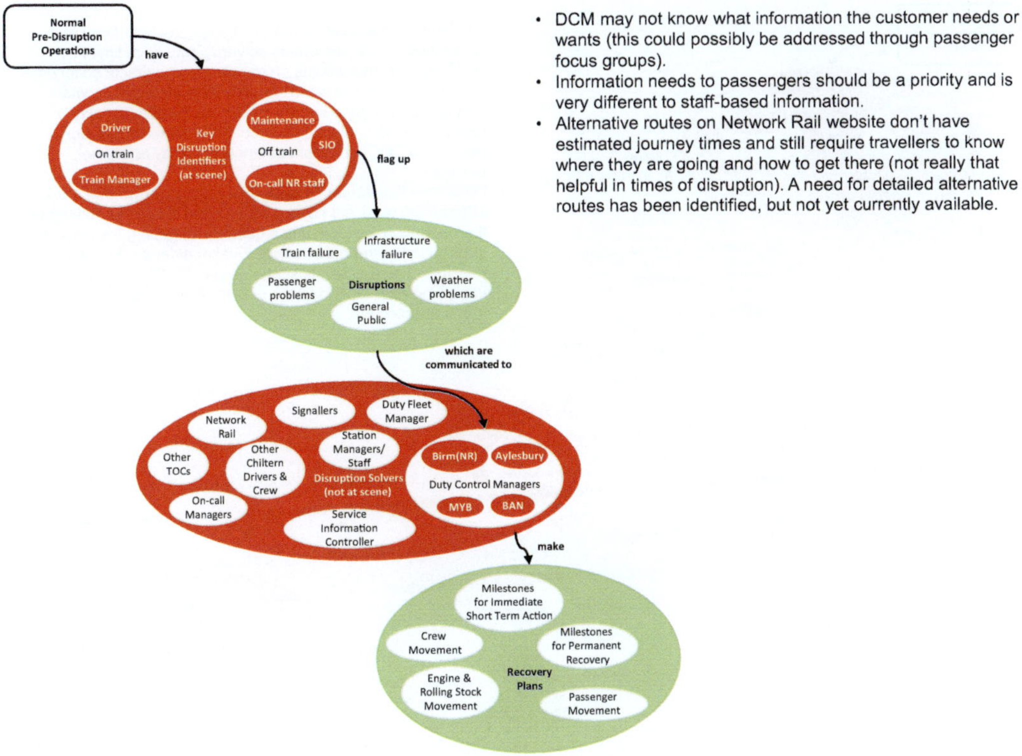

FIGURE 8.2 Scene 2 – Disruption Solvers (Duty Control Managers) Make Recovery Plans – with SSFs.

This game involves groups of staff working through rail disruption scenarios stage by stage to deal with typical questions from different types of passengers throughout an unfolding disruption; this is facilitated by pictures and data on a digital tablet. Several disruption scenarios were drawn as timelines: tunnel fire, landslide, breakdown, points failure, fatalities and power failures. Players are provided with partial information, which may change and be contradictory, representing experiences in a real disruption.

The Rail Disruption Game is challenging to play because players, the frontline staff, must work together to beat the clock and give passengers good quality answers to their questions, within a timed constraint, based on what is known about the disruption at a given time in a chosen scenario. Players must work together to give the best possible advice to customers. The board game embodies systemic success factors from the PrOH Modelling. Further details of how the game was conceived, designed and tested and implemented are detailed in Clegg et al. (2023a). The Rail Disruption Game is pictured in Figure 8.6. The rail disruption game became part of the PIDD process for reflection, learning and improvement for the rail operator's frontline staff.

Over a six-month period of use, the Rail Disruption Game generated 199 PIDD process improvement ideas. This compared to 34 ideas being produced in a previous six-month period using the original non-gamified PIDD management process involving approximately 800 employees, resulting in a 165-fold increase in improvement suggestions per full-time

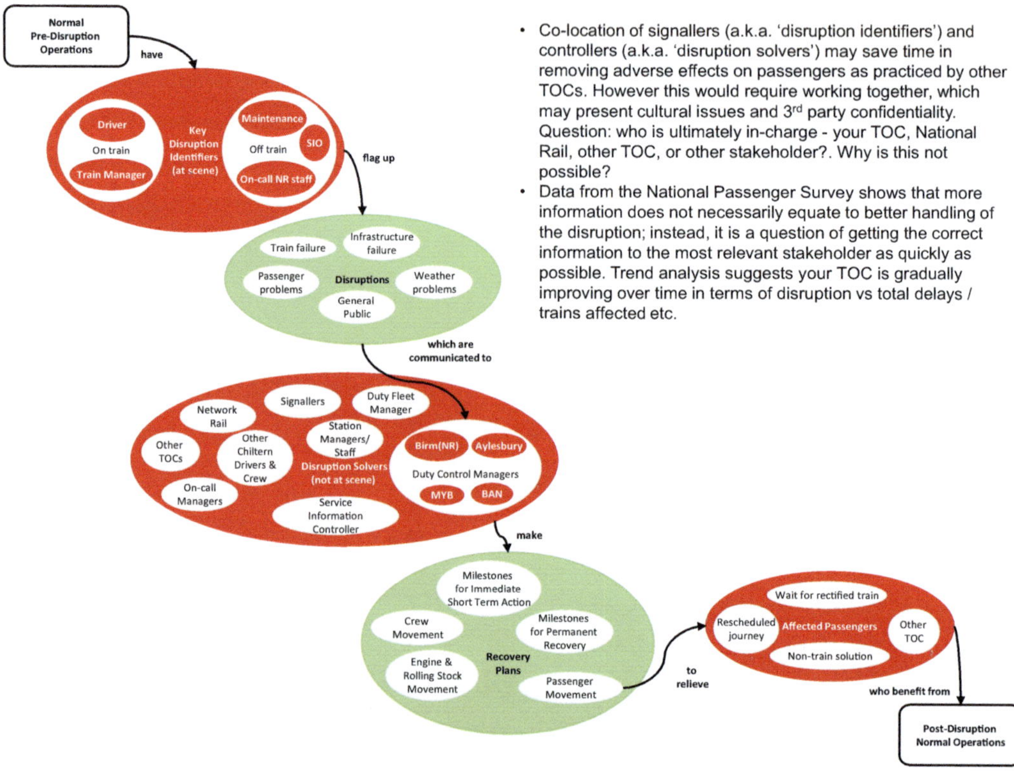

FIGURE 8.3 Scene 3 – Disruption Solvers (Duty Control Managers) Make Recovery Plans – with SSFs.

equivalent (FTE) employee over the same timeframe. This fact was acknowledged to be an astonishing achievement by the TOCs management team, who attributed it to the increased engagement of frontline staff in PIDD process training achieved by using the Rail Disruption Game. The authors of this book believe validation of the Rail Disruption Game's success, as the ultimate objective of this research, was to improve the PIDD management process. For this to happen, PIDD improvement suggestions had to come from PIDD managers: in other words, those who work in PIDD management daily and are responsible for sustained change. The massive increase in the number of suggestions came through increased *engageability* of staff and staff-to-staff *knowledge transfer* during the game – which did not previously happen before this game was implemented. In turn, the cause of this was better feedback in passenger satisfaction surveys held soon afterward.

Theoretical Considerations

This case presents the implementation and evaluation of the Rail Disruption Game. The aim of the case was to improve the management of passenger information during disruption (PIDD) via a safe and controlled environment, which became a gamified process by embedding a serious game (Orme et al., 2017) into it as a process improvement idea-generating instrument. This research suggests that through PrOH Modelling, serious games, founded on pedagogical

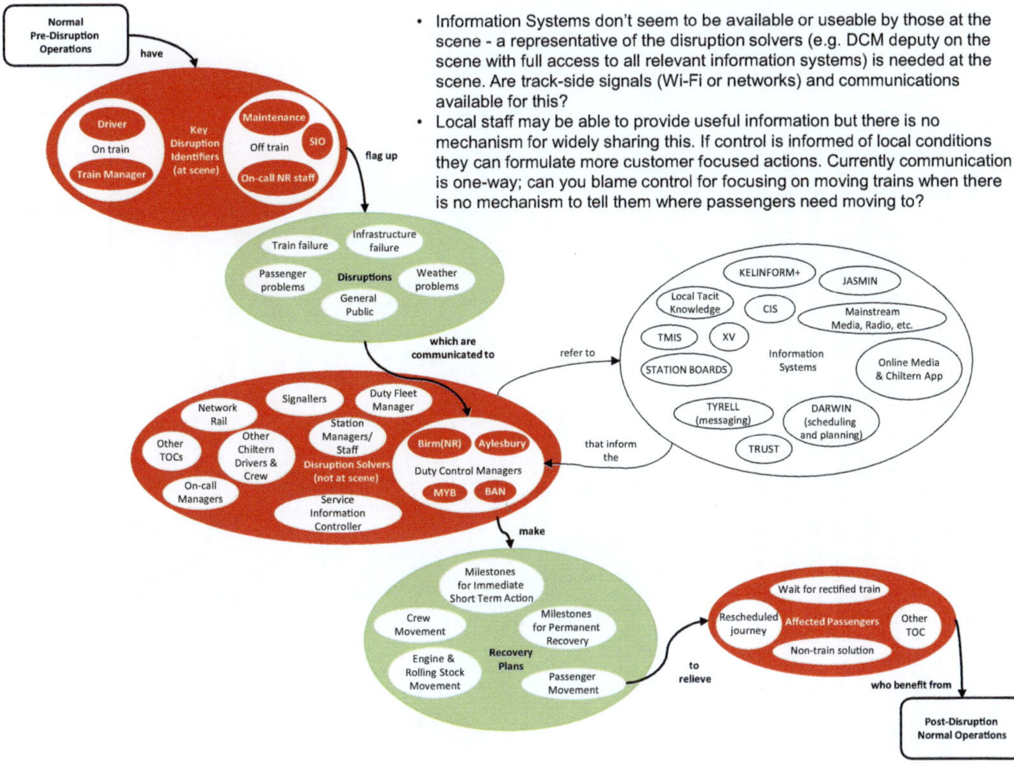

FIGURE 8.4 Scene 4 – Disruption Solvers (Duty Control Managers) Make Recovery Plans – with SSFs.

goals and the appropriate use of game mechanics and gamified processes, can be designed which engage, motivate, transfer knowledge and influence the behaviours of their users. This followed the SECI (Socialisation – Externalisation – Combination and Internalisation) cycle (Nonaka et al., 2000) to bring about the gamification of operational processes using this "serious game" for managers by **gamifying** learning.

Therefore, this case has abducted its findings to learning frameworks that help build serious games and gamify learning processes, especially to help

- develop mechanisms by which participants learned from the game given the nature of the PIDD scenario and how knowledge could be spread from one player's knowledge across the whole player cohort;
- maximise benefits gained by sharing tacit knowledge in risk-free discussions of PIDD scenarios in a non-confrontational game environment;
- generate systemic understanding of specific, representative and frequently occurring PIDD scenarios with non-player "avatars" representing a typology of different passengers;
- develop a game board and mechanisms capable of realistically representing the chosen scenario that is mobile and can be easily played in a railway station;

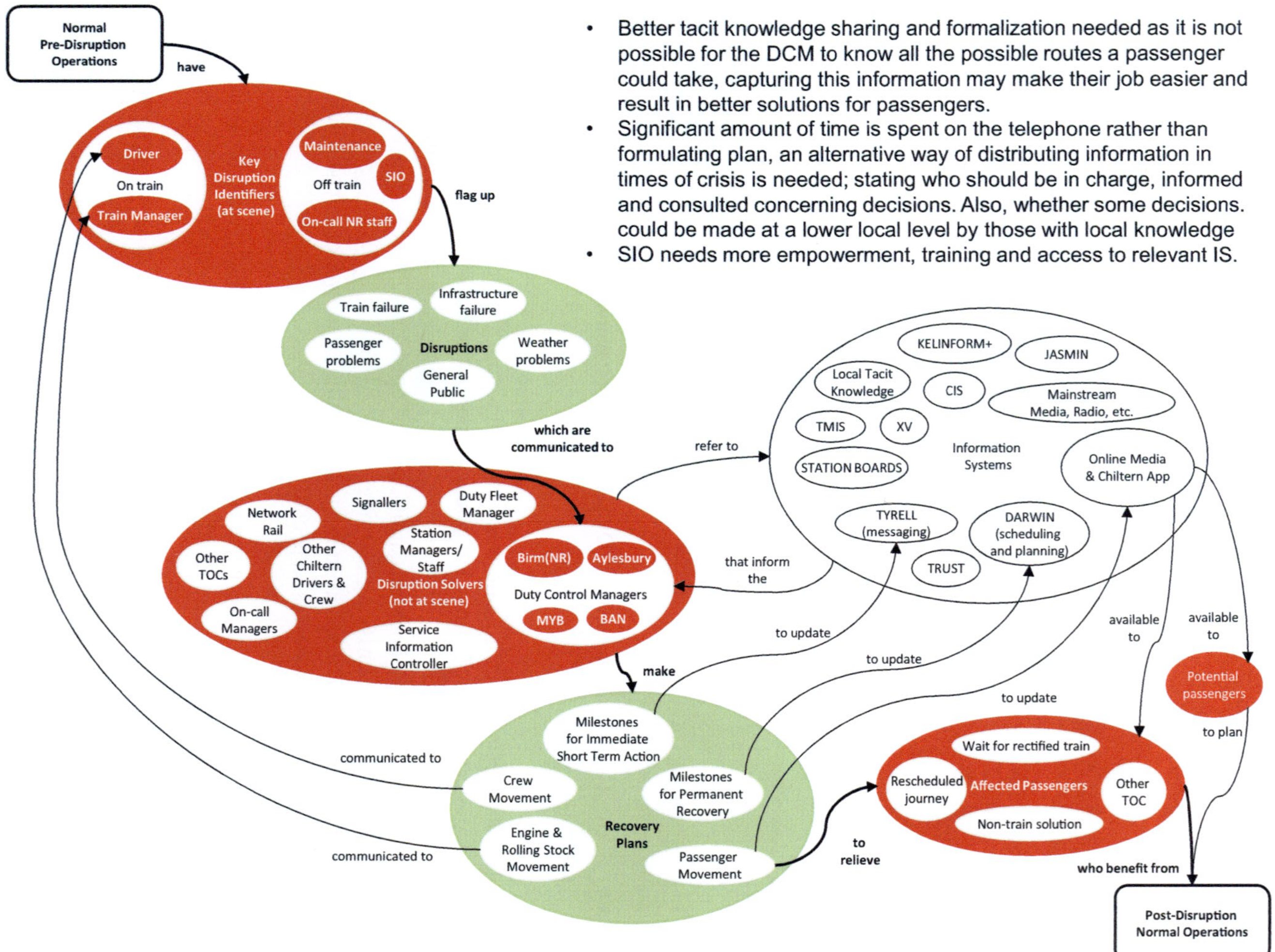

FIGURE 8.5 Scene 5 – Complete – Disruption Solvers (Duty Control Managers) Make Recovery Plans – with SSFs.

FIGURE 8.6 The Rail Disruption Game.

- instigate actions with supervisory management, social media teams, customer service as outcomes of gameplay;
- management and frontline staff get better insight into both the rail network and local interactions that are characteristic of PIDD scenarios;
- prompt discussion relevant to identified learning objectives;
- identify and recruit a facilitator to manage the game, or for players to self-facilitate; and
- design and conduct test runs of the game with the project team and subject matter experts to establish game playability and potential to stimulate desirable discussion.

The above frameworks were combined with relevant knowledge from other educational game developers (Fripp, 1993) and generic lessons taken from *a priori* frameworks on Mitigation, Planning, Reaction and Recovery (MPRR) endorsed by the Federal Emergency Management Agency (FEMA) and are used by the USA's Homeland Security to deal with disasters (Drabek, 1996; Fischer, 1998) – although rail disruptions are often less severe than disasters the disasters FEMA's MPRR was designed for, see Clegg et al, (2018) for further details.

Methodological Considerations

This case advocates that if serious game designers were able to apply increasingly user-centred design principles, as stated above, they could develop more purposeful games. One might think of this as action research, or intervention based research (IBR), where methods (M), theories (T) and problem situations (S) (e.g. ineffective PIDD management) are addressed simultaneously (Chandrasekaran et al., 2020); where moving "S" to state "S′" (S delta) as first envisaged at the onset of a project may not be the best route to proceed along, but something different such as "S*".

The authors of this book therefore demonstrate that "M" has been changed (revised NPD methodology for serious games and gamification (see Clegg et al., 2023a), and there are lessons learned on effective socialisation, externalisation, combination and internalisation of dynamic knowledge "T" (Nonaka et al., 2000), and the PIDD management process has improved from "S" (poor process) to "S′" (recognition of some kind of learning capability) to "S*" (a serious board game and gamified process) (Orme et al., 2017; Clegg et al., 2018).

Summary

As a result of this systems thinking and action research, many frontline staff became aware of how to resolve disruptions more quickly and with greater customer satisfaction, as discussed below. The Rail Disruption Game was awarded "highly commended" at the 2017 EurOMA conference (Orme et al., 2017) for teaching innovation, and papers based on it have been published in an academic journal (Clegg et al., 2018) and industry conferences focusing on the benefits of PrOH Modelling for helping to develop serious games in the context of gamified training and process improvement processes. For TOCs, the PrOH Modelling Methodology and the Rail Disruption Game have helped frontline staff to develop better heuristic decision making, perform better reviews of analysis, have more effective standard operating procedures (SOPs), engage staff in ongoing development, scan for new technology and develop more effective customer information channels to make better use of PIDD. Gamified learning was able to help in all stages of MPRR once the high-level systemic success factors were understood.

Further Reading

Clegg, B., Orme, R., and Petridis, P. (2023a), 'Developing a Serious Game for Rail Services: Improving Passenger Information During Disruption', *Information*, Vol. 14, Iss. 8, p. 464. https://doi.org/10.3390/info14080464

9

CASE 4: GMRDSL HOLARCHY OF PROH MODELS – ENRICHMENT FROM STRATEGIC LEVEL TO TACTICAL LEVEL

Part 2

Background Context

This chapter presents Part 2 of the GMRDSL action research case (see Chapter 6 for Part 1); it gives an overview of its set of models and shows how the **enrichment** of PrOH Models is done, going from a high strategic level into a lower tactical level. It builds on lessons from previous cases. It is essential that Part 1 of the GMRDSL case is read and understood before reading Part 2 of the GMRDSL case.

Figure 9.1 shows the holarchical set of PrOH Models for GMRDSL. The top-level strategic model is "The Factory", where inputs (potential order intake) are received from other business units (BUs) and outputs (assembled units) go to the end customer. Phases in the system of change for the "Factory" were identified as: "Order Intake", "Set-Up and Planning", "Manufacture" and "Order Completion".

The "Order Intake" tactical level phase was further enriched into "Estimating", "Quoting", "Customer Response" sub-phases at the operational level. **Dummy phases** can be used for phases that sit outside the system under observation but are still significant; for instance, a supplier's activities responding to an invitation to tender. The "Set-Up and Planning" tactical phase was further enriched into "Generate MMR" and "Generate MRP" sub-phases at the operational level. The "Manufacturing" tactical phase was further enriched into "Tooling, Purchasing and Loading" sub-phases at the operational level. And the "Order Completion" tactical phase was further enriched into "inspection and despatch", "customer response", "post-delivery" sub-phases at the operational level (Clegg et al., 1996a; Clegg et al, 1996b).

Enrichment of a top-level model can be done when a good understanding of it has been achieved and phases become conceivable by the PrOH Modeller using a **Process Matrix** that is used to list who does what in which phase of the system. At this point, it is not necessary to define logical dependencies within each phase. For GMRDSL, the **process matrix** for tactical phases that have been defined from the strategic PrOH Model seen in Chapter 6 (GMRDSL Part 1) is given in Table 9.1.

DOI: 10.4324/9781032650425-12

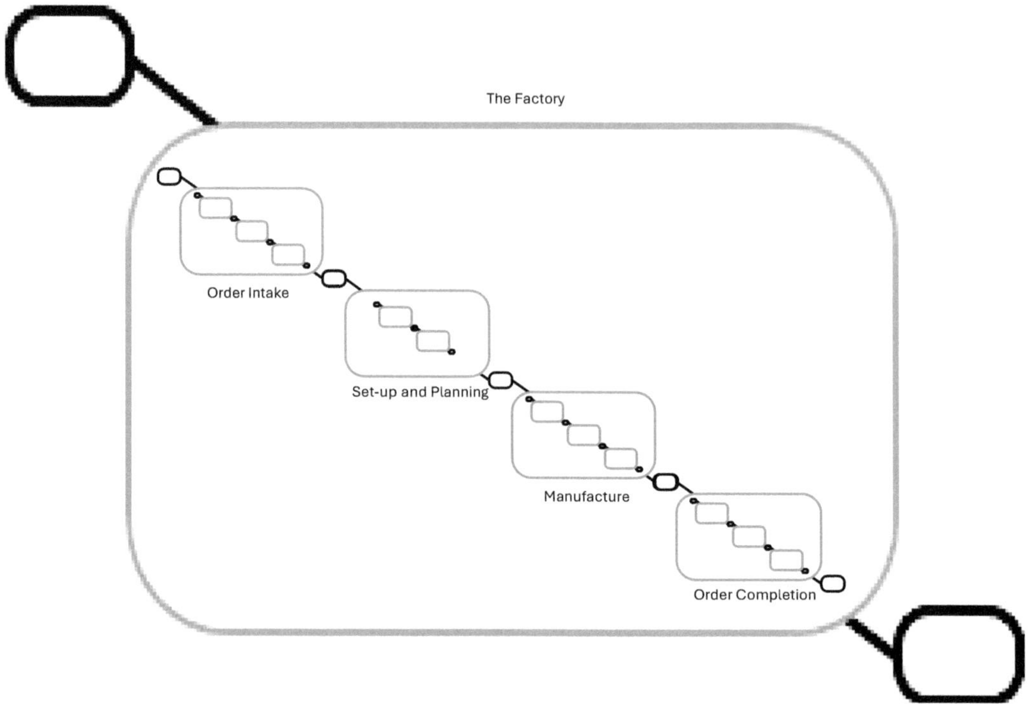

FIGURE 9.1 The Holarchy for the Set of PrOH Models for GMRDSL.

Modelling – Process Matrix, SIPOC Table and PrOH Models for Phases of Tactical Change

A **Process Matrix** helps a PrOH Modeller to think about who (agents: individual people or departments) does what in which phase of process change without having to think about the logical order of what is being done. Phases are based on the core process statement from the higher-level system; this helps the PrOH Modeller to go from a high and relatively superficial strategic level of understanding to a deeper tactical level of understanding, giving the potential to produce **enriched** PrOH Models.

From a completed **Process Matrix** (Table 9.1), the core process statements can then be formulated for each phase in a PrOH Model **SIPOC Table**. Value is created for the PrOH Modeller by going from the **Process Matrix**, which is a list of tasks done by agents without any logical dependencies, into a more carefully defined **SIPOC Table** that has logical dependencies (…inputs-activity-output/input-activity-output…) defined between each agent-task and input and output.

The purpose of Part 2 of the GMRDSL case study is therefore to show how **enrichment** happens in practice as described in Chapter 5. To this end, the SIPOC Table for each process change phase in the factory has been given, and the complete PrOH Model for each factory phase is given. In addition, even though the storyboard for each PrOH Model is not given as this would make this case too long, the Systemic Success Factors (SSFs) for change for each tactical phase PrOH Model are given. Modelling nuances for each factory phase are also discussed.

TABLE 9.1 Process Matrix for MRDSL Phase Matrix

NAME OF PROCESS PHASE	*Order Intake*	*Set-Up and Planning*	*Manufacture*	*Order Completion*
INPUTS	RFQ & bid data pack (LEO/SERPHA drawings, build state and mod. State, contract terms and conditions, bill of materials)	Purchase order & data pack (official order, LEO/SERPHA drawings, build state, contract terms & conditions, bill of materials)	MMR	Items ready for shipment
	ITP	Electronic spares requisition slip and build state received on Q&A database	MRP ECO	
AGENTS	**ACTIVITIES**	**ACTIVITIES**	**ACTIVITIES**	**ACTIVITIES**
Customer	* Issued ITP Supplied bid pack Receives bid to accept/reject	* Accepted bid and issued purchase order Supplied purchase order data pack	* May request contractual and design (ECR's, DSI's, CRI's) changes * Uses PM as a point of contact * May receive stage invoices * Must authorise design amendments * May inspect WIP	* Receive Finished Goods and Documentation * Signs and returns Consignment note * Receive final invoice
Contracts Department	* Initiates purchase order Sep-up and planning phase * Negotiate and indicate intention to bid * Review Bid Document * Advise on terms and conditions and possible stage payment plan	* Are recipients of purchase order ready * Vet contractual aspects and price of the purchase order against document * Negotiate contract amendments	* Negotiate contract amendments	* Raise purchase order/contract closure advice

TABLE 9.1 (Continued)

NAME OF PROCESS PHASE	*Order Intake*	*Set-Up and Planning*	*Manufacture*	*Order Completion*
Bid Manager	* Compiles bid * Requests estimates	* Is usually appointed as or will hand over to a Project Manager	*	*
Operations Department	* Analyse tooling and test requirements * Provide manufacturing time and cost estimates * Recommends provisional make versus buy decision	* Verifies manufacturing content of contract * Makes batching decision * Plan materiel allocation * Advises on MRP and technical content	* May raise manufacturing queries: ECRs, DSI's, * May request engineering support from customer * Carry out manufacture as defined in the MMR and related MECCA route cards/tags and as scheduled in the MRP * Refer to LEO drawing database and drawing database and drawings for manufacture detail	* Rework items that have failed final test
	*	*	* Re-work items that have failed test and inspection Embody design changes * Obtain kit detailed in MECCA route cards/TAGS from stores * Review progress in "sunrise meetings" * Submit items for tests and inspection Raise Advice of Delivery (AoD)	*
	*	*	* Reschedule as directed by PM to reduce critical path	*

(Continued)

TABLE 9.1 (Continued)

NAME OF PROCESS PHASE	*Order Intake*	*Set-Up and Planning*	*Manufacture*	*Order Completion*
Estimating Department	* Produce time and cost estimates in response to RFQ for commodities and manufacturing * Use Supercapes database to extract some price estimates * Request purchasing to obtain quotations for high value (T6) purchased/sub-contracted items	*	* Estimate any contract amendments	*
Purchasing Department	* Obtain quotations for high value (T6) purchased/subcontracted items	*	* Project procurement liaises with subcontractors obtaining three competitive quotes * Re-use estimates wherever possible * Pass prime contract terms and conditions down to sub-contractor * Expedite deliveries	*
Finance (NP)	* Provide overhead costs and labour rates * obtain from accounts order book turnover, claims and sales information recorded on SAWS database	*	* Obtain from accounts order book, turnover, claims and sales information recorded on SAWS database * Invoices customer	* Obtain from accounts order book, turnover, claims and sales information recorded on SAWS database * Invoices customer

(Continued)

TABLE 9.1 (Continued)

NAME OF PROCESS PHASE	*Order Intake*	*Set-Up and Planning*	*Manufacture*	*Order Completion*
Customer (Chelmsford Spares Department)	*	* Supply works requisition slip on Q&Q database	(see customer)	(see customer)
Programme Manager	*	* Organises order receipt/ start-up meeting * Request the MRP ECO report to be produced Requests the MECCA MMR to be produced * Issues purchasing requisitions * Bases the project plan on the MRP ECO report * Places actions to reduce critical path	* May request the CPR team to recommend critical path reductions * Places actions to reduce critical path * Uses a Q&A database to monitor contract plan changes * Main point of liaison with customer * Apply for MoD modification Kits on 714/715 products	* Apply for NSN * Complete required drawings * Ensure final cost claim is made * Request SPIS packing * Define completed build standard and declare as mod. Strike 0.
	*	* May request the CPR team to recommend Critical Path Reductions * Instructs Accounts to set-up MARCAS cost structure & budget * Main point of liaison with customer	* Use MECCA to monitor manufacture and purchasing progress of shop floor * Authorises expenditure for design changes	*
Configuration Department	*	* Manually load MRP system with MECCA data to produce a provisional schedule loading the shop floor * Cross check part identifies	* Use Q&A database for monitoring part identity changes * Produce MECCA tags/route cards and Missed Planning Report * Record all design changes	* Define final build standard

(Continued)

TABLE 9.1 (Continued)

NAME OF PROCESS PHASE	*Order Intake*	*Set-Up and Planning*	*Manufacture*	*Order Completion*
Quality Department	*	* Actioned to produce Quality plan * Attend project start-up reviews	* Authorise minor manufacturing concessions * Liaise with design authority for major concession * For MoD raise Form 77	* Authorise C of C's and 640's
CPR Team	*	* May attend project start-up meeting * Simulate potential critical path reductions on MRP schedule * Recommend critical path reductions to PM * Recommend MECCA data to be updated if improvements found	* Simulate potential critical path reductions on MRP schedule * Recommend critical path reductions to PM * Expedites actions for PM * Recommend MECCA data to be updated if improvements found	*
Spares Cell Manager	* Laise with Chelmsford BU	* Receives Q&A requisition slip directly from Chelmsford, data pack not required * Same as Programme Manager	(see Programme Manager)	(see Programme Manager)
Test and Inspection	*	*	* Inspection and test as Integral part of manufacture schedule * Performed special conditioned tests	* Build standard inspection

(*Continued*)

TABLE 9.1 (Continued)

NAME OF PROCESS PHASE	*Order Intake*	*Set-Up and Planning*	*Manufacture*	*Order Completion*
Dispatch Department	*	*	*	* Receipt of AoD signifies a shipment is ready to arrange transportation * Raise 640s for MoD purchase orders, and raise C of Cs, consignment note for all contracts given to PM
Accounts	*	* Set-up cost structure on MarCAS detailed in MMR * Produce local PMR, Site PMR and UBR packs	* Administrative project cost and budget on to MarCAS * Produce local PMR, site PMR and UBR packs	* Close project budget when CCA is received * Produce cost certificates when required
Directors	* Authorise high value bids	*	*	*
Stores	*	*	* Deliveries recorded on MECCA issue item to operations recorded on MECCA	*
AGENTS	**ACTIVITIES**	**ACTIVITIES**	**ACTIVITIES**	**ACTIVITIES**
Outputs	Purchase Order (and Data Pack)	MMR	Shippable Items	Dispatched Items
	*	MRP ECO	*	Dispatch Documentation

Order Intake Phase

Table 9.2 shows the **SIPOC Table** for the tactical order intake phase. The **core process statement** is given on the top line of the **SIPOC Table** that defines the focus of the system for change for how the project manager receives Requests for Quotations (RFQs) and aims to solicit Contractual Documents (Purchase Order and data pack).

The rest of the lines in the SIPOC Table in Table 9.2 describe the logical dependencies of activities in the real-world system under observation created from an amalgamation of interviews with stakeholders relating to the "Order Intake" process at GMRDSL.

Figure 9.2 gives the PrOH Model for "Order Intake". It follows the rules for enrichment given in Chapter 5 and the rules and guidelines for drawing a single PrOH Model given in Chapter 4. When presented to a group of stakeholders, it was shown in four scenes; the SSFs for each scene are stated.

Systemic Success Factors of Change: Order Intake

Scene 1 – core process statement:

- Project management functions duplicated at another (Chelmsford) business unit (BU) and at the SRL factory.
- At present enquiry turnaround takes four to eight weeks – it could be 50% quicker if Manufacturing Requirement Planning (MRP) was more accurate.
- Stop providing a full data pack with each request for quote (RFQ) as these take time and resources to produce; just define the build standard from the new bill of materials (LEO) database with the relevant engineering change requests (ECRs).
- BU should forewarn the factory that they have a manufacturing contract and when it will arrive.

Scene 2:

- The results of bidding decisions are not clearly promulgated (especially reasons for failure) to the factory.

Scene 3:

- Estimating and quoting functions are repeated at Frimley headquarters (London) and Chelmsford BUs.

Scene 4:

- Spare part production and repairs are also conducted at Frimley and Chelmsford BUs. The newly created manufacturing cell's advantages are that they (1) have a multidisciplinary

TABLE 9.2 SIPOC Table for "Order Intake" Phase

Supplier (agent and activity)	*Input*	*Agent*	*Activity*	*Output*	*Receiver (agent and activity)*
Customer (Chelmsford BU) (Other BU) specifies manufacturing requirement	**RFQ and data pack**	**project manager (programmes / bid dept) manager**	**negotiate to win the contractual documents (new PO/ SOW/ ITP), (PO/SOW amendment)**	**contractual documents (new PO/ SOW/ITP), (PO/SOW amendment)**	**Project (programmes / bid dept) (spares cell), (repairs cell) manager has responsibility to ensure the first MRP run (purchasing demands), (missed planning reports)**
SUO INPUT FROM CUSTOMER MANUFACTURING REQUIREMENT ENVIRONMENT: customer (Chelmsford BU) specifies manufacturing requirement	works requisition	project (spares cell), (repairs cell) managers	review the works requisition	accepted works requisition	**PHASE OUTPUT TO THE SET-UP AND PLANNING PHASE**: project (spares cell), (repairs cell) managers chairs a project start-up meeting
SUO INPUT FROM CUSTOMER MANUFACTURING REQUIREMENT ENVIRONMENT: customer (Other BU) specifies manufacturing requirement	RFQ and data pack	contracts dept (contracts manager), (contracts officer)	makes a bid decision (bid), (no bid)	OR: bid decision (bid)	contracts dept (contracts manager), (contracts officer) produces a customer advice note
					contracts dept (contracts manager), (contracts officer) will make an order forecast

(Continued)

TABLE 9.2 (Continued)

Supplier (agent and activity)	*Input*	*Agent*	*Activity*	*Output*	*Receiver (agent and activity)*
					project (programmes / bid dept) manager will sanction the estimate request
				OR: bid decision (no bid)	contracts dept (contracts manager), (contracts officer) produces a customer advice note
contracts department (contracts manager), (contracts officer)makes a bid decision (bid), (no bid)	bid decision (bid)	contracts dept (contracts manager), (contracts officer)	produces a customer advice note	customer advice note	customer becomes aware of the bidding decision
	bid decision (no bid)				
contracts dept (contracts manager), (contracts officer) produces a customer advice note	customer advice note	customer	becomes aware of the bidding decision	customer advice note	NO FURTHER ACTION
contracts department (contracts manager), (contracts officer) makes a bid decision (bid), (no bid)	bid decision (bid)	contracts dept (contracts manager), (contracts officer)	will make an order forecast	order forecast	finance dept (NP) calculate financial data (company order book), (overhead figures)
contracts dept (contracts manager), (contracts officer) will make an order forecast	order forecast	finance dept (NP)	calculate financial data (company order book), (overhead figures)	financial data (company order book), (overhead figures)	contracts dept (contracts manager), (contracts officer) work up the customer selling price

(Continued)

TABLE 9.2 (Continued)

Supplier (agent and activity)	*Input*	*Agent*	*Activity*	*Output*	*Receiver (agent and activity)*
contracts department (contracts manager), (contracts officer) makes a bid decision (bid), (no bid)	bid decision (bid)	project (programmes /bid dept) manager	will sanction the estimate request	estimate request	estimating dept (estimator) identify T6 outsourced items
					estimating dept (estimator) identify test estimate elements
					estimating dept (estimator) produce elements of and compile estimate (time and cost)
project (programmes / bid dept) manager will sanction the estimate request	estimate request	estimating dept (estimator)	identify T6 outsourced items	T6 outsourced items list	purchasing dept produce T6 purchase quotations
project (programmes / bid dept) manager will sanction the estimate request	estimate request	estimating dept (estimator)	identify test estimate elements	test estimate elements	test engineering define test requirements
project (programmes / bid dept) manager will sanction the estimate request	estimate request				
estimating dept (estimator) identify test estimate elements	test estimate elements	test engineering	define test requirements	tooling and test requirements	test engineering work up test estimates

(*Continued*)

TABLE 9.2 (Continued)

Supplier (agent and activity)	*Input*	*Agent*	*Activity*	*Output*	*Receiver (agent and activity)*
test engineering define test requirements	tooling and test requirements	test engineering	work up test estimates	(test estimates)	estimating dept (estimator) produce elements of and compile estimate (time and cost)
estimating dept (estimator) identify T6 outsourced items	T6 outsourced items list	purchasing dept	produce T6 purchase quotations	T6 purchase quotations	estimating dept (estimator) produce elements of and compile estimate (time and cost)
project (programmes / bid dept) manager will sanction the estimate request	estimate request	estimating dept (estimator)	produce elements of and compile estimate (time and cost)	estimate (test estimates)	contracts dept (contracts manager), (contracts officer) and project (programmes /bid dept) manager work up the authorised customer quotation (customer selling price)
purchasing dept produce T6 purchase quotations	T6 purchase quotations				
test engineering work up test estimates	(test estimates)				

(*Continued*)

TABLE 9.2 (Continued)

Supplier (agent and activity)	*Input*	*Agent*	*Activity*	*Output*	*Receiver (agent and activity)*
estimating dept (estimator) produce elements of and compile estimate (time and cost)	estimate (test estimates)	contracts dept (contracts manager), (contracts officer) and project (programmes / bid dept) manager	work up the authorised customer quotation (customer selling price)	authorised customer quotation (customer selling price)	contracts dept (contracts manager), (contracts officer) and project (programmes /bid dept) manager may need to negotiate with the customer to obtain contractual documents (new PO/SOW/ITP), (PO/ SOW amendment)
finance dept (NP) calculate financial data (company order book), (overhead figures)	financial data (company order book), (overhead figures)				
contracts dept (contracts manager), (contracts officer) and project (programmes /bid dept) manager work up the authorised customer quotation (customer selling price)	authorised customer quotation (customer selling price)	contracts dept (contracts manager), (contracts officer) and project (programmes / bid dept) manager	may need to negotiate with the customer to obtain contractual documents (New PO/SOW/ ITP), (PO/SOW amendment)	contractual documents (new PO/SOW/ ITP), (PO/SOW amendment)	**PHASE OUTPUT TO THE SET-UP AND PLANNING PHASE**: contracts dept (contracts manager), (contracts officer) vet documents (new PO/SOW/ITP), (PO/ SOW amendment) and record details in received order advice

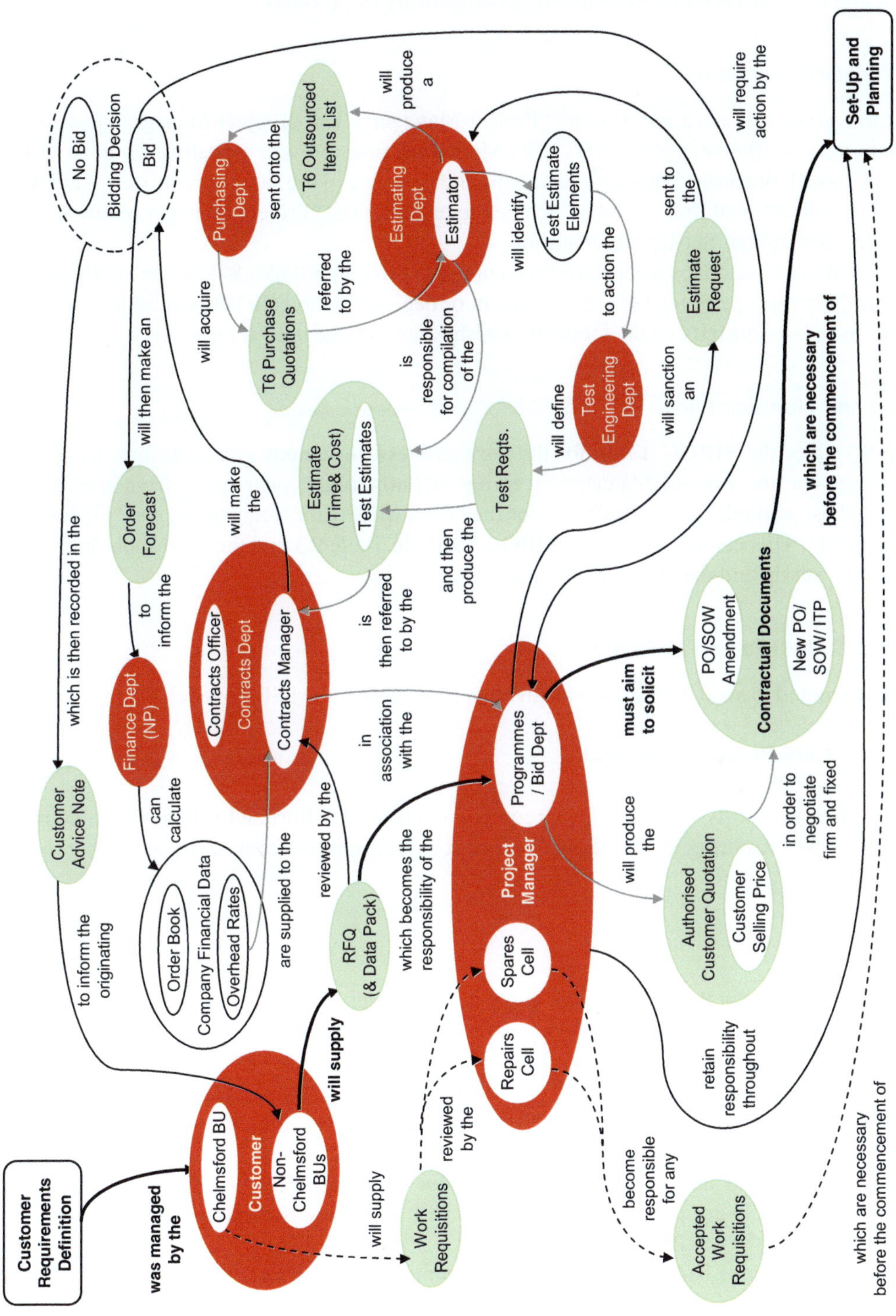

FIGURE 9.2 PrOH Model of "Order Intake" Phase – System for Change.

dedicated team, (2) reduce prioritising conflicts on the factory shop floor, (3) quick through-put and (4) have better ownership and accountability of products.

PrOH Modelling Nuances

- In this phase the main agent is the "Project Manager". The "Project Manager" is also the main agent in the next phase. As PrOH Modelling rules prevent repeating a bubble in the same model, the project manager cannot be shown twice in the same core process statement and so a directional link has been included to explain this. "Project Manager retain responsibility throughout Set-Up and Planning"
- There are two instances where two green tangible artefact bubbles follow one another without a different type of bubble (e.g., red agent or decision bubble) in between; this is inadvisable as the **systemicity** of the model diminishes but may be used if necessary.

Set-up and Planning Phase

Table 9.3 gives the **SIPOC Table** for the **core process statement** that describes the system for change for the Project Manager receiving "Contractual Documents" from the "Order Intake" phase and taking responsibility for the "First MRP Run" required by the "Operations Department". This can be seen in the **SIPOC Table** in Table 9.3 and the corresponding PrOH Model for "set-up and planning" is in Figure 9.3.

Systemic Success Factors of Change

When presented to stakeholders, it was given in four scenes; the SSFs for each scene are given.

Scene 1 – Core Process Statement

- The MRP system is very inflexible, requires much set-up effort and is believed to be inaccurate, often resulting in "stock-outs". More accuracy and less complexity are required.

Scene 2:

- Variances between the estimate, the quote and the order are checked for consistency by the contacts department, which should be unnecessary and needs to stop.

Scene 3:

- The MRP system that generates the MMR does not have reliable lead time, and many "dummy" details are put in to make it run. Bill of materials needs to be simplified and interface with the MRP.
- Batching decisions had not been made at the time of the estimate, which affects lead time and cost. Price breaks need to be given linked to batching or standard costs used for estimate and manufacture.

TABLE 9.3 Set-up and Planning Phase SIPOC Table

Supplier (agent and activity)	*Input*	*Agent*	*Activity*	*Output*	*Receiver (agent and activity)*
Project Manager (programmes/ bid dept) manager negotiates to win the contractual documents (new PO/ SOW/ITP), (PO/SOW amendment)	**contractual documents (new PO/ SOW/ITP), (PO/SOW amendment)**	**Project Manager (programmes/ bid dept), (spares cell), (repairs cell) manager**	**has responsibility to ensure the first MRP run (purchasing demands), (missed planning reports)**	**first MRP run (purchasing demands), (missed planning reports)**	**Operations Dept (production engineer), (team leader), (shop floor operatives), (materials planning manager) completes manufacture with assembled units and completed route cards**
PHASE INPUT FROM THE ORDER INTAKE PHASE MODEL: programmes (bid) dept manager may need to negotiate with the customer to obtain contractual documents (New PO/ SOW/ITP), (PO/SOW amendment)	contractual documents (new PO/SOW/ ITP), (PO/SOW amendment)	contracts dept (contracts manager), (contracts officer)	vet contractual documents (new PO/SOW/ ITP), (PO/SOW amendment) and record details in received order advice	amendments (CSP), (ECR's / CRI's)	contracts dept (contracts manager) and customer agree amendment type (CSP), (ECR/CRI's)
				received order advice	project (programmes dept) manager
contracts dept (contracts manager), (contracts officer) vet contractual documents (new PO/ SOW/ITP), (PO/ SOW amendment) and record details in received order advice	amendments (CSP), (ECR's / CRI's)	contracts dept (contracts manager) and customer	agree amendment type (CSP), (ECR/ CRI's)	received order advice	project (programmes dept) manager chairs a project start-up meeting

(*Continued*)

TABLE 9.3 (Continued)

Supplier (agent and activity)	*Input*	*Agent*	*Activity*	*Output*	*Receiver (agent and activity)*
contracts dept (contracts manager), (contracts officer) vet contractual documents (new PO/ SOW/ITP), (PO/ SOW amendment) and record details in received order advice	received order advice	project (programmes dept) manager	chairs a project start-up meeting	project start-up meeting	project (programmes dept) manager places project start-up actions
contracts dept (contracts manager) and customer agree amendment type (CSP), (ECR/CRI's)					
project (programmes dept) manager chairs a project start-up meeting	project start-up meeting	project (programmes dept), (spares cell), (repairs cell) manager	places project start-up actions	start-up actions (quality plan request)	quality dept draw up the manufacturing control documents (quality plan)
PHASE INPUT FROM THE ORDER INTAKE PHASE: project (spares cell), (repairs cell) managers review the works requisition	accepted works requisition			start-up actions (MMR request)	contracts dept (contracts officer) define the manufacturing control documents (MMR)

(*Continued*)

TABLE 9.3 (Continued)

Supplier (agent and activity)	*Input*	*Agent*	*Activity*	*Output*	*Receiver (agent and activity)*
project (programmes dept), (spares cell), (repairs cell) manager places project start-up actions	start-up actions (quality plan request)	quality dept	draw up the manufacturing control documents (quality plan)	manufacturing control documents (quality plan)	**PHASE OUTPUT TO THE MANUFACTURING PHASE**: operations dept (production engineer), (team leader), (shop floor operatives), (materials planning manager) reference manufacturing control documents (quality plan)
project (programmes dept), (spares cell), (repairs cell) manager places project start-up actions	start-up actions (MMR request)	contracts dept (contracts officer)	define the manufacturing control documents (MMR)	manufacturing control documents (MMR)	accounts dept load MarCAS (cost code structure)
					PHASE OUTPUT TO THE MANUFACTURING PHASE: operations dept (production engineer), (team leader), (shop floor operatives), (materials planning manager) reference manufacturing control documents (quality plan)
					MRP manager oversees production of manufacturing control documents (MRP EC0)

(Continued)

TABLE 9.3 (Continued)

Supplier (agent and activity)	*Input*	*Agent*	*Activity*	*Output*	*Receiver (agent and activity)*
contracts dept (contracts officer) define the MMR	MMR	accounts dept	load MarCAS (cost code structure)	MarCAS (cost code structure)	**PHASE OUTPUT TO THE MANUFACTURING PHASE**: accounts department produce PMR packs as required
contracts dept (contracts officer) define the MMR	MMR	MRP manager	oversees production of manufacturing control documents (MRP EC0)	manufacturing control documents (MRP EC0)	**PHASE OUTPUT TO THE MANUFACTURING PHASE**: operations dept (production engineer), (team leader), (shop floor operatives), (materials planning manager) reference manufacturing control documents (MRP EC0)
					project manager (programmes/ bid dept), (spares cell), (repairs cell) manager project manager sanctions the first MRP run (purchasing demands), (missed planning reports)
				lead-time reduction requirement	CPR team may produce a critical path report
MRP manager oversees production of manufacturing control documents (MRP EC0)	lead-time reduction requirement	CPR team	may produce a critical path report	manufacturing control documents (critical path report)	project manager (programmes/ bid dept), (spares cell), (repairs cell) manager project manager sanctions the first MRP run (purchasing demands), (missed planning reports)

(Continued)

TABLE 9.3 (Continued)

Supplier (agent and activity)	*Input*	*Agent*	*Activity*	*Output*	*Receiver (agent and activity)*
CPR team may produce a critical path report	manufacturing control documents (critical path report)	project manager (programmes/ bid dept), (spares cell), (repairs cell) manager	sanctions the first MRP run (purchasing demands), (missed planning reports)	first MRP run (purchasing demands)	**PHASE OUTPUT TO THE MANUFACTURING PHASE**: purchasing dept raise sub-purchase orders
MRP manager oversees production of manufacturing control documents (MRP EC0)	manufacturing control documents (MRP EC0)			first MRP run (missed planning reports)	**PHASE OUTPUT TO THE MANUFACTURING PHASE:** customer and the operations dept (production engineer), (team leader), (shop floor operatives), (materials planning manager) sorts out planning problems (modifications), (estimate queries), (DSI's), (test spec),

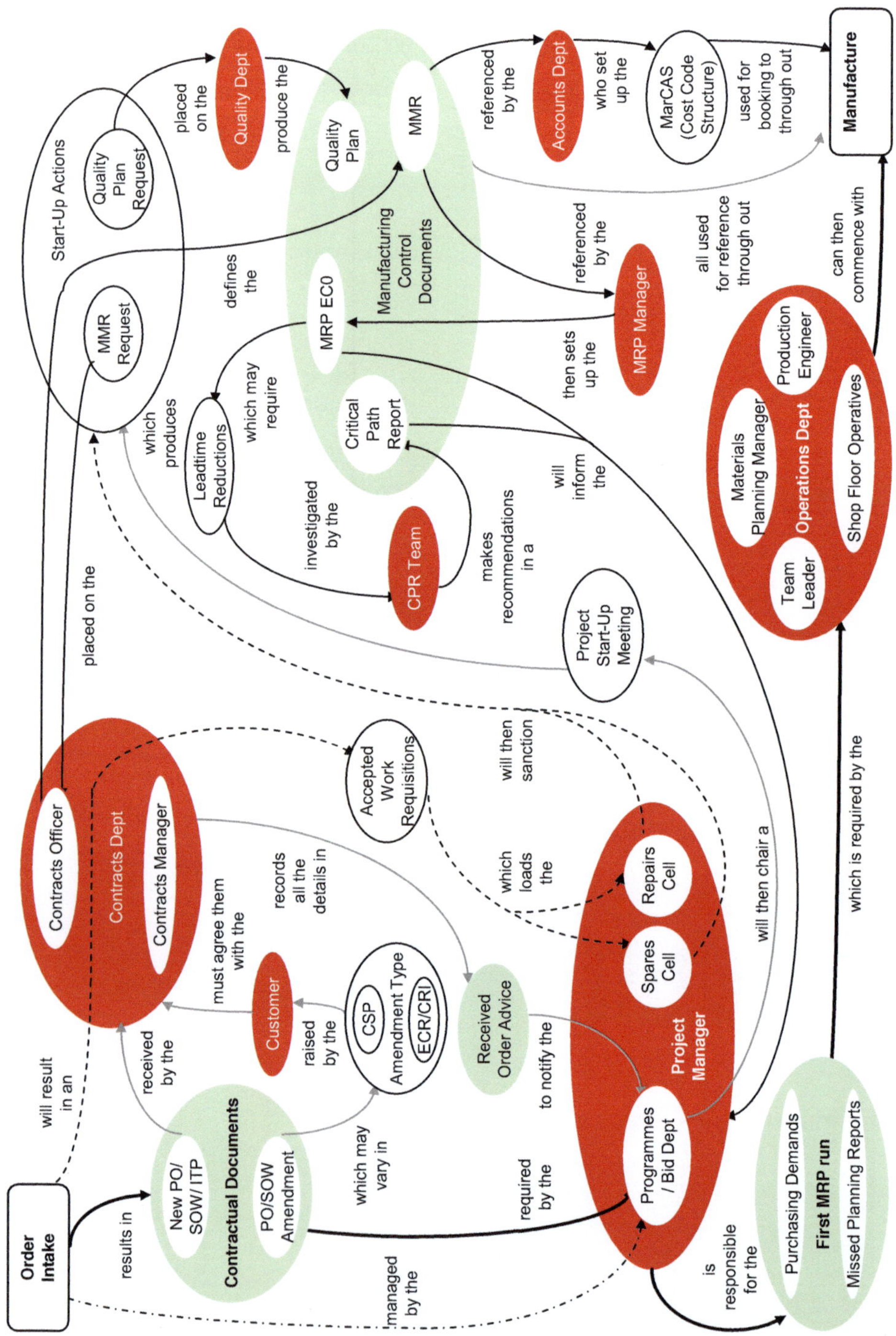

FIGURE 9.3 Set-Up and Planning Phase PrOH Model.

Scene 4:

- Multiple electronic databases that do not interface give multiple data entry. Need to eliminate standalone spreadsheet scheduling.

Modelling Nuances Explained

- The suppyling agent in the core process statement is the same as the main agent in this model, and so there are fewer bubbles in the core process statement. This is not best practice as each succeeding or proceeding phase should have a different most significant agent. However, sometimes this is not possible due to how phasing is defined. In this instance, bubbles are omitted and not repeated, which must be made clear in sentence description in the PrOH Model. For instance, "Order Intake managed by Programmes/Bid Department".
- Directional links have been shaded or dotted to make the PrOH Model to read.
- Red bubbles have been faded to white in the centre, which can make reading easier. These are the same as unfaded red bubbles.

GMRDSL Manufacture Phase

This phase describes the system of change for the manufacturing of GMRDSL's products (Radar Systems). The **SIPOC Table** for this tactical phase is given in Table 9.4 and its corresponding PrOH Model is given in Figure 9.4.

GMRDSL Manufacture Phase SSFs

The manufacture phase PrOH Model was presented to stakeholders in six scenes, the SSFs for each are given.

Scene 1 – core process statement

- The "spares cell" and the "repairs cell" were set-up to deal with high volume, low risk, low-cost manufacture independently from the main shop floor. They are to be an experiment to try out new process improvement initiatives before being implemented on the main shop floor.

Scene 2:

- Most manufacturing problems are caused by obsolescence in old designs and constantly changing customer requirements. Refits are given to new kit retrospectively; however, this practice must stop, and the correct build standard defined in the initial order.
- The control of "build standards" using "engineering change requests" (ECRs) is a critical success factor but not always used correctly. ECRs need to be reduced through better concurrent engineering, speeded up and better recorded.

TABLE 9.4 SIPOC Table for Manufacture Phase

Supplier (agent and activity)	*Input*	*Agent*	*Activity*	*Output*	*Receiver (agent and activity)*
Project Manager (programmes/bid dept) (spares cell), (repairs cell) has responsibility to ensure the first MRP run (purchasing demands), (missed planning reports)	**first MRP run (purchasing demands), (missed planning reports)**	**Operations Dept (production engineer), (team leader), (shop floor operatives), (materials planning manager)**	**completes manufacture with assembled units and completed route cards**	**assembled units with completed route cards**	**Project Manager (programmes/ bid dept) (spares cell), (repairs cell) closes out the project**
PHASE INPUT FROM THE SET-UP AND PLANNING PHASE: project manager (programmes/ bid dept), (spares cell), (repairs cell) manager project manager sanctions the first MRP run (purchasing demands), (missed planning reports)	first MRP run (purchasing demands)	purchasing dept	raise orders	orders	stored items (purchased parts)
purchasing dept raise sub-purchase orders	orders	suppliers	stored items (purchased parts)	stored items (purchased parts)	stores control stored items (purchased parts), (test equipment), (tooling) with MECCA

Supplier (agent and activity)	*Input*	*Agent*	*Activity*	*Output*	*Receiver (agent and activity)*
PHASE INPUT FROM THE SET-UP AND PLANNING PHASE: project manager (programmes/ bid dept), (spares cell), (repairs cell) manager project manager sanctions the first MRP run (purchasing demands), (missed planning reports)	first MRP run (missed planning reports)	operations dept (production engineer), (team leader), (shop floor operatives), (materials planning manager)	identifies planning problems (modifications), (estimate queries), (DSI's), (test spec),	planning problems (modifications), (estimate queries), (DSI's), (test spec),	customer and the operations dept (production engineer), (team leader), (shop floor operatives), (materials planning manager) solve planning problems (modifications), (estimate queries), (DSI's), (test spec),
FEEDBACK FROM: production testers declare assembled units with completed route cards	test results (fail)				
PHASE INPUT FEEDBACK FROM THE ORDER COMPLETION PHASE; quality dept conducts customer acceptance tests	customer acceptance tests (failures)				

Supplier (agent and activity)	*Input*	*Agent*	*Activity*	*Output*	*Receiver (agent and activity)*
operations dept (production engineer), (team leader), (shop floor operatives), (materials planning manager) identifies planning problems (modifications), (estimate queries), (DSI's), (test spec),	planning problems (modifications), (estimate queries), (DSI's), (test spec),	customer and the operations dept (production engineer), (team leader), (shop floor operatives), (materials planning manager)	solve planning problems (modifications), (estimate queries), (DSI's), (test spec),	(ECR's/CRI's)	MRP manager prints off MRP batch run (route cards/tags), (pick list)
					test engineering dept define and acquire stored items (test equipment)
					tooling engineer defines and supplies the stored items (tooling)
customer and the operations dept (production engineer), (team leader), (shop floor operatives), (materials planning manager) solve planning problems (modifications), (estimate queries), (DSI's), (test spec),	(ECR's/CRI's)	MRP manager	prints off MRP batch run (route cards/ tags), (pick list)	MRP batch run (route cards/tags), (pick list)	stores control stored items (purchased parts), (test equipment), (tooling) with MECCA

Supplier (agent and activity)	*Input*	*Agent*	*Activity*	*Output*	*Receiver (agent and activity)*
customer and the operations dept (production engineer), (team leader), (shop floor operatives), (materials planning manager) solve planning problems (modifications), (estimate queries), (DSI's), (test spec)	(ECR's/CRI's)	test engineering	dept define and acquire stored items (test equipment)	stored items (test equipment)	stores control stored items (purchased parts), (test equipment), (tooling) with MECCA
customer and the operations dept (production engineer), (team leader), (shop floor operatives), (materials planning manager) solve planning problems (modifications), (estimate queries), (DSI's), (test spec),	(ECR's/CRI's)	tooling engineer	defines and supplies the stored items (tooling)	stored items (tooling)	stores control stored items (purchased parts), (test equipment), (tooling) with MECCA
stored items (purchased parts)	stored items (purchased parts)	stores	control stored items (purchased parts), (test equipment), (tooling), (assembled units) with MECCA	production material (raw material), (kit)	operations dept (production engineer), (team leader), (shop floor operatives), (materials planning manager) conduct sunrise meetings
test engineering dept define and acquire stored items (test equipment)	stored items (test equipment)			MECCA records	

Supplier (agent and activity)	*Input*	*Agent*	*Activity*	*Output*	*Receiver (agent and activity)*
tooling engineer defines and supplies the stored items (tooling)	stored items (tooling)				
MRP manager prints off MRP batch run (route cards/tags), (pick list)	MRP batch run (route cards/tags), (pick list)				
FEEDBACK FROM: production testers test the assembled units	stored items (assembled units)				
stores control stored items (purchased parts), (test equipment), (tooling) with MECCA	production material (raw material), (kit)	operations dept (production engineer), (team leader), (shop floor operatives), (materials planning manager)	conduct sunrise meetings	sunrise meetings	project manager and operations dept ()...() reference manuf. control documents (quality plan) (EC0) (MMR) (CPR) to discuss manuf. issues (problems: kitting shortages, NCR's subcontract, plant, design/est) (stage claims), (concessions), (none)
stores control stored items (purchased parts), (test equipment), (tooling) with MECCA	MECCA records				

Supplier (agent and activity)	*Input*	*Agent*	*Activity*	*Output*	*Receiver (agent and activity)*
FEEDBACK FROM: operations dept (production engineer), (team leader), (shop floor operatives), (materials planning manager) must resolve manufacturing issues (kitting shortages), (NCR's), (subcontract), (plant), (design/est)	resolved manufacturing problems (kitting shortages), (NCR's), (subcontract), (plant), (design/est)				
FEEDBACK FROM: quality dept must authorise manufacturing issues (concessions)	authorised concessions				
operations dept (production engineer), (team leader), (shop floor operatives), (materials planning manager) conduct sunrise meetings	sunrise meetings	project manager and operations dept (production engineer), (team leader), (shop floor operatives), (materials planning manager)	reference manuf. control documents (quality plan) (EC0) (MMR) (CPR) to discuss manuf. issues (problems: kitting shortages, NCR's subcontract, plant, design/est) (stage claims), (concessions), (none)	manufacturing issues (kitting shortages), (NCR's), (subcontract), (plant), (design/est)	operations dept (production engineer), (team leader), (shop floor operatives), (materials planning manager) must resolve manufacturing issues (kitting shortages), (NCR's), (subcontract), (plant), (design/est)

Supplier (agent and activity)	*Input*	*Agent*	*Activity*	*Output*	*Receiver (agent and activity)*
PHASE INPUT FROM THE SET-UP AND PLANNING PHASE: contracts dept (contracts officer) define the MMR	manufacturing control documents (MMR)			manufacturing issues (concessions)	quality dept must authorise manufacturing issues (concessions)
PHASE INPUT FROM THE SET-UP AND PLANNING PHASE: quality dept draw up the manufacturing control documents (quality plan)	manufacturing control documents (quality plan)			manufacturing issues (none)	operations dept (production engineer), (team leader), (shop floor operatives), (materials planning manager) assemble units
PHASE INPUT FROM THE SET-UP AND PLANNING PHASE: MRP manager oversees production of manufacturing control documents (MRP EC0)	manufacturing control documents (MRP EC0)			manufacturing issues (stage payments)	finance (NP) issue stage claims
FEEDBACK FROM: accounts dept produce review packs (PMR) as required	review packs (PMR)			review packs (PMR)	**PHASE WIDTH OUTPUT**: accounts produce review packs (UBR)

Supplier (agent and activity)	*Input*	*Agent*	*Activity*	*Output*	*Receiver (agent and activity)*
project manager and operations dept ()…() reference manuf. control documents (quality plan) (EC0) (MMR) (CPR) to discuss manuf. issues (problems: kitting shortages, NCR's subcontract, plant, design/est) (stage claims), (concessions), (none)	manufacturing issues (stage payments)	finance (NP)	issue stage claims	stage claims	accounts dept produce review packs (PMR) as required
					PHASE OUTPUT TO ORDER COMPLETION PHASE: customer clears all claims
PHASE INPUT FROM THE SET-UP AND PLANNING PHASE: accounts dept load MarCAS (cost code structure)	MarCAS (cost code structure)	accounts dept	produce review packs (PMR) as required	review packs (PMR)	**FEEDBACK TO**: project manager and operations dept ()…() reference manuf. control documents (quality plan) (EC0) (MMR) (CPR) to discuss manuf. issues (problems: kitting shortages, NCR's subcontract, plant, design/est) (stage claims), (concessions), (none)

Supplier (agent and activity)	*Input*	*Agent*	*Activity*	*Output*	*Receiver (agent and activity)*
finance (NP) issue stage claims	stage invoices				
project manager and operations dept ()…() reference manuf. control documents (quality plan) (EC0) (MMR) (CPR) to discuss manuf. issues (problems: kitting shortages, NCR's subcontract, plant, design/est) (stage claims), (concessions), (none)	manufacturing issues (kitting shortages), (NCR's), (subcontract), (plant), (design/est)	operations dept (production engineer), (team leader), (shop floor operatives), (materials planning manager)	must resolve manufacturing issues (kitting shortages), (NCR's), (subcontract), (plant), (design/est)	resolved manufacturing problems (kitting shortages), (NCR's), (subcontract), (plant), (design/est)	FEEDBACK TO: operations dept (production engineer), (team leader), (shop floor operatives), (materials planning manager) conduct sunrise meetings
project manager and operations dept ()…() reference manuf. control documents (quality plan) (EC0) (MMR) (CPR) to discuss manuf. issues (problems: kitting shortages, NCR's subcontract, plant, design/est) (stage claims), (concessions), (none)	manufacturing issues (concessions)	quality dept	must authorise manufacturing issues (concessions)	authorised concessions	FEEDBACK TO: operations dept (production engineer), (team leader), (shop floor operatives), (materials planning manager) conduct sunrise meetings

Supplier (agent and activity)	*Input*	*Agent*	*Activity*	*Output*	*Receiver (agent and activity)*
project manager and operations dept ()…() reference manuf. control documents (quality plan) (EC0) (MMR) (CPR) to discuss manuf. issues (problems: kitting shortages, NCR's subcontract, plant, design/est) (stage claims), (concessions), (none)	manufacturing issues (none)	operations dept (production engineer), (team leader), (shop floor operatives), (materials planning manager)	assemble units	assembled units	production testers test the assembled units
operations dept (production engineer), (team leader), (shop floor operatives), (materials planning manager) assemble units	assembled units	production testers	test the assembled units	OR: test results (pass)	production testers declare assembled units with completed route cards
				OR: test results (fail)	**FEEDBACK TO**: operations dept (production engineer), (team leader), (shop floor operatives), (materials planning manager) identifies planning problems (modifications), (estimate queries), (DSI's), (test spec),

Supplier (agent and activity)	*Input*	*Agent*	*Activity*	*Output*	*Receiver (agent and activity)*
production testers test the assembled units	OR: test results (pass)	production testers declare assembled units with completed route cards	production testers declare assembled units with completed route cards	assembled units with completed route cards	**FEEDBACK TO**: stores control stored items (purchased parts), (test equipment), (tooling) with MECCA
					PHASE OUTPUT TO THE ORDER COMPLETION PHASE: quality engineer conducts customer acceptance tests

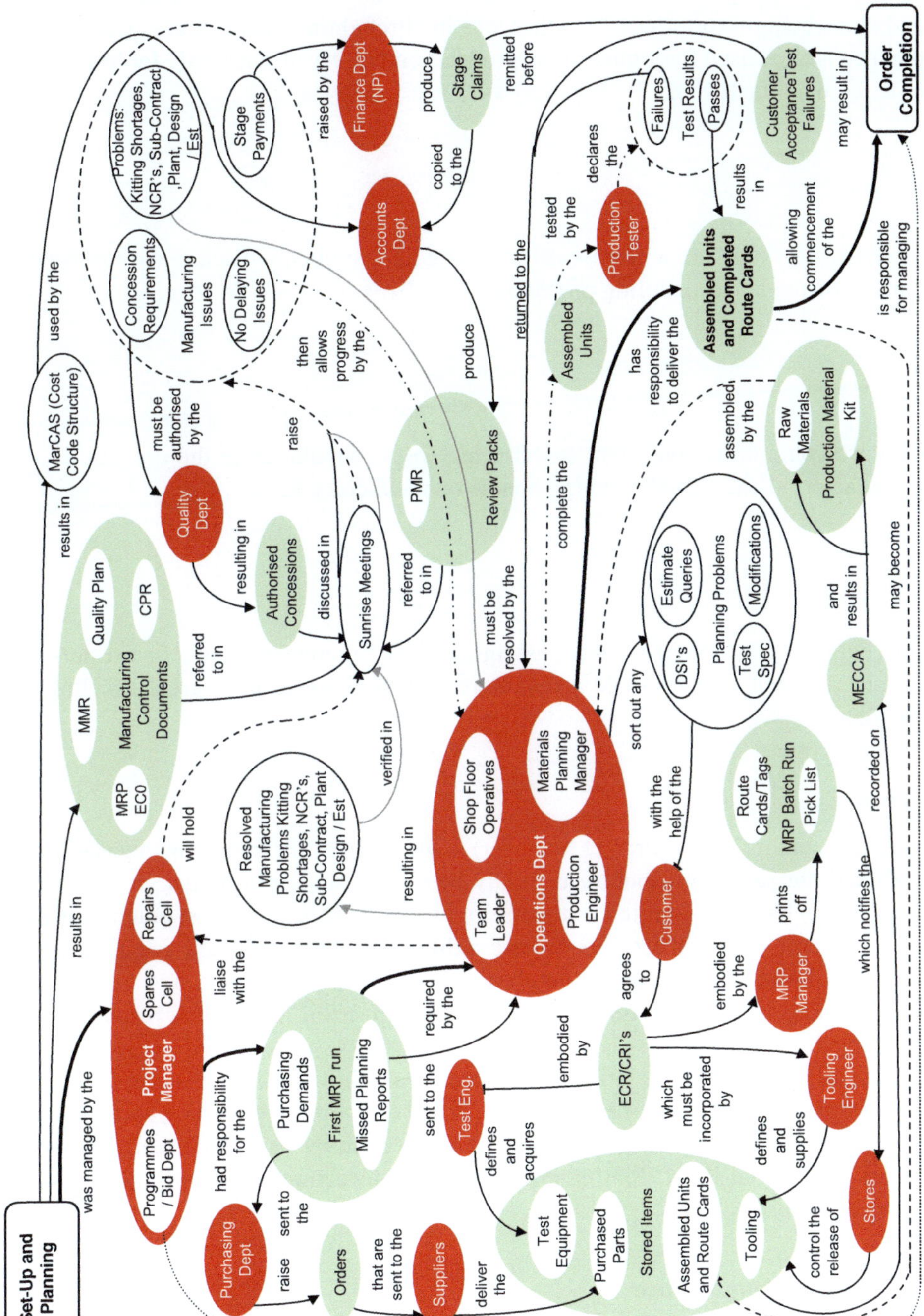

FIGURE 9.4 GMRDSL Manufacture Phase Model.

Scene 3:

- Kitting and assembly problems are caused by the factory stores being located at different sites and items being re-prioritised to other jobs in "firefighting" behaviours. More just-in-time practice is to be used for high-volume products and reserved stock only for low-volume project-based manufacturing.

Scene 4:

- New "sunrise meetings" are a new weekly meeting held to openly discuss and resolve current manufacturing and scheduling problems.

Scene 5:

- In the future communication from "sunrise meetings" should drive the communication within the factory using visual planning boards on the factory floor.

Scene 6:

- Plans are being made to "self-inspect" assembled units; therefore, production testers will no longer be required, which should install more pride in workers and a greater feeling that they are trusted.

Modelling Nuances Explained

- Because the receiving agent (Project Manager) is the same as the supplying agent (Project Manager) and the rule that a bubble can only be shown once in a model, it (the Project Manager bubble) has been omitted as the receiving agent. This is not best practice as each succeeding or proceeding phase should have a different most significant agent. However, sometimes this is not possible due to how phasing is defined. This nuance must be explained in the descriptions on the directional links, "Programmes/Bid Manager is responsible for Order Completion".
- As PrOH Models become more refined and contain more information, it is often necessary to show how different routes can be read from it and to keep some reading paths separate from others. In this model, as in others, this can be done by using differently patterned or coloured directional links. Joining and splitting of directional links has been used to increase readability.

GMRDSL Order Completion Phase

The Order Completion Phase presents the system of change for how the project manager could improve activities that take "Assembled Units and Routes Cards" to an "Order Completion" status required by the "Contracts Manager". This is once "Customer Acceptance Tests" and

TABLE 9.5 SIPOC Table for GMRDSL Order Completion Phase

Operations Dept (production engineer), (team leader), (shop floor operatives), (materials planning manager) completes manufacture with assembled units and completed route cards	*assembled units with completed route cards*	*Project Manager (programmes/ bid dept) (spares cell), (repairs cell)*	*closes out the project*	*closed order*	*SuO OUTPUT: future potential business*
PHASE INPUT FROM MANUFACTURE PHASE: production testers declare assembled units with completed route cards	assembled units with completed route cards	quality dept	conducts customer acceptance tests	OR: customer acceptance tests (passes)	project manager issues an advice of dispatch
FEEDBACK FROM: project manager must resolve failures customer acceptance tests failures	resolved failures			OR: customer acceptance tests (failures)	**PHASE OUTPUT FEEDBACK TO MANUFACTURING PHASE**: operations dept (production engineer), (team leader), (shop floor operatives), (materials planning manager) identifies planning problems (modifications), (estimate queries), (DSI's), (test spec)
quality dept conducts customer acceptance tests	customer acceptance tests (passes)	project manager	issues an advice of dispatch	advice of dispatch	configuration dept raises shipping paperwork

Operations Dept (production engineer), (team leader), (shop floor operatives), (materials planning manager) completes manufacture with assembled units and completed route cards	*assembled units with completed route cards*	*Project Manager (programmes/ bid dept) (spares cell), (repairs cell)*	*closes out the project*	*closed order*	*SuO OUTPUT: future potential business*
project manager issues an advice of dispatch	advice of dispatch	configuration dept	raise shipping paperwork	shipping paperwork (shipping report), (build state)	inspector authorises the shipping paperwork
configuration dept raises shipping paperwork	shipping paperwork (shipping report), (build state)	inspector	authorises the shipping paperwork	authorised shipping paperwork (shipping report), (build state)	project manager and contract manager may hold a wash-up meeting
inspector authorises the shipping paperwork	authorised shipping paperwork (shipping report), (build state)	project manager and contract manager	may hold a wash-up meeting	wash-up meeting	dispatch clerk raises dispatch paperwork (640's), (C of C's)
project manager and contract manager may hold a wash-up meeting	wash-up meeting	dispatch clerk	raises dispatch paperwork (640's), (C of C's)	dispatch paperwork (640's), (C of C's)	quality dept authorise the dispatch paperwork (640's), (C of C's)
dispatch clerk raises dispatch paperwork (640's), (C of C's)	dispatch paperwork (640's), (C of C's)	quality dept	authorise the dispatch paperwork (640's), (C of C's)	authorised dispatch paperwork (640's), (C of C's)	packers pack the goods
quality dept authorise the dispatch paperwork (640's), (C of C's)	authorised dispatch paperwork (640's), (C of C's)	packers	pack the goods	packaged goods (delivered), (ex-works)	customer responds with a customer acknowledgement

Operations Dept (production engineer), (team leader), (shop floor operatives), (materials planning manager) completes manufacture with assembled units and completed route cards	*assembled units with completed route cards*	*Project Manager (programmes/ bid dept) (spares cell), (repairs cell)*	*closes out the project*	*closed order*	*SuO OUTPUT: future potential business*
packers pack the goods	packaged goods (delivered), (ex-works)	customer	responds with a customer acknowledgement	customer acknowledgement	project manager may conduct project management review
customer responds with a customer acknowledgement	customer acknowledgement	project manager	may conduct project management review	project management review	inventory control will clear project inventories
					finance dept (NP) will make final claims and chase any outstanding stage claims
project manager may conduct project management review	project management review	inventory control	will clear project inventories	cleared project inventories	project manager can close the order
PHASE INPUT FROM MANUFACTURE PHASE: finance (NP) issue stage claims	claims (stage claims)	finance dept (NP)	will make final claims and chase any outstanding stage claims	claims (final claims)	customer clears all claims
project manager may conduct project management review	project management review				

Operations Dept (production engineer), (team leader), (shop floor operatives), (materials planning manager) completes manufacture with assembled units and completed route cards	*assembled units with completed route cards*	*Project Manager (programmes/ bid dept) (spares cell), (repairs cell)*	*closes out the project*	*closed order*	*SuO OUTPUT: future potential business*
finance dept (NP) will make final claims and chase any outstanding stage claims	claims (final claims)	customer	clears all claims	total remittance	project manager can close the order
customer clears all claims	total remittance	project manager	can close the order	closed order	**SuO OUTPUT**: future potential business
inventory control will clear project inventories	cleared project inventories				

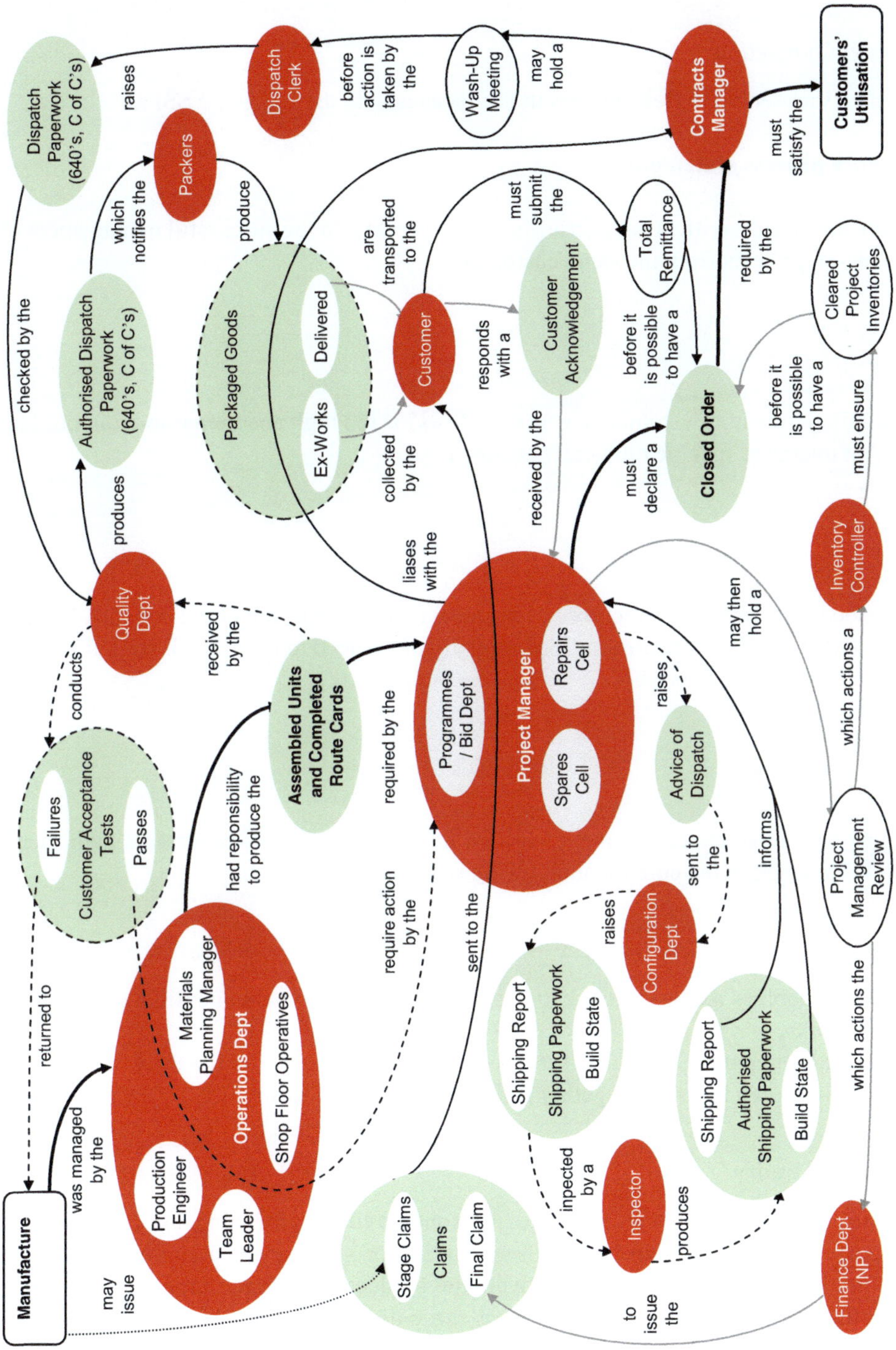

FIGURE 9.5 GMRDSL Order Completion Phase PrOH Model.

"Packaged Goods" have been collected and transported to the "Customer". Its SIPOC Table is given in Table 9.5, and its PrOH Model is given in Figure 9.5.

SSFs for Order Completion

This model was presented to stakeholders in four scenes with the following SSFs.

Scene 1 – core process statement

- These are not usually critical path activities but are crucial to the successful management of any follow-on projects from the same customer.

Scene 2:

- Current failure rate in "Customer Acceptance Tests" is too high and better up-front product design and tolerance specification must occur.

Scene 3:

- There is too much paperwork required to get an assembled unit "out of the door". Advice of Dispatch (AoDs) and Certificates of Conformity (CofCs) need to be merged. Digital ways of doing this need to be explored.

Scene 4:

- Packaging can be an expensive manufactured item and can be on the critical path; these need to be included in the core manufacturing schedule.

Explanation of Methodological Nuances

- Two decision bubbles are used. It is better practice if outcomes generate different paths for directional links.
- Colour coding and patterns are used for directional links to help read the PrOH Model.
- Directional links can be joined together if the text label is the same.

Abductions to Theory

This case further abducts to the principles of **concurrent engineering** as introduced in GMRDSL case Part 1. The main tenets of concurrent (or simultaneous) engineering are to design the product and the process that delivers the product at the same time, and ideally to also design the supply chain which is known as three-dimensional **concurrent engineering**

(Clegg and Boardman, 1996). Due to the many complex SSFs outlined above, it was difficult to achieve for GMRDSL. One of the primary reasons is the length of time it takes to design and build these highly complex and expensive products and the length of time they can be in service, which in many cases is more than 50 years.

Summary

This GMRDSL case, Part 2, has given a detailed example of how a system of change can be described in more depth by using a **Process Matrix** and following the **rules of enrichment** for PrOH Models given in Chapter 5, taking thinking from a strategic level to a more detailed tactical level. Four phases of systemic change were presented including their **SIPOC Tables**, their PrOH Models and the **Systemic Success Factors** for change associated with their storyboard scenes. PrOH Modelling nuances have been explained that will enable future PrOH Modellers to develop their own PrOH Models by reaching an acceptable level of rule adherence and guideline implementation during contextual adaptation to produce PrOH Models with high levels of **systemicity** and purposefulness.

Further PrOH Models were produced at a third **operational** level but are not included in this chapter.

Further Reading

Clegg, B. (1999), *A Systems Approach to Reengineering Business Processes Towards Concurrent Engineering Principles*. PhD Thesis. De Montfort University.

10

CASE 5: METAL ASSEMBLIES LTD (MAL)

Abstraction from Tactical to Strategic Level PrOH Models and Improving Leanness and Productivity in Automotive Manufacturing

Context

MAL is a company based in the UK Midlands; it produces pressed metal parts, machined components and welded assemblies for the automotive industry. It has over 60 years of experience in the automotive sector. It is a second-tier supplier, and its customers are high-volume first-tier suppliers to mainstream prestige original equipment manufacturers (OEMs) of well-known brands. The purpose of this case was to raise MAL's digital maturity of its strategic and operational processes from a basic level to become more advanced. Prior to this project, MAL used traditional manufacturing approaches with relatively little digitalisation.

At the time of this case, MAL had nine coil feed presses, several CNC tube manipulation machines, turning machines and robotic welding machines. MAL makes-to-print from its customers' designs and has its own tool-making facility. It employs approximately 40 full-time staff, mostly on the shop floor, and makes extensive use of casual labour. At the start of this case, digitalisation was limited to an Enterprise Resource Planning (ERP) system for sales order processing and a quality management system (QMS) to record production quality. These worked independently and relied on manual input, extraction and analysis of data. Some machines had a computer-controlled interface, but live data was not extracted.

Action Research, Systems Thinking and Systemic Success Factors

For its strategic performance, MAL defines eight core strategic KPIs and eight operational KPIs for shop floor activities. By using the PrOH Modelling Methodology, researchers were able to improve these KPIs by improving the production system and the technology used to measure it. This case used **socio-technical systems** theory in an abductive critique of practices at MAL.

This case began by modelling four system phases at a **tactical level**; this was deemed necessary as managers' most significant challenges lay at the interface of strategic office-based (e.g. ERP for sales order processing) systems and shop floor implementation (e.g. manufacturing

DOI: 10.4324/9781032650425-13

scheduling and tracking) systems. Subsequently, a strategic overview was required and so, through abstraction, a strategic level PrOH Model was produced. Furthermore, this case required deeper understanding about SSFs for manufacturing and therefore operational level models were developed to explicate these.

The full holarchy, in a set of PrOH Models, is shown in Figure 10.1. In order of creation, these were: four **tactical** level PrOH Models, one **strategic** PrOH Model abstracted from four **tactical** PrOH Models and two **operational** PrOH Models enriched from the tactical (Manufacturing) PrOH Model.

Tactical models for MAL are shown in Figures 10.2–10.5. The first of these is shown in Figure 10.2 and is called the "Win Customer Orders" phase.

Four story board scenes were created from the "Win customer orders" phase PrOH Model. The scenes are not shown in this case but the SSFs for each are given below:

Scene 1 – core process statement:

- Quoting (e.g. financial, commercial) process is driven by the managing director (also Chief Financial Officer and Operations Director) with support from the commercial and project manager, which causes a bottleneck.
- Build-to-print. Only the *process* of manufacturing is discussed with clients with little or no influence on product design.
- Seemingly little input from other functions, such as operations, in this phase, which can cause unnecessary reworking later.
- Shared server space for customer documentation is given but often without live system updates, causing version control issues.
- The materials requirement planning (MRP) part of ERP does not work as it should due to a lack of accurate shop floor data.

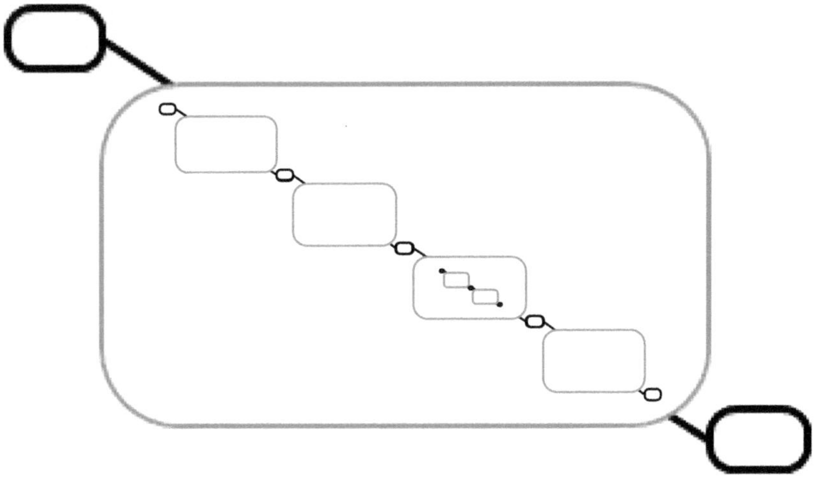

FIGURE 10.1 Picture of the Holarchy of PrOH Models for the MAL Case.

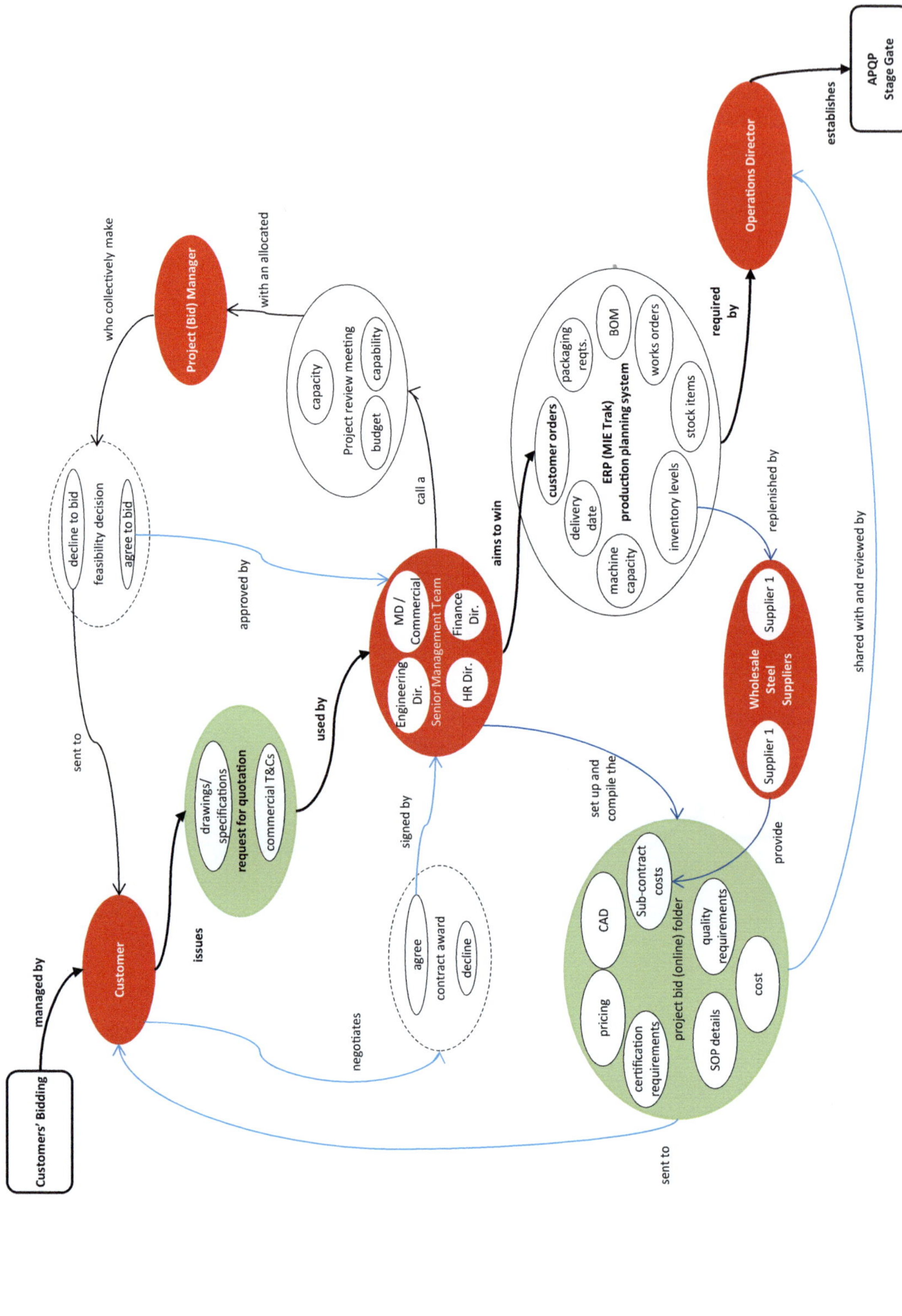
Customers' Bidding
managed by
Customer
issues
drawings/specifications
request for quotation
commercial T&Cs
used by
Engineering Dir.
MD / Commercial
Senior Management Team
HR Dir.
Finance Dir.
signed by
agree
contract award
decline
negotiates
sent to
decline to bid
feasibility decision
agree to bid
approved by
who collectively make
Project (Bid) Manager
with an allocated
capacity
Project review meeting
budget
capability
call a
aims to win
customer orders
packaging reqts.
BOM
delivery date
ERP (MIE Trak) production planning system
works orders
machine capacity
inventory levels
stock items
required by
Operations Director
establishes
APQP Stage Gate
replenished by
Supplier 1
Wholesale Steel Suppliers
Supplier 1
set up and compile the
provide
CAD
Sub-contract costs
pricing
project bid (online) folder
quality requirements
certification requirements
SOP details
cost
sent to
shared with and reviewed by

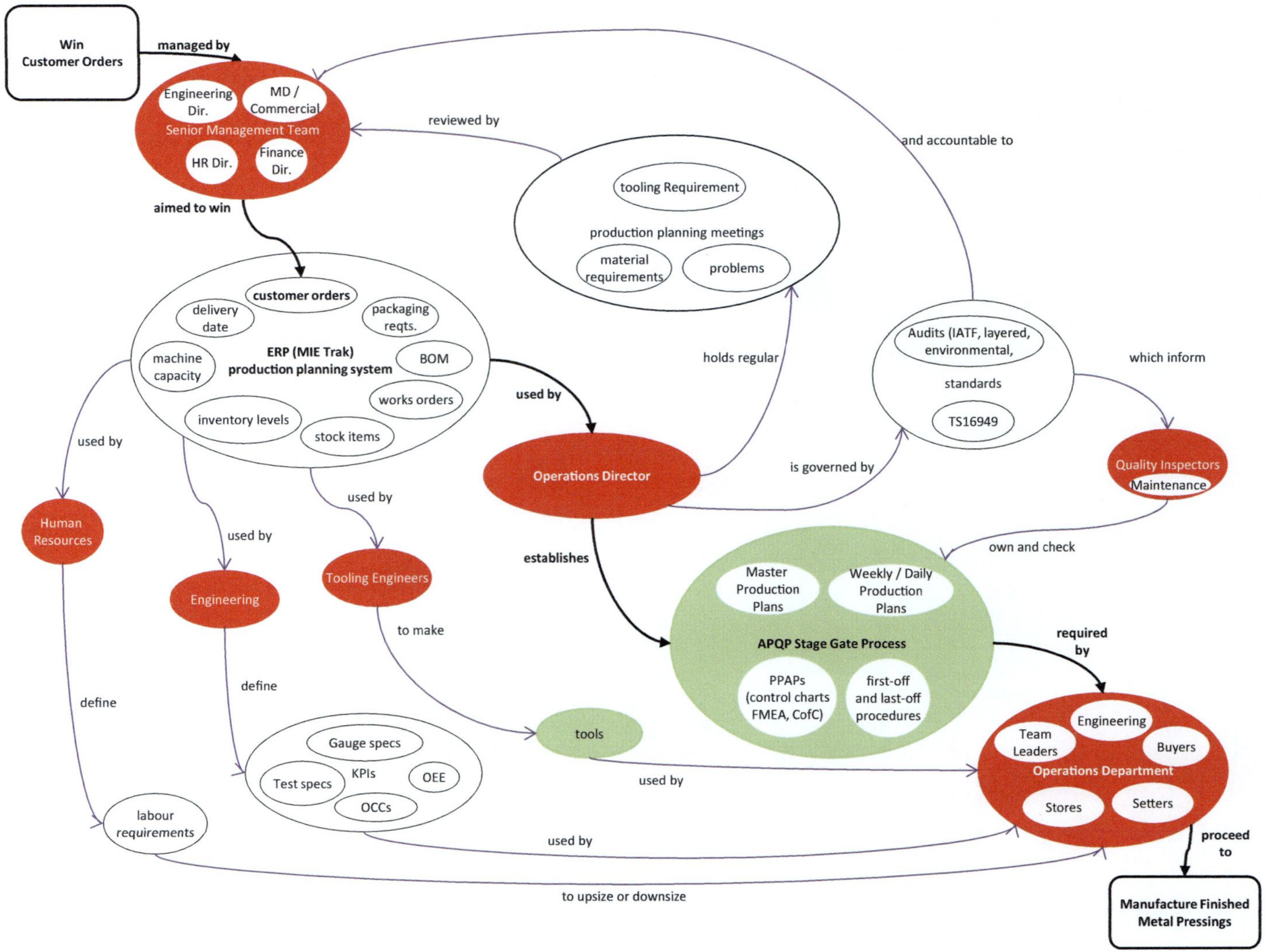

FIGURE 10.3 Tactical PrOH Model 2: Operations Director Establishes APQP Stage Gate Process.

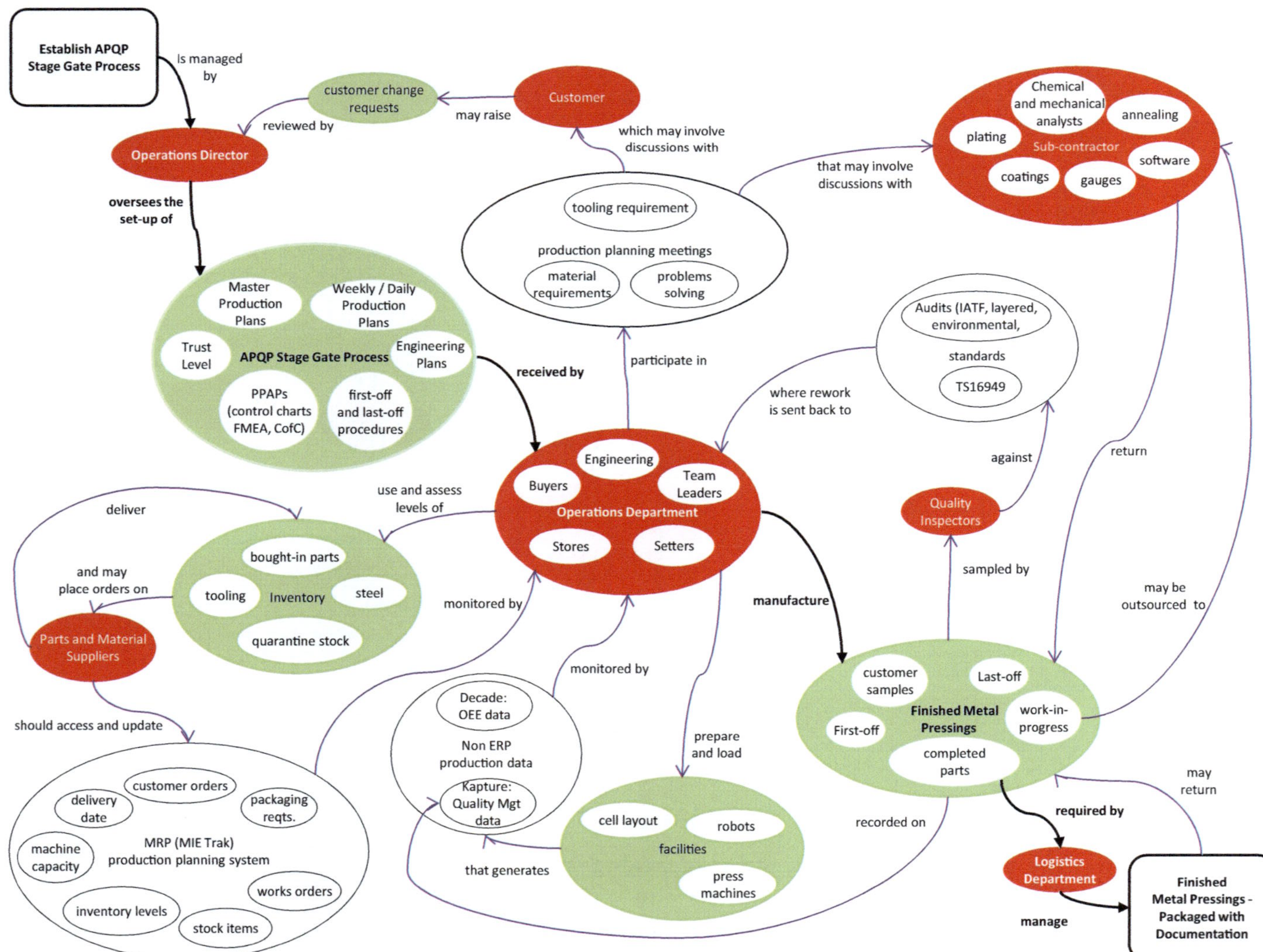

FIGURE 10.4 Tactical PrOH Model 3: Operations Dept. Manufacture Finished Metal Pressings.

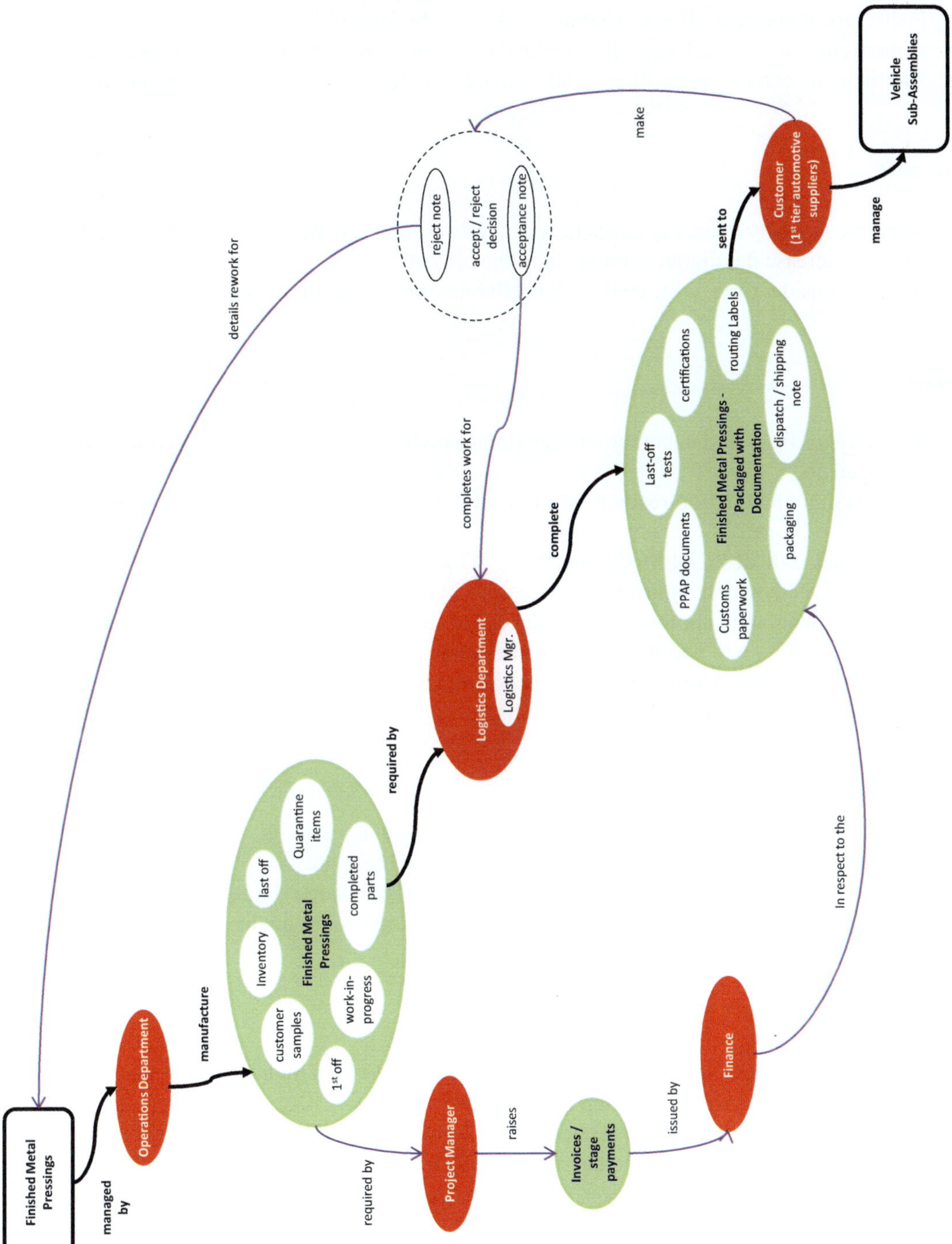

FIGURE 10.5 Tactical PrOH Model 4: Logistics Department Complete Finished Metal Pressings.

Scene 2:

- Is this repeat business? If not, what new risks may be incurred?
- Is there currently enough capacity to take the job, and how can we know this for certain?
- Are there the correct capabilities to take the job, and how can we know this for certain?

Scene 3:

- Need to constantly manually check the completeness and accuracy of data in project folders.
- Need to increase the digital component of the bid data.
- Need to consider time, cost, quality, dependability and flexibility.

Scene 4:

- Speeding-up links and accuracy of digital data exchange with customer build data would reduce errors.
- Get data more production-ready to hand over to the shop floor production managers.

The second tactical PrOH Model for MAL, “Operations Director establishes APQP Stage Gate Process”, is shown in Figure 10.3. APQP is the “Advanced Product Quality Planning” process used in manufacturing to ensure products meet customer requirements and consistently produce high quality and was developed by the Automotive Industry Action Group (AIAG).

SSFs from five storyboard scenes developed from “Operations Director Establishes APQP Stage Gate Process” PrOH Model in Figure 10.3 are:

Scene 1 – core process statement:

- Very inaccurate information in the MIETrak MRP system.
- MIETrak MRP system may not be fit for purpose for future needs.
- Production planning was paper-based but now moving towards digital (e.g. machine data collection via DECADE, analytics via PowerBI and Kapture for quality).

Scene 2:

- Very inaccurate information in MIE Trak MRP system due to a high degree of manual input required at high rates of production output.
- MIE Trak needs more digital interface with other systems with common interfaces.
- Manufacturing was paper-based but now moving towards digital (e.g. machine data collection – DECADE, analytics – PowerBI, Kapture – quality).

Scene 3:

- Operators should do hourly checks but don't always do these due to time pressures. Instead, these are done daily or weekly. The paper-based system is open to misuse but Kapture, or other similar QMSs, could force regular hourly checks to be made.
- 8D quality checks are needed for material goods received, but often are not done and disputes can then occur later (e.g. poor-quality materials).

Scene 4:

- Bluetooth measurement gauges are needed to collect data from machine settings and share with other systems.
- Barcodes are not used for tracking production but could give an accuracy improvement.
- Scrap rates need recording (can be addressed by Kapture).
- Need for more digital tablets to update systems – not enough computers in the hands of shop floor workers.

Scene 5:

- Digital Human Resources (HR) portal is needed, especially to manage agency staff (e.g. People HR).

The SSFs from five storyboard scenes created from the "**Operations Dept. Manufacture Finished Metal Pressings**" in Figure 10.4 are:

Scene 1 – core process statement:

- Operations department not making use of current IT who need more access and knowledge to Industry 4.0 technology.
- More data capture is needed from machines and more real-time, or near real-time, data analysis of machine data is needed (e.g. PowerBI for comparison of planned to actual progress).

Scene 2:

- Live data is not shared with customers. However, Decade can be shared off-line for customers who want to work on supplier improvement initiatives.
- Data is not shared with subcontractors. However, presently this is not necessary as they are also unready for digitalisation and Industry 4.0 technologies.

Scene 3:

- Layered audits take too long by hand or may occasionally be missed, which needs to be addressed by more automated quality management systems (QMSs) (e.g. Kapture).

- Tracking of work to and from subcontractors' factories is not done digitally. However, this is crucial for future developments to increase volume and quality of output.

Scene 4:

- MIETrak MRP not used on the shop floor and only for set-up with minimum functionality.
- No ERP access for suppliers.

Scene 5:

- DECADE now used for live data capture but not linked to MIETrak MRP.
- Kapture QMS now used for analysis of quality data, from manual entry on digital tablets.
- Decade and Kapture data can be fed to PowerBI.

The fourth tactical PrOH Model called "Logistics Dept. complete Finished Metal Pressings" is shown in Figure 10.5. Three storyboard scenes were produced from it. The SSFs attributable to these three storyboard scenes are:

Scene 1 – core process statement:

- Process is all done with manual paperwork.

Scene 2:

- Invoicing is now digitalised – done from MIETrak.

Scene 3:

- Delivery notes need to be digitalised and produced from MIETrak.
- Sign-on-glass is difficult as every page of the invoice needs signing, and delivery drivers change, but this can be possible soon.

Abstraction from four tactical PrOH shown in Figures 10.2–10.5 was performed in accordance with the PrOH Modelling Methodology given in Chapter 5. This case illustrates how to do **abstraction** and has created the strategic level PrOH Model seen in Figure 10.6 which contains all **core process** bubbles from the tactical models but has a unique **core process statement** of its own with new bubbles in it which relate to the new higher level of **abstraction**, and other bubbles in supporting statements which relate to the higher-level context. **Enrichments** previously shown in tactical models do not have to be shown.

The systemic success factors of change for the **strategic** level PrOH Model in Figure 10.6 are summarised in five storyboard scenes (Clegg et al., 2023) as follows.

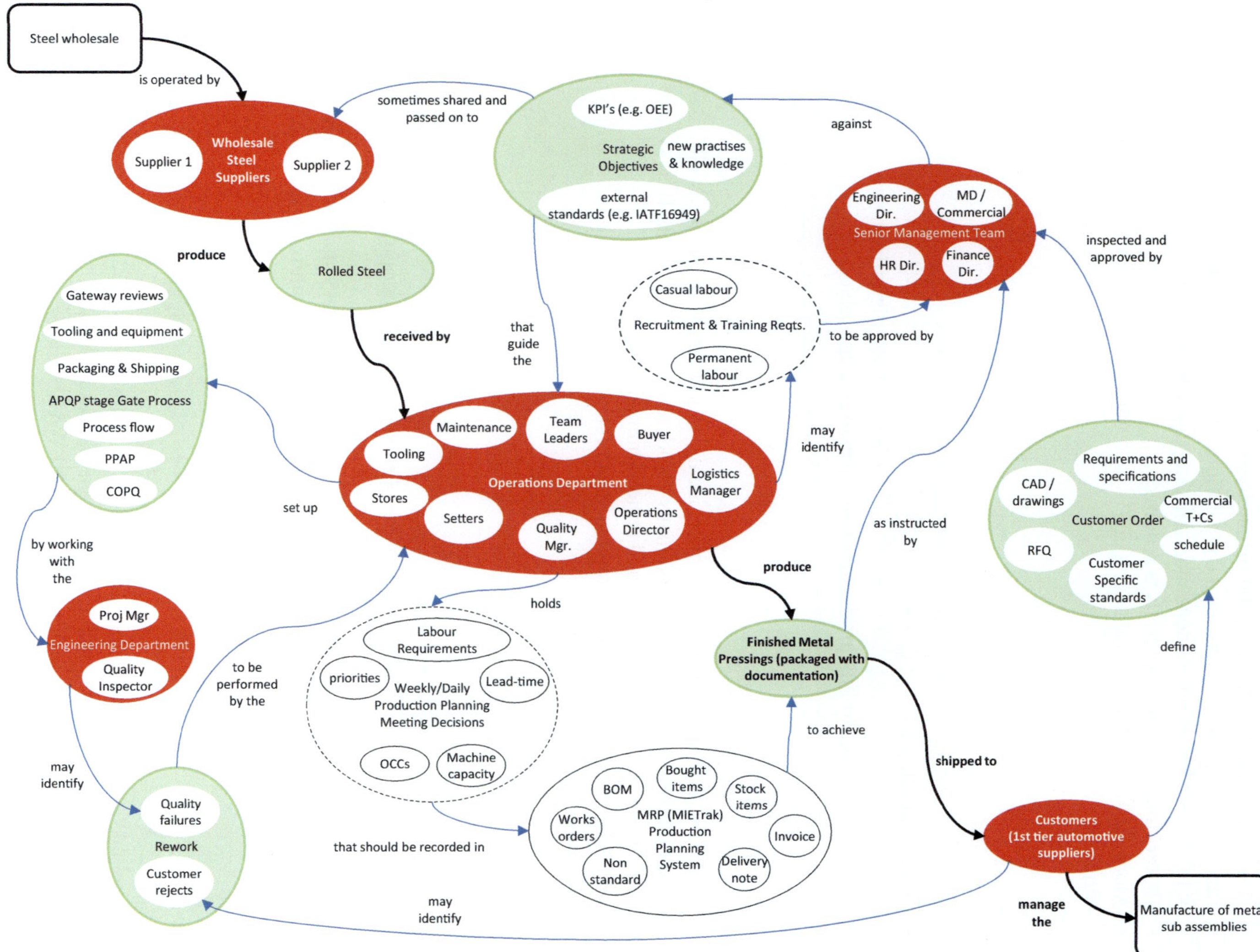

FIGURE 10.6 Strategic PrOH Model: Operations Department Produce Finished Metal Pressings.

Scene 1 – core process statement:

- Manufacturing is still fundamentally a "push" process and needs to be more of a "pull" system led from the shipping and dispatch department.
- Personal development plans for the Operations Department are not well developed.
- KPIs for vendor rating are done manually and could be automated.
- Better storage for raw materials is required.
- More electronic data interchange (EDI) links with external suppliers and customers are required.

Scene 2:

- Should be able to automatically import customer schedules.
- Need to develop KPIs that automatically update.
- Overall productivity (e.g. OEE) needs to be improved and digitalised.
- Need for live data to link production schedules to strategic objectives.

Scene 3:

- Need live production data on machines, ideally that is less than one week old.
- Manual set-up of MIETrak and too many "work arounds" for the MIETrak system.
- Need more accurate stock levels and remove human errors.
- DECADE (a programmable logic controller) for machine data capture needs integrating with other systems.

Scene 4:

- Need to monitor OEE and other KPIs.
- Closer links with maintenance and the tool room are needed for proactive maintenance.
- Digitalise Operational Control Chart (OCC) packs.
- Get rid of paper for quality management and use a digital QMS such as Kapture.
- Manual quality inspection checks need automating with Failure Mode Effects Analysis (FMEA).

Scene 5:

- Improve and automate Human Resources agency links.
- Develop an HR online portal for permanent and casual staff.
- Use a more mature HR system (such as TIMEWARE, Sage).

Benefits to the Company

SSF actions arising from this research had a significant impact on strategic and operational KPIs. On one hand, it was noticeable that some KPIs seemed to be adversely affected, which was due to increased accuracy and visibility of data in comparison to the previous manual paper-based estimates. On the other hand, some KPIs had immediately improved due to freeing up direct labour and management time. Overall, in this two-year project, MAL had no additional direct labour but was able to achieve a 15% increase in productivity by digitalising practices, which made the company leaner and achieved more from their existing machine resources, which were made smarter and by upskilling workers with digital competences, collectively creating an ecosystem of live accurate data as explicated by Rosin et al. (2020).

During further discussion of SSFs in the "Manufacture Finished Metal Pressings" phase, two more **operational** level PrOH Models called "First-off Manufacture" and "Last-off Manufacture" were created through **enrichment**. As with other pitches of the PrOH Modelling Methodology, their storyboards were constructed with SSFS, which were presented and discussed with operational team leaders to instigate further detailed changes.

Lessons learned from this case were on how internet-based technologies adoption is closely related to cultural practices. For instance, by making more information available more quickly and enabling widespread systems interoperability for middle management, it enabled middle management and shop-floor workers to work together, speed up and become more accurate in setting up, scheduling, and design for manufacturability of parts. In turn, this bettered cultural and social cohesions, leading to a propensity to want to do more digitalisation. This project also produced a virtual factory environment for training operators on how to set-up production pressing machines more quickly and safely (Panchal et al., 2024).

Methodological Nuances

The Process Matrix to establish tactical process phases, SIPOC Tables to establish PrOH Model logic, and storyboards are not shown in this case as the main pedagogical reason for this case is to demonstrate how **abstraction** is achieved from **tactical** to **strategic** levels as detailed in Chapter 5, and this creates valuable insights for a PrOH Modeller.

Theoretical Abduction for Wider Lessons Learned

The term "**sociotechnical system**" was first used by Trist and Bamforth in 1951 and since then **STS theory** has been adopted as a theoretical perspective in many empirical industrial studies, particularly in manufacturing (Soliman, 2018) and more lately in business platform ecosystems (Kapoor et al., 2021) and Industry 4.0 implementation (Nosalska et al., 2019). Even though STS theory was established in the 20th century it still provides a useful holistic, contemporary and open perspective for requirements gathering, change implementation, evaluation and testing of contemporary Industry 4.0 tools and techniques in pursuit of leanness, efficiency and growth. STS theory allows intervention-based action researchers to address SSFs of change via **abductive reasoning** (or rationalisation) from the observations and actions of stakeholders and their skills, organisational culture, manufacturing activities, process infrastructure and organisational goals (Bednar and Welch, 2019) within social, technical, work, organisational and environmental systems. This study explored MAL's STS systemic success factors (SSFs) in a **holarchy** of PrOH Models.

Findings emerged from four (tactically) **pitched** "meso-level" ("level N") PrOH Models that describe routines and capabilities to demystify the "black box" (Felin et al., 2012) of dynamic capabilities (Eisenhardt and Martin, 2000) arising from "micro-macro" foundations interactions within the "meso-level". As detailed by Felin et al. (2012) these models include individuals, processes, structural and interactive issues of macro (strategic) and micro (operational) level phenomena. Interactions between macro and micro levels are expressed using interconnecting meso-level (tactical) PrOH Models.

SSFs for the total system are described in transition to explain how changes in dynamic capability were catalysed from different levels at different time states. PrOH Modelling is therefore able to: (1) emphasise modelling the transience of dynamic change per se rather than the more traditional approach of contrasting an "**as-is**" state with a fictional future "**to-be**" state and (2) represent an organisation using holistic thinking rather than **hierarchical** thinking to reveal *performative and ostensive* behaviours (Feldman and Pentland, 2003). *By doing so, **aggregationism** and **reductionism** (or disaggregationism) are avoided in favour of **abstractive** and **enrichmental** thinking, and the burden of contrasting fictional models of real-world states in "**as-is**" and/or "**to-be**" states is avoided.*

Summary

Technical developments can undoubtedly contribute towards improved lean practice KPIs (Dornelles et al., 2022; Hines et al., 2004) but only because of increased interpretative abilities of real-time data (Senoner et al., 2022) and process quality (Rosin et al., 2020) as advocated and practised in lean and six sigma initiatives; especially if done incrementally (Minshull et al., 2022). Without broader human knowledge and experiential learning, fewer lean improvements would have occurred as **action research cycles** brought together technological and sociological work aspects and improved the adoption of "smart manufacturing" (Bokhorst et al., 2022; Cagliano et al., 2019) where micro and macro-level foundations and technical interoperability were strengthened in an improved "meso-level" understanding producing positive results for lean practice and increased quality levels.

Further Reading

Panchal, G., Clegg, B., Koupaei, E.E., Masi, D., and Collis, I. (2024), 'Digital Transformation and Business Intelligence for a SME: Systems Thinking Action Research Using PrOH Modelling', *Procedia Computer Science*, Vol. 232, pp. 1809–1818.

11

CASE 6: LAW SERVICE – HIGGS LLP

Transforming Legal Services for Greater Efficiency

Context and Challenge

The purpose of this case is to show:

- How PrOH Modelling can be applied to a professional services organisation in the private sector owned by its partners and operating in a tightly regulated industry.
- How a set of PrOH Models can be built in parallel and **abstracted** from to produce a higher-level PrOH Model following the rules and guidelines given in Chapters 4 and 5.
- How abductive rationalisation can be used at different modelling **pitches** to give broader contextual findings.

The UK's legal sector has faced unprecedented changes since the Legal Services Act (2007), which encouraged new entrants and increased competition. In response, Higgs LLP had to address internal inefficiencies, enhance workforce productivity and innovate pricing and service delivery. This involved improving processes and procedures that were inefficient and deeply ensconced in traditional non-customer-centric practices. The challenge was to remove the reticence of lawyers to approach clients directly and fully understand their needs, to improve competitive pricing with a multiplicity of fee arrangements and reduce their reluctance to sell additional services (Morris and Malhotra, 2002).

To meet these challenges, Higgs needed more expertise in streamlining operations for process optimisation and redesigning services, better people management practices to foster innovative thinking, assistance in designing new pricing strategies to replace or complement hourly billing, better project management for effectively delivering large and complex legal services and an innovative thinking team of managers to steer Higgs towards evolving client requirements. Higgs used the PrOH Modelling Methodology to catalyse these behaviours.

DOI: 10.4324/9781032650425-14

Systems Thinking, Action Research and Systemic Success Factors

The PrOH Modelling Methodology was delivered in **action research cycles**, enabling impactful changes within legal departments in a short span of 8–10 weeks. Five different legal services were modelled at a tactical level, which are summarised in Table 11.1. Each legal service was done in a different **action learning cycle (ARC)**.

The PrOH Modelling Methodology was used to understand the status quo of operations and the SSFs required to improve each. These legal services operate autonomously from one another at the tactical level as they are run like different business units overseen by the law firm partners, even though they share some joint support functions. An account of each service is given as a PrOH Model with its systemic success factors for change. The Process Matrix, SIPOC Tables and storyboards are not shown in this chapter as it focuses on **parallel abstraction** – which is a unique feature of this case not seen in other cases as previous sets of PrOH Models have been connected serially. PrOH Models in this case were built according to rules and guidelines in Chapters 4 and 5.

TABLE 11.1 Five Legal Services Modelled at a Tactical Level

Department/ARC	*Description*	*Operating Characteristics*
ARC 1 – Road Traffic Accident Claims	Road Traffic Accidents (RTA) are legal services within the broader Personal Injury department and accounted for a significant portion (90%) of the department's revenue.	High volume and low variety. Mass service delivery.
ARC 2 – Dispute Resolution/ Litigation	Dispute Resolution is a complex area of law overlapping with many other legal disciplines. Every case is unique requiring lawyers to tailor it to client's specific requirements and be well-versed in that niche of law.	Lowvolume and highvariety. Tailored services.
ARC 3 – Commercial Property Lease Transactions	The Commercial Property Services Department provides bespoke services in property-related legal matters. Lawyers act for both tenants and landlords.	Highvolume and highvariety.
ARC 4 – Corporate Services (e.g. Sale and Purchase Transactions)	Negotiating legal fees for corporate services (e.g. large management buyouts). This is notoriously challenging, as clients often supply the lawyers with insufficient knowledge at the outset.	Lowvolume and highvariety. Tailored services.
ARC 5 – Private Client Will Writing and Estate Administration	The work involves will writing, holding and executing. This is relatively high-volume routing work. Wills can become an asset for Higgs LLB once written and waiting to be executed.	Highvolume and lowvariety. Mass service delivery.

Road Traffic Accidents

Data was collected based on interactions with lawyers and support staff in the Road Traffic Accident (RTA) Department and five in-depth interviews lasting for 60–75 minutes. Raw data was a mixture of undisciplined charts and maps as well as **PrOH Modelling Process Matrix** and **SIPOC Tables.**

The RTA department had an inflow of 120–150 cases per month, and the majority are referrals from a major motor insurance company. These matters were distributed among the six fee earners. The case load on each fee earner is up to 200 at any given time, and a fee earner handles on average about 175 telephone calls per month from clients. A typical RTA requires interaction with 15 external organisations (e.g. third parties' insurers, triage assessors, medical experts, etc.), all of whom affect settlement timescales (up to 15 months), which makes it difficult to estimate timescales and maintain service expectations for clients, plan work accurately and measure performance effectively.

Figure 11.1 gives the PrOH Model of RTA's various stakeholders and their interactions where lawyers must liaise with and obtain essential knowledge from all external stakeholders to reduce processing time while preserving service quality. Process efficiency is crucial, and effective streamlining of operations helps to reduce costs.

The Systemic Success Factors (SSFs) of this professional service triad: professionals (lawyers), clients and the company are shown in the PrOH Model in Figure 11.1 and described in Table 11.2.

SSFs were assigned to lawyers and support staff to rectify in a set time and be accountable to partners for their achievement. According to Tinnilä and Vepsäläinen's (1995) typology of services RTA are "mass-transactions", and practical changes were made to:

- Eliminate time spent on photocopying, manually handling documents and increase process automation using systems for electronic filing and retrieving cases.
- Handle bills more efficiently.
- Reduce time chasing other external stakeholders.
- Provide flexible team-based secretarial support.
- Handle excessive workloads more accurately by correctly using a case management system.

Dispute Resolution

Dispute Resolution is a complex area of law as it overlaps with many other legal disciplines. Case volume is relatively low, and every case is unique requiring lawyers to tailor delivery to clients' specific requirements and be well-versed in legal details involving research to prepare detailed legal arguments. Dispute resolution also requires in-depth interaction with clients which makes managing the costs of litigation challenging, unpredictable and constantly prone to changes due to unexpected disclosures, counterclaims and submission of new expert evidence. Therefore, the process of delivering a dispute resolution matter can be unpredictable, leaving costs uncertain as unforeseen claims can be brought within the proceedings by an opponent. Levels of disclosure can be greater than expected and may be piecemeal. There may be interim applications along the way. Also, the number of witnesses impacting upon the

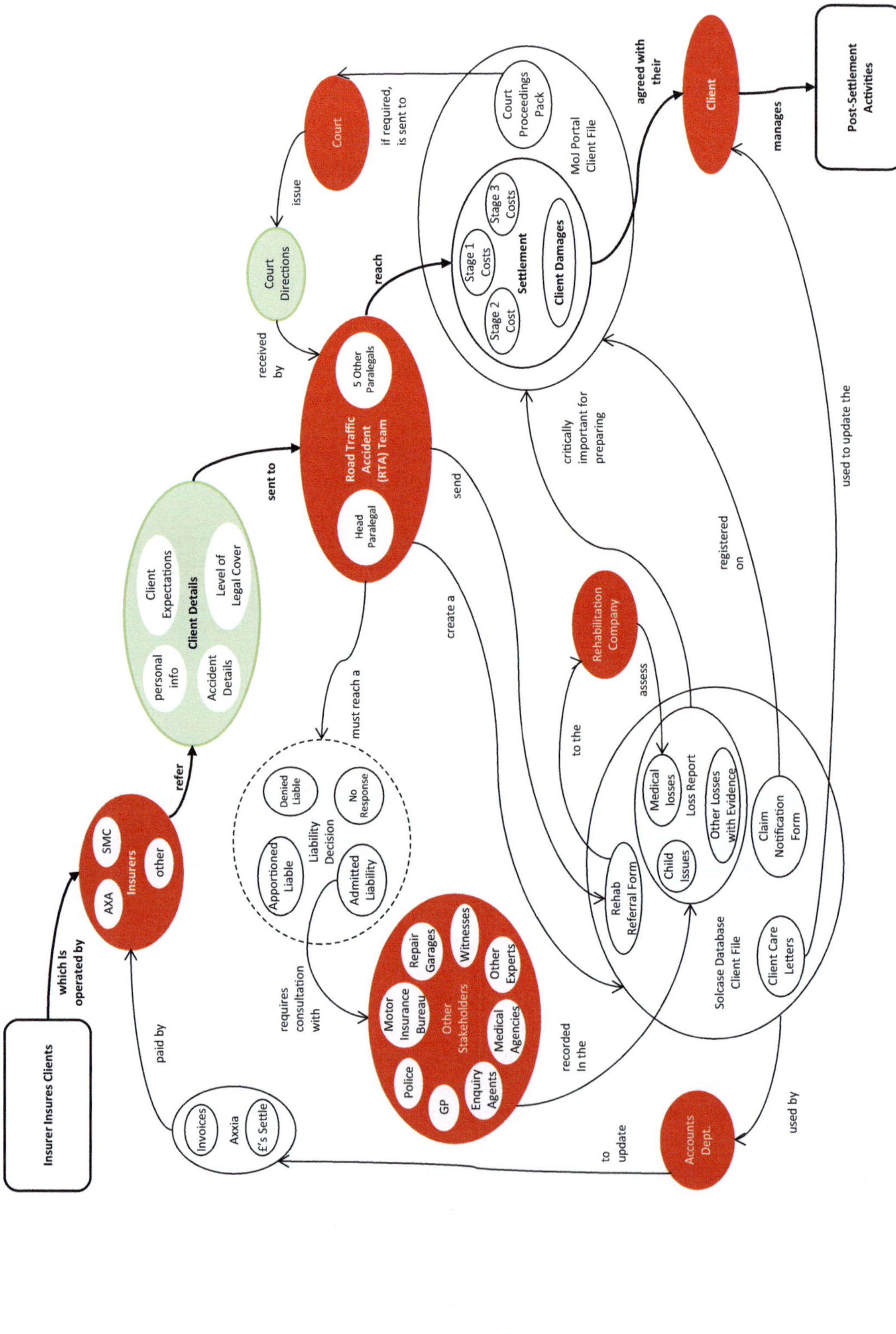

FIGURE 11.1 RTA Team Aiming to Reach a Settlement – Tactical PrOH Model.

TABLE 11.2 Road Traffic Accidents – Summary of SSFs

Systemic Success Factors		*Operational and Knowledge Challenges*
For Lawyer	*For Client*	
Complexity of the case – number of parties involved, claim amount, personal injury.	Recovery of damages (justice, claim amount, rehabilitation).	*Improving client experience – adhering to standard procedures whilst maintaining the same level of personal service.*
	Quicker settlement.	
Turnaround time for receiving documentation from outside parties.	Personal service – answer all queries, provide assurance and help recover damages to the best possible extent.	*Reducing turnaround time for reaching settlement.*
		Streamlining internal finance procedures.
		Understanding client needs and improving service quality.

length of trials and limited information available at the outset can lead to scope creep, disproportionate costs and a potentially negative experience all round. A partner said "litigation is like horse trading" which involves dealing with many unknowns creating difficulties in evaluating the merits of a case. With these challenges estimation of the legal costs has long been considered more of an art than a science, heavily reliant on experience and judgement. Thus, the emphasis of **systemic success factors** in this department must aim to build consensus with the client, work on indivisible tasks and manage distributed authority. These systemic issues are captured in the PrOH Model in Figure 11.2.

The systemic success factors (SSFs) of this professional service triad: professionals (lawyers), clients and the company are shown in the PrOH Model in Figure 11.2 and further described in Table 11.3.

Action teams were formed to take corrective action on these SSFs. While there is much written on organising high volume, low variety operations akin to service factories (Schmenner, 1986, 2004), there is less emphasis on low volume, high variety services such as Dispute Resolution. Findings indicate that despite high labour intensity, customer interaction and customisation in delivering this low volume, high variety legal service, there was potential for rationalising processes and improving efficiencies. This was possible by delineating administrative tasks from core legal service tasks and having better, more structured client engagement. For example, administrative tasks such as electronic filing, the ability to quickly generate Client Care Letters, due diligence searches on client credit and conflicts were separated and standardised.

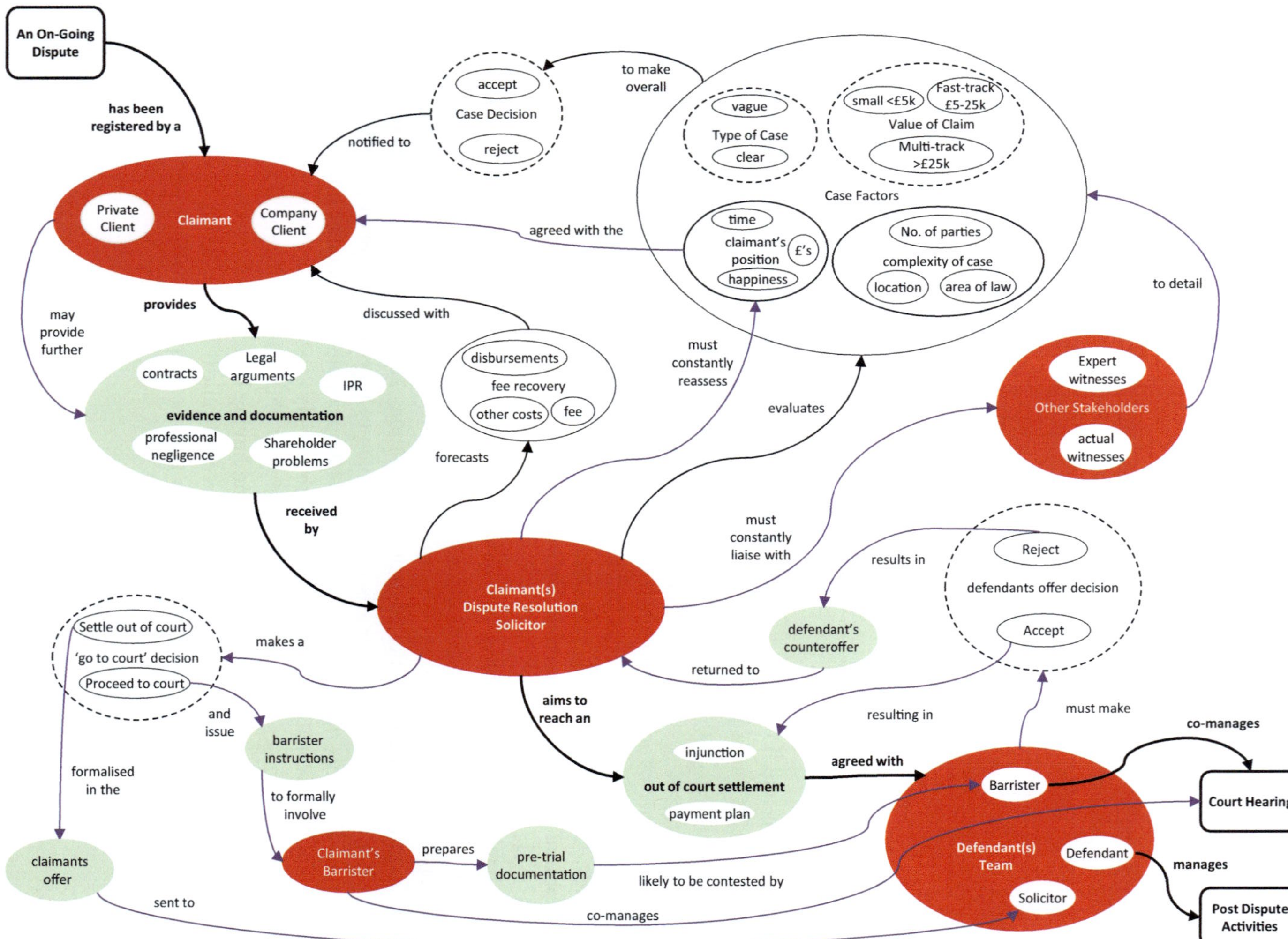

FIGURE 11.2 Claimant's Dispute Resolution – Tactical PrOH Model.

TABLE 11.3 Systemic Success Factors within the Dispute Resolution Department

Systemic Success Factors		*Operational Challenges*
For Lawyer	*For Client*	
Complexity of case – number of parties involved, area of law, location of client, value of claim, clear/vague documentation, merits of the case, witnesses required/not required. Client type – experience of litigation, technical knowledge, easy to advocate (expect clients to follow the advice). Managing client expectations throughout (impacts on fee recovery rate).	Positive outcome – expected route (settlement/go to court), expected value of settlement. Lawyer type – expect lawyer to be technically sound, strategic in dealing with other side. Cost of litigation – proportionate to the value of claim, transparent.	Need for better pricing, budgeting and scoping mechanism. Need for a robust process for factoring in soft issues such as managing client expectations and driving performance of fee earners. Understanding the typology of litigation cases to better estimate prices.

Commercial Property Lease Transactions

The Commercial Property Services Department provides bespoke services in a variety of property-related legal matters. Drafting lease documentation is a process-driven activity. Lawyers act for both tenants and landlords, and even though the service can differ hugely, depending on which side the lawyer is acting on, clients of both sides are increasingly demanding fixed-fee arrangements which forces property lawyers to be more accurate on cost estimates whilst simultaneously preserving suitably high levels of personal client contact. These are conflicting performance characteristics that need to be handled sensitively. Therefore, the success of this legal service lies in developing versatile empathic capabilities to cope with a high volume and high variety of cases for large business clients, individual landlords and private tenants. See Figure 11.3 for the tactical level PrOH Model of these systemic issues.

Research focused on the long-standing relationship with a leading national property company. Findings revealed that challenges for this department were to develop a much-needed unique selling point to develop a competitive edge in the eyes of new clients while preserving the existing client base by nurturing relationships and identifying windows of opportunity to sell additional services.

In three action teams new knowledge repositories were created, innovative ways of working were introduced and value added to both clients and lawyers' learning. Facilitating these were new case management tools, a client relationship plan, a new client on-boarding process, new work organisation within the group and finally administrative improvements. The systemic success factors (SSFs) of this professional service triad: professionals (lawyers), clients and the company are shown in the PrOH Model in Figure 11.3 and are described in more detail in Table 11.4.

Based on the Tinnilä and Vepsäläinen's (1995) typology of services, Commercial Property Lease Transactions are analogous to "Standard Contracts". This service type is characterised by the involvement of complex specifications but does not have extensive adaptations to an

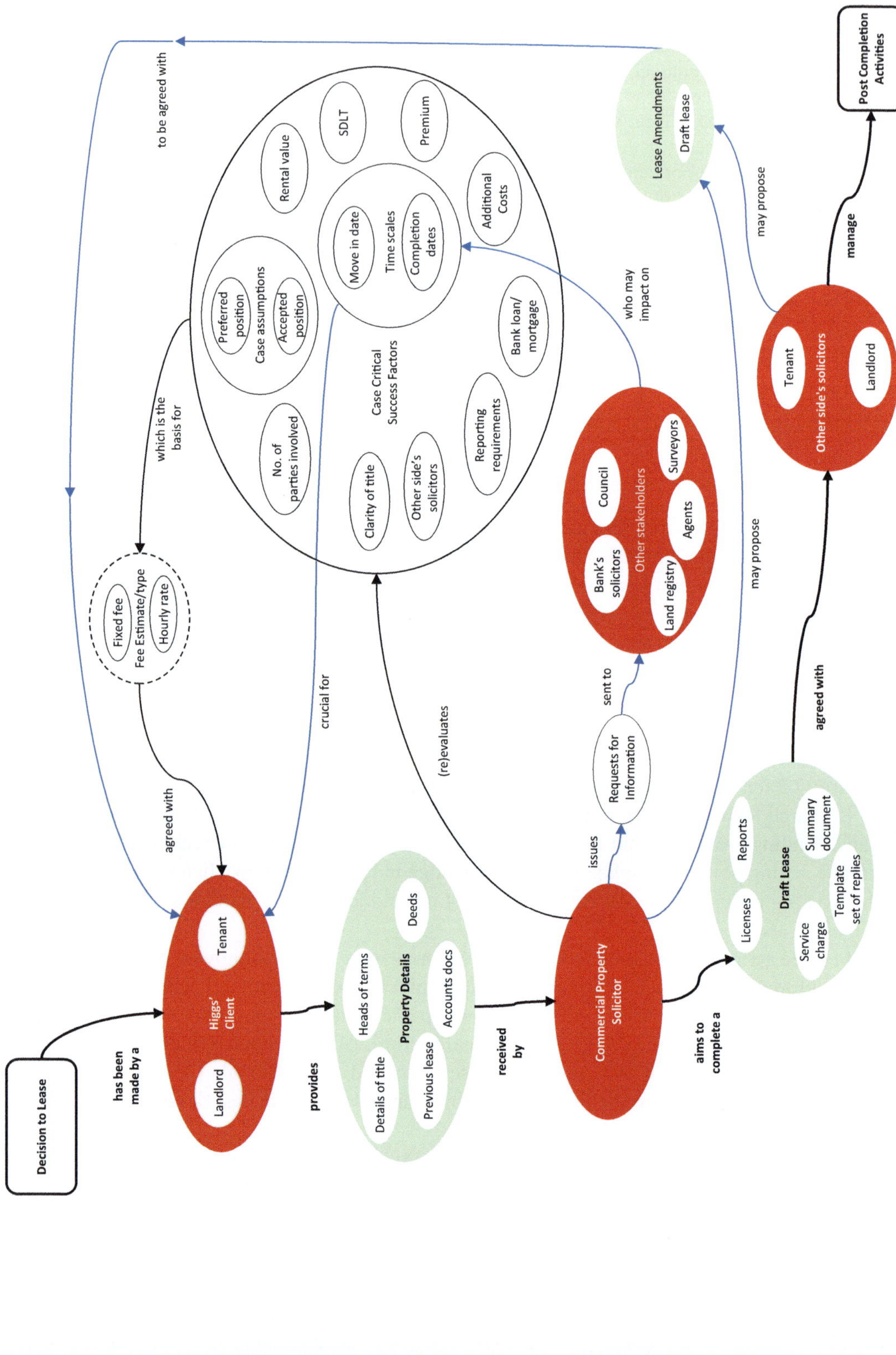
Decision to Lease
has been made by a
Higgs' Client
Landlord
Tenant
provides
Property Details
Details of title
Heads of terms
Previous lease
Accounts docs
Deeds
received by
Commercial Property Solicitor
aims to complete a
Draft Lease
Licenses
Reports
Service charge
Summary document
Template set of replies
agreed with
Other side's solicitors
Tenant
Landlord
manage
Post Completion Activities
may propose
Lease Amendments
Draft lease
to be agreed with
issues
Requests for Information
sent to
Other stakeholders
Bank's solicitors
Council
Land registry
Agents
Surveyors
who may impact on
may propose
(re)evaluates
crucial for
agreed with
Fee Estimate/type
Fixed fee
Hourly rate
which is the basis for
Case Critical Success Factors
Case assumptions
Preferred position
Accepted position
Rental value
SDLT
Premium
Time scales
Move in date
Completion dates
Additional Costs
No. of parties involved
Bank loan/ mortgage
Reporting requirements
Clarity of title
Other side's solicitors

TABLE 11.4 Systemic Success Factors within the Commercial Property Department

Systemic Success Factors		*Key Challenges*
For Lawyer	*For Client*	
Assumptions at the outset – Accepted/ preferred position of client. Completion timescale – move-in/move-out dates. Reporting requirements. Number of parties involved in the transaction. Lawyers of other side – amendments to documents, agreeing clauses. Fee type – hourly rate.	Fee type – fixed fee. Relationship with lawyer (institutional clients). Completion timescale – move-in/move-out dates.	Efficiency in process-driven transactions. Balancing personal service while operating on fixed fee. Improving relationship with institutional clients. Effective work division among senior and junior fee earners. Administrative routines to be standardised. Effective precedent and document management.

individual customer as there is a standard contract that specifies options and application to a client.

Corporate Services

Negotiating legal fees for corporate services (e.g. large management buyouts, mergers and acquisitions (M&A)) is notoriously challenging, as clients often supply the lawyers with insufficient knowledge at the outset. For example, information on claims, disputes, opponents and banks' lawyers may come to light only during the latter stages of the case and affect time spent by lawyers. In addition, there can often be excessive competitive pressure to win the work, and lawyers must provide attractive quotes to "out-do" the competition. In doing so, lawyers often have to make assumptions at the outset of a case to arrive at a price quote, which may contain uncertain estimates and inaccurate initial projections of time and effort, which may result in erosion of revenue contributions in the form of fee "write-offs". The ability to produce near-accurate projections of billable hours is the "holy grail" in negotiating, winning and sustaining legal business of this type. These **systemic success factors** for change are shown in the PrOH Model in Figure 11.4.

The systemic success factors (SSFs) of this professional service triad: professionals (lawyers), clients and the company are shown in the PrOH Model in Figure 11.4 and are summarised in Table 11.5. Actions teams were formed to make changes based on these.

This department was primarily concerned with mergers and acquisitions (M&A) services of corporate law, typically of low volume and high variety operations. Findings reveal the ability to produce near-accurate projections of billable hours based on experience is essential in quoting, negotiating and winning new business. As there is currently little support for lawyers in this process, there is a need to design new tools and approaches for acquiring and executing large corporate transactions. This **Action Research Cycle (ARC)** also explored and addressed some practical issues surrounding administrative tasks and handling documentation as well

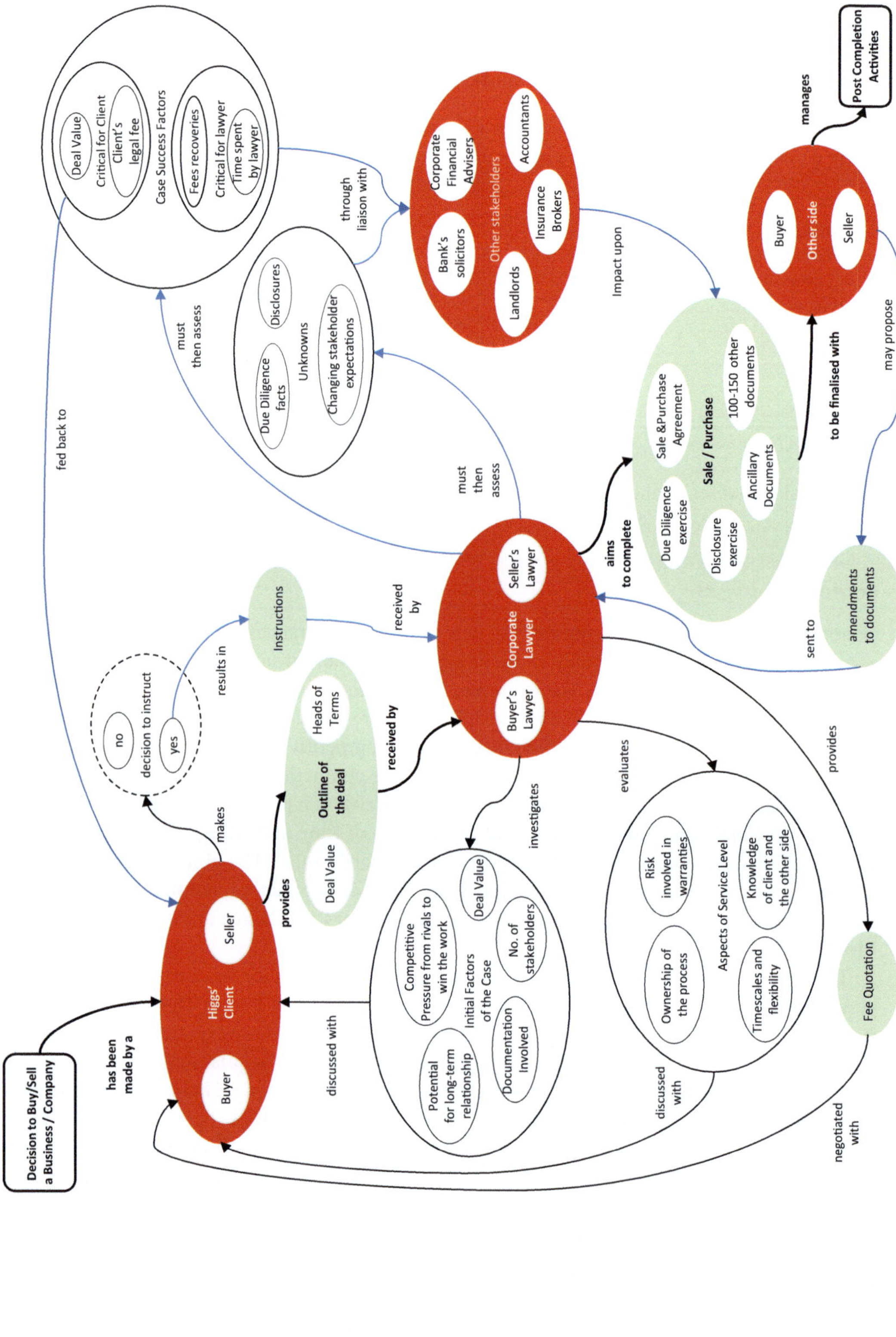

FIGURE 11.4 Corporate Solicitor Aims to Complete a Sale or Purchase

TABLE 11.5 Systemic Success Factors within the Corporate Department

Systemic Success Factors		*Key Challenges*
For Lawyer	*For Client*	
Case complexity – Unknowns at the outset (Due diligence facts, disclosures, expectations of clients), value of the deal (e.g. management buyout), number of stakeholders, volume of documentation, amendments to documents. Fee recovery – time spent by lawyer before being instructed. Timescales and flexibility. Knowledge of client and the other side.	Less involvement in the process and technicalities – expect lawyers to close the deal smoothly. Fee – transparent and proportionate.	Quoting and scoping the work. Need for training in negotiation skills. Administrative improvements in file opening, archiving, document management.

as the process of delivering pitch documentation and supporting lawyers with softer skills and knowledge, which led to process and knowledge management standardisation.

Using Tinnilä and Vepsäläinen's (1995) typology of services, the corporate M&A services are analogous to "Contingent Relations" which are characterised bycomplex problems, many interrelated activities and intensive communication. This type of service is characterised by risk sharing and requires close relationships with the client. Innovative tool solutions such as "client transaction guide", "flow of funds" tool and "fee see-saw" helped align client and lawyer's perspectives on value and impart a uniformity and consistency in service delivery.

Private Client Department – Will Production

In most cases drafting a legal will is a straightforward activity and can be standardised and is therefore easily affected by competitive market forces as semi-qualified specialist will writers and "supermarket law shops" pose an increasing threat to medium-sized law firms such as Higgs. The challenges facing this department are minimising cost of will production, building long-term relationships with clients, effective ability to cross-sell and provide additional value-adding services to clients. These issues are depicted in the PrOH Model in Figure 11.5.

The systemic success factors (SSFs) for each element of the professional service triad: the professionals (lawyers), the clients and the general company are shown in Figure 11.5 and described in more detail in Table 11.6.

As a result of the investigation and in conjunction with lawyers and support staff, various improvements were made to the current process to eliminate fail points, improve utilisation, productivity and enrich the clients' experience. It is estimated that Higgs holds approximately 20,000 wills which have been in the firm's repository (Will Bank), sometimes for decades. Changes in technology and the potential of electronic storage capability and the possibility to "fast track" any refreshing of personal information or new wishes open some practical challenges. For example, just keeping track of the client's changing circumstances is proving difficult due to the manual process involved in retrieving the will, verifying the current address and posting letters.

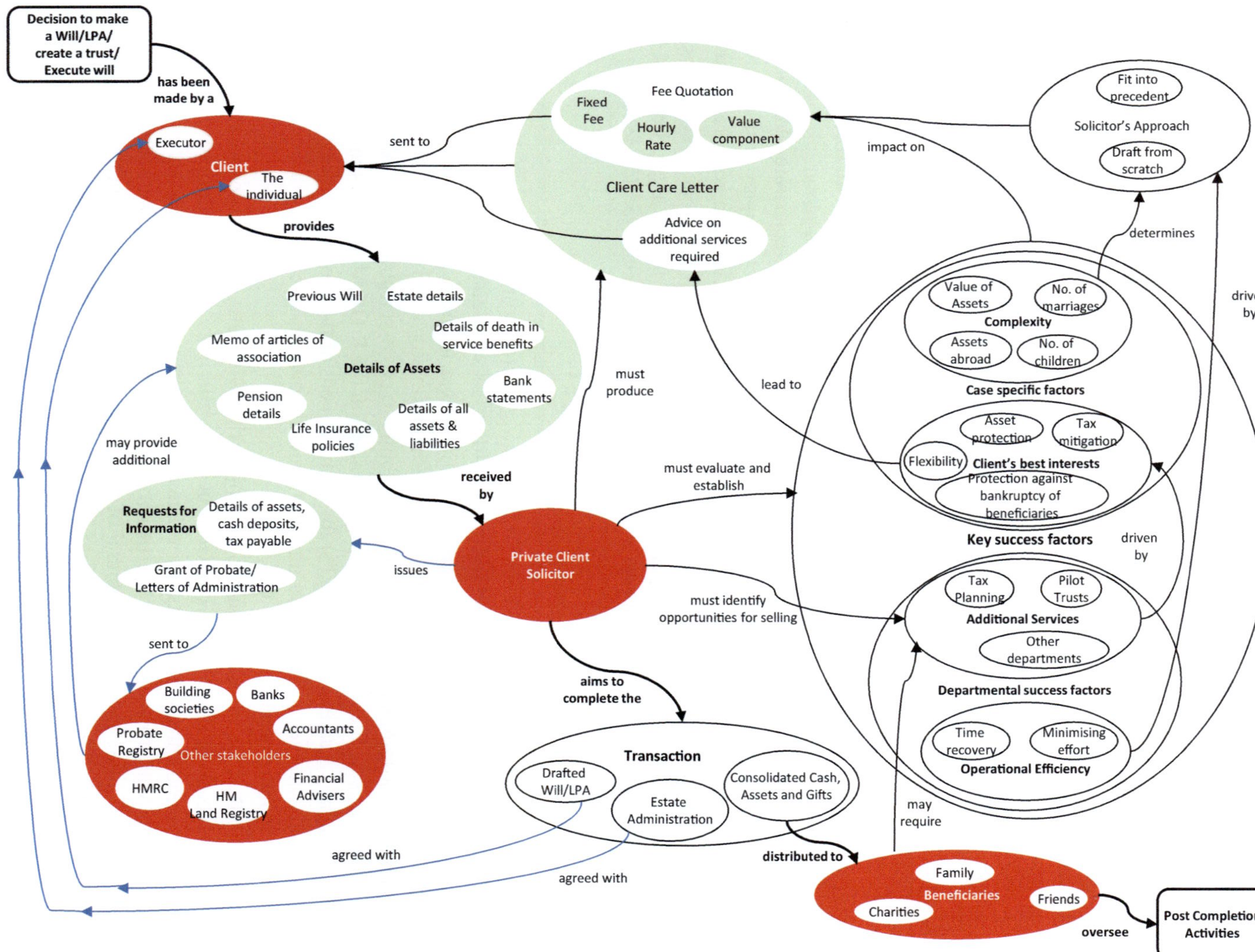

FIGURE 11.5 Private Client Solicitor Aims to Complete a Will, LPA or Probate.

TABLE 11.6 Systemic Success Factors and Challenges for Private Client Department at Lawyers Co

Systemic Success Factors			*Key Challenges*
For Lawyer	*For Client*	*For Firm*	
Case complexity – value of assets, assets abroad, number of children, etc. Information provision at the outset.	Flexibility, asset protection, tax mitigation. Speed of delivery.	Profitability Utilisation = (Actual hours billed / Total hours available) value = Realised fee per hour (Fees / Hours) Productivity = (Value) × (Utilisation) Selling additional services to clients	Improving client engagement whilst maintaining compliance. Improving time recovery. Document reusability and effective case management. Administrative routines to be standardised. Pricing and scoping complex probate matters. Work division and creation of new roles. Training and upskilling paralegals and lawyers.

Based on the Tinnilä and Vepsäläinen's (1995) typology of services categorised by the degree of service customisation, ranging from simple to complex, Private Client services such as Wills and Probate are analogous to "Mass-Transactions" as these are simple services with few options and little customisation opportunities in terms of delivery. They are routine tasks carried out according to market rules and at market price. The following practical changes were made:

- A system for identifying clients' best interests in initial and subsequent meetings to sell additional services.
- A system for scoping and budgeting for more complicated matters.
- A typology for determining the complexity of matters and taking necessary approaches to minimise time spent – for example, a case summary of critical factors and actions to take.
- Workflow management tool – that helps set reminders for necessary actions at each step and helps manage the process.
- An electronic database with contact details of all will holders and their next of kin or executors named in the will.

Overall Benefits to the Company

Practical benefits to Higgs were the development of innovative new tools changing lawyers' perspectives on pricing and service (e.g. the "case assessment radar" and the "fee seesaw") more direct engagement with clients so lawyers were able to see how their actions impacted the firm's overall performance, improved staff perception and orientation towards strategic change, time saved as a result of redesigned and streamlined processes, elimination of inaccurate pricing impacts on the top and bottom line, increased conversion rate in personal injury cases (67% to 93%), enhanced recoverable value of time recorded on accurately priced transactions and reduced time spent pursuing new opportunities.

The range of departments with different characteristics was selected using Schmenner's (1986, 2004) service volume and variety framework and observations and reflections were abductively rationalised using Tinnilä and Vepsäläinen's (1995) typology of services.

PrOH Modelling Methodology

By **abstraction** from these five legal service lines, a strategic top-level model was developed using the **abstraction** rules and guidelines outlined in Chapter 5 to create a PrOH Model shown in Figure 11.6. By using this strategic PrOH Model, it was possible to further **abduct** to strategic level theory using the strategic transformational framework developed by Pinnington and Morris (2003) to describe how a "Professional Partnership" (P2) practice can transition to a "Managed Professional Business" (MPB) (Balthu and Clegg, 2021) using a transformative framework.

Abductive rationalisation enables wider dissemination of company-based single-case transformation to a wider community interested in improving professional services.

The strategic PrOH Model in Figure 11.6 provides a high-level insight into legal processes, enabling visualisation, analysis and conceptualisation of end-to-end legal services. The PrOH Modelling Methodology's **storyboarding** facilitated structured inquiries with key stakeholders, enabling data gathering for service process redesign (Clegg et al., 2020).

Methodological nuances in this case:

- Three levels of **containment bubbles** (e.g. bubbles within bubbles within bubbles) to show grouping of entities in a PrOH Model.
- **Complex bubbles** that contain **decision bubbles** and **containment bubbles**.

Abductive Learning

Two levels of modelling were done, going from five **parallel** tactical models abstracted in-parallel up into one strategic level PrOH Model. Each level being pertinent to different theories through abductive rationalisation. In this case:

- Pinnington and Morris's P2 MPB framework (2003) at the strategic level.
- Tinnilä and Vepsäläinen's (1995) typology of services at the tactical level.

This demonstrates how **abstraction**, and **enrichment**, is useful for **abductively** generalising to theories and how different theories can simultaneously co-exist at different levels. This practice of simultaneously rationalising against two different theories which may at times conflict with one another is in line with emerging ideas on **quantum systems thinking** (Finkelstein, 1993). This is a controversial area of research that could be further considered in socio-technical systems using **abstraction** and **refinement** of holonic-based holarchies using the PrOH Modelling Methodology.

Summary

This case is of special interest, because it is from a professional service environment (Harvey et al, 2016) and uses parallel abstraction. It also uses different theories at each level to explain its findings and actions taken. It would be interesting from a systems perspective to conduct further examples of parallel PrOH Modelling, and see if other behaviours and theoretical frameworks could be applied **abductively**. More details about this case can be read in Balthu (2021) and and Balthu andClegg (2021).

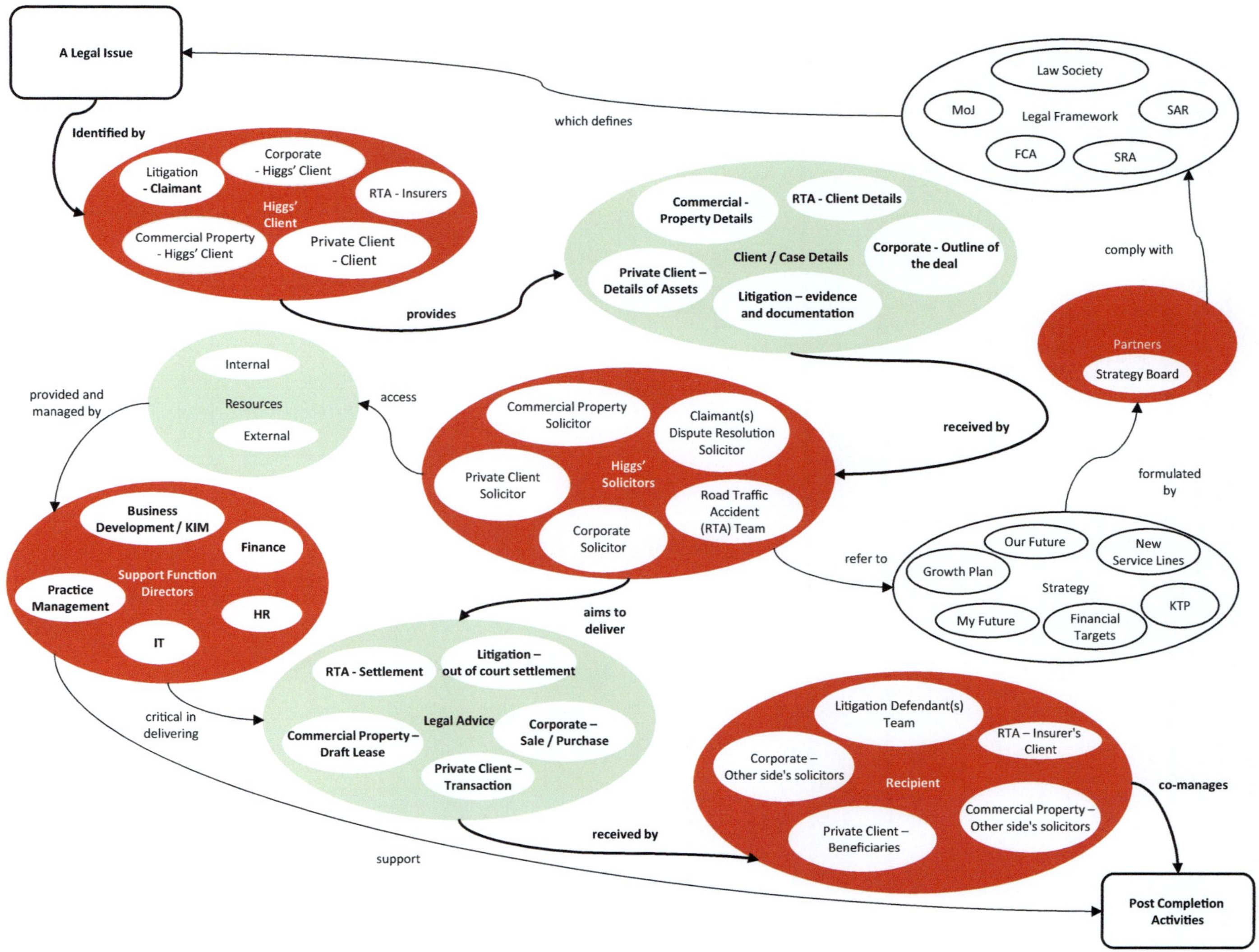

FIGURE 11.6 Higgs Solicitors Aim to Deliver Legal Advice – Strategic Level PrOH Model Produced by Abstraction from Five Tactical PrOH Models.

Further Reading

Balthu, K. (2021), *Applying Systems Thinking to Improve Professional Service Operations*. Ph.D Thesis, Aston University.

Balthu, K., and Clegg, B. (2021), 'Improving Professional Service Operations: Action Research in a Law Firm', *International Journal of Operations and Production Management*, Vo. 41, Iss. 6, pp. 805–829.

12

CASE 7: QUALITY MANAGEMENT

SigmaPro

Context and Background

This case is a less conventional business improvement challenge and more of a business development opportunity for SigmaPro, as an action research partner, which wanted to develop its services and products. SigmaPro is a franchisee delivering **lean six sigma** (LSS) training (Pepper and Spedding 2010; Clegg et al., 2010; Clegg et al., 2013) from a US-based parent organisation. The US parent company provides marketing for its services and training materials that are adapted by SigmaPro for different clients according to requirements. To differentiate itself from other providers of the same material, SigmaPro wanted to develop a unique model to measure lean six sigma maturity levels that could be used to explain to clients what level they currently were at and where they could be in a particular timeframe to enable a training plan to be conceived and delivered. Data was collected from SigmaPro's clients. PrOH Modelling provided a means to show the Systemic Success Factors (SSFs) for how to get from a lower level of LSS maturity to a higher level of LSS maturity to increase organisational perfromance (Shafer and Moeller, 20.

At the time of doing this case, there was much uncertainty in the economic environment that meant organisations were increasingly under pressure to meet their customers' needs while maintaining cost competitiveness to reduce wasteful practices and eliminate errors. To achieve this, many organisations tried to implement LSS approaches; however, despite some well-publicised successes, results were often not realised and despite lean six sigma's popularity in practice and extensive literature on the subject, there is no definitive maturity model for how to do this. Therefore, at the time, it remained unclear how lean, and six sigma are best combined and customised to achieve maximum impact. Moreover, literature suggests that to be successful, lean six sigma should be implemented and investigated from a systemic perspective (Clegg and Orme, 2010). Therefore, the integration of lean and six sigma thinking in a systems-based maturity assessment model set a challenge for the PrOH Modelling Methodology in the context of an **action research** project.

DOI: 10.4324/9781032650425-15

Action Research and Systems Thinking

Questions asked by this research were (1) How does the literature suggest organisations should implement lean six sigma? (2) How is it possible to measure the implementation of a lean six sigma programme? (3) How do organisations choose to systemically and systematically integrate lean and six sigma approaches in practice? (4) How can "soft" and "hard" systems approaches be integrated to allow qualitative and quantitative aspects of lean six sigma to be implemented?

This research started with an extensive literature review of lean six sigma (Orme, 2016, pp.17–73) which is summarised in a "maturity" model table, criteria versus levels, as seen in Figure 12.1. Related research on the **cost of quality (CoQ)** indicates a higher maturity of organisational improvement practice results in a more desirable cost of quality profile (Sower et al., 2007). Therefore, the **cost of quality** can indicate the capability level of an organisation and its ability to evolve (Bessant et al., 2001) and can serve as a means of comparing different lean six sigma programmes and their performance across different organisations (Bititci et al., 2015).

Phase one of the research consisted of the **inductive** development of a maturity model, based on an extensive literature review outlining four levels:

- Level 1: no process exists/action is taken on the element.
- Level 2: a process exists, but it is not highly explicit or regularly adhered to.
- Level 3: a clear process exists, but it is not always adhered to.
- Level 4: a clear process exists, and it is always adhered to.

The lower levels of LSS maturity were found to be associated with higher levels of **cost of quality** and the higher levels of LSS maturity with lower levels of **cost of quality**. However, in practice, lower maturity quality systems could not make these measurements with any confidence, so this is difficult to prove.

Data was collected from seven different SigmaPro clients who were at the time in the process of applying LSS. The output of this was a PrOH Model for each client's case (not shown in this chapter). Each case was able to be assessed against Table 12.1 and once a PrOH Model had been constructed, in accordance with rules and guidelines given in Chapter 4, it was rated 1–4 in terms of its LSS maturity (see Table 12.1). Case 1 was rated at 3.3, Case 2 at 3.0, Case 3 at 2.7, Case 4 at 2.7, Case 5 at 2.7, Case 6 at 2.5 and Case 7 at 2.3. From these seven PrOH Models a generic PrOH Model, as seen in Figure 12.1, was produced (Clegg and Orme, 2012). Further details of these client cases are given in detail in Orme (2016, p.139 onwards).

Use of Theory

This case differs from others as it started with LSS, a known body of knowledge spanning theory and practice (Gutiérrez Gutiérrez et al, 2009), and through inductive thinking produced a reference table for LSS levels and applied this to practice by producing a PrOH Model for each different client case.

The reason for giving this application of the PrOH Modelling Methodology is because PrOH Modelling has been used in a different context – to benchmark one client case against another using reference (Table 12.2) constructed from literature before cases were chosen and

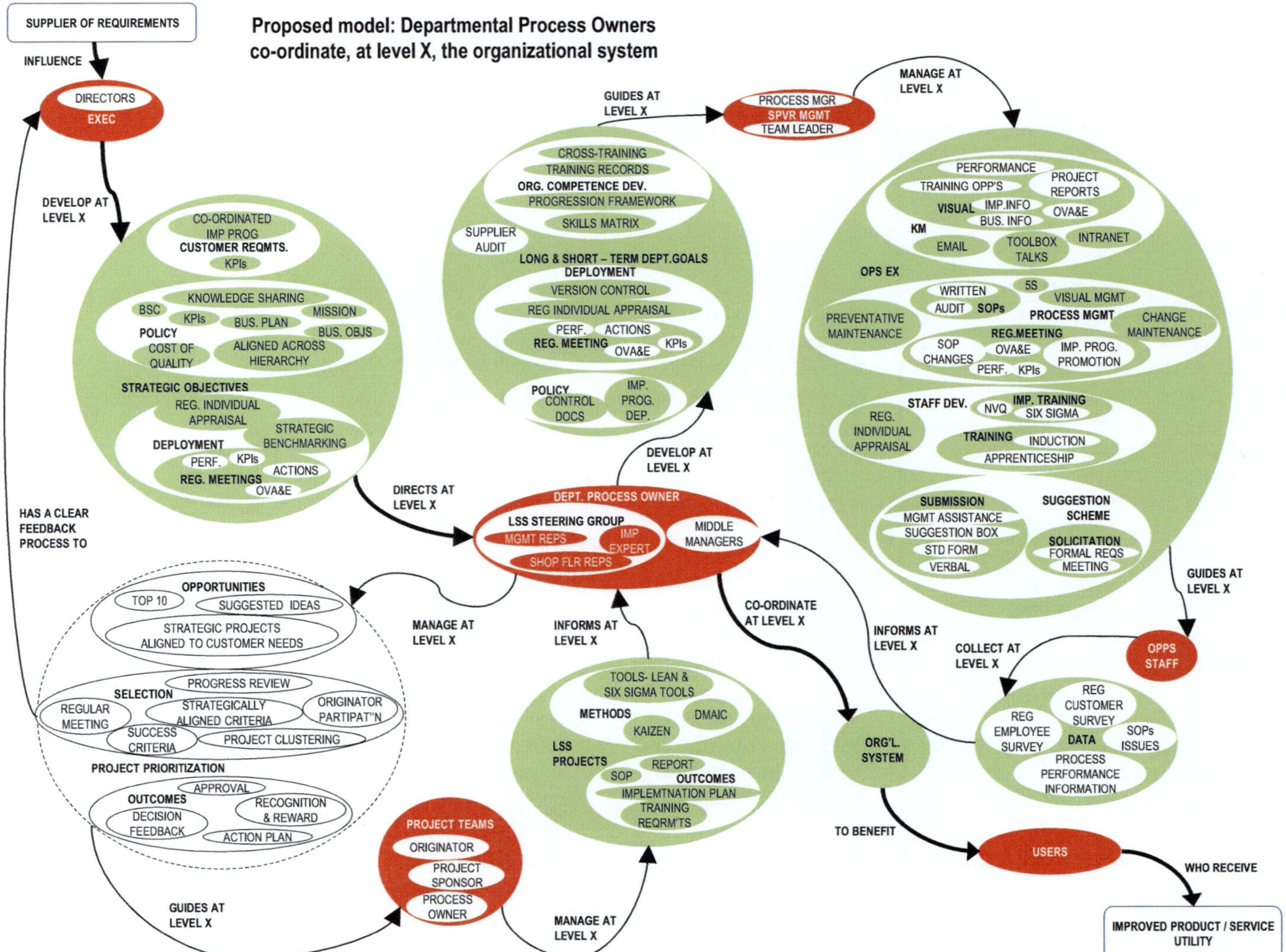

FIGURE 12.1 LSS Maturity PrOH Model.

Source: Orme, 2016, p.209.

TABLE 12.1 Lean Six Sigma Maturity Model

Criteria	*Level 1*	*Level 2*	*Level 3*	*Level 4*
Strategic Thinking				
Leadership	Senior management has little or no involvement in improvement activity.	Senior management involvement is limited to the allocation of resources.	Senior management allocates resources and are personally involved in aspects such as progress reviews.	They are fully involved and promote improvement effort as a key strategic initiative
Organizational values, attitudes and ethics	There is no clear outline of what values, attitudes and ethics are expected within the organization.	There is limited communication and adherence to organizational values, attitudes and ethics.	There is effective communication of organizational values, attitudes and ethics but organizational adherence is limited.	There is effective communication of organizational values, attitudes and ethics and organizational adherence.
Strategy	Business Plans are financial only for next 12 months.	Business plans define financial, strategy and short-term goals.	Business plans cover the next 5 years and include both financial and non-financial goals.	Business plans cover 1,5 and 10 years. There are clear improvement targets for all strategy areas
Deployment	There is no process for communicating business goals and targets; it is not seen as important.	The need for goal deployment is recognised but business goals and targets are communicated in an ad-hoc way.	There is a clear process for communicating goals and targets, employees are aware of them but there is no formal review process.	Goal deployment and performance management exists for all employees linking day to day activities to strategic goals and targets.
Improvement Approach				
People Deployment	Employees are focused on own job only, there is no structured improvement approach	Some employees are involved in part time improvement effort	Some employees are involved part-time and there are some full-time projects being run by senior management.	Improvement effort is part of everyday activity for all employees in all key strategic areas, including a mix of project and local activity.

Criteria	*Level 1*	*Level 2*	*Level 3*	*Level 4*
Project Prioritization	There is ad-hoc selection of projects by management; they are not linked to strategy.	Projects are selected through discussion but there are no clear selection criteria.	Strategic projects are selected using clear criteria, but local project selection is ad-hoc.	Projects are prioritized at all levels and selected using defined criteria.
Improvement Processes	There are no formal problem-solving methods used; we rely on experience	There are some basic tools used, for example Pareto	Basic tools are used, and when required, statistics to solve more complex problems.	A range of different approaches are used, including complex statistical tools, to solve operational problems and reduce risk in new product introduction.
Improvement tracking	The performance of the improvement programme is not tracked.	Performance tracking limited to operational aspects such as numbers trained	KPIs link programme to some aspects of organizational objectives but not all customer, financial, process and people impact are tracked.	KPIs link programme to all aspects of organizational objectives including tracking of customer, financial, process and people impact.
Operational Excellence				
Environment	Generally, the workplace is untidy.	The work environment is generally tidy but is not actively maintained; 5S or similar used in some areas	The workplace is mostly well organized, clean and actively maintained. We use 5S or similar in all operational areas.	Everywhere is well organized, clean and maintained continuously, 5S or similar is used across all areas to increase efficiency and effectiveness and add value
Staff Development	There is no formal approach to people competences and employee development. Employees do not feel involved.	There are training programmes in some areas to develop staff. There is some focus on employee involvement and teambuilding.	There are staff development plans for everyone. Employees focus on teamwork and are empowered to make changes.	There are staff development plans in place for everyone and succession planning in operation for all key roles. Improvement activity is self-sustaining.

Criteria	*Level 1*	*Level 2*	*Level 3*	*Level 4*
Processes	Processes are not defined. There is a reliance on the experience of the people carrying out the work.	Documentation and SOPs exist to define main tasks, but this is not fully utilized.	There are clear and concise operating procedures for all operational areas, but adherence is limited.	Clear and concise operating procedures exist for all key activities which are fully adhered to. These are created as part of new product / process introduction and maintained and updated as part of continuous improvement.
Systems perspective	The operational focus is on individual tasks and functions.	Processes are recognized and managed but not in a connected way. Departmental targets are not aligned.	Processes managed with consideration of other processes but at a sub-system level. Some departmental targets are aligned.	The organization understands the interconnectedness of individual processes and manages them from a holistic perspective. All departmental targets are fully aligned.
Supplier relationship management	Suppliers are not involved in any aspect of planning or development	Suppliers are involved but only in terms of specifications and demand planning	Suppliers have regular contact to ensure flow of processes but are treated at arm's length.	Suppliers are partnered with and developed to provide competitive advantage.
There are attempts to capture improvements and best practice, but co-ordination is limited.	Best practice and improvement outcomes are captured and made explicit, but active knowledge sharing is not facilitated.		Best practice and improvement are captured and communicated to relevant stakeholders. Knowledge sharing is encouraged and active. Market leadership through best practice is paramount.	
Change	The organization sees no need for change	The need for change is recognized but activities are uncoordinated	Change is encouraged but tends to be reactive in nature and is not always maintained.	The need for proactive change is seen as key for competitive advantage and changes are actively maintained.

Criteria	*Level 1*	*Level 2*	*Level 3*	*Level 4*
Knowledge management	There is no process for capturing or communicating best practice or improvement.	There are attempts to capture improvements and best practice, but co-ordination is limited.	Best practice and improvement outcomes are captured and made explicit but active knowledge sharing is not facilitated	Best practice and improvement are captured and communicated to relevant stakeholders. Knowledge sharing is encouraged and active. Market leadership through best practice is paramount
Data				
Tracking	Tracking is limited to financial with little or no other data	Financials and some KPI's exist but these are not aligned with business goals.	Some KPI's aligned with strategy but not for all areas. KPI's not systematically tested for validity.	Strategically aligned and validated KPI's drive day-to-day improvement and breakthrough improvement.
Data Accuracy	Financials are audited but data accuracy is not questioned	There is recognition that data may have inaccuracies, but this is not acted upon	Some performance data is systematically tested for accuracy	All key performance data is systematically tested for accuracy and the risks of inaccurate data are understood.

Source: Adapted from Orme, 2016, pp.72–73.

modelled. Each PrOH Model for each case was a *separate* standalone PrOH Model unconnected from any other PrOH Model. All PrOH Modelling was at the same pitch of modelling. Abstraction was not used to produce the generic PrOH Model.

If the **Logic Compass** (Figure 2.4, Chapter 2) is applied to this action research project, the initial phase predominantly exhibits **inductive logic** to produce the reference table; the middle phase predominantly exhibits **analogous logic** to classify and compare the maturity of client cases against the *a priori* framework and the final phase produced a generic PrOH Model of LSS through **deductive logic** by amalgamating known theory and empirical case evidence, resulting in a generic version of a LSS Maturity PrOH Model being proposed in Figure 12.1.

Methodological Contribution

Additionally, through this research, a novel integrated systems methodology, combining PrOH and Systems Dynamics, was developed and tested, constituting a new contribution to systems thinking (Orme, 2016).

Although not covered in detail in this chapter, it is important to note that the PrOH Model SIPOC Tables were instrumental in achieving more than one type of modelling, as they are able to form a dataset for different forms of systems modelling and simulation, taking research to "harder" directions if more quantitative data is added, or "softer" directions with more text-based qualitative analysis.

Summary

It would be interesting to experiment using PrOH Modelling in different types and sequences of logic, as given in the **Logic Compass** (Figure 2.4, Chapter 2) to see how these might encourage innovative and creative solutions for LSS or other similar management practices.

Further Reading

Clegg, B., and Orme, R. (2012), 'System of Systems: Pure and Applied to Lean Six Sigma', In System of Systems Gheorghe, A.V. Ed., Intech. http://www.intechopen.com/books/system-of-systems/system-of-systems-pure-and-applied-to-lean-six-sigma

Orme, R.A. (2016), *A Systems Approach to Developing a Unified Methodology and Deployment Model to Help Maximize Impact of Lean Thinking and Six Sigma in Organizations.* PhD Thesis, Aston University.

13

CASE 8: REASSESSING A UNIVERSITY SCHOOL'S PORTFOLIO DELIVERY

Organisational Context and Challenge

This case improved the efficacy and efficiency of professional support services and teaching processes in a leading UK university to align better with changing academic requirements and external market forces. The challenge was that one school in the university, the Languages and Social Sciences (LSS) School, had declining numbers of students and an increasingly diverse range of course offerings with fewer students in each. Delivery of courses was becoming untenable from financial and operational perspectives, and the **systemic success factors** of change needed to be more carefully understood, consensus built around change and remedial action taken.

Action Research, Systems Thinking and Action Research

The PrOH Modelling Methodology was used to simultaneously review strategic and operational processes, because this enabled roles, processes and tasks to be more purposefully redefined and reengineered to meet endogenous organisational requirements and exogenous market forces (Clegg, 2020). As always with PrOH Modelling, numerous stakeholders with a diverse range of backgrounds were interviewed. These included staff involved in teaching, research and management as well as student representatives and members of the University's Executive. PrOH Models were created which unified different stakeholder perspectives and which were later presented to a broader audience in the school and central university services using the PrOH Modelling story boarding technique.

This case study involved a **holarchical** set of PrOH Models consisting of one tactically pitched model representing the views of the Dean and senior management team called "School of LSS Deliver an Educational Experience" as given in Figure 13.1 which shows the overall customer-facing process starting by taking newcomers to the university as an input and producing educated students as an output.

DOI: 10.4324/9781032650425-16

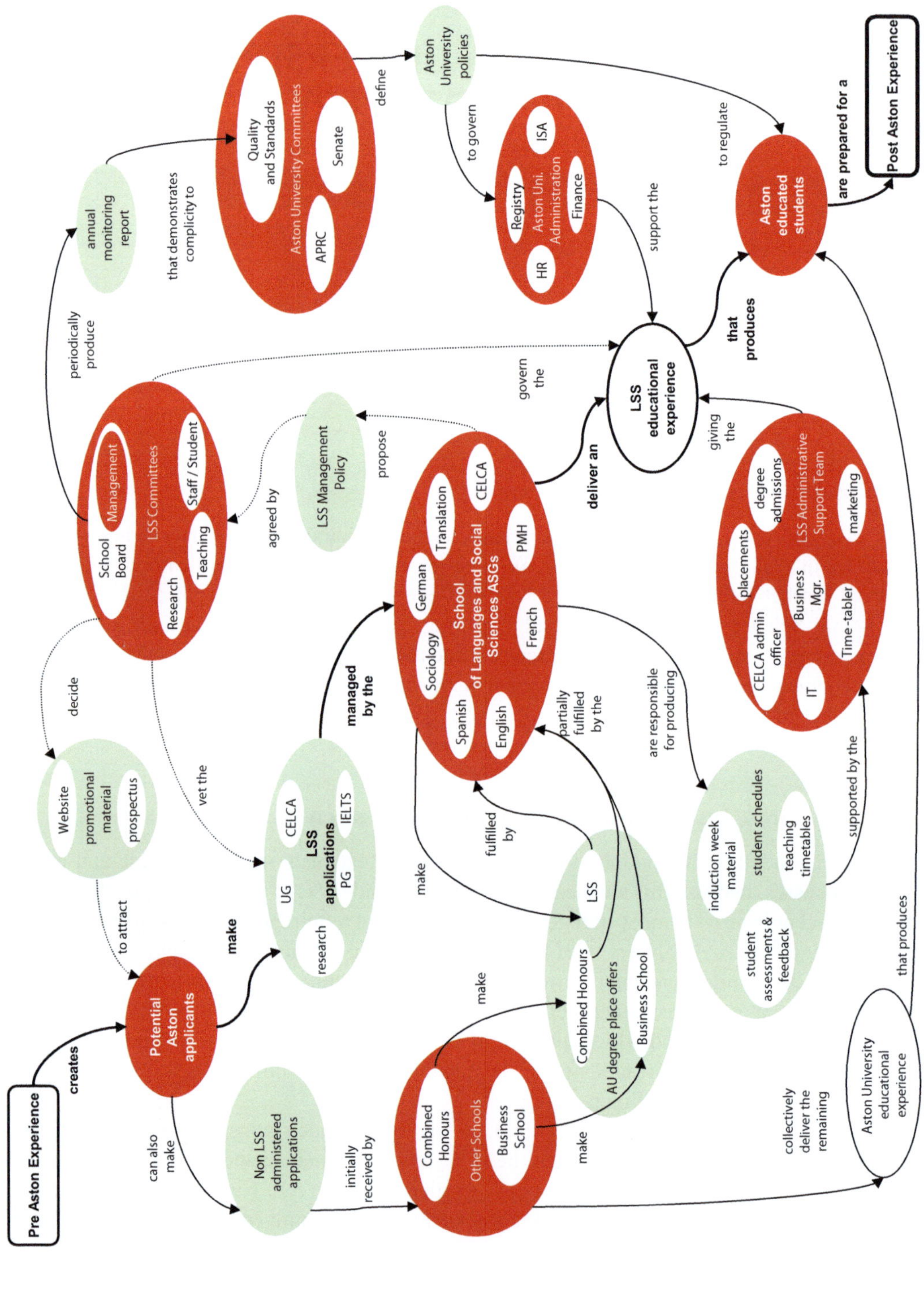

FIGURE 13.1 School of Language and Social Science (SLSS) Delivers an Educational Experience.

The systemic success factors associated with the tactical-level view in Figure 13.1 are as follows:

- Each Academic Subject Group (ASG) in the School of LSS creates an administrative workload that needs to be better aligned to support staff provision and achieve a clearer demarcation of roles.
- Education provision needs to be increasingly thought of as product/service delivery.
- Applications for the School of LSS come from many routes other than just the LSS. An overall university experience needs to be presented for integrated courses, and the interfaces with these other parts of the university need to be improved.
- Annual planning horizons should be declared and used by all, increasing the use of partial, provisional and firmed-up versions of timetables where possible. These need to be driven by a university-wide calendar.
- LSS policy and procedures must be available to all staff and students. Decision making should be devolved to operational staff with authority for decision-making responsibilities, including budgetary devolution where appropriate.
- External promotion and marketing of the LSS must set realistic expectations for potential students.
- IT systems are fragmented; better compatibility and integration are required to speed up data exchanges.
- Functional divisions within ASGs must be removed to achieve more collective strategising.
- Support for faculty-wide research programmes must be improved.
- The quality and standards of staff performance (via student, peer and line-manager feedback) must be measured against volume (load levels) and responsibilities (actions).

The tactical PrOH Model in Figure 13.1 was enriched by producing two lower-pitched, operational PrOH Models called:

- "LSS Make LSS Place Offers" describing activities that occur before and during recruitment.
- "LSS Complete the LSS Educational Experience" describing activities occurring after the students have been recruited and are in attendance.

The **holarchy** diagram for this case and its set of PrOH Models is shown in Figure 13.2. All three PrOH Models were storyboarded and presented to LSS with systemic success factors assigned to each scene in a town-hall meeting attended by more than 100 LSS School members.

A strategic PrOH Model linking the LSS to other schools (e.g. the business school or the science and engineering school) and the overall university strategy (via a college structure) could also have been produced through abstraction if required.

Benefits to University

This project resulted in some rationalisation of courses and departmental groups and later led to the LSS School merging with other schools into a college to gain efficiency from economies of scale in their back-office operations and marketing functions, which strengthened their combined teaching portfolio and research centre presence. The project had positive international implications as many more students were recruited from outside the UK.

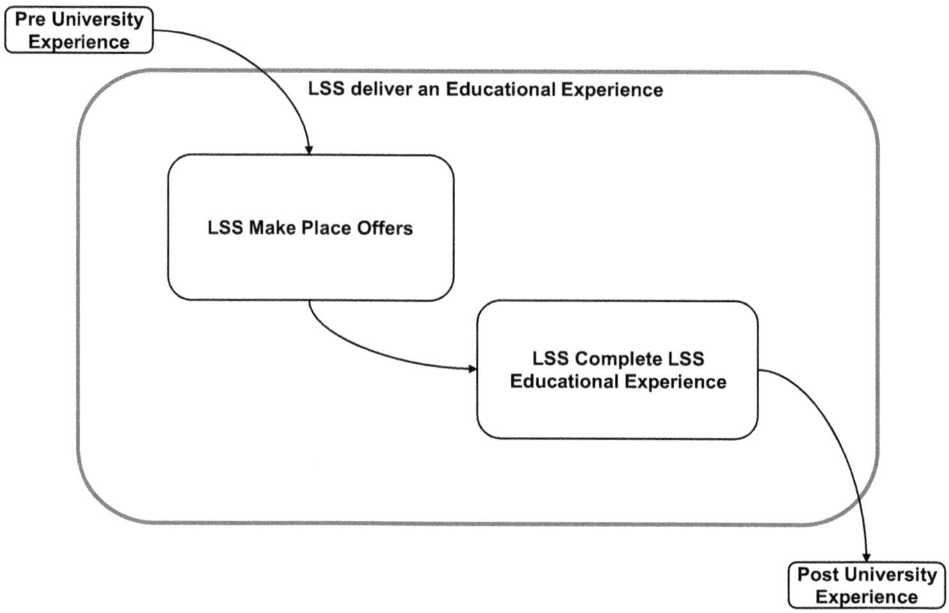

FIGURE 13.2 Holarchy Model for Set of PrOH Models in the LSS Case.

Theoretical Abductions

Hayes and Wheelwright's (1979a, 1979b) volume and variety conceptual framework and Silvestro et al.'s (1992) adaptions for services are used in this study as a framework to abductively rationalise and explain findings from a theoretical perspective, via abductive logic (Lawson, 1998; Sætre and Van de Ven, 2021a, 2021b) to explain shifts in operational delivery.

Because new departments and new academics joined the LSS and because the number of students increased, an overall increase of throughput was placed on the school's incumbent administrative processes. These processes reached a critical breaking point, because they lacked efficacy and efficiency and were under- and inappropriately resourced. This action research project highlighted many of the **systemic success factors** for change and recommended corrective interventions. These are discussed below using the 4Vs (variety, variation over time, volume and visibility) theoretical framework that provide a useful and relevant typology of operations management characteristics (Slack et al., 2004, pp.20–25).

Broadly, this case shows that higher education organisations need to plan more strategically and be as good at data and knowledge processing as they are at delivering pedagogical content. The 4Vs' model was used to explain recent changes in LSS. First, student volumes initially increased in an unplanned way from 2012 to 2014 and led to too much organisational complexity and cost. Second, corrective actions took place during 2015–2016, reducing cost and complexity in educational service delivery and in LSS's organisation. Third, it demonstrates why future directions must lie in a conscious decision to go with either (1) high volume and lower variety value-based strategy associated with relatively low visibility and smoothed variation or (2) a higher variety and lower volume premium-priced strategy with greater visibility and unsmoothed variation. Going for both options ("(1)" and "(2)") is not considered possible by the 4Vs' framework. The 4Vs' framework also advises against high volumes and high variety, because it leads to overly complex processes and high cost of delivery and advises against low volumes and low variety, because it is unlikely that sustained delivery is possible. Figure 13.3 shows these transitionary paths, where between 2012 and 2014, delivery had started to move away from the best fit line (from i to ii) and then return towards it (from ii to iii) because of planned changes made in 2015–2016.

PrOH Modelling was used in this case to clarify the positive and negative effects of change processes and facilitate transitional recommendations for improvements. The PrOH Modelling Methodology's holistic properties were useful to show where new roles should be created (e.g. new marketing and admissions roles); show where specific tasks and roles would be better consolidated (e.g. research and quality activities and executive officer and business manager roles); help with improving continuous flow (e.g. more connectivity between online ICT); suggest more suitable division or fragmentation of roles (e.g. dedicated administrators for each ASG, better use of sessional staff, and a dedicated role for managing assessments) and show where to add further resources to the process (e.g. to help level loads and deal with lumpy demand patterns). These systemic insights were made possible by simultaneously considering the tactically pitched LSS model and the lower-pitched operational models – provided collectively by the set of three **holarchical** PrOH Models – which catalysed change recommendations from detailed examination of operational practices and the creation of new strategic level visions.

Because this case study led to a significant redefinition of roles and tasks, we can see that the perceived misalignment between academic requirements and administrative support was substantiated and remedied. Additionally, by collectively redefining the school's **systemic success**

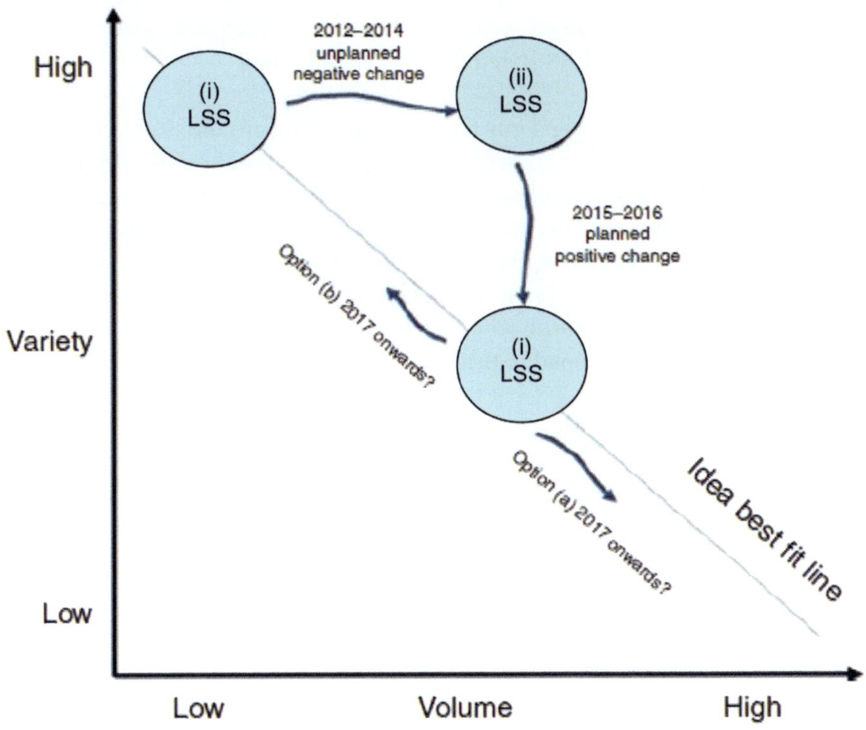

FIGURE 13.3 Changes Made LSS in the Context of the 4Vs' Theoretical Service Delivery Concept: A Summary of Phases and Time Lapses.

factors, it was possible to fundamentally change reporting structures, power and authority and enhance the culture in LSS. This was achieved by using a holistically composed multi-pitched set of systems thinking models produced using the PrOH Modelling Methodology.

Methodological Contribution

Previously, PrOH Modelling had predominantly been used in the private sector for engineering and manufacturing activities. This study showed how PrOH Modelling can be used in abductive rationalisation against conceptual frameworks, such as the 4Vs' model to stimulate thinking about roles and tasks in processes (Rytmeister, 2009) and how they can be merged through abstracted thinking or rethought through **enriched** understanding.

Together, collective decision making and action taking moved LSS towards a "collective consciousness" that enabled frontline staff and the management team to view themselves differently (Hodgkinson and Brown, 2003). The key to doing this was effective individual and group learning "in" action, reflection "on" action and reflection "for" action, as embodied in PrOH Modelling and other leading systems intervention approaches (e.g. Revans, 1982; Kolb, 1984; Senge, 1990). In this case, the top-down "tactical" modelling view was more formal, overt and management-led, whereas the bottom-up view was more latent and heartfelt. Bringing both views together increased the novelty of action taking, the credibility and confidence of all staff and the relevance of actions taken in response to exogenous market forces and political changes. For frontline staff, this diminished scepticism and suspicion of the senior management team's motives, and for the senior management team, it improved the overall collegiality of the school. This meant that changes were more readily accepted and easier to implement.

In early 2017, the head of the LSS stated that this exercise had

> [...] really helped us to understand our processes, clarify our core mission and know what our peripheral activities were. It showed us how we could build on our strengths to deliver courses efficiently, effectively and most importantly with financial sustainability, which considering recent budgetary cuts and regulatory changes, by the UK Government, is our primary concern. What was particularly interesting is that by using the "4Vs' framework" as a theoretical framework we found that those in strategic positions were less directly affected by "V-changes" than those who were in operational positions – who had the least authority and least time to respond to them and change them [...].

This is a phenomenon that the authors refer to as the 4Vs' latent whipping effect:

> [...] Therefore we should always take a holistic view of our school at every level and at every stage of our delivery; and by doing so we will be in a stronger position to tackle upcoming challenges. We would use these techniques again in the future to reassess our constantly changing situation.

The changes made will hopefully make the delivery of modern foreign languages more resilient, efficient and effective and increase the percentage of native English-speaking students working in non-Anglophonic countries.

Summary

This action research activity was considered by those involved to have a positive and instrumental effect on instigating change. It was probably successful partly because it took the view that "[...] the future of [a] university is contingent on how well internal adaption processes to external changes are implemented [...]" (Sporn, 1995, p.72). In summary, this holistic thinking

- raised awareness of systemic school-level issues and reduced inertia to create change at the strategic, tactical and operational levels;
- freed up academics from administrative duties so that they could devote more time to teaching and research activities while simultaneously reducing bureaucracy;
- provided clarification of core processes, roles and responsibilities so that a customer-facing process focus was adopted and reporting structures were unequivocal;
- made sure that the support structure met the new academic requirements;
- ensured that critical events in the academic year were fully resourced along with a contingency to deal with any unforeseen circumstances; and
- increased professionalism and collectivism for teaching and professional staff, allowing discretionary behaviour to flourish.

A full discussion of these can be found in Clegg (2020) as it discusses the whole case in detail.

Further Reading

Clegg, B.T. (2020), 'Improving Systemic Success Factors in a University to Achieve More Effective and Efficient Operations: Using the PrOH Modelling Methodology', *Business Process Management Journal*, Vol. 26, Iss. 2, pp. 630–654.

PART IV

Reflection and Future Research

Abstract

Part Four gives practical next steps for action researchers planning to use the PrOH Modelling Methodology and future developments in PrOH Modelling.

Chapter 14 reintroduces the PrOH Modelling Methodology as introduced in Chapter 4. Each part of the PrOH Modelling Methodology is taken in turn and practical aspects such as engaging with clients, managing the project, and getting impactful deliverables are discussed.

Chapter 15 looks at the future directions of action research and systems thinking such as methodological and theoretical developments and new application areas.

14

REFLECTIONS ON OVER 25 YEARS OF USING THE PROH MODELLING METHODOLOGY IN ACTION RESEARCH

Introduction

The purpose of this chapter is to give you, the reader and potential user of PrOH Modelling, a summary of practical things to look out for and do when using the PrOH Modelling Methodology in **action research** projects. This chapter is not intended to replicate theory covered in Parts I and II or cases given in Part III but gives pragmatic, hands-on tips from experienced users of PrOH Modelling who have worked in action research projects.

Before **action research** can begin, a "case company" is required. These are found by networking in industry events, having a website that promotes you and your skills and presenting a professional approach to undertaking the work. Cases are set-up by agreeing on a *value proposition* from the action researcher to the "client organisation". Proficiency in methodology is essential, and some background knowledge of the relevant sector is important although the researcher must realise they will never become as expert in the case organisation as those in it and so must make contributions as a methodologist and systems thinker with broader industry experiences brought in from having done other cases.

The PrOH Methodology – Practical Guidance

The PrOH Modelling Methodology in Figure 14.1 (as introduced in Chapter 4, Figure 4.1) is used to structure further stage-by-stage guidance given in Table 14.1.

To reiterate the basics:

1. **Planning**: Scope granularity of real-world human activity system in an organisation (e.g. process) and define minimum viable elements of the system and reason(s) for change.

   Researching – secondary planning to contextualise practical study in a wider field of use using secondary research.

DOI: 10.4324/9781032650425-18

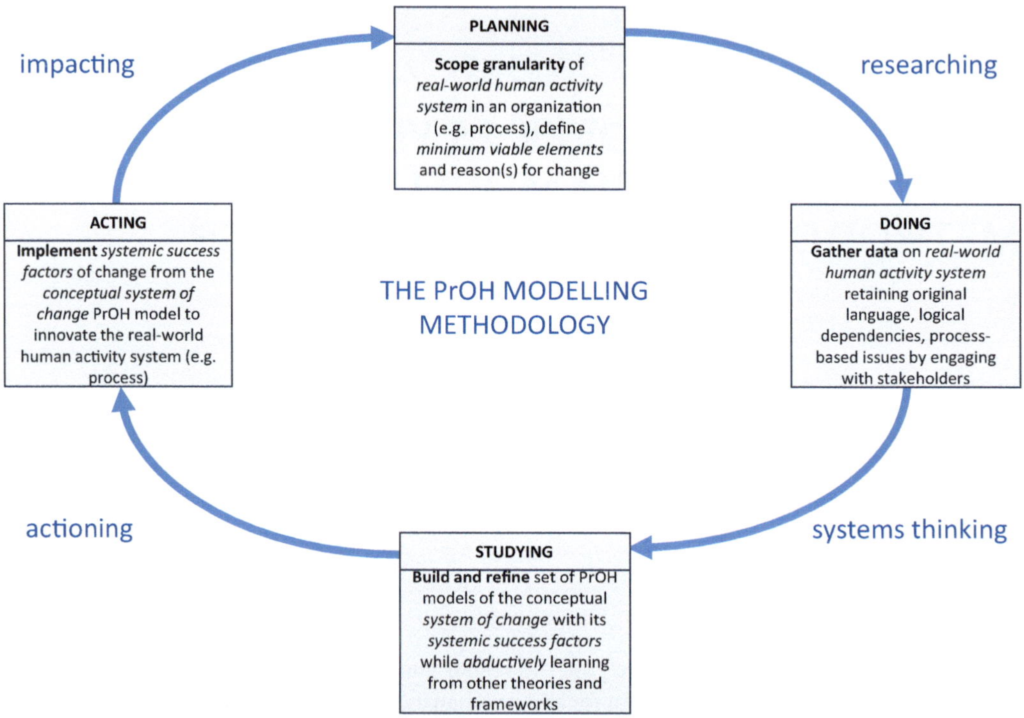

FIGURE 14.1 The PrOH Model Methodology.
(Reprise of Figure 4.1 from Chapter 4.)

2. **Doing**: Gather data on real-world human activity systems retaining original language, logical dependencies and process-based issues by engaging with stakeholders.

   Systems Thinking – conceptualising a system of change from the real-world system under observation (e.g. process) of "as-is" and "to-be" thinking into a conceptual system of change.

3. **Studying**: Build and refine a (set of) PrOH Models of the conceptual system of change with its systemic success factors while abductively learning from other theories and frameworks.

   Actioning – drawing on best practice research from other sources.

4. **Acting**: Implement the *systemic success factors* of change from the PrOH Model of the *conceptual system of change* to innovate the real-world human activity system (e.g. process).

   Impacting – practical knowledge transfer and imbibition of actions into practice.

TABLE 14.1 Summary of Practical Do's and Don'ts of PrOH Modelling Methodology in Action Research

Stage	*Do's*	*Don'ts*
Planning	Ideally get your project funded by a company in-kind and better still with a financial contribution, so the case company values your findings.	Don't do work that is not valued by the "client" organisation.
	Get the scope of the action research project defined and managed as a project using all good project management practices, tools and techniques.	Don't forget this is a project that could last up to three years (e.g. length of a PhD) and will need to be managed as a project.
	Be clear on what the client wants out of the project and what you, the action researcher, wants from the project.	Don't forget to define project stages and stage gates with objectives, deliverables, intended outcomes and intended impacts.
	Sign a contract, or memorandum of understanding, with a delivery plan and stage payments.	Don't forget to formalise the **action research** as a project.
	Get ethical approval from client and researchers' organisation for the work.	Don't forget that ethical considerations will be important if you wish to publish your work.
	Remember to get a non-disclosure agreement (NDA) signed.	Don't forget to establish if you need to anonymise names, facts and figures.
	Make sure you are covered with professional indemnity insurance.	Make sure that recommendations have "buy-in" from the "client".
Researching	Keep an open mind about challenges one might find with organisational issues. Be prepared to change.	Don't forget that in **action research** the problem you think you were researching when you embarked may change as new knowledge is revealed.
	Begin to get involved in case study organisational activities, strategic and operational, as much as possible. Try to arrange time to spend in the organisation; for instance, block visits and/or regular on-line and face-to-face meetings as required.	Don't forget to do background reading on company, sector and industry to increase your ability to understand the case.
Doing	Keep data recorded in a format that is accessible and useable by others (diagrams, spreadsheets, videos interviews, voice recording, documents, etc.).	Don't forget that getting primary data from organisation is difficult, time consuming and personal skills in networking, setting up meetings, collecting data are very important.
	Store data on a secure cloud-based platform.	Don't forget to back up all data and write up research thoughts as you go for reports and publications.
	Have contingency plans if things don't work out as initially envisaged.	Have a work plan that has autonomous interrelated **action research cycles** that can be flexibly applied.

(*Continued*)

TABLE 14.1 Continued

Stage	*Do's*	*Don'ts*
Systems thinking	Model the system of change and the SSFs using systems thinking in **action research cycles**.	Don't model an "as-is" and "to-be" model and don't use a linear chronological approach.
	Use exploratory soft systems methodological thinking.	Don't fall into the trap of being a **hard** methodologist wanting to optimise a well-defined problem.
Studying	Use existing theories in literature reviews focused on the topic area and be clear on the type of logic you are using – use the "**logic compass**" to support your rationalisation.	Don't forget that this is where your contribution to theory will occur, and the remainder of the project will feed into theoretical explication or development of theory or theories.
	Models are meant as a way of understanding change and are not the end purpose.	Don't forget that by using a defined methodology with real data you might be able to make a methodological contribution.
Actioning	Use methodological techniques to engage with the case company (e.g. storyboards and games) and find reasons to have other meaningful discussions.	Don't forget to make the project engaging and linked to other ongoing work in the organisation to keep the case company interested. Join in with extra activities if invited.
	Keep your study interesting for your case sponsor/champion. Drip-feed findings from each **action research cycle (ARC)**.	Don't forget to bring in new insights into discussion to inform and educate stakeholders throughout your case. Don't wait until the end to give your findings.
Acting	Be prepared to deal with political issues in the organisation and resistance to change. An up-front financial contribution, a contract and plan of work helps to lower resistance.	Don't forget that actions will include people, process and technological changes that are likely to cost the company money and time.
	Place and track actions that arise from workshops.	Don't forget that often a business case will have to be made at the end of each action research cycle.
Impacting	Gather the effects of SSF changes on organisational performance. Use quantitative and qualitative measures and try to monetise these.	Don't forget that impact is the effect on the system (organisation) you are working with, as your case, and not the theoretical contributions you might make to scholarly outputs.

The Do's and Don'ts of the PrOH Modelling Methodology

Table 14.1 summarises some of the practical "do's and don'ts" for each part of the PrOH Modelling Methodology; these are by no means a complete list. Many of these relate to effective project management of the **action research** being done.

If the PrOH Modelling Methodology is used correctly, it should enable users to make strong practical contributions to a case organisation creating a positive impact from knowledge transfer. In reciprocation, new knowledge learned by working with case companies can contribute to knowledge in new publications and learning materials. A methodological contribution to systems thinking and action research is also likely.

Supportive Use of Technologies

There are standard office software packages that are fundamental to support the PrOH Modelling Methodology which have been mentioned throughout this book, and you will need to be able to use these effectively. For instance:

- MS PowerPoint for drawing PrOH Models.
- MS Excel for structuring SIPOC data for PrOH Models.
- MS Visio for drawing unstructured raw data pictures of "as-is" processes that can be put into SIPOC diagrams and maybe operationalising future "to-be" processes and procedures.
- Use of voting software (such as Vevox or Mentimeter) can be used to present PrOH Models and their SSFs to large audiences in a lecture format to see how an audience agrees or disagrees with each and the results from such voting can then be used in further quantitative analysis. These voting tools have been used in some recent cases to good effect and experimentation continues.

Alternative more bespoke PrOH Modelling software can be used as found on prohmodel.org:

- PrOH Tool© – that uses a bespoke downloadable MS Excel-based SIPOC table that can be uploaded to create the beginnings of a PrOH Model in MS PowerPoint and hence saves time by doing a data-to-picture conversion for you. PrOH Tool uses a large language model library and artificial intelligence to do this conversion.
- PrOH Game© – a PrOH Model turned into a game that helps people to begin to think more systemically.

It is likely that future PrOH Modelling tools will be able to make greater use of artificial intelligence (AI) and generative AI with the PrOH Tool© by developing large libraries of PrOH Model data as it is used more widely.

Future versions of PrOH Tool© may also be able to automatically create **abstracted** or **enriched** PrOH Models that will be able to suggest SSFs and remedies to SSFs based upon learning from previous PrOH Models that have been uploaded into the PrOH Tool©, which will act as training material for future PrOH Models. Therefore, as more SIPOC data gets entered into the PrOH Model Tool ©, the better it will become at **abstracting** and **enriching** PrOH Models. This is a general principle that could assist other soft systems modelling. The authors invite you to become part of the future of PrOH Modelling by actively uploading your data into PrOH Tool©.

Summary

This chapter serves as a short summary overview of the PrOH Modelling Methodology and the "do's and don'ts" of each stage. It also points the way forward for future support tool use.

Further Reading

Innovate Uk, Knowledge Transfer Projects. https://iuk-ktp.org.uk/
Meredith, J.R., Shafer, S.M., and Mantel, S. (2021), *Project Management: A Managerial Approach*, 11th ed. Chichester: Wiley.
prohmodel.org (formerly prohmodeller.org). For PrOH Tool© and PrOH Game©.
prohmodel.com. For Other PrOH Modelling Services.

15

YOUR JOURNEY AS AN ACTION RESEARCHER WHILE USING SYSTEMS THINKING

Introduction

This chapter reflects on the journey of the action researcher doing **action research** using the PrOH Modelling Methodology, and therefore contrasts with Chapter 14 that reflects directly on the PrOH Modelling Methodology.

Action research has become a well-recognised approach for researchers to transform, empower and emancipate individuals and communities through collaborative enquiry and intervention. A central tenet of action research is to generate learning and new knowledge through numerous cycles of action and reflection. Yet traditional **action research** methodologies are limited in their ability to fully extract learning from action due to an underdeveloped understanding of a researcher's role and their evolving identity throughout the research process. Such limitations undermine the depth of engagement with the problem context and the potential for a researcher to reflect and generate learning in real-time in engaged scholarship (Van de Ven, 2007).

Based on multiple in-depth longitudinal case studies conducted over decades of work, this book argues for the **emancipation**, or freedom of thought, for action researchers and those being researched through a new **Situated Emancipatory Action Research (SEAR)** Framework that has been developed and based on dozens of Process Oriented Holonic (PrOH) Modelling Methodology applications in action research projects.

The **SEAR Framework** seeks to overcome the limitations inherent in **action research** by emphasising the importance of researchers' cognitive journey, moving from a primarily detached observer to an immersed agent of change, while continuously *reflecting in action*. Authors of this book propose that this allows for more innovation via **abductive rationalisation**.

This chapter demonstrates how the **SEAR Framework** enables the **emancipation** of both the *researcher* and the *researched* through an intertwining and mutually complementary process of *deepening* and *widening* understanding through successive **action research cycles (ARCs)**. The new **SEAR Framework** facilitates action researchers to become **emancipated**

DOI: 10.4324/9781032650425-19

from their precepts, biases and identity, towards better engagement with problem situations and extraction of new knowledge.

This chapter recommends further investigation and experimentation using the **SEAR Framework** to refine and improve its application in wider **action research** settings. The **SEAR Framework** is another unique aspect developed by using the PrOH Modelling Methodology.

Future developments of the **SEAR Framework** may include the use of other **action research** methodologies and combinations with forms of systems thinking in a hybrid approach. Together, the PrOH Modelling Methodology and the **SEAR Framework** have many application areas which are suggested below.

From a Situated-Reflective-Agent Concept to a Situated Emancipatory Action Research Framework

To further illustrate the role of a researcher in action research, authors of this book have coined the term "**Situated-Reflective-Agent**" **(SRA)** as a proxy to "action researcher", to try to address the concept of cognitivist bias as well as to enhance reflection in action (Balthu and Clegg, 2021). The concept of "**situatedness**" refers to an agent embedded in the environment, emphasising the importance of direct engagement with the research in context. This means that a researcher, immersed in the "problem situation", reflects upon their experiences and actions within the context, allowing their understanding to evolve. In doing so, a researcher's identity is shaped by their engagement in the research process and by its participants, leading to a more dynamic, adaptive role that goes beyond simple observation and decreased detachment (Schon, 1983).

The philosophical basis for the Situated-Reflective-Agent (SRA) model is discussed along with a detailed explanation of an individual's cognitive journey in a recent paper by Balthu and Clegg (2021). The SRA concept is presented in Figure 15.1 to provide the background for the more comprehensive SEAR Framework presented later.

Previous research proposes that the essence of the "**Situated-Reflective-Agency**" (SRA) concept was to initially position a researcher in the place of a detached observer (at Point A) which is akin to Schein's (1999) *pure inquiry*, where a researcher is rather like an objective "gamekeeper of knowledge" observing what is going on. As a researcher becomes more immersed and reflective in the process of inquiry, progressing to Point B, their transition from being an outsider to "going native" and becoming a "poacher of knowledge" within the organisation occurs as a researcher gains deeper engagement and understanding. This journey is akin to Polanyi's (1966) concept of *tacit knowledge* as a researcher develops in situ and then gradually emerges at Point C through an upward journey as a **Situated-Reflective-Agent** to become a "reformed gamekeeper", fully integrated within an organisation through praxis while continuously being able to reflect-in-action.

The SRA concept provides a valuable stepping stone for conducting rigorous action research by emphasising the importance of embedding the researcher into the organisational context and adopting an intentional reflective practice. However, the **SRA** concept stops short of providing concrete guidance on translating its principles into **action research cycles (ARCs)** that can support impactful organisational transformation; therefore, there is an opportunity to build on the SRA concept to address the limitations of action research approaches as highlighted above.

Thus, the remainder of this section explains how the **SEAR Framework** has been developed from the original **SRA Concept** to allow for use in **action research cycles**. The SRA was

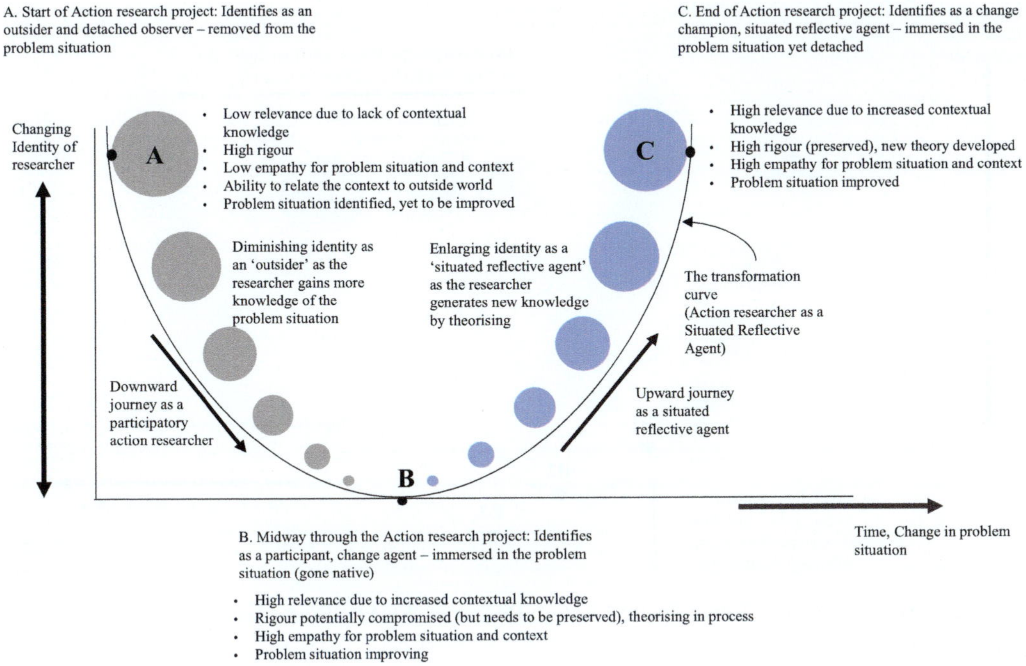

FIGURE 15.1 Evolving Identity of an Action Researcher into a "Situated-Reflective-Agent".

Source: Balthu and Clegg (2021).

initially **inducted** from the law firm case study (Chapter 11) and extended into the new **SEAR Framework** using further subsequent case studies given in Part III.

The **Situated Emancipatory Action Research (SEAR) Framework** presented in Figure 15.2 offers a logical next step for enacting successive, iterative **action research cycles** of inquiry in applied settings. Specifically, the **SEAR Framework** integrates emancipatory intent, expanding cycles of PrOH Modelling and flexible adaptation based on real-time learning.

The emancipatory focus allows the **SEAR Framework** to challenge restrictive organisational assumptions and structures through a process of critical empowerment, supported by PrOH Modelling. Expanding **action research cycles** enable progressively deeper understanding of the problem situation and broader impact over time. Integrating participatory methods like PrOH Modelling brings forth stakeholder perspectives through participation, knowledge co-creation and innovative solution design.

Specifically, in Figure 15.2, in the first **action research cycle (ARC 1)**, a researcher is immersed within the organisation through engaging employees in collaborative PrOH Modelling workshops. This immersion grants deep experiential insight into the initial problem situation, allowing a researcher to recognise and confront their biases as they interact with stakeholders and observe diverse perspectives. As a researcher then initiates ARC 2 and ARC 3 flowing directly from ARC 1, they can build upon their immersion (embedding) established through the first **ARC** of PrOH activities, leading to the subsequent design of new PrOH Models, action teams and associated solutions.

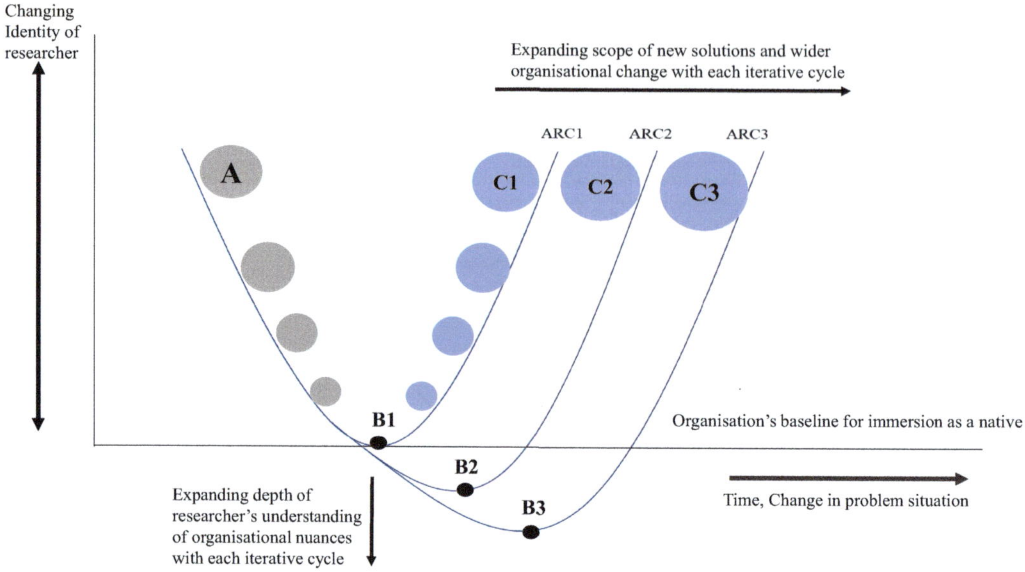

FIGURE 15.2 The Situated Emancipatory Action Research (SEAR) Framework.
Source: Balthu and Clegg (2025).

In Figure 15.2, the **SEAR Framework** illustrates a reduced need for complete re-embedding of the researcher in each **ARC**, allowing more in-depth analyses at an accelerated pace (flowing down the y-axis from point A); this gives stronger **agency** to the researcher through more insightful and impactful interventions. This expanding depth is depicted on the y-axis of the **SEAR Framework** from points B1 to B2 and B3. Immersion in the problem situation grows along the y-axis, demonstrating the maturing of *situatedness.* With each iterative cycle, the researcher *deepens* their understanding of organisational nuances and tests new solutions to address defined problems.

Additionally, the x-axis width corresponds to the widening problem scope enabled as the **action research cycles** progress. Instead of retaining a static focus, the compounding insights gained from repeated PrOH Modelling iterations and SSF implementations encourage broader change ambitions across iterative cycles, which is depicted in the increasing size of C from A → C1 to A → C2 and A → C3. The Point C indicates how the action researcher turns into a more effective *change agent* with greater *agency* to deliver highly relevant yet rigorous research-based change leading to higher levels of emancipation for client stakeholders due to their continual involvement throughout each ARC. More extensive organisational transformation becomes possible as perspectives of researchers evolve. Points A, B and C, as discussed in the SRA model (Figure 15.1), remain central to the **SEAR Framework** (Figure 15.2) establishing the temporal nature of change in action researchers' *weltanschauung,* towards a more evolved and powerful **agency** of change embedded into the problem situation – yet cleansed of cognitivist biases and able to generate rigorous knowledge through cycles of action and reflection.

The **SEAR Framework** supports rigorous and empowering interventions that foster emancipation for both the *researcher* and the *researched,* enabling the delivery of authentic transformation. Emancipation for the *researcher* occurs through the process of *deepening* along the y-axis in successive **ARC** iterations from B1 to B3, allowing action researchers to gain deeper insights into organisational dynamics. Emancipation for the *researched* occurs through the process of *widening* along the x-axis as staff participation in collaborative problem-solving activities and the exploration of alternative solutions lead to organisational changes.

These two facets of the **SEAR Framework**, *deepening* and *widening*, align with calls for action research to solve real-world problems, integrate diverse views, build change capacity and catalyse researcher agency and participant evolution through critical reflection (Bradbury-Huang, 2010). The **SEAR Framework** therefore develops the **SRA Concept** into an extended and more comprehensive framework for conducting emancipatory action research.

The **SEAR Framework** also aligns with foundational thinking on **action research** and its core principles advocated by previous research (Eden and Huxham, 1996; Reason and Bradbury, 2001; Bradbury-Huang, 2010). Specifically, Bradbury-Huang (2010) advocate core principles of participation, solving real-world problems, integrating diverse views and building capacities for change. In line with **Mode 3** action research, as discussed by Grundy (1988), the **SEAR Framework** emphasises the active participation of both the researcher and the researched, fostering a collaborative, reflexive process that not only aims for problem-solving but also promotes emancipation and transformation for both parties involved. The underlying principles of the **SEAR Framework** are (1) transforming researchers' identities to overcome detached observation, (2) situating researchers to embed them within an organisational context and (3) engaging in **reflexivity** to *reflect-in-action.*

The **SEAR Framework** presents a logical approach to iterative **action research** based on two PrOH Modelling case studies and may need additional development regarding real-world application, flexibility, pacing, integrating evaluation, metrics and further methodological developments. Thus, an opportunity exists in this area for further research and validation.

Use of Hybrid Approaches

Another future area of research for **action research** using the PrOH Modelling Methodology is the use of hybrid methodologies. While no single methodology can perform all types of analysis, the weaknesses of each can sometimes be diminished by using more than one methodology together. For instance, even in the field of systems thinking, the weaknesses of more qualitative approaches (e.g. Checkland's SSM, VSM and PrOH Modelling) can be complemented by the more quantitative approaches of Systems Dynamics (and perhaps types of simulation). For instance, Orme (2016) has experimented with combining Systems Dynamics models and PrOH Modelling using the same dataset based on data from **SIPOC Tables**. Likewise, Balthu has experimented with combining PrOH Modelling with Checkland's SSM (Balthu, 2021). Current research is exploring combinations of PrOH, Systems Dynamics and Viable Systems Modelling.

Moving out of the systems thinking field, the PrOH Modelling Methodology has also been combined with text coding methods such as Grounded Theory (Glaser and Strauss, 1967; Strauss and Corbin, 1998) and Decision Trees (Balthu, 2021) and Sentiment Analysis to help generate Systemic Success Factors (SSFs).

Creations of multi-methods are a hotbed for future research as both **action research** and **systems thinking** readily lend themselves to extension, adaptation and recontextualisation. Authors of this book welcome such work, particularly in the context of **action research** and believe this can be done in the context of the **SRA Concept** and its **SEAR Framework**, at its different points as discussed above, that may well enable greater depths and breadths of understanding about cases and reflexive **abductive thinking** to either explicate or extend theorising from cases.

Topics for Future Systems Thinking and Action Research

Future topics to investigate using the PrOH Modelling Methodology in organisations would be:

- **Digitalisation** – of service operations, production and supply chains to use new emerging technologies such as artificial intelligence, machine learning and cloud-based systems.
- **Circular economy** – for the reduction, reuse and recycling of material to reduce long-term environmental damage to the planet.
- **Internationalisation** – to explore the tensions of either expanding supply networks or the near-shoring or on-shoring in times of global crises.
- **Artificial Intelligence (AI)** – applications to organisational efficiency, productivity and effectiveness.

On an economy-wide scale, topics would include:

- **Humanitarian response** – looking at how emergency response systems can more effectively deliver aid and expertise to disaster zones. This would include work in the voluntary, charitable third sector of the economy.
- **Public services** – in the not-for-profit sector looking at challenges of meeting delivery commitments against volatile political environments and uncertain financial planning (e.g. health services, public transport, education, etc.).
- **United Nations' sustainability development goals (SDGs)** – which embody a huge planet-wide systemic challenge for fairness and equality, better health, justice and energy issues. https://sdgs.un.org/goals.

Summary

The authors would argue for what they call "**holonic realisation**" where people have a better understanding of *systems for change* rather than constantly focusing on the status quo and potential hypothetical future states, are able to think systemically rather than linearly, can explore with an open mind rather than optimise easy-to-fix small problems and be able to use inclusive methods that are transparent for users and provoke thought, creativity and innovation. Surely, this is what we are all living for?

The dawn of "**holonic realisation**" and the end of **solipsism**, where people stop denying issues of the existence of anything outside of their own consciousness, is hopefully nearly here. The authors believe that the PrOH Modelling Methodology has made some positive contributions in these areas and will continue to do so in the future.

Further Reading

Balthu, K.C., and Clegg, B. (2025), From Canonical to Emancipatory Action Research: Using PrOH Modelling to Enhance Reflexivity', *Systemic Practice and Action Research*, Vol. 38, Iss. 6. pp.1–29

Balthu, K., and Clegg, B. (2021), 'Improving Professional Service Operations: Action Research in a Law Firm', *International Journal of Operations and Production Management*', Vol. 41, Iss. 6, pp. 805–829.

United Nations Sustainability Goals. https://sdgs.un.org/goals

ANSWERS TO ACTION BOXES AND THINKING BOXES

Box Number	*Question*	*Answer*
Part 1		
Thinking Box 1	n/a	Read on in Chapter 1 but try to keep in mind organisational systems that you are familiar with and what a system for changing these would consist of.
Action Box 1	1.	Hard and soft – as a socio-technical system
	2.	Soft – predominantly a human centred system
	3.	Hard – predominantly a mechanistic system
	4.	Soft – soft – predominantly a human centre system
	5.	Hard – predominantly a mechanistic system
	6.	Hard – a product design.
Thinking Box 2	n/a	This is a personal preference, but the type of logic needs to suit the type of research being done.
Action Box 2	1.	Abductive
	2.	Deductive
	3.	Inductive
	4.	Analogous
	5.	No logic so not applicable.
Thinking Box 3	1.	"Win new business", "Deliver Customer Service", "Manufacture Products", "Conduct Market Research" would all be core business processes. There are many others. Further to question 1 the corresponding systems of change for these organisational
	2.	processes might be "Improve the amount of business won", digitalise customer service, "improve leanness of manufacturing" and "Conduct more effective market research". These focus on the conceptual system of change rather than a "real" operational process.

Box Number	*Question*	*Answer*
Action Box 3	n/a	This is difficult to answer. One way is to learn the PrOH Modelling Methodology. Other possible options maybe SSM, VSM or Systems Dynamics (SD). It would not be suitable to use hard systems methodologies (HSMs).
Part 2		
Thinking Box 4		Read "Ghost in the Machine" and other works by Koestler and his contemporaries. It is radically different to conventional thinking.
Action Box 4		It is common for change managers to model real-world processes, and these are prone to failure because it is not almost possible to do this. Modelling a system of change that is conceptual is possible to do but the difficulty is conceiving what should be in it, and this can only be decided by stakeholders facilitated by an experience systems thinker and soft systems modeller.
Thinking Box 5	n/a	Read more about holarchical thinking, holons and holarchy especially for modelling conceptual systems of change. It might change your whole perception of modelling and change.
Action Box 5	(1)	A classic design sequence would be: "requirements generation", "concept design", "detailed design", "prototyping".
	(2)	A classic set of parallel services in a law company would be, "road traffic accidents", "dispute resolution", "litigation" and "mergers and acquisitions".

GLOSSARY OF KEY TERMS

Term	*Definition*
Abstraction	The process of simplifying a complex system by focusing on essential features and omitting detailed elements, enabling understanding at a higher conceptual level. In PrOH Modelling, abstraction helps move from detailed to higher-level models to demonstrate emergent properties. Can be done form a set of **serial** models or **parallel** models.
Abductive logic/reasoning/ rationalising	Abductive reasoning starts with an observation similar to inductive reasoning but then uses preexisting explanations similar to deductive reasoning to group observations for the best possible explanation.
Action research	A participative and iterative approach to research that involves stakeholders collaboratively identifying problems, implementing solutions and reflecting on outcomes to drive systemic change.
Action research cycles (ARCs)	Action research methodological loops that repeat throughout an action research project. Each can focus on a different aspect of the project.
Active agent	A person (or artificial intelligence) found in the central columns of a SIPOC table. This is the origin of the active verb phrases to go into the **core process statement** of a PrOH Model.
Agency	The capacity of individuals or groups to act independently and make choices that influence a system.
Agent(s)	People or groups of people (e.g. departments, business units, etc.) in a real-world system that effect system change by having agency.
Aggregation (Aggregationism)	Joining entities together without creation of extra emergent properties in a system. Opposite of abstraction.

Term	*Definition*
Analogous reasoning	A problem-solving method where knowledge or patterns from one domain are applied to understand or address challenges in another, similar domain.
Ashby's law of requisite variety	The rule that states a control system must have more variety in it than the system it controls.
"As-is"	Modelling or understanding a current system
Autopoietic systems	Self-sustaining systems that maintain and reproduce their own organisation and boundaries through internal processes, as seen in living organisms and certain social systems.
CATWOE Root Definition	A way to define the essential elements of a system under observation by **Customer**, **Agent**, **Transformation**, **Weltanschauung**, **Owner** and **Environment** in Checkland's SSM.
Causality – direct	A simple relationship that can be expressed as a person/agent does something to give an outcome.
Causality – indirect	A complex relationship where a person/agent may do something that will cause indirect changes to a systems outcome through a sequence of implied events that may require wider tacit knowledge to understand.
Chronological thinking (chrono-logicalism)	Where logic in a model is portrayed as a chronological (time and date) sequence of event as found in a flow chart
Chrono-holonical-logicalism	A modelling approach in PrOH Modelling where holons are linked in both a logical and chronological sequence to depict temporal flows of systemic activity.
Coarse	PrOH Modelling. A PrOH Model that needs more refining.
Coercive system	A system in which control and compliance are maintained primarily through authority, rules and external enforcement rather than voluntary participation.
Concurrent Engineering	Sometime known a "simultaneous engineering". Designing the product and the process that will deliver the product at the same time.
Complex bubbles	PrOH Modelling can be of two types: **Containment bubbles** or **Decision bubbles**.
Core Process Statement (for a PrOH Model)	The main statement in a PrOH Model defining relationships between previous process phase, inputs, receiving agent of current phase, key agent of current process phase, outputs, receiving agent of outputs in the next process phase and the next process phase. It is the main construct in a **PrOH Model Template**.
"Could 'n' Should"	A model of change – the transition between "as-is" and "to-be".
Critical (systems) thinking	The disciplined process of actively conceptualising, analysing, synthesising and evaluating information to guide belief and action. In (systems) thinking, it enables practitioners to reflect on assumptions and make sound judgements within complex contexts.
Cybernetic paradigm	A theoretical framework that studies systems through feedback, control, communication and regulation to maintain stability and adapt to changes.

Term	*Definition*
Containment Bubbles	PrOH Modelling. Inclusive sub-bubbles where all sub-bubbles are part of the larger bubble that they are inside. Solid outer line. Can be bubbles of any colour; red, white or green.
Cybernetic systems	Systems characterised by closed-loop feedback mechanisms that enable self-regulation and adaptation to achieve stability and desired outcomes.
Deductive logic	Deductive reasoning typically starts off with a logical theory or hypothesis that is then examined to reach a specific conclusion.
Double-loop learning	A concept focused on improving not just actions, but also the underlying rules, assumptions and goals (e.g. metrics) that guide those actions.
"Drop-off" point	Where a model of an organisational system ends.
Decision bubbles	Mutually exclusive sub-bubbles with outer dotted lines. Can be of any type (e.g. colour). Not all outcomes are possible as some sub-bubbles are mutually exclusive of others.
De-refinement	When detail is stripped out of a PrOH Model to make it coarser.
Dummy phase	A phase of a system of change that sit outside the system of observation but significantly effects it (e.g. a supplier's response to an invitation to tender).
Emergent properties	Properties found at a higher level of modelling but not at a lower level.
Emancipation	Freedom of thought during research.
Enrichment	The process of adding additional descriptive detail to a model at a lower level, revealing hidden properties and supporting a deeper understanding of complex systems. Enrichment contrasts with reductionist breakdown and is central to building a holarchy in PrOH Modelling.
Epistemology	The study of knowledge: its nature, origin and limits. In soft systems methodology, epistemology underpins the interpretive, subjective approach to understanding human activity systems and constructing defensible models.
Gamification	A technique for turning learning into fun, with a competitive element, so players learn things almost without realising they are learning.
Gestalt	German: the general shape or form of an entity; English: *psychology*, an organised whole that is perceived as more than the sum of its parts as per Oxford English Dictionary online.
General Systems Theory (GST)	Developed by biologist Ludwig von Bertalanffy in the 1950s–1960s, is an interdisciplinary framework for studying systems as organised, holistic entities rather than isolated parts.
Goal-seeking	A key property of cybernetic and purposeful systems where the system acts to maintain or achieve a specific objective or state, often using feedback mechanisms to self-correct deviations.
Granularity of a process	The level of content description of a process; typically having a strategic, tactical or operational pitch.

Term	*Definition*
Hermeneutics	An approach that holds that the most basic fact of social life is the meaning of an action.
Hidden properties	Properties found at a lower level of modelling but not at a higher level.
Hierarchy (Hierarchical)	A structure that is reductionistic in its composition formed through reductionism and aggregation, and in modelling terms implies "child-parent" inheritance of properties. **Hidden properties** and **emergent properties** not recognised.
Holarchy	A set of **holonic** models.
Holon	A conceptual modelling construct used to depict a system for change to systems under observation found in the real world. A holon contains other holons and is part of a larger holon.
Holonic	Having properties of a **holon**.
Holonic realisation	When people have a better understanding of *systems for change* rather than focusing on the status quo and potential hypothetical future states
Holonical-logicalism	Where logic of system is portrayed within a holonic construct.
Human Activity System	A system composed of people undertaking purposeful activities. Human activity systems exhibit high levels of complexity and unpredictability due to human decision-making and are a core focus of soft systems thinking and PrOH Modelling.
Hypothetico-deductive	A scientific reasoning process where a hypothesis is proposed and then tested by deducing consequences and comparing them with empirical observations. While soft systems methodology is largely interpretive, hypothetico-deductive logic underpins some structured approaches within systems thinking.
Inductive logic	Inductive reasoning, instead, starts off broadly from a specific observation, which is then analysed for patterns resulting in propositions and theoretical generalisations.
Inheritance of properties	Seen in hard systems methodologies when properties of a lower-level model must be directly derived from a higher-level model; and vice versa.
Information Systems Engineering (ISE)	A multidisciplinary approach to designing, developing and managing information systems that support organisational processes, business needs and technical solutions.
Interpretivism	An epistemological stance emphasising understanding the subjective meanings and experiences of individuals within complex human activity systems.
Job shop	A low production environment where workers are multiskilled and work on one product at a time.
Lebenswelt	Lifeworld (German) may be conceived as a universe of what is self-evident or given, a world that subjects may experience together.
Length of a model	In PrOH Modelling, the extent of a business process from its starting "**pick-up**" point to its ending "**drop-off**" point, focusing on including only relevant elements that contribute to the system's purpose.

Term	*Definition*
Machine age	Thinking that applies an analytical approach and takes a viewpoint where the relationships that govern "reality" follow the doctrine of mechanism which can be understood through the application of reductionism.
Maturity model	A framework that assesses the degree of development or capability of a system or process, usually across progressive stages of improvement or evolution.
Minimum viable elements	The elements found in the core process statement of a PrOH Model.
Mode 1 research	Traditional academic research driven by theoretical and disciplinary concerns, often conducted within universities with a focus on scientific rigour.
Mode 2 research	Context-driven, problem-focused research carried out in collaboration between academics and practitioners in real-world settings.
Mode 3 (action) research	Research integrating multi-stakeholder participation across societal levels. It addresses complex, systemic problems by combining transdisciplinary knowledge and focusing on co-production of solutions that are context-specific yet contribute to wider theoretical understanding. Mode 3 reflects the principles of systemic intervention, boundary critique and reflexivity within action research.
Multiple tenable viewpoints	Different **agents** in a system can have different opinions of a system that are simultaneously valid.
Natural language	Language that is considered normal in everyday speech and writing.
Ontology	Ontology comes from two Greek words: on, which means "being", and logia, which means "study", so ontology is the study of being alive and existing.
Open systems	**Systems** that continuously interact with their external environment through the exchange of information, energy or material.
Organisational cybernetics	The application of cybernetic principles (feedback, control, communication) to understand and manage complex organisations as self-regulating systems.
Parallel abstraction	When a set of parallel PrOH Models of the same pitch are summarised at a higher-level modelling pitch in a single model.
Parallel enrichment	When a single higher-level model is expressed in enhanced detail as a set of lower-level models. It is the reverse of parallel abstraction.
Parallel models	PrOH Models that are at the same level of organisational pitch and run autonomously from one another at that level but may be connected at other levels.
Participatory (action) research	A collaborative research methodology where researchers and participants jointly diagnose problems, implement interventions and reflect on outcomes to create actionable knowledge.
"Pick-up point"	Where the model of an organisational system begins.

Term	*Definition*
Pitch of a model	In PrOH Modelling, the organisational level at which the model is constructed (e.g. strategic, tactical or operational), influencing the granularity of the model.
Phenomenology	A philosophical approach focusing on the lived experiences and perceptions of individuals to understand phenomena as they are experienced, used in interpretive research.
Physical artefacts	Tangible objects produced by or used within a system, such as documents, tools or equipment, often considered as outputs in process modelling.
Primary data	Data collected specifically for the exercise currently being undertaken.
Primary task (SSM)	The task which an enterprise must perform if it is to survive.
Process under observation	The real-world system being researched. In PrOH Modelling this will be an organisational process.
Problem contexts (Jackson)	**Mechanical-unitary**, **systemic-unitary**, **mechanical-pluralist** and **systemic-pluralist.**
Process Matrix /Matrices	A tool used in PrOH Modelling to define phases within the system, or in systems thinking terms **holons** within **holons**, where each column lists, without sequence, what activities are in each phase. Similarly, it can be used to do identify **Sub-phases** from **Phases**.
"Producer-product" effect	Cause is necessary but not sufficient for the effect.
Process oriented holon	A part of a change process that is both a whole system and a part of a larger system (holarchy), central to PrOH Modelling.
PrOH Model	A model of a system of change using holonic principles and developed using the PrOH Modelling Methodology.
PrOH Model Icon	A thumbnail picture that represents the PrOH Model Template in a holarchical diagram.
PrOH Model Template	A structure that represents the essential elements of a process oriented holon as a model using the PrOH Modelling Methodology.
Provenance of origin	Seen in soft systems methodologies when properties of a lower-level model do not have to be directly derived from a higher-level model and vice versa.
Quantum systems thinking	Where different explanations of systems phenomena are simultaneously viable even though they may be contradictory.
Quality Function Deployment (QFD)	A structured analysis to match functional features of a technical solution to a design requirement.
Reductionist (reductionism)	An analytical approach that simplifies complex systems by breaking them down into smaller, isolated components, often criticised in soft systems thinking for overlooking emergent (and hidden) properties. Opposite of **enrichment**.
Refinement	The act of adding more supporting process descriptions to a core process description beyond the minimal viable elements.
Reflexive (or self-reflexive). Reflexivity	The process by which researchers critically examine their own role, assumptions and influence within the research process, essential in action research and **SSM**.

Term	*Definition*
Research paradigm	A framework into which the theories and practices of your discipline fit to create the research plan. This foundation guides all areas of your research plan, including the aim of the study, research question, instruments or measurements used and analysis methods.
Scope of model	A model defined in terms of its real-world position in and organisational reporting structure (see **pitch**), finish and start (see **length**) and amount of digression from the core process statement (see **width**).
Secondary data	Data already available and not collected specifically for an exercise being undertaken.
Serial models	PrOH Models that connect to one another at the same pitch of modelling by their inputs and outputs. Models follow in a chain as "previous phase", "current phase" and "next phase".
Serial abstraction	When a set of serial PrOH Models of the same pitch are summarised at a higher-level modelling pitch in a single model.
SEAR Framework	A way of combining successive **Action Research Cycles (ARCs)** of increasing depth and breadth in a project.
Situatedness	An action researcher's extent of embeddedness in their environment.
Situated-Reflective-Agent (SRA)	The conceptual cognitive journey of a research using **action research** and **systems thinking** (PrOH Modelling).
Socio-technical systems (STS) (theory)	Organisational systems that consist of both social elements (people, culture) and technical elements (processes, technology), requiring integrated design and analysis.
Soft Systems Methodology (SSM)	A participatory, systemic approach to explore and improve complex, ill-defined problems through stakeholder-driven modelling and debate.
Solipsism	Denying the existence of issues outside of one's own consciousness.
Span-of-enrichment	Number of models created at a lower level from a higher-level model.
Sponsor (and/or champion)	Person, agent or company wanting the change to happen. They may be paying and/or driving the change.
Systemic	Relating to a system, inherent in a system.
Systems Age	Built based on expansionism, teleology and "systems thinking".
System under observation (SuO)	The specific system being studied and modelled, particularly in soft systems methodology where the boundaries and purposes of the system are defined by stakeholders.
System phase	In PrOH Modelling system phases are used to model different parts of the system for change which can be connected in **series** or in **parallel**.
Systemic success Factors (SSFs) of change	Properties that influence change within a system and its wider context while still being a parsimonious construct.
Systemicity	The degree or quality of being systemic and the application of **systemic** thinking used to demonstrate systemic success factors.

Term	*Definition*
Systems engineering/systems analysis	A structured interdisciplinary approach to designing and managing complex systems, focusing on requirements, functionality and lifecycle performance.
Teleology	The philosophical study of purpose or goal-directedness, in systems thinking, it relates to the purposeful behaviour of systems aimed at achieving specific ends.
"To-be"	Modelling or understanding a future system.
Validation	Making sure that a model adequately represents an intended system under observation (conceptual or real).
Validation – authentication	Model validation given to those who contributed the original data.
Validation – dissemination	A model validation exercise given to those not contributing to the original data but who operate in the system under observation.
Validation – promulgation	Given to those who neither contributed the raw data, operate in the system under observation but have a related interest, such as those who may work in different phases of the process; earlier or later.
Variety engineering	The purposeful design and regulation of a system's internal variety to match the complexity of its external environment (**Ashby's Law of Requisite Variety**).
Verification/Verifiable	Something that that it follows a set of prescribed rules and guidelines defined in a methodology.
Viable Systems Model (VSM)	A modelling approach developed by Stafford Beer (1979) describing the necessary functions and structures required for an organisation to remain viable and adaptable in a changing environment.
Wicked problem	A complex, ill-defined problem with no clear solution, where stakeholders may have conflicting views and solutions may generate unforeseen consequences.
Width of a model	In PrOH Modelling, the range of supporting activities included in a model to complement the core business process, contributing to a richer understanding of the system under observation.

REFERENCES

Abdulmalek, F.A., and Rajgopal, J. (2007), 'Analyzing the Benefits of Lean Manufacturing and Value Stream Mapping Via Simulation: A Process Sector Case Study', *International Journal of Production Economics*, Vol. 107, Iss. 1, pp. 223–236.

Ackoff, R.L. (1961), 'Systems, Organisations and Interdisciplinary Research', *Systems: Research and Design*, pp. 26–42.

Ackoff, R.L. (1971), 'Towards a System of System Concepts', *Management Science*, Vol. 17, Iss. 11, pp. 661–671.

Ackoff, R.L. (1974a), *Redesigning the Future: A Systems Approach to Societal Problems*. New York: John Wiley and Sons.

Ackoff, R.L. (1974b), 'The Social Responsibility of OR', *Operational Research*, Vol. 25, pp. 403–414.

Ackoff, R.L. (1981a), *Creating the Corporate Future: Plan or Be Planned For*. New York: John Wiley & Sons.

Ackoff, R.L. (1981b), *Creating the Corporate Future*. New York: Wiley.

Ackoff, R.L. (1981c), 'The Art and Science of Mess Management', *Interfaces*, Vol. 11, pp. 20–26.

Ackoff, R.L. (2006), 'Why Few Organizations Adopt Systems Thinking', *Systems Research and Behavioural Science*, Vol. 23, pp. 705–708.

Ackoff, R.L. (2010), *Systems Thinking for Curious Managers*. Axminster: Triarchy Press.

Albliwi, S.A., Antony, J., and Lim, S.A.H. (2015), 'A Systematic Review of Lean Six Sigma for the Manufacturing Industry', *Business Process Management Journal*, Vol. 21, Iss. 3, pp. 665–691.

Albliwi, S., Antony, J., Lim, S.A.H., and van der Wiele, T. (2014), 'Critical Failure Factors of Lean Six Sigma: A Systematic Literature Review', *International Journal of Quality & Reliability Management*, Vol. 31, Iss. 9, pp. 1012–1030.

Alfieri, A., Cantamessa, M., and Montagna, F. (2012), 'The SoS Approach for Lean Manufacturing Systems', *International Journal of Technology Management*, Vol. 57, Iss. 1–3, pp. 149–165.

Allen, T., and Starr, T. (1982), *Hierarchy: Perspectives for Ecological Complexity*. Chicago: University of Chicago Press.

Alvesson, M., and Kärreman, D. (2004), 'Interfaces of Control. Technocratic and Socio-Ideological Control in a Global Management Consultancy Firm', *Accounting, Organizations and Society*, Vol. 29, Iss. 3, pp. 423–444.

Andreewsky, E., and Bourcier, D. (2000), 'Abduction in Language Interpretation and Law Making', *Kybernetes*, Vol. 29, Iss. 7/8, pp. 836–845.

Ang, C.L., and Gay, R.K.L. (1993), 'IDEF0 Modelling for Project Risk Assessment', *Computers in Industry*, Vol. 22, pp. 31–45.
Argyris, C., Putnam, R., and Smith, D. (1985), *Action Science.* San Francisco: Jossey-Bass.
Argyris, C., and Schön, D. (1974), *Theory in Practice: Increasing Professional Effectiveness.* San Francisco: Jossey-Bass.
Argyris, C., and Schön, D.A. (1978), *Organizational Learning: A Theory of Action Perspective.* Reading: Addison-Wesley.
Argyris, C., and Schön, D.A. (1991), 'Participatory Action Research and Action Science Compared – A Commentary', In Whyte, W.F. (Ed.), *Participatory Action Research*, London: Sage Publications, pp. 85–96.
Arnheiter, E.D., and Maleyeff, J. (2005), 'The Integration of Lean Management and Six Sigma', *The TQM Magazine*, Vol. 17, Iss. 1, pp. 5–18.
Aronson, D. (1996), An Overview of Systems Thinking. https://community.mi.temple.edu/mis3534sec001spring2022/files/2021/12/Overview-of-Systems-Thinking.pdf
Ashby, W.R. (1956), *An Introduction to Cybernetics.* London: Methuan.
Assarlind, M., Gremyr, I., and Bäckman, K. (2013), 'Multi-Faceted Views on a Lean Six Sigma Application', *International Journal of Quality & Reliability Management*, Vol. 30, Iss. 4, pp. 387–402.
Avison, D.E., and Wood-Harper, A.T. (1990), *Multiview.* Oxford: Blackwell.
Balogun, J., and Hope Hailey, V. (2008), *Exploring Strategic Change.* London: Prentice Hall.
Balthu, K. (2021), *Applying Systems Thinking to Improve Professional Service Operations.* Ph.D. Thesis, Aston University.
Balthu, K., and Clegg, B. (2021), 'Improving Professional Service Operations: Action Research in a Law Firm', *International Journal of Operations and Production Management*, Vol. 41, Iss. 6, pp. 805–829.
Balthu, K.C., and Clegg, B. (2025), 'From Canonical to Emancipatory Action Research: Using PrOH Modelling to Enhance Reflexivity', *Systemic Practice and Action Research*, Vol. 38, Iss. 6. pp.1–29.
Barlas Y. (1996), 'Formal Aspects of Model Validity and Validation in System Dynamics', *System Dynamics Review*, Vol. 12, Iss. 3, pp. 183–210.
Barton, J., and Haslett, T. (2007), 'Analysis, Synthesis, Systems Thinking and the Scientific Method: Rediscovering the Importance of Open Systems', *Systems Research and Behavioural Science*, Vol. 24, Iss. 2, pp. 143–155.
Baskerville, R., Baiyere, A., Gregor, S., Hevner, A., and Rossie, M. (2018), 'Design Science Research Contributions: Finding a Balance Between Artifact and Theory', *Journal of the Association for Information Systems*, Vol. 19, Iss. 5, pp. 358–376.
Baskerville, R., and Lee, A. (1999), 'Distinctions Among Different Types of Generalizing in Information Systems Research', In Ngwenyama, O., et al. (Eds.), *New IT Technologies in Organizational Processes: Field Studies and Theoretical Reflections on the Future of Work.* New York: Kluwer Academic Publishers.
Battista, J.R. (1977), 'The Holistic Paradigm and General Systems Theory', *General Systems*, Vol. XXII, pp. 65–71.
Becker, W.M., Herman, M.F., Samuelson, P.A., and Webb, A.P. (2001), 'Lawyers Get Down to Business', *The McKinsey Quarterly*, Vol. 2, pp. 45–55.
Beckett, J.A. (1971), *Management Dynamics.* New York: McGraw-Hill.
Bednar, P.M., and Welch, C. (2019), 'Sociotechnical Perspectives on Smart Working: Creating Meaningful and Sustainable Systems', *Information Systems Frontiers*, Vol. 22, Iss. 2, pp. 281–298.
Beer, S. (1959), *Cybernetics and Management.* London: English University Press.
Beer, S. (1972), *Brain of the Firm; Allen Lane.* London: The Penguin Press.
Beer, S. (1979), *The Heart of Enterprise.* Chichester: Wiley.
Beer, S. (1984), 'The Viable System Model: Its Provenance, Development, Methodology and Pathology', *The Journal of the Operational Research Society*, Vol. 35, Iss. 1, pp. 7–25.
Beer, S. (1985), *Diagnosing the Systems for Organisations.* Chichester: Wiley.
Benedettini, O., and Neely, A. (2012), *Complexity in Services: An Interpretative Framework.* Chicago: POMS 23rd Annual Conference.
Bennis, W.G., and O'Toole, J. (2005), 'How Business Schools Lost Their Way', *Harvard Business Review*, Vol. 82, pp. 96–104.
Bertalanffy, L. (1968), *General Systems Theory.* New York: Brazillier.
Bertalanffy, L. (1969), *General Systems Theory: Foundations, Development, Applications.* New York: George Braziller.

Bessant, J., Caffyn, S., and Gallagher, M. (2001), 'An Evolutionary Model of Continuous Improvement Behaviour', *Technovation*, Vol. 21, Iss. 2, pp. 67–77.

Bierau, F., Perlo, P., Müller, B., Gomez, A., Coosemans, T., and Meyer, G. (2015), 'Opportunities for European SMEs in Global Electric Vehicle Supply Chains in Europe and Beyond', In Schulze, T., Müller, B., and Meyer, G. (Eds.), *Advanced Microsystems for Automotive Applications 2015, Smart Systems for Green and Automated Driving.* Switzerland: Springer. International Publishing, pp. 223–235.

Bititci, U.S., Garengob, P., Atesc, A., Sai, S., and Nudurupati, S.S. (2015), 'Value of Maturity Models in Performance Measurement', *International Journal of Production Research*, Vol. 53, Iss. 10, pp. 3062–3085.

Bititci, U.S., and Spanellis, A. (2024), *Systems Thinking for Business and Management.* London: Kogan Page.

Blair, R.N., and Whitson, C.W. (1971), *Elements of Industrial Systems Engineering.* Englewood Cliffs: Prentice Hall.

Blichfeldt, B.S., and Andersen, J.R. (2006), 'Creating a Wider Audience for Action Research: Learning from Case-Study Research', *Journal of Research Practice*, Vol. 2, Iss. 1, Article D2.

Boardman, J.T., and Clegg, B.T. (2001), 'Structured Engagement in the Extended Enterprise', *International Journal of Operations and Production Management*, Vol. 21, Iss. 5–6, pp. 795–811.

Bogdanov, A.A. (1913–1917 [1996]), In Dudley, P. (Ed.), *Bogdanov's Tektology.* Hull: Centre for Systems Studies Press.

Bokhorst, J.A., Knol, W., Slomp, J., and Bortolotti, T. (2022), 'Assessing to What Extent Smart Manufacturing Builds on Lean Principles', *International Journal of Production Economics*, Vol. 253, pp. 108599.

Born, G. (1994), *Process Management to Quality Improvement.* Chichester: Wiley.

Boulding, K.E. (1956), 'General Systems Theory – The Skeleton of Science', *Management Science*, Vol. 2, Iss. 3, pp. 197–208.

Bradbury-Huang, H. (2010), 'What Is Good Action Research? Why the Resurgent Interest?', *Action Research*, Vol. 8, Iss. 1, pp. 93–109.

Brocklesby J. (2007), 'The Theoretical Underpinnings of Soft Systems Methodology—Comparing the Work of Geoffrey Vickers and Humberto Maturana', *Systems Research and Behavioural Science*, Vol. 24, Iss. 2, pp. 157–168.

Brown, C. (2019), 'Why and How to Employ the SIPOC Model', *Journal of Business Continuity and Emergency Planning*', Vol. 12, Iss. 3, pp. 198–210.

Buchel, A., et al. (1984), 'Comparison of Design Methodologies: Characteristics and Deficiencies', In Hubner, H. (Ed.), *Production Management Systems.* Austria: IFIP.

Bulow, I. (1989), 'The Bounding of a Problem Situation and the Concept of a System's Boundary in Soft Systems Methodology', *Journal of Applied Systems Analysis*, Vol. 16, pp. 35–41.

Burgess, N., and Wake, N. (2013), 'The Applicability of the Viable Systems Model as a Diagnostic for Small to Medium Sized Enterprises', *International Journal of Productivity and Performance Management*, Vol. 62, Iss. 1, pp. 29–46.

Cabrera, D., Cabrera, L., and Midgely, G. (Eds.). (2024), *The Routledge Handbook of Systems Thinking.* London: Routledge.

Carr, W., and Kemmis, S. (1986), *Becoming Critical: Education, Knowledge & Action Research.* Victoria: Deakin University Press.

CCTA. (1990), *SSADM Version 4 Reference Manuals.* Manchester: NCC/Blackwell.

Cecil, J.A., Srihari, K., and Emerson, C.R. (1992), 'A Review of Petri Applications in Manufacturing', *International Journal of AMT*, Vol. 7, pp. 168–177.

Chandrasekaran, A., Treville, S., and Browning, T. (2020), Editorial: Intervention-Based Research (IBR)—What, Where, and How to Use It in Operations Management, *Journal of Operations Management*, Vol. 66, Iss. 4, pp. 370–378.

Chapman, J, (2004), *System Failure Why Governments Must Learn to Think Differently.* London: Demos.

Chase, R.B., and Tansik, D.A. (1983), 'A Customer Contact Model for Organizational Design', *Management Science*, Vol. 29, Iss. 9, pp. 1037–1050.

Checkland, P.B. (1971), 'A Systems Map of the Universe', Journal of Systems Engineering, Vol. 1, Iss. 2, pp. 107–114.

Checkland, P.B. (1972), 'Towards a System Based Methodology for Real World Problem Solving', *Journal of Systems Engineering*, Vol. 3, Iss. 2, pp. 87–116.

Checkland, P.B. (1975), 'The Development of Systems Thinking by Systems Practice: A Methodology from an Action Research Project', In Trappl, R., and Hanika, F. (Eds.), *Progress in Cybernetics and Systems Research*, Vol. II. Washington: Hemisphere Publishing Corporation.

Checkland, P.B. (1978), The Origins and Nature of "Hard" Systems Thinking', *Journal of Applied Systems Analysis*, Vol. 5, pp. 99–110.

Checkland, P.B. (1979), 'Techniques in "soft" Systems Practice Part 1: Building Conceptual Models', *Journal of Applied Systems Analysis*, Vol. 6, pp. 33–40.

Checkland, P.B. (1980a), '"Primary Task" and "Issue Based" Root Definitions in Systems Studies', *Journal of Applied Systems Studies*, Vol. 7, pp. 51–54.

Checkland, P.B. (1980b), 'The Systems Movement and the "Failure" of Management Science', *Cybernetics and Systems: An International Journal*, Vol. 11, pp. 317–324.

Checkland, P.B. (1981), *Systems Thinking, Systems Practice*. Chichester: Wiley.

Checkland, P.B. (1983), 'O.R., and the Systems Movement: Mappings and Conflicts', *Journal of the Operational Research Society*, Vol. 34, Iss. 8, pp. 661–675.

Checkland, P.B. (1985), 'Achieving "Desirable and Feasible" Change: An Application of Soft Systems Methodology', *Journal of Operational Research Society*, Vol. 36, Iss. 9, pp. 821–831.

Checkland, P.B. (1988a), 'Information Systems and Systems Thinking: Time to Unite?', *International Journal of Information Management*, Vol. 8, pp. 239–248.

Checkland, P.B. (1998), 'Soft Systems Methodology: An Overview', *Journal of Applied Systems Analysis*, Vol. 15, pp. 27–30.

Checkland, P.B. (1989), 'Soft Systems Methodology', *Human Systems Management*, Vol. 8, pp. 273–289.

Checkland, P.B. (1991), 'From Framework Through Experience to Learning: The Essential Nature of Action Research', In Nissen, H.-E., Klein, H.K., and Hirschheim, R. (Eds.), *Information Systems Research*. Amsterdam: Elsevier.

Checkland, P.B. (1993), *Systems Thinking: Systems Practice*. Chichester: John Wiley, pp. 286–293.

Checkland, P.B. (1995), 'Model Validation in Soft Systems Practice', *Systems Research*, Vol. 12, Iss. 1, pp. 47–54.

Checkland, P.B. (1999), *Systems Thinking Systems Practice: A 30-Year Retrospective*. New York: John Wiley.

Checkland, P.B., Forbes, P., and Martin, S. (1990), 'Techniques in Soft Systems Practice Part 3: Monitoring and Control in Conceptual Models and in Evaluation Studies', *Journal of Applied Systems Analysis*, Vol. 17, pp. 29–37.

Checkland, P.B., and Poulter, J. (2006), *Learning for Action: A Short Definitive Account of Soft Systems Methodology and its use for Practitioners, Teachers and Students*. Chichester: John Wiley & Sons Ltd.

Checkland, P.B., and Scholes, J. (1990), *Soft Systems Methodology in Action*. Chichester: Wiley.

Checkland, P.B., and Wilson, B. (1980), '"Primary Task" and "Issue Based" Root Definitions in Systems Studies', *Journal of Applied Systems Analysis*, Vol. 7, pp. 51–54.

Checkland, P.B., and Holwell, S. (1998), 'Action Research: Its Nature and Validity', *Systemic Practice and Action Research*, Vol. 11, Iss. 1, pp. 9–21.

Churchman, C.W. (1968), *The Systems Approach*. New York: Dell Publishing, p. 11.

Churchman, C.W., Ackoff, R.L., and Arnoff, E.L. (1957), *Introduction to Operations Research*. New York: Wiley.

Clegg, B.T. (1999), *A Systems Approach to Reengineering Business Processes Towards Concurrent Engineering Principles*. PhD Thesis. De Montfort University.

Clegg B.T. (2006), 'Business Process Orientated Holonic (PrOH) Modelling', *Business Process Management Journal*, Vol. 12, Iss. 4, pp. 410–443.

Clegg, B.T. (2007), 'Building a Holarchy Using Business Process Orientated Holonic (PrOH) Modeling', *IEEE Systems, Man and Cybernetics: Part A*, Vol. 31, Iss. 1, pp. 23–40.

Clegg, B.T. (2020), 'Improving Systemic Success Factors in a University to Achieve More Effective and Efficient Operations: Using the PrOH Modelling Methodology', *Business Process Management Journal*, Vol. 26, Iss. 2, pp. 630–654.

Clegg, B.T., Balthu, K., and Morris, G. (2020), 'Changing Professional Service Archetypes in a Law Firm Using Process Orientated Holonic (PrOH) Modelling', *Knowledge Management Research and Practice*, Vol. 18, Iss. 1, pp. 38–52.

Clegg, B.T., and Boardman, J.T. (1996), 'Process Integration and Improvement Using Systemic Diagrams and a Human-Centred Approach', *Concurrent Engineering*, Vol. 4, Iss. 2, pp. 119–136.

Clegg, B.T., and Boardman, J.T. (1997), 'Systemic Analysis of Concurrent Engineering Practice: The technology Exploitation Process', *Fifth International Conference on Factory 2000*. IET. (No. 435)

Clegg, B.T., and Boardman, J.T. (1998a), 'A Soft Systems Methodology to Support Business Process Change Towards Concurrent Engineering', INCOSE '98. Vancouver. July.

Clegg, B.T., and Boardman, J.T. (1998b), 'Achieving Strategic Change Towards Concurrent Engineering by using a new Soft Systems Methodology', The World Innovation and Strategy Conference '98. Sydney. August.

Clegg, B.T., Boardman, J.T., and Buckingham, A.D. (1996b), 'Factory Process Improvement Using a Human-Centred Approach', International Conference Proceeding Concurrent Engineering '96. September, Toronto.

Clegg, B.T., Eslamian, E., Masi, D., Collis, I., and Panchal, G. (2023), 'A Systems Thinking Action Research Approach for the Digitalisation of a Manufacturing SME', Euroma '23. Leuven, Belgium. 2–6 July.

Clegg, B.T., Gholami, R., and Omurgonulsen, M. (2013), Quality Management and Performance: A Comparison Between the UK and Turkey. *Production Planning & Control*, Vol. 24, Iss. 12, pp. 1015–1031.

Clegg, B.T., and Orme, R. (2012), 'System of Systems: Pure and Applied to Lean Six Sigma', In System of Systems Gheorghe, A.V. Ed., Intech. http://www.intechopen.com/books/system-of-systems/system-of-systems-pure-and-applied-to-lean-six-sigma

Clegg, B.T., Orme, R., Owen, C., and Albores, P. (2018), 'Analysis of a Train-Operating Company's Customer Service System During Disruptions: Conceptual Requirements for Gamifying Frontline Staff Development', *Journal of Rail Transport Planning & Management*, Vol. 8, pp. 56–77.

Clegg, B.T., Orme, R., and Petridis, P. (2023a), 'Developing a Serious Game for Rail Services: Improving Passenger Information During Disruption', *Information*, Vol. 14, Iss. 8, p. 464. https://doi.org/10.3390/info14080464

Clegg, B.T., Rees, C., and Titchen, M. (2010), 'A Study into the Effectiveness of Quality Management Training: A Focus on Tools and Critical Success Factors', *TQM Journal*, Vol. 22, Iss. 2, pp. 188–208.

Clegg, B.T., and Shaw, D. (2008), 'Using Process-Orientated Holonic (PrOH) Modelling to Increase Understanding of Information Systems', *Information Systems Journal*, Vol. 18, pp. 447–477.

Clegg, B.T., Wingrove, S.J., and Boardman, J.T. (1996a), 'Improving Process Management Performance Using Systemic Methods and Tools', *IEE Colloquium: 'Systemic Methods for Improving Business Performance*, Digest No. 1996/075.

Coghlan, D., and Brannick, T. (2014), *Doing Action Research in Your Own Organization*. 4th ed. London: SAGE.

Coughlan, P., and Coghlan, D. (2002), 'Action Research for Operations Management', *International Journal of Operations & Production Management*, Vol. 22, Iss. 2, pp. 220–240.

Coughlan, P., Draaijer, D., Godsell, J., and Boer, H. (2016), Operations and Supply Chain Management: The Role of Academics and Practitioners in the Development of Research and Practice', *International Journal of Operations & Production Management*, Vol. 36, Iss. 12, pp. 1673–1695.

Coghlan, D., and Shani, A. (2014), 'Creating Action Research Quality in Organization Development: Rigorous, Reflective and Relevant', *Systemic Practice and Action Research*, Vol. 27, Iss. 6, pp. 523–536.

Coulson-Thomas, C. (1994), *Business Process Reengineering*. London: Kogan-Page.

Coyle, G. (2000), 'Qualitative and Quantitative Modelling in System Dynamics: Some Research Questions', *System Dynamics Review*, Vol. 16, Iss. 3, pp. 225–244.

Davison, R.M., Martinsons, M.G., and Kock, N. (2004), 'Principles of Canonical Action Research', *Information Systems Journal*, Vol. 14, Iss. 1, pp. 65–86.

Deming, E.W. (1986), *Out of the Crisis*. Cambridge: Massachusetts Institute of Technology Press, p. 88.

Deming, E.W. (1993), *The New Economics*. Cambridge: Massachusetts Institute of Technology Press, p. 35.

De Marco, T. (1978). *Structured Analysis and System Specification*. New York: Yourdon Inc.

Detty, R.B., and Yingling, J.C. (2000), 'Quantifying Benefits of Conversion to Lean Manufacturing with Discrete Event Simulation: A Case Study', *International Journal of Production Research*, Vol. 38, Iss. 2, pp. 429–445.

Dicesare, F.P. (1993a), *Practice of Petri Nets in Manufacturing*. London: Chapman and Hall.

Dicesare, F.P. (1993b), 'Re-Engineering to Achieve a Concurrent Engineering Environment', *Journal of Design and Manufacturing*, Vol. 3, pp. 75–89.

Dong, J.J., et al. (1995), 'A Holonic Manufacturing Framework for Concurrent Engineering and Enterprise Integration', Concurrent Engineering: A Global Perspective. Conference Proceeding. CE95, pp. 151–161.

Dornelles, J., Ayala, N.F., and Frank, A.G. (2022), 'Smart Working in Industry 4.0: How Digital Technologies Enhance Manufacturing Workers' Activities', *Computers & Industrial Engineering*, Vol. 163, Article 107804.

Doumeingts, G. (1984), *Methode GRAI, Methode de Conception des Systems en Productique.* State Thesis, university Bordeau, France.

Drabek, T.E. (1996), *Sociology of Disaster Course Instructor Guide, Federal Emergency Management Agency (FEMA).* Emmitsburg: National Emergency Training Center.

Eden, C. (1995), 'Using Cognitive Mapping for Strategic Options Development and Analysis (SODA)', In Rosenhead, J. (Ed.), *Rational Analysis for a Problematic World.* Chichester: Wiley, pp. 21–42.

Eden, C., and Huxham, C. (1996), 'Action Research for Management Research', *British Journal of Management*, Vol. 7, Iss. 1, pp. 75–86.

Eden, C., Jones, S., and Sims, D. (1983), *Messing About in Problems, an Informal Structured Approach to their identification and Management.* Oxford: Pergamon.

Eikeland, O. (2012), 'Action Research - Applied Research, Intervention Research, Collaborative Research, Practitioner Research, or Praxis Research?', *International Journal of Action Research*, Vol. 8, Iss. 1, pp. 9–44.

Eisenhardt, K.M. (1989), 'Building Theories from Case Study Research', *Academy of Management Review*, Vol. 14, pp. 532–550.

Eisenhardt, K.M. (2000), 'Paradox, Spirals, Ambivalence: The New Language of Change and Pluralism', *The Academy of Management Review*, Vol. 25, Iss. 4, pp. 703–705.

Eisenhardt K.M., and Martin, J.A. (2000), 'Dynamic Capabilities: What Are They?', *Strategic Management Journal*, Vol. 21, Iss. 10/11, pp. 1105–1122.

Feldman, M.S., and Pentland, B.T. (2003), 'Reconceptualizing Organizational Routines as a Source of Flexibility and Change', *Administrative Science Quarterly*, Vol. 48, pp. 94–118.

Felin, T., Foss, N.J., Heimeriks, K.H., and Madsen, T.L. (2012), 'Micro-Foundations of Routines and Capabilities: Individuals, Processes, and Structure', *Journal of Management Studies*, Vol. 49, Iss. 8, pp. 1351–1374.

Filion, L.J. (1994), 'Visionary Systems Thinking (VST) as a Support to Creativity in the Quality Management (TQM) Process', *Systems Research*, Vol. 11, Iss. 1, pp. 125–133.

Finkelstein, D. (1993), 'Thinking Quantum', *Cybernetics and Systems: An International Journal*, Vol. 24, Iss. 2, pp. 139–149.

Fischer, H.W. (1998), 'The Role of the New Information Technologies in Emergency Mitigation, Planning, Response and Recovery', *Disaster Prevention and Management: An International Journal*, Vol. 7, Iss. 1, pp. 28–37.

Fitzgerald, B. (1996), 'Formalised Systems Development Methodologies: A Critical Perspective', *Information Systems Journal*, Vol. 6, pp. 3–23.

Flood, R.L., and Jackson, M.C. (1991), *Creative Problem Solving: Total Systems Intervention.* Chichester: Wiley, p. 6.

Fojcik, T.M. (2013), 'Exploitation, Exploration and the Ambidextrous Design Choice in the Transition to Electric Vehicles: An Analysis of Small and Medium-Sized Automotive Suppliers in Germany', *International Journal of Automotive Technology and Management*, Vol. 13, Iss. 4, pp. 354–371.

Fripp, J. (1993), *Learning Through Simulations: A Guide to the Design and Use of Simulations in Business and Education*, McGraw-Hill Training Series. London: McGraw Hill.

Gane, C., and Sarson, T. (1979), *Structured Systems Analysis: Tools and Techniques.* New York: Improved Systems Technologies Inc.

Gatenby, D.A., Lee, P.M., and Howard, R.E. (1994) 'Concurrent Engineering: An Enabler for Fast, High Quality Product Realisation', AT&T Technical Journal., January/February pp. 34−47.

Gauch, H.E. (2015), *Scientific Method in Practice*', Cambridge: Cambridge University Press, pp. 269–326.

Gerard, R.W. (1964), 'Entitation, Animorgs and Other Systems', in Mihajlo D. Mesarovic, *Views on general systems theory,* New York, Wiley, 1964, pp. 120−1

Giannakis, M., et al. (2018), 'The Design and Delivery of Modular Legal Services: Implications for Supply Chain Strategy', *International Journal of Production Research*, Vol. 56, Iss. 20, pp. 6607–6627.

Glaser, B.G., and Strauss, A.L. (1967), *The Discovery of Grounded Theory: Strategies for Qualitative Research.* New York: Aldine.

Greenwood, D.J., and Levin, M. (1998), *Introduction to Action Research: Social Research for Social Change*. Thousand Oaks: Sage Publications, Inc.
Gregory, F.H. (1993), 'Soft Systems Methodology to Information Systems: a Wittensteinian Approach', *Journal of Info Systems*, Vol. 3, pp. 149–168.
Gregory, F.H. (2003), 'Mingers on the Classification of Philosophical Assumptions', *The Journal of the Operational Research Society*, Vol. 54, Iss. 12, pp. 1301–1302.
Grundy, S. (1988), 'Three Modes of Action Research', In Kemmis, S., and McTaggert, R. (Eds.), *The Action Research Reader*, 3rd ed. Geelong: Deakin University Press.
Guba, E.G. (1990), *The Paradigm Dialogue*. Newbury Park: Sage Publications.
Guba, E.G., and Lincoln, Y.S. (1994), 'Competing Paradigms in Qualitative Research', In Denzin, N.K., and Lincoln, Y.S. (Eds.), *Handbook of Qualitative Research*. Thousand Oaks: Sage, pp. 105–117.
Gutiérrez Gutiérrez, L.J., Lloréns-Montes, F.J., and Bustinza Sánchez, O.F. (2009), 'Six Sigma: From a Goal-Theoretic Perspective to Shared-Vision Development', *International Journal of Operations & Production Management*, Vol. 29, Iss. 2, pp. 151–169.
Habib, B. (2015), 'The Relationship Between Factors of Quality Models and Attributes of Process Models: Represented Through Venn Diagram', *International Journal of Computer Applications*, Vol. 129, Iss. 1, pp. 37–47.
Hall, A.D. (1962), *A Methodology for Systems Engineering*. Princeton: Van Nostrand.
Harvey, J., Heineke, J., and Lewis, M. (2016), 'Editorial for Journal of Operations Management Special Issue on "Professional Service Operations Management (PSOM)"', *Journal of Operations Management*, Vol. 42, pp. 4–8.
Hayes, R.H., and S.C. Wheelwright, S.C. (1979a), Link Manufacturing Process and Product Life Cycles'. *Harvard Business Review*, Vol. 57, Iss. 1, pp. 133–140.
Hayes, R.B., and Wheelwright, S.C. (1979b), 'The Dynamics of Process-Life Cycles', *Harvard Business Review*, Vol. 57, Iss. 2, pp. 127–136.
Hayes, R.H., and Wheelwright, S.C. (1984), *Restoring Our Competitive Edge: Competing Through Manufacturing*, New York: John Wiley
Heikkinen, H.L.T., Huttunen, R., and Syrjala, L. (2007), 'Action Research as Narrative: Five Principles for Validation', *Educational Action Research*, Vol. 15, Iss. 1, pp. 5–19.
Hines, P., Holweg, M., and Rich, N. (2004), 'Learning to Evolve: A Review of Contemporary Lean Thinking', *International Journal of Operations & Production Management*, Vol. 24, Iss. 10, pp. 994–1011.
Hitch, C.J. (1985), 'An Appreciation of Systems Analysis', In Optner, S.L. (Ed.), *Systems Analysis*. Englewood Cliffs: Prentice Hall, pp. 19–36.
Hodgkinson, M., and Brown, G. (2003), 'Enhancing the Quality of Education: A Case Study and Some Emerging Principles', *Higher Education*, Vol. 45, pp. 337–352.
Jackson, M.C. (1982), 'The Nature of "Soft" Systems Thinking: The Work of Churchman, Ackoff and Checkland', *Journal of Applied Systems Analysis*, Vol. 9, pp. 17–39.
Jackson, M.C. (1983), 'The Nature of "Soft" Systems Thinking: Comment on the Three Replies', *Journal of Applied Systems Analysis*, Vol. 10, pp. 109–113.
Jackson, M.C. (1984), 'A System of System Methodologies', *Journal of the Operational Research Society*, Vol. 35, Iss. 6, pp. 473–486.
Jackson, M.C. (1985), 'Social Systems Theory and Practice: The Need for a Critical Approach', International Journal of General Systems, Vol. 10, pp. 135–151.
Jackson, M.C. (1990), 'Beyond a System of Systems Methodologies', *The Journal of the Operational Research Society*, Vol. 41, Iss. 8, pp. 657–668.
Jackson, M.C. (1991), 'The Origins and Nature of Critical Systems Thinking', *Systems Practice*, Vol. 4, Iss. 2, pp. 131–149.
Jackson, M.C. (1995), 'Beyond the Fads; Systems Thinking for Managers', *Systems Research*, Vol. 12, Iss. 1, pp. 25–42.
Jackson, M.C. (2000), *Systems Approaches to Management*. New York: Plenum/Kluwer.
Jackson, M.C. (2003), *Creative Holism: Systems Thinking for Managers*. Chichester: John Wiley and Sons.
Jackson, M.C. (2003a), 'Deeper Complementarism: A Brief Response to Ulrich', *Journal of the Operational Research Society*, Vol. 54, Iss. 11, pp. 1225–1226.
Jackson, M.C. (2006), 'Creative Holism: A Critical Systems Approach to Complex Problem Situations', *Systems Research and Behavioural Science*, Vol. 23, pp. 647–657.

Jackson, M.C. (2019), *Critical Systems Thinking and the Management of Complexity: Responsible Leadership for a Complex World.* Chichester: Wiley.

Jackson, M.C. (2020), *Critical Systems Thinking and the Management of Complexity.* Chichester: Wiley.

Jackson, M.C. (2024), *Critical Systems Thinking: A Practitioner's Guide.* Chichester: Wiley.

Jackson, M.C., and Keys, P. (1984), 'Towards a System of System Methodologies', *Journal of the Operational Research Society,* Vol. 35, Iss. 6, pp. 473–486.

Jacob, F. (1974), *The Logic of Living Systems.* London: Allen Lane.

Johannesson, P., and Perjons, E. (2021), *An Introduction to Design Science*. Cham: Springer.

Juran, J.M. (1988), *Quality Control Handbook*, 4th ed. New York: McGraw Hill.

Kalaitzi, D., Matopoulos, A., and Clegg, B. (2019), 'Managing Resource Dependencies in Electric Vehicle Supply Chains: A Multi-Tier Case Study', *Supply Chain Management: An International Journal*, Vol. 24, Iss. 2, pp. 256–270.

Kapoor, K., Bigdeli, A.Z., Dwivedi, Y.K., Schroeder, A., Beltagui, A., and Baines, T. (2021), 'A Sociotechnical View of Platform Ecosystems: Systematic Review and Research Agenda', *Journal of Business Research*, Vol. 128, pp. 94–108.

Kast, F.E., and Rosenzweig, J.E. (1979), *Organisation and Management: A systems and Contingency Approach*, 3rd ed. New York: McGraw-Hill.

Khisty, C.J. (1993), *Citizen Participation Using a Soft Systems Perspective, Transport Research.* Record 1400. Washington: Transport Research Board.

Khisty, C.J. (1995), 'Soft Systems Methodology as a Learning and Management Tool', *Journal of Urban Planning and Development*, Vol. 121, Iss. 3, pp. 91–107.

King, N. (2004), 'Using Templates in the Thematic Analysis of Text', In Cassell, C., and Symon, G. (Eds.), *Essential Guide to Qualitative Methods in Organizational Research.* London: Sage.

Koestler, A. (1967), *The Ghost in the Machine*. London: Hutchinson.

Kolb, D.A. (1984), *Experiential Learning.* Englewood Cliff: Prentice Hall.

Koufteros, X., Vonderembse, M., and Doll, W. (2001), 'Concurrent Engineering and Its Consequences', *Journal of Operations Management*, Vol. 19, Iss. 1, pp. 97–115.

Kruger, K., and Basson, A.H. (2018), 'Evaluation Criteria for Holonic Control Implementations in Manufacturing Systems', *International Journal of Computer Integrated Manufacturing,* Vol. 32, Iss. 2, pp. 148–158.

Lambiotte, J.G., et al. (1989), 'Multirelational Semantic Maps', *Educational Psychology Review*, Vol. 1, pp. 331–367.

Lane, D.C. (1999), 'Social Theory and System Dynamics Practice', *European Journal of Operational Research*, Vol. 113, Iss. 3, pp. 501–527.

Lane, D.C. (2000), 'Should System Dynamics be Described as a 'Hard' or 'Deterministic' Systems Approach?', *Systems Research and Behavioural Science*, Vol. 17, pp. 3–22.

Lane, D.C. (2001), 'Rerum Cognoscere Causas: Part II—Opportunities Generated by the Agency/ Structure Debate and Suggestions for Clarifying the Social Theoretic Position of System Dynamics', *System Dynamics Review*, Vol. 17, Iss. 4, pp. 293–309.

Lane, D.C., and Jackson, M.C. (1995), 'Only Connect! An Annotated Bibliography Reflecting the Breadth and Diversity of Systems Thinking', *Systems Research*, Vol. 12, Iss. 3, pp. 217–228.

Lane, D.C., and Oliva, R. (1998), 'The Greater Whole: Towards a Synthesis of System Dynamics and Soft Systems Methodology', *European Journal of Operational Research*, Vol. 107, Iss. 1, pp. 214–235.

Lawson, T. (1998), 'Clarifying and Developing the Economics and Reality Project: Closed and Open Systems, Deductivism, Prediction, and Teaching', *Review of Social Economy*, Vol. 51, pp. 356–375.

Lee, N., and Lings, I. (2008), *Doing Business Research.* London: Sage.

Legal Services Act 2007. (2007) https://www.legislation.gov.uk/ukpga/2007/29/contents (Accessed: 20 October 2025)

Lewis, M.W., Brown, A. (2012), 'How Different Is Professional Service Operations Management', *Journal of Operations Management*, Vol. 30, Iss. 1–2, pp. 1–11.

Maclean, D., MacIntosh, R., and Grant, S. (2002), 'Mode 2 Management Research', *British Journal of Management*, Vol. 13, pp. 189–207.

Mandahawi, N., Al-Shihabi, S., Abdullah, A.A., and Alfarah, Y.M. (2010), 'Reducing Waiting Time at an Emergency Department Using Design for Six Sigma and Discrete Event Simulation', *International Journal of Six Sigma and Competitive Advantage*, Vol. 6, Iss. 1–2, pp. 91–104.

Marca, D.A., and McGowan, C.L. (1987), *SADT: Structured Analysis and Design Technique.* New York: McGraw-Hill Book Company.

Martin, C., and Metcalf, M. (2011), 'Implementation Processes: A Boolean Analysis', *Journal of the Operational Research Society*, Vol. 62, Iss. 1, pp. 21–28.
Martin, J. (1986), *Information Engineering: Volumes I-III.* Lancs: Savant.
Martin, J., and McClure, C. (1988), *Structured Techniques: The Basis for CASE.* Englewood Cliffs: Prentice-Hall.
Mason, R.O., and Mitroff, I.I. (1981), *Challenging Strategic Planning Assumptions.* New York: Wiley.
McFarlane, D.C., and Bussman, S. (2000), 'Developments in Holonic Production Planning and Control', *Production Planning and Control*, Vol. 11, Iss. 6, pp. 522–536.
McHugh, P., Merli, G., and Wheeler, W.A. (1997), *Beyond Business Process Reengineering: Towards the Holonic Enterprise.* Chichester: Wiley.
McLoughlin, P. (1986), 'SSM - Its Role in Management Services: or Finding a Nut to Fit the Spanner', *Management Services*, Vol. 30, Iss. 8, pp. 16–20.
Midgley, G. (2003), 'Five Sketches of Post Modernism: Implications for Systems Thinking and Operational Research', *Journal of Organisational Transformation and Social Change*, Vol. 1, Iss. 1, pp. 47–62.
Miles, M.B. (1979), 'Qualitative Data as an Attractive Nuisance: Problem ofAnalysis*Administrative Science Quarterly*, Vol. 24, pp. 590–600.
Miles, R.K. (1985), 'Computer Systems Analysis: The Constraint of the Hard Systems Paradigm', *Journal of Applied Systems Analysis*, Vol. 12, pp. 55–65.
Miles, R.K. (1988), 'Combining "Soft" and "Hard" Systems Practice: Grafting or Embedding?', *Journal of Applied systems Analysis*, Vol. 15, pp. 55–60.
Mingers, J. (2000), 'Variety Is the Spice of Life: Combining Soft and Hard OR/MS Methods', *International Transactions in Operational Research*, Vol. 7, Iss. 6, pp. 673–691.
Mingers, J. (2003), 'A Classification of the Philosophical Assumptions of Management Science Methods', *Journal of the Operational Research Society*, Vol. 54, Iss. 6, pp. 599–570.
Mingers, J. (2005), 'Classifying Philosophical Assumptions: A Reply to Ormerod', *Journal of the Operational Research Society*, Vol. 56, Iss. 4, pp. 465–467.
Mingers J., and Brocklesby, J. (1997), 'Multimethodology: Towards a Framework for Mixing Methodologies', *Omega*, Vol. 25, Iss. 5, pp. 489–509.
Minshull, L.K., Dehe, B., and Kotcharin, S. (2022), 'Exploring the Impact of a Sequential Lean Implementation Within a Micro-Firm–a Sociotechnical Perspective', *Journal of Business Research*, Vol. 151, pp. 156–169.
Modi, S.B., and Mabert, V.A. (2007), 'Supplier Development: Improving Supplier Performance Through Knowledge Transfer', *Journal of Operations Management*, Vol. 25, Iss. 1, pp. 42–64.
Moen, R.D., and Norman, C.L. (2010), 'Circling Back: Clearing Up the Myths About the Deming Cycle and Seeing How It Keeps Evolving', Qualityprogress.com
Moorcroft, J. (2004), 'Mental models and learning in system dynamics practice', in Pidd, M. (Ed.), Systems modelling: theory and practice, John Wiley and Sons Ltd, Chichester.
Morris, T., and Malhotra, N. (2002), Towards Managerialism: Analysing the Process of Change in Professional Service Organisations. Paper Presented at the 4th Biennial Workshop on Professional Service Firms, Alberta, August.
Morrison, E.W., and Milliken, F.J. (2000), 'Organizational Silence: A Barrier to Change and Development in a Pluralistic World', *The Academy of Management Review*, Vol. 25, Iss. 4, pp. 706–725.
Myers, M.D. (2009), *Qualitative Research in Business & Management.* London: Sage Publications Ltd.
Nonaka, I., Toyama, R., and Konno, N. (2000), 'SECI, Ba and Leadership: A Unified Model of Dynamic Knowledge Creation', *Long Range Planning*, Vol. 33, pp. 5–34.
Nosalska, K., Piatek, Z.M., Mazurek, G., and Rzadca, R. (2019), 'Industry 4.0: Coherent Definition Framework with Technological and Organizational Interdependencies', *Journal of Manufacturing Technology Management*, Vol. 31, Iss. 5, pp. 837–862.
Novak, J., and Gowin, D.B. (1984), *Learning How to Learn.* Cambridge: Cambridge University Press.
Näslund, D. (2008), 'Lean, Six Sigma and Lean Sigma: Fads or Real Process Improvement Methods?', *Business Process Management Journal*, Vol. 14, Iss. 3, pp. 269–287.
Näslund, D. (2013), 'Lean and Six Sigma – Critical Success Factors Revisited', *International Journal of Quality and Service Sciences*, Vol. 5, Iss. 1, pp. 86–100.
Orme, R.A. (2016), *A Systems Approach to Developing a Unified Methodology and Deployment Model to Help Maximize Impact of Lean Thinking and Six Sigma in Organizations.* Ph.D. Thesis, Aston University.

Orme, R.A., Clegg, B., Poole, A., Yeoman, A., Owen, C., Petridis, P., and Albores, P. (2017), A Gamified Approach to Improving Customer Service Delivery in a Train Operating Company. In Proceedings of EurOMA Conference, Edinburgh, Scotland, 1–5 June.

Ormerod, R.J. (1992), 'Combining Hard and Soft Systems Practice', *Systemist*, Vol. 14, Iss. 3, pp. 160–165.

Panchal, G., Clegg, B., Koupaei, E.E., Masi, D., and Collis, I. (2024), 'Digital Transformation and Business Intelligence for a SME: Systems Thinking Action Research Using PrOH Modelling', *Procedia Computer Science*, Vol. 232, pp. 1809–1818.

Pasmore, W.A., Woodman, R.W., and Simmons, A.L. (2008), 'Toward a More Rigorous, Reflective, and Relevant Science of Collaborative Management Research', In Shani, A.B., Mohrman, S.A., Pasmore, W.A., Stymne, B., and Adler, N. (Eds.), *Handbook of Collaborative Management Research.* SAGE Publications, Thousand Oaks, pp. 567–582.

Passenger Focus Report 2014. (2014), Rail Passengers' Priorities for Improvements. https://www.transportfocus.org.uk/research-publications/publications/rail-passengers-priorities-for-improvements-october-2014/

Patching, D. (1987), 'Soft Systems Methodology & Information Technology', *Management Sciences.*

Paton, S., Clegg, B., Pilkington, A., and Hsuan, J. (2021), *Operations Management*, 2nd ed. London: McGraw-Hill. Higher Education.

Pender, B., Currie, G., Delbosc, A., and Shiwakoti, N. (2012), 'Planning for the Unplanned: An International Review of Current Approaches to Service Disruption Management of Railways', In Australasian Transport Research Forum. ATRF, Perth 35th.

Pepper, M.P.J., and Spedding, T.A. (2010), 'The Evolution of Lean Six Sigma', *The International Journal of Quality & Reliability Management*, Vol. 27, Iss. 2, pp. 138–155.

Peterson, J.L. (1981), *Net Theory and Modelling of Systems.* Englewood Cliff: Prentice Hall.

Pidd, M. (1996), *Tools for Thinking: Modelling in Management Science.* Chichester: Wiley.

Pidd, M. (2004), *Computer Simulation in Management Science*, 5th ed. Chichester: John Wiley & Sons Ltd.

Pinnington, A., and Morris, T. (2003), 'Archetype Change in Professional Organizations: Survey Evidence from Large Law Firms', *British Journal of Management*, Vol. 14, Iss. 1, pp. 85–99.

Polanyi, M. (1966), *The Tacit Dimension.* London: Routledge and Kegan Paul.

Prasad, B., and Strand, N. (1993), 'A Flow-Chart-Based Methodology for Process Improvement', Quality Concepts '93 World Class Manufacturing. Michigan: Engineering Society of Detroit, pp. 53–74.

Ramage, M., and Shipp, K. (2009), *Systems Thinkers.* London: Springer.

RAND Corporation. (2025). https://www.rand.org/about/history/rand-by-the-decade.html

Rapoport, R.N. (1970), 'Three Dilemmas in Action Research', *Human Relations*, Vol. 23, Iss. 6, pp. 499–513.

Reason, P. (2006), 'Choice and Quality in Action Research Practice', *Journal of Management Inquiry*, Vol. 6, Iss. 15, pp. 187–203.

Reason, P., and Bradbury, H. (Eds.) (2001), *Handbook of Action Research: Participative Inquiry and Practice.* London: SAGE.

Revans, R.W. (1982), 'The Enterprise as a Learning System in the Origins and Growth of Action Learning', In Pedler, M. (Ed.), *Action Learning in Practice*, 2nd ed. Aldershot: Gower Publishing.

Rice, A.K. (1958), *Productivity and Social Organisation: The Ahmedabad Experiment.* London: Tavistock Publications.

Rice, A.K. (1963), *The Enterprise and Its Environment: A systems Theory of Management Organisation.* London: Tavistock.

Richmond, B. (1987), *Systems Thinking: Critical Thinking Skills for the 1990s and Beyond.* Waltham: Pegasus Communications.

Robinson, S., Radnor, Z.J., Burgess, N., and Worthington, C. (2012), 'SimLean: Utilizing Simulation in the Implementation of Lean in Healthcare', *European Journal of Operational Research*, Vol. 219, Iss. 1, pp. 188–197.

Rodríguez-Ulloa, R.A., Montbrun, A., and Martínez-Vicente, S. (2011), 'Soft System Dynamics Methodology in Action: A Study of the Problem of Citizen Insecurity in an Argentinean Province', *Systemic Practice and Action Research*, Vol. 24, Iss. 4, pp. 275–323.

Rosenhead, J., and Mingers, J. (Eds.) (2001), *Rational Analysis for a Problematic World Revisited*, 2nd ed. Chichester: John Wiley and Sons.

Rosin, F., Forget, P., Lamouri, S., and Pellerin, R. (2020), 'Impacts of Industry 4.0 Technologies on Lean Principles', *International Journal of Production Research*, Vol. 58, Iss. 6, pp. 1644–1661.

Rytmeister, C. (2009), 'Governing University Strategy: Perceptions and Practice of Governance and Management Roles', *Tertiary Education and Management*, Vol. 15, Iss. 2, pp. 137–156.

Sætre, A.S., and Van de Ven, A. H. (2021a), 'Generating Theory by Abduction', *Academy of Management Review*, Vol. 46, Iss. 4, pp. 684–701.

Sætre, A.S., and Van de Ven, A.H. (2021b), 'Abductive Theorizing Is More Than Idea Generation: Disciplined Imagination and a Prepared Mind', *Academy of Management Review*, Vol. 49, Iss. 2, pp. 454–457.

Saunders, M. (2003), *Research Methods for Business Students*, 3rd ed. Harlow: Pearson Education Limited.

Savage, A., and Mingers, J. (1996), 'A Framework for Linking SSM and Jackson System Development (JSD)', *Information Systems Journal*, Vol. 6, pp. 109–129.

Schein, E.H. (1999), *Process Consultation Revisited: Building the Helping Relationship.* Reading: Addison-Wesley.

Schmenner, R.W. (1986), 'How Can Service Businesses Survive and Prosper?', *Sloan Management Review*, Vol. 27, Iss. 3, pp. 21–32.

Schmenner, R.W. (2004), 'Service Businesses and Productivity', *Decision Sciences*, Vol. 35, Iss. 3, pp. 333–347.

Schon, D. A. (1983), *The Reflective Practitioner.* London: Temple Smith.

Schwaninger, M. (2006), 'System Dynamics and the Evolution of the Systems Movement', *Systems Research and Behavioral Science*, Vol. 23, pp. 583–594.

Selener, D. (1997), *Participatory Action Research and Social Change: Cornell Participatory Action Research Network.* Ithaca: Cornell University.

Senge, P. (1990), *The Fifth Discipline: The Art & Practice of the Learning Organization.* New York: Doubleday.

Senoner, J., Netland, T., and Feuerriegel, S. (2022), 'Using Explainable Artificial Intelligence to Improve Process Quality: Evidence from Semiconductor Manufacturing', *Management Science*, Vol. 68, Iss. 8, pp. 5704–5723.

Shafer, S.M., and Moeller, S.B. (2012), 'The Effects of Six Sigma on Corporate Performance: An Empirical Investigation', *Journal of Operations Management*, Vol. 30, Iss. 7–8, pp. 521–532.

Shah, R., and Ward, P.T. (2007), 'Defenginand Developing Measures of Lean Production', *Journal of Operations Management*, Vol. 25, Iss. 4, pp. 785–805.

Singhal, K., and Singhal, J. (2012a), 'Imperatives of the Science of Operations and Supply-Chain Management', *Journal of Operations Management*, Vol. 30, Iss. 3, pp. 237–244.

Singhal, K., and Singhal, J. (2012b), 'Opportunities for Developing the Science of Operations and Supply-Chain Management', *Journal of Operations Management*, Vol. 30, Iss. 3, pp. 245–252.

Silvestro, R., Fitzgerald, L., Johnston, R., and Voss, C. (1992), Towards a classification of service processes. International Journal of Service Industry Management, Vol. 3, Iss. 3, pp. 62–75.

Sinn, J.S. (1998), 'A Comparison of Interactive Planning and Soft Systems Methodology: Enhancing the Complementarist Position', *Systemic Practice and Action Research*, Vol. 11, Iss. 4, pp. 435–453.

Slack, N., Chambers, S., and Johnston, R. (2004), *Operations Management*, 4th ed. Harlow: FT. Prentice Hall.

Small, C., Baines, R., and Colquhoun, G. (1998), The Use of Graphical Modelling Methods in the UK Manufacturing Industry. 14th NCMR. September. Conference Derby University.

Snabe, B., and Größler, A. (2006), 'System Dynamics Modelling for Strategy Implementation – Case Study and Issues', *Systems Research and Behavioral Science*, Vol. 23, Iss. 4, pp. 467–481.

Soliman, M., Saurin, T.A., and Anzanello, M.J. (2018), 'The Impacts of Lean Production on the Complexity of Sociotechnical Systems', *International Journal of Production Economics*, Vol. 197, pp. 342–357.

Soltani, E., Ahmed, P., Liao, Y.Y., and Anosike, P.U. (2014), 'Qualitative Middle-Range Research in Operations Management', *International Journal of Operations and Production Management*, Vol. 34, Iss. 8, pp. 1003–1027.

Sower, V.E., Quarles, R., and Broussard, E. (2007), Cost of Quality Usage and Its Relationship to Quality System Maturity', *International Journal of Quality and Reliability Management*, Vol. 24, Iss. 2, pp. 121–140.

Spangler, D. (2025), https://www.sociocracy.info/holon-and-holarchy/

Sporn, B. (1995), 'Adaptation Processes at Universities: Organizational Implications of a Complex Environment', *Tertiary Education and Management*, Vol. 1, Iss. 1, pp. 72–75.

Sterman, J.D. (2000), *Business Dynamics: Systems Thinking and Modelling for a Complex World.* London: Irwin McGraw-Hill.

Strauss, A., and Corbin, J. (1998), *Basics of Qualitative Research: Techniques and Procedures for Developing Grounded Theory.* Thousand Oaks: Sage Publications.

Susman, G.L., and Evered, R.D. (1978), 'An Assessment of the Scientific Merits of Action Research', *Administrative Science Quarterly*, Vol. 23, Iss. 4, pp. 582–603.

Tinnilä, M., and Vepsäläinen, A. (1995), 'A Model for Strategic Repositioning of Service Processes', *International Journal of Service Industry Management*, Vol. 6, Iss. 4, pp. 57–80.

Trist, E.L., and Bamforth, K.W. (1951), 'Some Social and Psychological Consequences of the Longwall Method of Coal-Getting', *Human Relations*, Vol. 4, Iss. 1, pp. 3–38.

Trist, E.L., Higgin, G., Murray, H., and Pollock, A. (1963), *Organisational Choice: Capabilities of Groups at the Coalface under Changing Technologies.* London: Tavistock.

U.S. Air Force. (1981), 'Integrated Computer Aided Manufacture (ICAM)'Functional modelling Manual (IDEF0)', Air Force Laboratory, Wright Patterson AFB, Ohio, Report # AFWAL-TR-81-4023.

U.S. Air Force. (1982), 'Integrated Computer Aided Manufacture (ICAM) Architecture Part II Information Modelling Manual (IDEF 1X)', Air Force Materials Laboratory, Wright Patterson AFB, Ohio, Report # AFWAL-TR-85-4032.

Ulrich, W. (1983), *Critical Heuristics of Social Planning.* Bern: Haupt.

Van Aken, J., Chandrasekaran, A., and Halman, J. (2016), 'Conducting and Publishing Design Science Research: Inaugural Essay of the Design Science Department of the Journal of Operations Management', *Journal of Operations Management*, Vol. 47–48, Iss. 1, pp. 1–8.

van der Aalst, W.M.P., and van Hee, K.M. (1994), *Business Process Redesign: A Petri-Net-Based Approach.* Internal Report. Dept. of Mathematics and Computer Science. Eindhoven University of Technology, The Netherlands.

Van de Ven, A. (2007), *Engaged Scholarship.* Oxford: Oxford University Press.

Vidgen, R., Rose, J., Wood, B., and Wood-Harper, A.T. (1994), 'Business Process Reengineering: The Need for a Methodology to Re-Vision the Organisation', In Glasson, B.C., et al. (Eds.), *BPR: Information Systems Opportunities and Challenges.* Holland: Elsevier Science.

Warren, K. (2008), *Strategic Management Dynamics.* Chichester: John Wiley and Sons Ltd.

Wastell, D.G., White, P., and Kawalek, P. (1994), 'A Methodology for Business Process Redesign; Experiences and Issues', *Journal of Strategic Information Systems*, Vol. 3, Iss. 1, pp. 23–40.

Watson, R., and Smith, R. (1988), 'Applications of the Lancaster Soft Systems Methodology in Australia', *Journal of Applied Systems Analysis*, Vol. 15, pp. 3–26.

Weinburg, G.M. (1975), *An Introduction to General Systems Thinking.* London: John Wiley.

Weiner, N. (1948), *Cybernetics: Or Control and Communication in the Animal and the Machine.* London: Wiley.

Wilson, B. (1984), *Systems: Concepts, Methodologies and Applications.* New York: John Wiley and Sons Ltd.

Wilson, B. (2001), *Soft Systems Methodology: Conceptual Model Building and Its Contribution.* Chichester: John Wiley and Sons.

Woodburn, I. (1988), 'The Idea of "System" and Its Use in 'Hard" and "Soft" Systems Approaches', *Journal of Applied Systems Analysis*, Vol. 15, pp. 49–53.

Woodcock, L. (1996) '*Moving to Process Management*'. KPMG.

Yin, R.K. (2009), *Case Study Research: Design and Methods*, 4th ed. Thousand Oaks: Sage.

Yourdon, E., and Constantine, L. (1978), *Structured Design*, 2nd ed. New York: Yourdon Press.

Zaff, B.S. (1991), 'An Integrated Methodology for Knowledge and Design Acquisition', IEEE CH3007-2/91/0000-00779.

INDEX

Note: Page numbers in bold reference tables and Page numbers in italics reference figures

For Product Safety Concerns and Information please contact our EU representative GPSR@taylorandfrancis.com Taylor & Francis Verlag GmbH, Kaufingerstraße 24, 80331 München, Germany